MW00439992

PERSONALITY ASSESSMENT
IN MANAGED HEALTH CARE

PERSONALITY ASSESSMENT IN MANAGED HEALTH CARE

Using the MMPI-2 in Treatment Planning

Edited by

JAMES N. BUTCHER

New York   Oxford
Oxford University Press
1997

Oxford University Press

Oxford   New York
Athens   Auckland   Bangkok   Bogota   Bombay   Buenos Aires
Calcutta   Cape Town   Dar es Salaam   Delhi   Florence   Hong Kong
Istanbul   Karachi   Kuala Lumpur   Madras   Madrid   Melbourne
Mexico City   Nairobi   Paris   Singapore   Taipei   Tokyo   Toronto   Warsaw

and associated companies in
Berlin   Ibadan

Copyright © 1997 by Oxford University Press, Inc.

Published by Oxford University Press, Inc.
198 Madison Avenue, New York, New York 10016

Oxford is a registered trademark of Oxford University Press

All rights reserved. No part of this publication may be reproduced,
stored in a retrieval system, or transmitted, in any form or by any means,
electronic, mechanical, photocopying, recording or otherwise,
without the prior permission of Oxford University Press.

Library of Congress Cataloging-in-Publication Data
Personality assessment in managed health care : using the MMPI-2 in
   treatment planning / edited by James N. Butcher.
      p.   cm.
   Includes bibliographical references and index.
   ISBN 0-19-511160-5
   1. Minnesota Multiphasic Personality Inventory.   2. Managed mental
health care.   I. Butcher, James Neal, 1933–
RC473.M5P47   1997
362.2'0425—dc20   96-9456

9 8 7 6 5 4 3 2 1

Printed in the United States of America
on acid-free paper

Contents

Contributors

Ann Leslie Albanese, M.Ed., is a graduate student in the Counseling/Clinical/School Psychology Program at the University of California, Santa Barbara, where she is specializing in clinical psychology. She is currently completing her predoctoral internship at the Counseling and Career Services Center at UCSB. Areas of special interest include eating disorders, families coping with psychological disorders, and matching treatment to client.

Peter A. Ambrose, Jr., Ph.D., M.B.A., is the Clinical Director of Managed Mental Health for Alliance Blue Cross Blue Shield in St. Louis, Missouri. Dr. Ambrose is a licensed psychologist having received his doctorate from the University of Missouri-Columbia. He has been an Assistant Professor in the Departments of Neurology, Pediatrics, and Psychiatry at Washington University School of Medicine in St. Louis and the University of Arkansas for Medical Sciences. Dr. Ambrose's family includes his wife Ann and their children Megan and Brendan.

Mary Baker, M.A., received her master's degree in Counseling Psychology and is currently in a Counseling/Clinical/School Psychology doctoral program emphasizing in Clinical Psychology at the University of California in Santa Barbara. She has published and/or presented papers in the areas of empirically validated treatments, managed health care, and social interactions in children with autism. She has special interests in patient treatment matching for psychiatric disorders, childhood disorders (primarily autism), and families with developmentally disabled children.

Cynthia D. Belar, Ph.D., is the director of the doctoral program in clinical psychology at the University of Florida, President of the Division of Health Psychology of the American Psychological Association, and Chair of the Council of University Directors of Clinical Psychology. She received her Ph.D. in clinical psychology from Ohio University in 1974 after an internship at Duke University Medical Center. From 1974 to 1984 she was on the faculty of the Department of Clinical and Health Psychology at the University of Florida Health Science Center, where she developed the Pain and Stress Management Laboratory as well as the Medical Psychology service and training component of the doctoral and internship programs. From 1983 to 1990 she served as Chief Psychologist and Clinical Director of Behavioral Medicine for the Kaiser Permanente Medical Care Program in Los Angeles. Her research has been in the area of pain, stress management, and biofeedback.

Larry E. Beutler, Ph.D., is Professor and Director of the Counseling/Clinical/School Psychology Program at the University of California, Santa Barbara. He obtained his Ph.D. from the University of Nebraska in 1970 and subsequently served on the faculties of Duke University Medical School, Stephen F. Austin State University, Baylor College of Medicine, and the University of Arizona. Dr. Beutler is a Diplomate of the American Board of Professional Psychology (ABPP), a past international President of the Society for Psychotherapy Research (SPR), and President-Elect of the Division of Psychotherapy (American Psychological Association). His is also the outgoing Editor of the *Journal of Consulting and Clinical Psychology*, the Co-Editor of the *Journal of Clinical Psychology*, and a fellow of the American Psychological Association, The American Psychological Society, and the International Fellowship of Eclectic Psychotherapists. He is the author of approximately 250 scientific papers and chapters, and he is the author, editor, or co-author of eleven books on psychotherapy and psychopathology.

James N. Butcher, Ph.D., is Professor of Psychology in the Department of Psychology at the University of Minnesota. He received an MA in experimental psychology in 1962 and a Ph.D. in clinical psychology in 1964 from the University of North Carolina at Chapel Hill. He was awarded Doctor Honoris Causa from the Free University of Brussels, 1990. He is a member of the University of Minnesota Press' MMPI Consultative Committee. He is currently the Editor of *Psychological Assessment* and serves as consulting editor for numerous other journals in psychology and psychiatry. He is a fellow of the American Psychological Association and the Society for Personality Assessment.

Ralph H. Earle, Ph.D., A.B.P.P., is a noted family therapist and psychologist, author, and lecturer. He is past national President of the American Association of Sex Educators, Counselors and Therapists. He is a national authority on sexual addiction with over 25 years' experience working with sexual problems and works extensively with sex offenders. He has many media credits and is the author of several books including *Lonely All the Time: Recognizing, Understanding and Overcoming Sex Addiction* and *Come Here, Go Away*. He is the co-author of a book published in 1995 entitled *Sex Addiction: Case Studies and Management*. Dr. Earle is an ordained minister and serves on the Board of Directors of the Interfaith Sexual Trauma Institute of St. John's University, Minneapolis, MN. He is the Director of Psychological Counseling Services in Scottsdale, AZ.

Stephen E. Finn, Ph.D., is the Director of the Center for Therapeutic Assessment in Austin, Texas—an institute devoted to studying the beneficial effects of psychological assessment on clients. He is also an Adjunct Assistant Professor at the University of Texas at Austin, where he taught graduate courses in assessment for eight years and was the Associate Director of the Clinical Psychology Training Program. Dr. Finn is the author of many articles and chapters on psychological assessment and is co-author, with Mary Tonsager, of *Therapeutic Assessment: Using Psychological Testing to Help Clients Change*, to be published by the American Psychological Association. His other recent book, *A Manual for Using the MMPI-2 as a Therapeutic Intervention*, was published by the University of Minnesota Press. Dr. Finn lectures frequently around the world on topics related to assessment.

Daniel R. Fisher is a doctoral student at the Counseling/Clinical/School Psychology Program at the University of California, Santa Barbara. He is currently on internship at New York Hospital–Cornell Medical Center, Department of Psychology. He has previously co-authored articles on graduate training models in psychology, the effects and forms of resistance in psychotherapy, and clinical decision making in a managed care environment.

T. Mark Harwood is a doctoral student specializing in clinical psychology in the Counseling/Clinical/School Psychology Program at the University of California–Santa Barbara. He is presently completing his predoctoral internship at the VA Medical Center, Palo Alto, CA. Areas of special interest include: common and specific psychotherapeutic factors, prescriptive psychotherapies, geropsychology, severe psychopathology, and substance abuse. He has published and/or presented papers in the area of prescriptive psychotherapies.

Kelly Klump, M.A., received her Bachelor of Arts degree from Michigan State University. She recently earned her Master of Arts degree in Clinical Psychology from the University of Minnesota, where she is currently a fourth-year student in the Clinical Psychology doctoral program. Kelly's primary research interests are in the genetic and environmental contributions to eating disordered behavior.

Hale Martin, Ph.D., is a licensed psychologist in Colorado who specializes in psychological assessment as well as cognitive/behavioral and psychodynamic therapy. He recently moved from Austin, TX, to Denver, CO, to practice and teach at the University of Colorado at Denver. In Austin he served as Associate Director for the Center for Therapeutic Assessment and as adjunct assistant professor at the University of Texas at Austin. He received his doctoral degree in clinical psychology from the University of Texas at Austin, completing a clinical internship at Michael Reese Hospital and Medical Center in Chicago and a post-doctoral fellowship in psychological and neuropsychological assessment at the University of Texas Health Science Center at San Antonio. His research interests include therapeutic assessment, personality measurement, and masculinity–femininity. He is currently finishing a book on masculinity–femininity with Stephen Finn, Ph.D., for the University of Minnesota Press.

John C. Norcross, Ph.D., is Professor and former Chair of Psychology at the University of Scranton and a clinical psychologist in part-time independent practice. Author of more than 125 scholarly articles, Dr. Norcross has written or edited 10 books, the most recent being *Changing for Good* (with James Prochaska and Carlo DiClemente), the *Handbook of Psychotherapy Integration* (with Marvin Goldried), *An Insider's Guide to Graduate Programs in Clinical and Counseling Psychology* (with Tracy Mayne and Michael Sayette), and the third edition of *Systems of Psychotherapy: A Transtheoretical Analysis* (with James Prochaska). He has served on the editorial board of 10 journals, as a co-developer of the APA Psychotherapy Videotape Series, and as a clinical and research consultant to a number of organizations, including the National Institute of Mental Health. John lives, works, and plays in the northern Pocono Mountains with his wife, two children, and slightly deranged Weimaraner.

Steven Vay Rouse, M.S., is a doctoral candidate at the University of Minnesota. He earned his M.S. in clinical psychology at Abilene Christian University and gained professional experience in a wide variety of settings, including a university psychological testing office, the behavior therapy unit of a state school, and an outpatient substance abuse clinic. He is currently working toward his Ph.D. in the Personality Research division of the psychology department and is involved in several MMPI-2 research projects. Following completion of his degree, Steven plans to continue research on clinical personality assessment.

Monica Sandowicz, M.A., is a graduate student in the Counseling/Clinical/School Psychology at the University of California, Santa Barbara, where she is specializing in Clinical Psychology. She is currently completing her predoctoral internship at Oregon Health Sciences University, Portland, OR. Areas of special interest include systematic treatment selection, resistance in psychotherapy, and child psychotherapy.

Jill Sullivan, B.A., a graduate of the University of Michigan, is currently a doctoral student in clinical psychology at the University of Minnesota, where she is studying the pathophysiology and concomitant psychopathology in adolescents and young adults with phenylketonuria (PKU).

Jeanette Taylor, B.A., received her Bachelor of Arts degree in psychology in 1993 from the University of Colorado in Boulder, Colorado. She graduated *summa cum laude* and was inducted into Phi Beta Kappa in her senior year at the University of Colorado. She is currently in her second year of the Clinical Psychology program at the University of Minnesota in Minneapolis, Minnesota. Her research interests revolve around the main theme of criminal behavior and associated psychopathology.

Roxanne R. Witte, Ph.D., is a licensed clinical psychologist who currently has private practices at New Leaf Counseling Center in Flagstaff, Arizona and at Psychological Counseling Services in Scottsdale, Arizona. Roxanne developed her interest in the use of the MMPI during her doctoral program when, completing her dissertation, she used the MMPI as a measure of personality and how obtained personality profiles interacted with reports of marital satisfaction and communication styles. She has continued to use the MMPI in her clinical work as an integral component of the assessment process and in the development of treatment goals for her clients. Dr. Witte has been a clinic director in the Oklahoma State Guidance System, a school psychologist in Las Vegas, Nevada, and has specialized in child psychology for the past eight years. As part of her work with children and their families, Dr. Witte also specializes in the treatment of children and women who have been sexually abused. In addition, Dr. Witte sees couples for relationship and marital counseling and runs an ongoing couple's group.

Part I

IMPLICATIONS OF MANAGED CARE
FOR PERSONALITY ASSESSMENT

1

Assessment and Treatment in the Era of Managed Care

James N. Butcher

Mental health services are currently undergoing considerable change. Health service providers are evolving new approaches for funding mental health services and developing new modes of documentation and ways of assessing accountability. Mental health practitioners are being forced to modify their treatment strategies and are being encouraged to treat patients in a reduced number of sessions. As a result, many clinical practitioners consider the current mental health scene to involve an unfortunate reduction in the quality and amount of services to clients. Clients with extensive or long-term problems may not be allowed enough sessions to resolve them. Many mental health professionals have found themselves pressed to alter or give up their traditional practices because insurance carriers have reduced or denied reimbursement for treatment for their patients. Some are even seeking alternative practice or career directions such as employment screening or forensic assessment where fees for services are more certain and less vulnerable to the reductions in financial support that have recently impacted independent psychotherapy practice.

The shift in power in mental health services delivery from the mental health professional to accounts managers (who might or might not be knowledgable about therapy) has clearly impacted the availability, type, quality, and quantity of mental health services open to patients in need of psychotherapy. Third-party payers have imposed a "new accountability" and are monitoring, controlling, and denying services and, in some cases, even determining who provides them.

In the provision of mental health services, three traditional fields of endeavor intersect: business management to coordinate funding resources, the practice of psychotherapeutic intervention, and personality assessment technology. In the past, these three mental health professional groups have followed parallel lines of development, although addressing the same human problems and concerned with the same people. They have focused on very disparate aspects of health services delivery. In approaching mental health services from such diverse perspectives, each approach has evolved a different set of realities—and each has not always been sufficiently conversant with the activities and contribution of the other. In today's mental health climate the working relationships are likely to be closer than in the past, even though not always positive.

The guiding purpose of this book is to explore and provide working examples of the effectiveness of psychological treatment in the context of managed care when it is based on a sound foundation of personality assessment information. Before we get into the specific techniques of incorporating assessment into effective therapy and the plan of this book to address them, we need to explore the present situation from the perspective of these three diverse forces in mental health service provision.

The Managed Care Perspective

An important revolution has been occurring in health care delivery. The case management "responsibility" in mental health services, at least in terms of decisions about reimbursement or treatment length, has shifted from the traditional health service professional to the financial manager. A new emphasis on accountability has evolved and there is a reluctance to expend the mental health dollar on so-called superfluous or ineffective services. Managed care corporations have brought about a new set of procedures with which the mental health professional must contend. For the past decade, health service delivery has been evolving into greater accountability for dollars spent and freedom of establishing a treatment program limited by watchful evaluation procedures.

Health care dollars have seemingly shrunk to the point that more cost-containing measures are required to streamline services to ensure that society's health needs can be met more cost effectively. In the past, health service providers have not generally been sufficiently concerned with the cost containment for services and in many cases may have perpetuated inefficient or nonworking but costly procedures in the hopes of obtaining an ameliorating effect. Many insurance carriers appear to encourage a "telescoping" of treatment into fewer sessions because it reduces the overall total cost of the procedure—cheaper is better! For example, some therapists may now provide therapy without the benefit of important elements of the treatment such as pretreatment personality assessment or therapeutic follow-up because the HMO case representative did not authorize payment to cover such items.

Actually, there is no single program of mental health care provision in the United States and no single-minded philosophy as to what, if any, psychological therapy will be funded and for how long. Moreover, different health care providers cover services differently. For example, some systems actually cover assessment-based therapy by reimbursing the full cost (see Chapter 8) while others simply pay a flat fee, varying in amount between providers, for a procedure such as an MMPI-2 or other personality inventory. The idea of a national health plan is highly politicized and (at least at this writing) seemingly remote. New health plans to revolutionize health care have advanced only to be criticized or shunted aside as alternative models are offered. No single national program has evolved to satisfy all of the diverse situations found across the country today. It is likely that in the immediate future mental health care funding for assessment and therapy will resemble a patchwork quilt with many shapes and colors present. No two regions or psychological practices have the same experiences. It is clear also that mental health services that are supported depend to a great extent on the individual experiences and forceful negotiations between the health professional and the HMO case representative.

It is difficult to find fault with the concept of greater accountability in expenditures for health services. Accountability is particularly important in a field where procedures are somewhat "soft" and where results may be somewhat more difficult to gauge compared with other procedures such as surgery. The case can clearly be made that this accountability in the mental health system is probably overdue and that an explicit accounting of *what* is being provided and *what* benefits are obtained for the dollars expended is timely. Mental health professionals need to make greater efforts to demonstrate the efficacy of their procedures. If a procedure doesn't work or cannot be empirically verified, then it needs to be altered to work more effectively in the present climate or it will be eliminated or surpassed. In health service delivery, accountability should be the rule rather than the exception. Yet, it is also important to avoid undue stifling of services or procedures that potentially can serve to ameliorate mental health problems just because their full efficacy is unknown or unrecognized by the payer. Being "penny wise and pound foolish" with respect to health care reimbursement can come at a great cost to society over the long term by undermining the development of treatment approaches or in failing to offer needed services to some of its citizens. There needs to be a balance between true service to society and expending resources on unnecessary elements of the treatment. And there needs to be a clear communication between line service personnel, researchers, and the accountants to make sure that everyone views the issue of appropriate cost for service rendered with congruence.

There is a clear danger of having clinical treatment plans be determined solely on the basis of economics (some would say crass accountability) rather than by persons involved in the treatment who are cognizant of the problems and possibilities. An effective procedure that could lead the practitioner to make appropriate, effective treatment decisions could be minimized or treated as "superfluous" on financial grounds but have clear effectiveness on clinical grounds. An administrative decision not to pay for a psychological assessment in the initial stages of therapy could have a deleterious effect on the therapy itself. For example, if the therapist proceeds in treating a client who presented with depression without recognizing that the true problem is substance abuse disorder, the psychotherapy, no matter how well intended or competently administered, will likely be for naught. If, in exercising the goals of cost saving, the case manager thoughtlessly eliminates crucial procedures such as pretreatment assessment, the therapy can become more inefficient or ineffective because major problems are missed and not accounted for in the early stages of treatment (see Klump & Butcher in Chapter 7). Moreover, the absence of a pretreatment assessment essentially *guarantees* that treatment effectiveness *cannot* be adequately assessed because there is no base line of personality information from which to assess change—a situation that sound managed care administrators should actually discourage.

The Therapist's Perspective

In today's clinical practice, therapists face a number of challenges in addition to their usual tasks of trying to help their clients understand and change their behavior. Many therapists are currently feeling the need to operate in "quick time" in order to manage the time constraints or the limited numbers of available sessions allocated in each case by the third-party payers. Moreover, therapists have the additional challenge in that they feel they must conduct therapy under a "glass bubble" today, given the fact that peer review of treatment practices and progress has become an industrywide standard. Therapists need to feel comfortable working in an environment with someone looking over their shoulder.

In today's mental health service environment, with the reduction or limitations in fees to cover more than a few sessions, some therapists appear to be reducing the amount of time they typically devote to the initial phase of pretreatment evaluation and are limiting or eliminating the follow-up sessions so needed as patients try out new behaviors. At the front end of treatment, the psychological assessment that is often considered crucial to the formulation of the case problem is often eliminated altogether or only cursorily done. Therapists tend to focus their attention instead on devoting the few precious (allowable) sessions to implement an intervention (often a "manualized therapy" or standardized treatment protocol) without a clear understanding or full appreciation of the client's problems. This can result in a problematic situation—the application of a mechanized treatment approach without knowing whether the procedures will actually fit or benefit the particular client. Norcross and Beutler, in Chapter 3, recommend against the mechanistic application of treatment procedures without determining their suitability for the particular client.

As noted above, the decision not to spend the time or billable resource to conduct an initial assessment can be problematic and can lead to inefficient treatment. Therapists who are seeing a complicated case, particularly one with potentially treatment destructive elements, should not be easily put off by a case managers recriminations against "superfluous" testing. Instead, the therapist can press the case representative for sufficient resources. Interestingly, in many cases (as noted by Ambrose in Chapter 4), making a request for additional time to evaluate the client is often supported by the HMO case manager and results in obtaining needed approval if the reasons are clearly stated.

The Assessment Psychologist's Perspective

Psychological assessment is not the new kid on the block in the clinical setting, nor is it an area of the clinical intervention that can be summarily dismissed or ignored for long. As Norcross and Beutler (Chapter 3) noted, psychological assessment has a long tradition in applied psychology. There has been over 100 years of theoretical development and technological refinement in assessment methods. Psychological assessment has been a substantial contributing partner in the clinical interaction over the past several decades—even though it has been ignored by some theoreticians and criticized by others as being of lesser importance in treatment. Clinical assessment appears, in many respects, to be the activity that is readily sidestepped when belt tightening is implemented in the psychological treatment process. Yet, despite its seeming expendability to some professionals in the current managed care environment, assessment has several important contributions to make in treatment planning.

Assessment psychologists have long been aware of the importance of having a solid knowledge base of personality and cognitive functioning in advance of making major dispositions or recommendations about a client. Personality factors and the dynamic characteristics that make up the problems (and hopefully the solutions) the patient brings to treatment are key elements for the therapist to get a grip on. In most psychotherapeutic approaches, trait assessment and a dynamic formulation of the client's problems early in therapy are central processes. Even behavior therapy, which has traditionally been less concerned with personality structure or dynamics, can be subverted by unrecognized destructive personality characteristics the client might possess. Regardless of treatment approach, psychological assessment information can be a valuable asset in effective goal setting and structuring of therapy.

Assessment as a Key Step in Accountability

Reduction in the assessment orientation in clinical practice would be an unfortunate situation in the present managed care environment for reasons other than its value in impacting the treatment itself. In many respects, early assessment is one of the most crucial elements in clinical practice when it comes to accountability. Without assessment information, both the clinical intervention and empirical accountability can be impaired substantially. Psychological assessment also becomes integral in treatment intervention when it comes time to evaluate the effects of therapy. Evaluation of effectiveness, a buzz word in the vocabulary of managed care officials, is the "home court" of assessment, thereby making it a very key element in mental health intervention. When one asks the question "Is treatment effective?" they are really asking "Has the patient benefited or changed positively as a result of the treatment?" The need to assess change necessitates that problems, symptoms, and personality be evaluated at both the beginning and end of the treatment.

Most assessment-oriented psychologists are aware that the field of psychological assessment has a very substantial experience base and has much to contribute to the provision of psychological services. As Rouse et al. (Chapter 10), for example, discovered in their recent review of one instrument, the MMPI/MMPI-2, there was a vast database of treatment-oriented research (over 1000 relevant articles) exploring the field of personality assessment and treatment planning. Such a storehouse of relevant empirical research and theoretical development should prove valuable to the task of treatment planning and in providing psychological treatment if the other professions in the treatment field (the therapists and accounts managers) are made aware of it.

However, managed mental health care representatives and some therapists have not been fully apprised of the contribution that psychological assessment can make in structuring and shortening the process of therapy. Unfortunately, assessment psychologists have been somewhat remiss in communicating the efficacy of their procedures with professionals outside their area as to the benefits and values of assessment derived information in impacting psychological treatment. Research and theoretical articles devoted to explaining the costs/benefits of assessment in treatment planning are virtually absent from the research literature. In Chapter 7, Klump and Butcher provide a discussion of the values and benefits of personality information in treatment planning and describe possible deleterious effects of conducting treatment without an objective personality evaluation.

About This Book

The idea for this volume on assessment and treatment planning emerged from recent discussions of the role of psychological assessment in managed care at the 1995 session of the 30th Annual Symposium on Recent Developments in the Use of the MMPI-2 and took further shape in discussions with Larry Beutler and John Norcross. At the MMPI-2 symposium, assessment psychologists and managed care experts were asked to address pertinent issues related to providing assessment services in the area of managed care. In the fruitful discussions that ensued, it became apparent that proponents of managed care were challenging mental health practitioners to *account* for their procedures in terms of benefits for the cost incurred. This challenge (Ambrose, 1995; Stenmark, 1995) stimulated considerable discussion among assessment psychologists and prompted us to muster evidence on the power of one instrument, the MMPI-2, to demonstrate how and when assessment can produce benefit in the clinical intervention.

The task of providing mental health services to a person with psychologically based problems is often difficult and requires the use of objective methods of appraisal to clearly define problems and point to achievable goals in treatment. The goal of this book is to explore the potential contribution of objective personality assessment to treatment planning in a managed care context.

Impact of Managed Care on Psychotherapy

In the initial treatment chapter (Chapter 2), Beutler and his colleagues provide a panoramic view of psychological treatment along with a guide for practitioners working in the current system, pointing out many facets of the health care system. The authors include in their analysis a historical perspective on the evolving systems of managed care and discuss the range of managed care options currently available. These approaches range widely in terms of their quality and types of services offered.

The challenges facing managed care systems are presented along with the issues as to their survivability and viability in the face of the requirement of objective evaluation and patient monitoring. Moreover, they note that managed care programs are operating in a rather arbitrary manner without established (well-founded) criteria of what services work and how much of particular services is needed. Beutler and his colleagues describe the role of "manualized therapy" or the use of standardized treatment protocols in providing treatment.

Beutler and his colleagues, recognizing the value of assessment in treatment planning, discuss the importance of overcoming the ambivalent (if not negative) attitude some people seem to have toward pretreatment assessment in the present era of managed care. In their view, it is important for managed care programs to incorporate sound assessment strategies into service offerings if the system is going to thrive in the current environment. In their view, an active educational program incorporating objective information will be central to the provision of mental health services in the future health care system.

Ingredients of Planned Therapy: Role of Assessment

The chapter by Norcross and Beutler (Chapter 3) gets at the heart of the contribution of assessment to treatment planning and managed care. The necessity of conducting personality assessment in treatment planning is succinctly stated: "Infusing objective psychological assessment and research-informed models of treatment selection into practice are two vital antidotes to the afflictions of managed care." It is their view, as it is mine, that an early personality assessment can add immeasurably to the therapist's effectiveness with a particular client. Norcross and Beutler provide a "treatment selection model that is rooted in objective psychological assessment and empirical outcome research." We know a great deal about the patient characteristics and treatment elements that bring about ameliorative effects. Norcross and Beutler review four key elements (referred to as "four plus client markers") or patient characteristics that operate to make treatment successful: patient expectancies, being at an appropriate stage of change, being at a low level of reactance or resistance, and having the capability to form relationships. As you will see in Chapter 3, these four central elements in pretreatment planning can be very successfully assessed by objective personality tests like the MMPI-2 in pretreatment assessment.

Managed Care: Altering the System to Fit the Client

An insightful view of the managed care system from the inside is provided in Chapter 4 by Peter Ambrose. Ambrose provides the clinician with an inside track to the often necessary negotiations that are required between the practitioner and the health provider representative, the case management professional, in order to obtain reimbursement for a particular client. Ambrose provides the practitioner with tactics that can effectively be employed to negotiate service liability on cases. The health provider makes a number of assumptions that the practitioner needs to address in order to get coverage for psychological assessment. For example, if the therapist wants to include a computer-based psychological evaluation into the treatment, the practitioner needs to "massage" the case manager to approve the service. This can be done by educating the case manager about the benefits of the service and providing a clear rationale for its use.

Implementation of Assessment Services in a Managed Care Environment

In her seven years as Chief Psychologist at Kaiser-Permanente in California, Cynthia Belar worked extensively with psychological assessment in a managed care context. The MMPI was a central element in psychological evaluations for cases that called for a personality evaluation. Belar makes a strong case for using psychological assessment in managed care and sees an expanded role for assessment in the future. In her view, assessment is likely to play an important role in measurement of behavior—an important component of psychological services. She also feels that the role of assessment information in providing test feedback to patients is an important contribution to the therapy itself.

In the chapter by Ralph Earle and Roxanne Witte (Chapter 6), the incorporation of psychological assessment in the context of an independent practice of psychology (Beigel, Earle, Fleischman, & D'Andrea, 1990) is addressed and illustrated. Earle and his colleagues provide extensive psychological services both within and outside the managed care environment. (They provide mental health consultation to corporations, court assessments, and couples counseling not normally reimbursed in the current health model.) Many of their patient contacts incorporate an MMPI-2 assessment because they feel the need to have a clear understanding of the client's problems and dynamics early in the clinical intervention to know well the problems they are dealing with. They provide a case example of how the MMPI-2 can be incorporated into treatment.

Objective Personality Assessment and Treatment Planning: The Role of the MMPI-2

Turning more specifically to the use of the MMPI-2 in providing personality-based information about patients, the chapter by Klump and Butcher (Chapter 7) brings into focus the rationale for a therapists use of assessment data in treatment planning. The sensitive use of the MMPI-2 in assessment can have an important effect in conveying to the patient that the therapist sees an important need to learn and understand their personality and problems through an objective assessment. Patients in therapy usually appreciate the fact that a therapist employs objective means to understand his or her problems and personality factors and does not simply rely on superficial impressions.

Clearly, one the most beneficial aspect of MMPI-2-based assessment in treatment planning is that an early assessment provides the therapist with a view of fruitful pathways to follow in the treatment as well as showing a map of potential "minefields" within the client's personality—the areas of treatment resistance or possible treatment destructive areas. Assessment can aid the therapist in understanding the patient's personality structure (defenses and vulnerabilities) and provides a key to the therapist's appraisal of the problems and resistances that need addressing. For example, "Does the client have disabling anxiety or depression?" "Does the client have features of an addictive disorder?" "Are there personality problems that could undermine the therapy?"

Costs and Benefits of Assessment

Klump and Butcher also provide a theoretical analysis of the factors involved in appraising the costs involved in psychological assessment in relation to the benefits of having psychological assessment information in treatment planning. This analysis serves to stake out the territory and point directions for further understanding and appreciating what an objective evaluation, early in treatment, can contribute to the treatment process.

Assessment Therapy: An Effective Response to Managed Care

Not all psychotherapists are cowed by the draconian developments in mental health care service delivery. Finn and his colleague's approach to psychological intervention has capitalized on the extensive information available through psychological assessment, the need to incorporate a *greater* amount of personality information in the treatment, and the readiness to which objective personality assessment can be explained to insurers. Finn and colleagues have developed "assessment therapy," a treatment approach that incorporates the use of test feedback in the early stages of therapy to provide the client with a more focused treatment approach. In this technique, patients are readily engaged into the process of understanding their problems early in the treatment process through direct and therapeutically oriented test feedback. This therapeutic approach brings about remarkable treatment change in an abbreviated time frame.

The key element in Finn's assessment-therapy approach is that he has conducted the research on treatment efficacy in his practice and can demonstrate to health care providers that his treatment has beneficial results and works efficiently (cost effectively).

Importance of Timeliness in Assessment

One of the assumptions underlying the use of using psychological assessment information in treatment is that therapy can be more effectively implemented when timely personality-based information is available for establishing treatment goals and tasks. The earlier in the treatment the therapist has test information available, the more powerful the effect of test feedback in therapy will be and the more quickly the intervention can begin. Timeliness of the evaluation can be critical to an effective intervention. Assessments can often be incorporated into the therapy within the first or second session if the test can be quickly processed. Computer-derived test reports can be obtained quickly and cost-effectively and, moreover, can provide the therapist with (a) objectively derived and highly accurate (Berah et al., 1993; Gillet et al., 1996; Butcher et al., 1997) personality description that can be employed to indicate problem areas that need to be addressed and (b) personality problems that might require confrontation early in the process.

Survey of Treatment-Related Assessment Research

In order to explore the broad base of information available in the present treatment literature, Rouse, Taylor, and Sullivan conducted a survey of MMPI-2-based treatment research and found approximately 1000 research studies related to psychotherapy and the MMPI/MMPI-2. They provide a very user-friendly introduction to this extensive research literature by categorizing the articles according to content area and summarizing the key articles in the area. In their introduction to the literature review they include a listing of many of the relevant studies underlying MMPI/MMPI-2 usage in treatment planning.

References

Ambrose, P. (1995, March). Role of objective personality assessment in managed care: A forum presentation. Presented at the 30th Annual Symposium on Recent Developments in the Use of the MMPI/MMPI-2, St. Petersburg, Florida.

Beigel, J. K., Earle, R. H., Fleischman, L., & D'Andrea, R. (1990). *Successful private practice in the 1990's.* New York: Brunner/Mazel.

Berah, E., Butcher, J., Miach, P., Bolza, J., Colman, S., & McAsey, P. (1993). Computer-based interpretation of the MMPI-2: An Australian evaluation of the Minnesota Report. Presented at the Australian Psychological Association Meetings, Melbourne, October.

Butcher, J. N., Berah, E., Ellertsen, B., Miach, P., Lim, J., Nezami, E., Guelfi, J. D., Pancheri, P., Cheung, F., Derksen, J., & Almagor, M. (1997). Objective personality assessment: Computer-based MMPI-2 assessment in international clinical settings. In C. Belar (Ed.), *Handbook of clinical psychology: Cultural factors.* New York: Elsevier.

Butcher, J. N., Sullivan, J., & Kerwin, C. (1997). Accuracy of computer-based MMPI-2 reports: A field study of psychotherapist ratings. Presented at the 31st Annual Symposium on Recent Developments in the Use of the MMPI/MMPI-2, Minneapolis, Minnesota.

Gillet, I., Simon, M., Guelphi, J., Baun, A., Monier, C. Seunevei, F., & Svarna, L. (1996). The MMPI-2 in France. In J. N. Butcher (Ed.), *International Adaptations of the MMPI-2: A handbook of research and clinical applications.* Minneapolis, MN: University of Minnesota Press.

Stenmark, D. (1995); & Ambrose, P. (1995, March). Role of objective personality assessment in managed care: A forum presentation. Presented at the 30th Annual Symposium on Recent Developments in the Use of the MMPI/MMPI-2, St. Petersburg, Florida.

2

Clinical Decision Making in Managed Health Care

T. Mark Harwood
Larry E. Beutler
Daniel Fisher
Monica Sandowicz
Ann Leslie Albanese
Mary Baker

Clinical Decision Making in Managed Health Care

While approximately 30% of the U.S. population qualify for one or more psychiatric diagnoses (Regier et al., 1988), only one in five of these individuals actually seeks and receives mental health treatment (Castro, 1993). Over the last decade, health care costs have escalated at an astounding rate, averaging from two to three times the rate of inflation; even more dramatically, in view of the number of eligible individuals receiving services, mental health care expenditures have increased over 30% per year (Giles, 1993). Psychiatric patients currently account for approximately one-quarter of all hospital days in America (Kielser & Sibulkin, 1987). National efforts to respond to these needs have converged to create a proliferation of diverse managed health care programs. The nature and structure of these programs often change at such a rapid rate that systematic evaluations of their impact are frequently out of date by the time they are completed. Each change is intended to correct the assumed failures of the preceding one, but there is little evidence that these efforts either have stemmed the increasing costs of health care or have addressed the needs that gave rise to managed health care systems in the first place.

The first-generation managed care systems of the 1970s were established in order to (1) increase the availability of high-quality health services, (2) control unnecessary health care expenditures, and (3) provide a vehicle for the practice of preventive measures (Karon, 1995). In spite of some early success, many believe that con-

13

temporary systems are too frequently driven by the incentive of controlling costs to successfully reach the ternary goals that gave rise to early health care systems (Karon, 1995). Psychotherapists often resent what they perceive to be financially motivated treatment restrictions, and patients are often dissatisfied with the minimal services provided by a health care system that seems only to be interested in cost (Karon, 1995). While yet to be realized, managed health care is both a reality and a potentially positive method of maintaining costs while ensuring access to service. To balance these economic and service delivery forces, however, treatments must become more focused, brief, and effective than they currently are.

One timely, efficient, and effective strategy to accomplish these goals is to comprehensively and systematically individualize mental health care. That is, we must be able to identify the patient characteristics and presenting problems that require, and will benefit from, treatment and then use this knowledge to discriminately assign treatment settings, therapists, strategies, and procedures. We must work to obtain the information that will allow us to (1) prescribe treatment settings that are no more restrictive than needed for the particular patient and problem presented, (2) identify the point at which treatment can be safely terminated, (3) employ providers that are the least expensive among those with the skills necessary to address the patient's problems, and (4) achieve the maximal benefit possible for the time involved. Doing this means reversing the general tendency among managed health care institutions to eschew the role of initial evaluation and, instead, to participate with clinicians and researchers to develop evaluation processes that identify qualities of patients and environments that are directly related to making these decisions. Judging from contemporary literature that describes the relationships among patient characteristics and treatment outcomes, this will probably mean reducing the reliance on categorical diagnostic formulations and increasing the reliance on environmental and dimensionalized qualities of patients that can effectively be used to vary the levels and components of care (Beutler & Clarkin, 1990; Beutler & Harwood, 1995a). Systematic pretreatment assessment can be an avenue for informing the selection of the most appropriate treatment for the individual's unique problem(s) and characteristics (Beutler & Harwood, 1995b). However, the nature of the assessment is dictated as much by the types of services provided as by the nature of the patient's condition. Thus, to review the relationship between patient needs and optimal treatments is of little value without knowing the nature of the services that are or can be provided in managed health care programs.

In the following pages, we will (1) review the evolution and nature of managed health care models as these apply to defining the nature of mental health treatments that are available, (2) discuss some of the issues that stem from efforts to provide treatment within a system of care that is in a continued state of flux, and (3) suggest some methods and models for individualizing patient assessment in a way that will improve the effectiveness and efficiency of treatment.

History of Managed Health Care

In the United States, health care costs are rising more rapidly than any other segment of our economy, more than doubling the general rate of inflation (Resnick &

DeLeon, 1995). Estimates are that health care costs will consume 20% of our gross national product by the year 2000 (Resnick & DeLeon, 1995). Although the recent expansion of managed health care is, in large part, a response to medical/social economics (Hersch, 1995); the emergence of managed health care may be traced back to the early 1900s (DeLeon et al., 1991).

In 1906, two physicians established the Western Clinic in Tacoma, Washington, the first prepaid group practice. This clinic contracted with the lumber industry providing medical care to lumber employees at the rate of $0.50 per individual per month (DeLeon et al., 1991). A later notable event took place in 1929 when the Ross–Loos Medical Group contracted with employees and families of the Los Angeles County Department of Water and Power for a consumer-controlled comprehensive health plan (DeLeon et al., 1991).

The next wave of noteworthy historical developments in managed health care was initiated by Kaiser Permanente in the 1930s (DeLeon et al., 1991). This program was initiated because Henry J. Kaiser, one of the principle builders in the development of the Hoover Dam, had difficulty recruiting construction crews to relocate their families to the desert due to the paucity of available medical care. Dr. Sidney Garfield offered to sell the necessary services to Kaiser at a cost to the corporation of $0.05 per employee work hour (DeLeon et al., 1991). The Kaiser Permanente Health Plan thrived after going public following the end of World War II. The success of this plan depended on the timeliness of its promise to provide comprehensive health coverage and preventative services at relatively low subscriber rates and without the exclusions, limitations, and high deductibles that were customary at that time (DeLeon et al., 1991).

Until 1937, most managed health care programs were on the west coast. However, in 1937 the Group Health Association (GHA), the first HMO on the east coast, opened its doors in Washington, D.C. (DeLeon et al., 1991). As of 1989, GHA was comprised of approximately 150,000 members or covered individuals; 55% of its membership were commercial or corporate group employees, 40% were federal employees, and the remaining 5% were direct payers or individuals with personal coverage (DeLeon et al., 1991).

The Nixon administrations' stance on national health care (Nixon's 1971 and 1972 Health Message to Congress) coupled with the HMO Public Service Act of 1973 encouraged the development and expansion of managed health care programs by providing federal funding for their development and initiated a *federal qualification* certification process for identifying those HMOs that met financial and organizational standards (DeLeon et al., 1991; Resnick et al., 1994). To address the joint needs of cost-savings and quality, this legislation mandated that mental health services provided by federally chartered HMOs must offer at least 20 sessions of outpatient mental health care (short-term evaluation and crisis intervention) and medical-care/appropriate referral services for chemical dependency (Richardson & Austad, 1994).

From its inception, managed health care has been a source of affordable yet high-quality care available to many and has generally enjoyed popular support. To address lingering problems with quality, however, the past two decades have seen the progressive evolution through three health care generations. The first-generation managed health care model relied on telephone review and offered limited benefits. The second generation of managed health care embodied these same characteristics with the additional feature of initiating unmanaged provider networks that were administered through a negotiated and discounted fee for service. The current, third generation of managed health care expanded availability of benefits through the use of brief, focused therapies administered by preferred providers trained in time-limited treatment. Now emerging within this third generation is the "prime provider" or "retained provider," a system of identifying panels of professionals who have demonstrated their efficacy and efficiency in providing a wide range of services (Cummings, 1995).

Contemporary Managed Health Care Models (HMO, PPO, EAP, etc.)

Until the 1980s, managed health care was synonymous with Health Maintenance Organizations (HMOs). Managed health care has recently evolved into several different models of which HMOs and their derivatives are subtypes (DeLeon et al., 1991). HMOs may be classified into four basic types: staff, group, independent practice associations, and network/direct contract models (Austad & Hoyt, 1992; Resnick et al., 1994). Other models of managed health care include those offered as preferred provider organizations (PPOs) and employee assistance programs (EAPs). While our discussion will be limited to these major models, it is instructive to note that mixed models of managed health care exist and may include various features of all of the foregoing models (Hillman, 1988).

Managed health care, in its various forms, is essentially an organized system of securing health care services from hospitals, physicians, and other providers/workers for a designated population (Resnick et al., 1994). Various systems arrange and market their health care plan to employers or individuals by recruiting bids and contracts from providers and provider groups, based on estimates of the projected costs of identified health services. For a fixed prepaid fee, employers and individuals subscribe to an HMO, for example, entitling them to the services provided by that health plan (Resnick et al., 1994). Open-panel HMOs grant some autonomy to patients in their selection of providers and allow great participation from any qualified professional in the community (Resnick et al., 1994). Closed-panel HMOs typically limit the selection of providers to those health professionals employed or identified by the HMO itself. Benefits vary from plan to plan and often incorporate limits on the maximum amount of care provided or services available. In effect, all MHC programs require systems for (1) collecting fees and (2) distributing payments.

Collecting Fees   Three basic payment structures have been used by managed health care systems to manage costs: fee-for-service, prospective payment, and capitation. To some extent, these payment systems distinguish among HMOs, PPOs, and other models of care. Fee-for-service financial arrangements typically involve the provider submitting a bill directly to the consumer for the time spent delivering services. Traditional indemnity insurance providers have used this method and the consumer was required to submit the bill to the insurance carrier for reimbursement. A modification of this arrangement involves the managed care agency negotiating a reduced price directly with the provider, in order to control costs, and the provider then bills the health service organization for the time spent. PPOs generally still utilize this latter payment structure (Richardson & Austad, 1994) since this system does not pose inordinate financial risks to the provider.

Capitation is a system of payment where a provider or group of providers contract to deliver all the necessary health care services required by a specified population for a fixed cost (flat fee) per enrolled member or employee (Richardson & Austad, 1994). In order to keep costs low, contemporary HMOs and IPAs (independent practice associations) usually employ this system, but it requires them to assume some "risk." Risk, in this context, is defined as the difference between subscribers fees and the actual cost of health services. HMOs incur a financial loss if the cost of provided services exceeds premiums/prepayment amounts (DeLeon et al., 1994). In this system, providers have a financial disincentive to refer to or consult with outside specialty providers due to the additional cost of utilizing such services. Since subscribers may leave the system if they are dissatisfied, HMOs often have the delicate task of balancing quality care with cost containment under the burden of legal obligations to accept any enrollee regardless of prior medical history or health status while providing all necessary medical services for a capitated fee (Resnick et al., 1994). Under this type of plan, most HMOs offer only the minimal mental health benefits that are mandated by their national charters or state laws (Resnick et al., 1994).

The third system of prospective payment employs diagnostic-related groups (DRGs) as their basis for establishing fixed treatment prices. Fees are set as the average cost of treating patients with a given diagnosis. Because of the low correspondence between diagnosis and cost, this procedure is just beginning to be applied to mental health conditions and cannot adequately be evaluated for strengths and weaknesses (Richardson & Austad, 1994).

Distribution of Payments   In all managed care systems, the procedures for determining the distribution of money to the providers (i.e., case management and/or utilization review) have frequently been a problem for psychologist-providers (Resnick et al., 1994). The gate-keeper to reimbursement is often a medical generalist, unskilled in psychiatric disorders or psychosocial interventions, who controls access to, duration of, and, sometimes, type of treatment (Resnick et al., 1994). In some systems of managed care, the gatekeeper has operated as an encumbrance demanding that the psychologist periodically justify treatment decisions to a gatekeeper who has little or no background in mental health. Adversarial roles frequently develop and patients may be deprived of appropriate and necessary care (Resnick et al., 1994).

The staff model HMO employs a cohort of providers as salaried employees or contractors operating out of HMO-owned facilities instead of distributing money on the basis of service delivery. In this model, providers are salaried; however, financial incentives may be provided if performance and increased profits for the HMO warrant. Non-staff providers are generally excluded from the "in-house" or closed panel business arrangements that typify the staff model (Resnick et al., 1994).

Another variation of procedures for distributing payments to providers is the group model, which involves the establishment of a contractual agreement between the HMO and a finite group of specified practitioners. This defined group of providers is much the same as the exclusive closed panel feature in the staff model, and outside providers are usually excluded from the group model business system. The HMO arranges a capitated per-subscriber fee that remains constant regardless of the number of treatment visits made. This creates a financial incentive to minimize services/increase efficiency and/or avoid incurring additional costs by utilizing outside consultation or referral to psychologists or other specialty providers (Resnick et al., 1994). The principle difference between the group model and the staff model is that services in the former model may be provided in either a centralized location or, as is usually the case, in the various offices of contracted practitioners.

Considered an open-panel system, the independent practice association (IPA) model provides health care from within the practitioner's private office. The IPA contracts with a large network of professionals to deliver specific services for a reduced fee or capitated payment. The IPA, in turn, contracts with an HMO on a slightly higher capitated basis to provide services to the HMO members (Austad & Hoyt, 1992; Resnick et al., 1994).

The network/direct contract model, a variant of the group model and also an open panel system, is more commonly found in rural areas (Resnick et al., 1994). HMOs network throughout surrounding communities and contract with the individual practitioner or with small groups of professionals. In this model, many individual practitioners are recruited into the HMO system. HMO members are generally treated in the provider's private office with little or no reliance on clinics or centralized multispecialty practices (Resnick et al., 1994). This model is similar to a PPO model in that the providers may be organized by an administrative marketing organization, functioning as a broker between groups of providers and patients/subscribers. In some instances, PPOs may be organized by a group of professionals. When professionals form the PPO, they may assume the underwriting risk for the provision of services, something that is uncommon to PPOs in general. In the PPO, risk is essentially the same as in the HMO system, being the difference between the actual cost of delivering professional services and the fees paid to the HMO (Resnick et al., 1994).

Two broad types of PPOs exist: provider-based and third-party-sponsored. Although there are variants of the models, in provider-based PPOs, professionals generally operate from their private offices. In this model, fee-for-service care is combined with financial incentives that encourage patients to use an established panel of selected providers (Austad & Hoyt, 1992). The fee is usually some specified percentage below that which is the customary and reasonable rate; however, fees are negotiable (Resnick et al., 1994). In some PPOs, patients may use nonpreferred providers (practitioners not on the preestablished panel) for a higher (nondiscounted) fee (Austad & Hoyt, 1992). PPOs offer the following advantages to psychologists: (1) prompt payment of services, (2) steady flow of referrals, (3) the opportunity for psychologists to sit on the board of directors for PPO policy, and (4) the flexibility to act as a broker and participate in PPO profits. In the third-party-sponsored model, contracts between payors and providers are negotiated by a third party (Resnick et al., 1994).

EAPs are often not considered to be managed care organizations (Resnick et al., 1994). However, EAPs often function like typical capitated programs to provide restricted types and amounts of mental health care to employees and their families. EAPs frequently contract with independent providers or groups that may deliver services at the employment site or the providers' office (Resnick et al., 1994). They place a premium on the rapid identification and alleviation of those employee problems that have the potential for negative financial and organizational impact. Generally, EAPs provide for crisis intervention, problem assessment, and brief counseling. EAPs also provide referral to private and community-based resources for more enduring problems of employees and their families (Resnick et al., 1994). Substance abuse counseling, educational programs targeting occupationally relevant health and life-style issues, and psychotherapy for stress-related problems may be provided by EAPs (Resnick et al., 1994).

A diversity of program models and services fall under the auspices of EAPs; however, for our purposes, EAPs will be separated into two broad models of service delivery: internal and external. Dependent on the actual model, a variable mix of professionals, paraprofessionals, and even nonprofessionals comprise the staff of EAPs (Resnick et al., 1994). The internal model EAP is typically housed administratively within a department associated with human resources, and psychologists may act as administrators or providers. In this model, staff may operate on-site or from offices located nearby and are directly employed either by the organization or by company-contracted on-site independent consultants (Resnick et al., 1994). Although easy accessibility is available with internal models, employees may have concerns regarding privileged information; therefore, confidentiality and professionalism are important qualities that must be established and ensured to overcome any potential reluctance/fear associated with internal models.

External models of EAPs may provide services from an individual practitioner or a variety of independent practitioner groups, private consulting firms, or nonprofit agencies (Resnick et al., 1994). Ordinarily, services are received off-site. However, providers may operate on-site, thus accessing the important advantages of observing the work-site-related stress and organizational culture.

Monitoring and Controlling Treatments

Managed care programs vary widely in the quality and even the type of mental health services provided. While the intent of programs is to provide the most effective treatments available, decisions about what treatments to provide are often based on less than optimal information. Not infrequently, the nature of services provided are based on external factors, initial costs, and relationships that are assumed to exist between patient diagnoses and treatment outcomes in the absence of truly empirical data. Overly cost-conscious management, to the neglect of the patient, has given a bad name to the managed care industry in general (cf. Karon, 1995; Hoyt & Austad, 1992; Schreter et al., 1994).

The wide array of mental health treatments utilized by managed care organizations may be separated into two broad modal groupings: medical/somatic treatments and psychosocial treatments. Regardless of the modality or format, appropriate treatment may be defined as the least intrusive treatment that is necessary to be effective.

Medical Treatments

Medical/somatic mental health treatments include pharmacotherapy, convulsive treatment (e.g., insulin treatment), electroconvulsive treatment (ECT), and psychosurgery. Pharmacotherapy is the most frequently utilized form of mental health treatment within the domain of medical/somatic interventions. Approximately 10% of the population in the United States and other urbanized industrial societies receive a prescribed psychoactive medication each year (Klerman et al., 1994). Not surprisingly, some managed health care systems have advocated or promoted the use of medical interventions in an attempt to contain costs. Gibson (1994) notes that Federal Employees Blue Cross reviewers once used guidelines favoring the use of radical procedures (psychosurgery, insulin therapy, high-dosage drug therapy, and ECT) over psychosocial interventions and low-dosage pharmacotherapy.

The major forms of pharmacotherapy include antidepressant, antimanic, anxiolytic/antianxiety, and antipsychotic or neuroleptic medications. Psychomotor stimulants, sedative hypnotics, antipanic, and antiobsessional medications are also available. Since the 1950s, pharmacotherapy has greatly expanded in both class and type of compound; that is, various psychotropic medications (mostly synthetic) have been developed for a growing range of mental health problems (Klerman et al., 1994). Research interests and funding for the study of psychopharmacotherapeutic agents have also grown in recent decades, contributing to this expansion.

Although studies have produced inconsistent and contradictory results, the efficacy of pharmacotherapy for certain patient groups has received a great deal of empirical support (e.g., Elkin et al., 1989, McLean & Taylor, 1992, Sotsky et al., 1991). The difficulty continues to be selecting the best medication from an extensive armamentarium of drugs for a particular patient. Treatment decisions are largely based on patient diagnosis, the clinician's limited familiarity with available drugs, and unvalidated clinical lore. Treatments may be offered without a clear understanding of the mechanism of action, the length of effect, or the efficacy of available alternatives. From a cost–benefit perspective, pharmacotherapy may, at first blush, look quite attractive to managed care organizations; the administration of psychotropic medications is not labor intensive, often produces rapid symptom reduction, and may quickly return the patient to premorbid levels of functioning.

The "quick-fix" promise of pharmacotherapy is attenuated by several factors. Many patients are refractory to pharmacotherapy or prove unresponsive to the various psychotropic medications, treatment noncompliance and dropout rates are very high; and there are often unpleasant and complicating side effects of medication, especially among neuroleptics (e.g., tardive dyskinesia and parkinsonism). Medications also frequently interact with one another in iatrogenic ways, complicating treatment further and even introducing new problems. The fundamental concern of many, however, is that patients learn little about how to cope and adapt from medication and may require psychosocial training and psychotherapy to help establish more effective lives (Beutler & Clarkin, 1990).

ECT has generated much controversy and apprehension due to its indiscriminate use and unrefined practice in the 1940s and 1950s. Today, ECT is often seen as a "last resort" treatment for patients that are suffering from severe depression and have proven unresponsive or refractory to other forms of treatment (e.g., pharmacotherapy). This status, though, may reflect the presence of negative attitudes about the procedure rather than being a clear statement about the value of the procedures. Refinements such as the use of muscle relaxants, anesthetics, and administration of the least amount of electrical current required to produce seizure have decreased the discomfort or trepidation surrounding ECT and have greatly reduced the possibility of physical injury and memory loss (Sackeim et al., 1985).

Although the therapeutic mechanisms of ECT are not completely understood, it is known that ECT-induced seizures result in substantial neurotransmitter release. Deficiencies in various neurotransmitters have been implicated in the etiology of depression (Hollister & Csernansky, 1990). Despite our present lack of understanding regarding its palliative mechanisms, ECT has proven effective in bringing many patients out of severe depression faster than pharmacotherapy (Janicak et al., 1985).

Psychosurgery, too, is extremely controversial and rarely used. It is a radical procedure designed for the selective destruction of specific brain areas. Nerve tissues connecting the frontal lobe with the limbic system and/or hypothalamus are the most frequently selected areas for incision because of their implicated role in emotional regulation. The possibility of iatrogenesis (e.g., intellectual impairment) with this procedure is relatively high due to the complexity and delicacy of brain structures; however, improved techniques and greater knowledge of the central nervous system have begun to reduce risks and provide relief for otherwise refractory acutely suicidal/severely depressed patients or those suffering from intractable pain (Valenstein, 1980). Again, the absence of support for such treatments may rest more with their lack of acceptance in the political and medical communities than in their empirically established rates of effectiveness.

Psychosocial Treatments

Included among the psychosocial treatments are individual, group, and family formats of variable duration and frequency and myriad strategies (e.g., cognitive, experiential, eclectic therapies) under which manifold techniques are subsumed (Beutler & Clarkin, 1990). These fine distinctions, often considered important to theoreticians and clinicians, are largely ignored by MHC. Instead treatments are defined and distinguished on the basis of method of delivery (individual, group, family), general intensity (time and frequency), and setting (inpatient, outpatient, and partial care). Beyond these rough distinctions, psychosocial treatments are generally treated, within MHC, as being rather amorphous and homogeneous.

Individual psychotherapy, although the least economical, is the most commonly sought psychosocial format by patients/clients due, at least in part, to the intimate and confidential nature such a format provides. In contrast, group treatments are looked upon favorably and encouraged in managed care systems due to their assumed efficacy, diversity of applications, and potential savings (Richardson & Austad, 1994).

The nature of the group format promotes its efficiency and efficacy. One therapist may see several patients in a short amount of time, and group members become involved in their own and others progress when they assume a therapeutic role for others as providers of support and advice (Beutler & Clarkin, 1990). Group formats are extremely therapeutic for certain presenting problems, and treatment manuals have been developed for use in the group format (e.g., "*Agoraphobia*," Barlow and Waddell, 1985).

Family treatment formats are not often approved under managed care programs. In companies where it is covered, family therapy is approved for situations where the family dynamic or situation is seen as a treatment factor that must be addressed in the pursuit of effective and efficient treatment. That is, the family system is either deteriorating or in some type of dysfunctional equilibrium and contributing/causing/maintaining the presenting problem(s). The burden of long-term treatment is often placed on family members by the exclusive focus on acute conditions, and little opportunity is afforded by MHC for providing family support and therapy to offset these stresses. In some managed care partial and inpatient care programs, family groups are encouraged to facilitate patient discharge, help prevent relapse, and educate members on general and appropriate mental health issues.

It should be noted that managed mental health systems may support the use of several psychosocial treatment formats (perhaps even a wide array of them) for some types of patients, particularly if there is little evidence that any specific treatments are efficacious and if the problem has defied clear understanding. Thus, treatment of substance abusers may include varieties of group and individual therapy along with self-help programs, medication, hospitalization, and "intervention," even though several of these component treatments contain elements or implied philosophies that are diametrically opposed to other methods within the same treatment program. The presence of such conceptual muddiness in the application of treatments is not restricted to MHC systems, but characterizes the field of mental health delivery more generally. It is a problem that must be addressed if treatment costs are to be contained.

Also assigned in the service of containing costs are various other ways in which treatment intensity is controlled and monitored. Generally speaking, long-term mental health treatments are discouraged among managed health care organizations; that is, most managed care entities only approve short inpatient stays (3–10 days) and only approve four to six sessions of outpatient mental health coverage at a time. Managed health care organizations have generally adopted the model of focused, brief, intermittent mental health treatment maintained throughout the life cycle (Cummings, 1995; Hoyt & Austad, 1992) for most problems. Contrasting with the prevailing model of long-term care among independent practitioners, the focus of MHC is on short-term treatment of acute stress, with correspondingly less effort devoted to chronic conditions and to identifying the specific treatment procedures or guiding philosophies that best work with different patient groups.

Once resolution of the acute episode is achieved, patients are taken out of therapy with the option of returning if further treatment is deemed necessary. The strength of this model lies in its goal-oriented, directive, and problem-solving approach designed to quickly return the patient to premorbid levels of functioning/productivity with minimal disruption to daily living. The model's systemic weakness resides in the failure to adequately prevent recurrence and address the needs of those with either subclinical or chronic problems. Patients that require longer treatments are typically not well served in managed care organizations (Gabbard, 1994). Long-term treatments are typically necessary for persons suffering from complex (perva-sive) and chronic (long-standing) problems (Beutler & Clarkin, 1990). Those pa-tients with severe character disorders (e.g., borderline personality disorder) are included as candidates for long-term or unlimited therapy (Kernberg, 1984).

The intensity of treatment offered by MHC also varies as a function of treatment setting. The number of outpatient sessions allowed per year in managed mental health varies slightly, and the usual allotment is 20 sessions. Inpatient services also vary with regard to approved length of stay, with 3–10 days being the usual allot-ment for each stay. Outpatient treatment is typically seen as a cost-effective tradeoff for more expensive inpatient stays (Schreter, 1994). When inpatient care is approved, as it may be for those with severe functional impairment, individual treatment is recommended and stays are generally brief (Harbin, 1994). Inpatient care is looked on as reserved for acute medical necessity, usually leading to rapid pharmacologi-cal stabilization and discharge within 7–10 days (Gabbard, 1994). The acute-stabilization philosophy often produces a revolving door situation where the ulti-mate costs of many brief stays exceed the cost of one extended, comprehensive, and focused treatment (Gabbard, 1994).

Challenges of Managed Health Care Systems

The success and survivability of MHC programs depends on the abilty to control access to treatment and to monitor the use of services. It is noteworthy, however, that few, if any, of the decisions regarding setting, intensity, or modality are guided di-rectly by empirically established criteria. Decisions to cover eight sessions, twenty sessions, or more are quite arbitrary and often seem capricious both to the practi-tioner and to the patient. The decisions rest on uncertain assumptions and foster an attitude of distrust regarding the need to improve patient evaluation procedures. There is no consistently accepted set of criteria for selecting among the wide vari-ety of psychosocial interventions or, for that matter, for determining when to pro-vide various combinations of psychosocial and medical treatments. The absence of such guidelines and corresponding or supporting research represents the major challenge to controlling costs in contemporary systems. Several developments are collapsing to further place pressure on health care systems to increase service qual-ity while controlling costs. The future depends on the success of MHC to come to grips both with internal pressures and weaknesses of the system and to accommo-date external developments and advances in research.

Internal Constraints on the Efficacy
of Mental Health Delivery in MHC

The issues surrounding mental health delivery within managed care systems are manifold and may only be addressed superficially within the parameters of this chapter. In general, concerns centering around the quality of care (efficacy, efficiency), autonomy of the provider/clinician, and managed care profit margins comprise the bulk of controversy.

The dilemmas in managed mental health care stem, at least partially, from the basic marketing and characteristic limitations of the system. That is, patients are promised high-quality care while purchasers (usually employers concerned with profits/health care expenses) are promised reduced costs (Schreter, 1994). As one would expect, it is difficult to simultaneously achieve both goals. Yet, it is important to remember that the quality of services provided and the financial bottom line must achieve a balance or dissatisfied patients/employers will switch to a better managed system of health care (Zimet, 1994).

Despite arguments and resistance by some patients and professionals, managed care has continued to proliferate, indicating a degree of necessity and marketability/satisfaction. In time, managed care may be expected to improve satisfying greater numbers of patients and professionals alike; however, for now, controversy will continue to surround managed mental health care as systems struggle to achieve an equilibrium between the financial bottom line and the therapeutic bottom line.

Those disapproving of managed care argue that there is no convincing evidence it controls costs (Gabbard, 1994) or that there is no scientific support for limited benefit design (England, 1994). Another argument against managed care centers around administration. That is, the cost of administration in managed care is enormous and it is estimated that one-quarter of the United States health care spending goes to managed care administration (Gabbard, 1994). Moreover, the quality of services has come under question, offering little consolation to cost-conscious consumers (Karon, 1995).

Time/Costs   Many managed care companies are "for profit" and therefore it is logical that they have a primary concern with the financial bottom line (Karon, 1995; Schreter, 1994). Recently, managed care was forced to carefully scrutinize its role in mental health because in the last 15 years mental health care costs have doubled as a percentage of the overall health care dollar (Hersch, 1995). In answer to the current trend in mental health, aggressive cost control strategies have been implemented in attempts to cope with the growing financial burden of managed mental health care. Such strategies include case management/utilization review, increased co-payments, increased deductibles, caps on sessions, caps on both expenditures per year and lifetime, exclusion of certain diagnoses, and exclusion of various treatment formats such as marriage and family therapy (Hersch, 1995).

Behavioral health "carve-outs" (i.e., the separation of mental health and substance abuse care from major medical benefits) is an example of an innovative and aggressive cost-control strategy. With carve-outs, care is purchased from another vendor (i.e., a provider/company at risk) promising to provide improved cost and quality controls (England, 1994). Carve-out companies bid for contracts and make assumptions regarding the intended covered populations' demand (e.g., monthly demand) for mental health services. These companies compete for contracts, quoting wildly different rates and various combinations of services provided (England, 1994). Underbidding is problematic to patients because they are often denied necessary services.

Aggressive cost control has persisted in mental health care (Karon, 1995) even though there is no evidence to suggest that what is cheapest in the short term maintains its advantage over the long term (Patterson, 1994) and despite the increasing evidence of medical cost-offset (Pallak et al., 1993). Medical cost-offset refers to the reduction in medical expenditures (and eventual savings in the long run) that results when patients receive psychological treatment for emotional problems instead of inappropriately utilizing nonpsychiatric and often ineffective services for emotional distress (Pallak et al., 1993). Estimates are that 60% of all visits to primary care physicians are stress-related (VandenBos & DeLeon, 1988), suggesting that effective mental health treatments might be effectively used in a wider variety of circumstances than currently covered by most MHC.

As many managed care organizations are for-profit, the concomitant financial considerations often constrain therapeutic decision making. Although cost control is paramount for the managed care organization, quality of care must remain high; that is, patients deserve high-quality and effective treatment in their own right (Beutler & Harwood, 1995b). The aforementioned underscores the need for prescriptive treatments—that is, focused, empirically validated/highly effective, and efficient/brief therapies that increase the likelihood of treatment success.

External Regulation   Prior to the recent expansion of managed care, mental health professionals generally were trusted to set reasonable and customary fees and to regulate their own treatment loads. The diagnosis and treatment plan was established by the provider and generally went unquestioned. This degree of autonomy has been lost in today's managed health programs. Restrictions are imposed by MHC policies, not only on the length and type of treatment that can be provided but also on the use of assessment procedures that, paradoxically, can be used to increase treatment efficiency (e.g., Butcher, 1990). Under today's managed care, clinical decisions may be subject to the constraints of regulatory agencies (typically external) with a vested interest in cost control (Karon, 1995).

Case management and utilization review (UR) are managed care's primary regulatory mechanisms designed to eliminate unnecessary expenses and efficiently promote the expected treatment outcome. While the provider decides on the type and intensity of treatment, case management companies and UR determine which, if any, services will be covered by the insurance or health care plan (Reinhardt & Shepherd, 1994). Case management differs from its earlier predecessor, UR, in that it is intended as a more comprehensive and detailed approach to treatment planning/service monitoring and is most appropriate for complicated cases (Reinhardt & Shepherd, 1994).

Confidentiality between clinician and patient, once sacrosanct, no longer exists under case management or UR, and review requirements often create additional administrative burden for providers. The disruption of confidentiality in managed care has resulted in flagrant legal and ethical violations, the interested reader is referred to Higuchi (1994) for a discussion of confidentiality and other legal issues in managed mental health care.

Adversarial relationships have developed between behavioral health care professionals and managed care administrators when less trained personnel or personnel lacking a day-to-day knowledge of the patient challenge and/or constrain criti-cal psychiatric or psychological decisions (Gabbard, 1994; Harbin, 1994). Some patients may feel conflicting pressures due to the review process itself; that is, pa-tients may feel that they must improve quickly or else the reviewer will decide that the patient cannot benefit from treatment, and at the same time they may also feel that their mental health care will be terminated prematurely if they show any im-provement at all. One case example described a situation in which the clinician eventually added the review process to the medical record problem list because the reviewer's scrutiny had become a major stressor to the patient and was judged a barrier to effective treatment (Gabbard, 1994).

Although not as prominent today, secret criteria (i.e., undisclosed review crite-ria for inpatient and outpatient services) still exist in some companies (Gabbard, 1994; Schreter, 1994). Without public criteria on treatment approval/coverage, clinicians are left uncertain regarding the provision of relevant information and frustrated by management decisions often seen as arbitrary and inconsistent. Re-cent legislative pressure and provider lobbying has resulted in most managed care companies making public their criteria on medical necessity (Harbin, 1994). The control of treatment, once held by the provider, has shifted and those with control in managed care may not understand psychological services as they apply to the patient; that is, diagnosis alone does not inform treatment decisions (Beutler & Harwood, 1995b). One must consider the complexity of the clinical situation, in-cluding comorbidity and the unique characteristics that inform alternative treat-ment selection and ultimately affect therapeutic outcome. While problems with managed care regulatory agencies exist, many review systems function well and may actually provide effective and high-quality care in a cost-efficient manner (Reinhardt & Shepherd, 1994). Good and effective case management (and UR to a lesser degree) considers the array of patient characteristics and alternative treatment modalities/formats/intensities before identifying the most efficacious and efficient combination (Butcher, 1990, 1995a), recognizing that short-term costs may be increased by managed care if long-term savings are projected (Reinhardt & Shep-herd, 1994).

Consumer Satisfaction   Much as there is division regarding the efficacy of man-aged care among professionals, there exists a similar division among patients re-garding satisfaction of mental health services, with consumers giving mixed reviews to managed care. That is, patients with problems amenable to the treatment model favored by managed care (e.g., noncomplex, situation-specific, and treatable in a brief, symptom-focused prescriptive fashion) typically give good ratings to their companies when managed correctly. Patients with problems not easily treated within the managed care model (e.g., complex and chronic) are less likely to be satisfied with treatments. Furthermore, underbidding among carve-out companies has often resulted in denial of services and/or diminished quality of services (England, 1994) and disgruntled consumers.

Attendance to the financial bottom line has created some questionable practices by a few managed care companies and may contribute to consumer dissatisfaction. For example, some managed care companies have inappropriately rewarded reviewers for denying care (Harbin, 1994). In addition, prevention efforts have generally been ignored in managed health care because this involves spending money now on an uncertain future; that is, managed care is primarily concerned with this year's budget and not the budget in years ahead (Karon, 1995). Moreover, there may be an over-reliance on medication to circumvent the need to provide more than six sessions of psychotherapy (Karon, 1995).

External Developments That Affect Effective Mental Health Delivery in MHC

Manualized Treatments (Standardized Protocols)   Financial risk among many managed health care systems has created a disincentive to provide more than the minimal services necessary. Identifying the nature of treatment is complicated by the presence of over 300 brand-name therapies (Beutler, 1991), each of which is offered by a clinician primarily as a function of familiarity rather than effectiveness (Clarkin & Hurt, 1988). MHC has only partially dealt with this problem by encouraging the use of brief and intermittent treatment models for both inpatient and outpatient services (Carson, 1993, Cummings, 1995). As Carson (1993) recognizes, treatments of short duration and specific focus must be of especially high quality to be effective and clinicians must develop expertise in the appropriate selection and implementation of brief psychotherapies.

To ensure such quality, attention is turning to the advantages of using brief therapies that have been manualized and that have received scientific support of efficacy. Manualized therapies are now the standard in quality psychotherapy research due in part to their purity of treatment delivery, empirical validation, and aid to replication. Treatment manuals are comprised of written materials that guide the clinician's decisions regarding treatment factors—for example, treatment intensity, procedures, techniques, identification of patient themes and the selection of focal targets of change (Beutler & Clarkin, 1990; Kazdin, 1994). In other words, manuals specify both the prescribed and proscribed aspects of therapy (Lambert & Bergin, 1994). The inherent structure of treatment manuals may provide a safeguard against the negative effects of therapist-induced treatment inconsistency (Beutler et al., 1994) as suggested by evidence that use of treatment manuals produces more consistent results and less negative effects than does non-use (Henry et al., 1993; Piper et al., 1990). Another positive aspect of treatment manuals is that they can speed up the therapist training process (Lambert & Bergin, 1994).

A number of time-limited, manualized treatments have been found to be clinically efficacious and effective (Giles, 1993). The need to distinguish between scientifically credible treatments and those that lack empirical support led the Division of Clinical Psychology of the American Psychological Association to establish a task force to identify those manualized treatments that meet certain criteria of efficacy. The task force has published a list of treatments and corresponding patient problems for which there is empirical support of efficacy (Task Force on Promotion and Dissemination of Psychological Procedures, 1995). While this task force eschews the temptation to use this list as a means of identifying what treatments should be supported by MHC, it is likely that cost considerations will result in providers being encouraged to demonstrate that their treatments are those that have been supported by research studies of efficacy. This move also will likely force gatekeepers and MHC administrators to become more familiar with the various models of psychotherapy than they currently are.

There are two dangers in this movement to recommend contemporary manuals for patients with different diagnostic conditions, however. First, the models supported by contemporary efficacy research are probably not representative of those methods usually utilized in practice. Research studies utilize criteria and procedures to ensure both compliance with the model and skill in its implementation. Concomitantly, most studies find that a large number of practitioners fail to achieve the levels of skill and compliance demanded by research. To incorporate such prescriptions into MHC programs will require a system of monitoring not only the training of practitioners but also their levels of compliance and skill. The expected tendency for all practitioners to verbally endorse models of treatment for which insurance coverage is offered without substantially altering their practices in correspondent ways will be difficult to address.

A second problem with this approach is that contemporary manuals are designed to be quite inflexible. They are applied in the same way to all patients of a given diagnosis (major depression, anxiety, etc.) without regard for the wide differences among patients that exist in any diagnostic group (Beutler, 1991). The desirability of manuals that are flexible enough to address the wide variety of people who have any given diagnosis has not been addressed to date by the task force on empirical treatments.

Presently, manuals are uniformly constructed from a single theoretical framework, some of which (e.g., cognitive therapy, interpersonal therapy, etc.) are unfamiliar to many practitioners. The exclusive reliance on such manuals does not address the possibility that effective interventions may combine procedures from several different theories. Similarly, defining the conditions for which treatments are effective in diagnostic terms is inconsistent with the empirical evidence that suggests that diagnosis and problem type account for inconsequential proportions of variance in determining the effects of treatment. Most therapies are transportable across different diagnostic conditions, with some modification, and nondiagnostic characteristics of patients may be more important than diagnostic ones in defining the limits of using any given approach. Indeed, conceptually, aspects of patient response styles, conceptual levels, severity, intellect, and so on, may be much more important both in serving as indicators/contraindicators and in predicting what treatment will work than the diagnosis or problem initially presented (see Butcher, 1990).

Prescriptive Therapies for Patient-Treatment Matching   Concern with the foregoing problems have fostered the development of models and manuals for prescriptive treatment selection (e.g., Goldstein & Stein, 1976; Beutler, 1983; Beutler & Clarkin, 1990; Beutler et al., 1991b; Beutler & Harwood, 1995a). As initially formulated by Arnold Lazarus (1967), the goal of what have become "prescriptive interventions" is to apply the most empirically sound procedures available, based upon patients' presenting problems and styles of relating, regardless of the theoretical viewpoint from which these procedures derive. The various models of treatment that constitute "prescriptive treatment" emphasize that the procedures of psychotherapy can effectively be applied independently of much, if not most, of the theory in which they are embedded. The commitment to empirical evidence over theoretical models prevails in contemporary renditions of the several approaches to prescription (Norcross & Goldfried, 1992; Stricker & Gold, 1993).

Available prescriptive models vary in several ways, including (a) whether they focus on mental health treatment generally or only on the specific domain of psychotherapy, (b) the availability of a manualized form of the prescribed interventions, (c) the nature and identity of the patient dimensions considered to be important, (d) whether the focus of integration among treatments is at the level of theory, strategy, or techniques, and (e) the amount of research generated by the approach.

Three models of integrating the diversity of psychosocial treatment have achieved critical levels of visibility. The most widely recognized is that proposed by Arnold Lazarus (1981) under the name *multimodal therapy* (MMT). MMT was the original technical eclectic therapy, and it retains the distinction of being most closely focused on the selection and use of specific techniques, among the prescriptive treatments.

MMT begins with a careful and systematic assessment of the patient, the patient's strengths and weaknesses, and the context in which the problems occur. The assessment is guided by a structured procedure that systematically gathers data that are relevant to seven domains of experience. These domains are identified by the acronym BASIC-ID and include aspects of behavioral (B), affective (A), sensory (S), imaginal (I), cognitive (C), interpersonal (I), and biologic/neurophysiologic (D = drugs) functioning. Unique to multimodal therapy is the use of a modality profile, which is an inventory used by the clinician to gain information on all seven areas of client functioning in order to design a comprehensive and individualized treatment program. In addition, the multimodal approach emphasizes the importance of observing the client's predominant pattern of generating negative affect. For example, some people tend to dwell first on aversive images (I), followed by unpleasant sensations (S), to which they attach negative cognitions (C), leading to maladaptive behavior (B) (Lazarus, 1992). This I–S–C–B "firing order" may require a different treatment plan than, for example, a C–I–S–B sequence. Thus, Lazarus recommends that clinicians select techniques from across a wide range of theoretical approaches in accordance with the client's particular response pattern and associated symptoms.

Transtheoretical psychotherapy (Prochaska, 1984) has chosen to focus on the level of strategy rather than specific technology. Thus, it is much more closely focused on a theory of behavior and behavior change than MMT. The foundation for this approach is a theoretically derived stage model of readiness to change. Initially, four stages of change were hypothesized, but this list has expanded to five with the infusion of research (Prochaska & DiClemente, 1992), each identifying a stage of progress and readiness to effect change.

From an assessment of the patient's readiness for change, the transtheoretical clinician identifies both a class of therapeutic processes that are expected to be especially adept at affecting the motivation to proceed to the next level of readiness, and a level of focus for the intervention. Thus, stages vary from precontemplative, through contemplative, preparation, action, and maintenance; the ten basic processes of change correspond to such means as consciousness raising (for the precontemplative patient), self-evaluation (for the contemplative patient), self-liberation (for the patient in preparation for change), contingency management, and relationship facilitation (for those in action and maintenance stages). These methods are applied to levels of desired change that are identified as symptom/situational, maladaptive cognitions, interpersonal conflicts, family systems conflicts, and intrapersonal conflicts.

Prochaska and DiClemente (1992) indicate that in order to assess the client's readiness for change, the clinician must take into account both the client's perception of the problem and actions he has taken to address the problem. In addition, the clinician should assess the degree of effort the client has invested in negotiating the challenges associated with earlier stages of change. For example, a client who appears to be in the preparation stage of change presumably has engaged in the consciousness-raising and self-evaluation processes associated with the contemplative stage. In order to determine if this is in fact the case, the clinician would assess the client's level of awareness and understanding regarding the problem.

Once the the client's present stage of change has been determined, the clinician proceeds to assess (a) the levels at which change must occur and (b) the order in which these levels should be addressed. Both the client's and therapist's perspectives should be considered in assessing these levels. Ideally, Prochaska and DiClemente suggest that the initial intervention should occur at the symptom/situational level, due to the probability that change will occur most quickly at this level. Furthermore, the problem as identified at this level often represents the primary reason for the client's distress. In addition to a clinical interview, these authors indicate that at least several questionnaires have been investigated empirically for use in assessing the stages, levels, and processes of change.

Systematic treatment selection (STS; Beutler & Clarkin, 1990) derived from two separate efforts to define patient indicators and contraindicators for applying a variety of treatment approaches. It combined the breadth of Francis et al. (1984) and the specificity of Beutler (1983) with other integrative models, including the stages of readiness embodied in transtheoretical psychotherapy (Prochaska, 1984). Empirical literature was scoured to define patient dimensions that had prognostic value, especially those that characterized research programs that had compared two or more forms of treatment. Four levels of clinician decisional process were defined, arranged in sequence to produce a graduated and increasingly fine-grained set of decisions about treatment. The first level of decision making represents the assessment phase. The clinician evaluates and judges the patient's status on a series of dimensions that have predictive properties to the decisions that follow. Initially, a large number of patient characteristics were defined, but these have been reduced to a half-dozen major dimensions with the passage of time and the accumulation of research evidence (Beutler & Consoli, 1992; Gaw & Beutler, 1995). These dimensions include: problem severity, problem complexity, coping style, reactance potential, motivational distress, and social support.

From an assessment of these initial patient dimensions, decisions are made regarding the context of treatment (setting, intensity, modality, format, etc.), the method of developing a working relationship (role induction, support versus confrontation, use of self-disclosure, etc.), and the particular procedures and goals to be pursued (outcomes, intermediate goals, strategies, and techniques). In particular, the patient dimensions of reactance potential, coping style, problem complexity, and motivational distress have been identified as important variables in making specific treatment choices. Specifically, these dimensions serve as indicators or contraindicators for the use of directive and nondirective procedures, insight versus behavioral procedures, systemic versus symptomatic goals, and the use of supportive versus arousal evocation procedures.

Methods of assessment for the patient dimensions vary, as does the empirical evidence for the validity of these methods. In the interest of brevity, we will confine ourselves here to providing a brief description of some approaches to assessing some of those dimensions that have been supported by empirical evidence as important in matching treatments to patients.

Interpersonal reactance may be defined as one's sensitivity and resistance to the influence of others. General patient reactance is best assessed by observing a patient's response to the demand characteristics of the therapy environment. Once this is observed, the therapist is well advised to counterbalance the patient's level of reactance with procedures that deemphasize the therapist's power and efforts to change the patient. The use of nondirective, supportive, self-management and paradoxical interventions are examples of procedures that may serve this function. Formal measures of reactance potential also exist, notably the Therapeutic Reactance Scale (Dowd et al., 1991).

Coping style consists of the collection of conscious and unconscious methods a person uses both to manage anxiety or threat and to compensate for problems in everyday functioning. Perhaps the most frequently cited empirical measurements of coping style are derived from the MMPI-2. For example, specific subscales of the MMPI-2 are associated with a tendency for the patient to manifest either an externalizing or an internalizing coping style (Butcher, 1995b). Once again, these measures are the notable examples among a number of formal assessments that have been used to assess coping style and its correlates.

Problem severity represents a continuum of functioning ranging from little or no impairment or incapacitation (Gaw & Beutler, 1995). Severity is an external dimension and is assessed in terms of objective measures of functional impairment. These measures include the Beck Depression Inventory (BDI; Beck et al., 1961), the Hamilton Rating Scale for Depression (HRSD; Hamilton, 1967), the Symptom Check List 90-R (SCL 90-R; Derogatis et al., 1976), and the State–Trait Anxiety Inventory (STAI; Spielberger et al., 1970).

While MMT is a strong advocate of the importance of using empirical evidence, there has been little systematic use or testing of the model among adult patients with clinical disorders. There is research on child and school-based behaviors, but this research provides ambiguous results and the diversity of procedures used does not permit a concise statement of efficacy. A major contribution of the transtheoretical approach has been in the development of methods for identifying readiness for change and for identifying the nature of change processes that may be linked to each stage of readiness (Prochaska & DiClemente, 1992). It has also been applied successfully to studies of smoking cessation.

Systematic treatment selection has provided an organizing model for both initiating and consolidating a great deal of research (Beutler & Clarkin, 1990; Beutler et al., 1991a). The dimensions used in this model were selected on the basis of an empirical rather than theoretical criteria, quite unlike either MMT or transtheoretical psychotherapy (Beutler, 1979, 1991). As such, there is reasonable post hoc support for the use of some indicators that derive from a variety of unrelated sources that has been complemented by a prospective research program (Beutler et al., 1991b).

Patient Dimensions that Predict Treatment Response

As a member of the APA task force on empirically established treatments, the second author and colleagues recently conducted an extensive review of literature, with special but nonexclusive focus on the treatment of clinical depression. Several hundred references were extracted from various sources and scoured for compliance with the general criteria used by the original task force to distinguish treatments that have been empirically validated for effects. These criteria included (1) two independent, random assignment studies offering support of the matching dimension and (2) the presence of a manual that guided treatment. We sought evidence of the nature of relevant patient variables that distinguished between the effects of two or more treatments.

The following paragraphs present a very brief synopsis of those dimensions of patient and treatment that we believe meet these criteria at the present time. These conclusions are framed as statements that set the targets for assessing patient qualities that will enhance their ability to respond to treatments that vary in strategy and technique. We conclude that three patient variables, interpersonal reactance, coping style, and problem severity or functional impairment, can be used as indicators for varying treatments in specified ways. We will summarize the status of three sets of therapeutic strategies and the associated patient dimensions with which they are differentially effective. The classes of therapy intervention that are predisposed by the patient variables are as follows: (1) antidepressant medication plus psychotherapy versus psychotherapy alone, (2) directive versus nondirective treatments, and (3) behavioral versus insight-oriented treatments.

Antidepressant Medication Plus Psychotherapy versus Psychotherapy Alone

There is little question that antidepressant medications are an effective intervention for many forms of depression. There are many classes of medication and a plethora of effects associated with various of these. The current review surveyed evidence for the possibility that the concomitant use of medication and psychotherapy is more effective for some patients than for others. We addressed this issue by reviewing the results of studies in which medication plus some form of psychotherapy was compared to psychotherapy-only and medication-only groups of depressed patients. We particularly looked for patient conditions and attributes in which differential effects were observed.

The results of our survey provided criteria level support for the following conclusion:

1. Unipolar depressed patients with high levels of functional impairment tend to respond better to psychotherapies that are supplemented with tricyclic antidepressants than to psychotherapy alone.

The most extensive treatment of this issue has been the NIMH Treatment of Depression Collaborative Research Program (Elkin et al., 1989) in which imipramine along with supportive therapy was compared to a pill placebo, cognitive therapy (Beck et al., 1979), and interpersonal psychotherapy (Klerman et al., 1984). Several different analyses of functional impairment (external ratings of impaired functioning) suggest that especially among those with moderate and severe depression, tricyclic antidepressants along with supportive psychotherapy exert at least modestly superior effects to the various psychotherapies. Specifically, for example, Sotsky et al. (1991) reported that among patients with moderate to severe clinical ratings of depression at intake, imipramine was more effective than the psychotherapies. Among those with mild to moderate depression severity, however, interpersonal psychotherapy (Klerman et al., 1984) was the more effective treatment.

This finding was generally supported by Prusoff et al. (1980), who compared amitriptyline alone and in combination with interpersonal psychotherapy for those with major depression. Among those with moderate and severe levels of major depression, the combination of medication with psychotherapy was most effective; but among those with mild and moderate levels of initial depression, interpersonal psychotherapy alone was as effective as any of the other treatments.

Directive versus Nondirective Treatments

Interventions that rely on the direct transmission of knowledge or instructions from therapist to patient through interpretations, homework assignments, or directed awareness also seem to be differentially effective when compared to procedures that rely on patient initiation. Moreover, this relationship cuts across patient diagnosis. The patient quality with which therapist directiveness interacts is embodied in states and traits that are usually described by the terms "resistant" or "reactant." This literature, along with the methods of measuring patient states and traits, has been recently summarized quite extensively (Beutler et al., 1996). This literature supports the following conclusion:

2. Directive interventions are indicated for patients whose resistant states and traits are low, but contraindicated for those whose resistant states and traits are high.

A number of studies support this conclusion, including two separate studies, conducted by two different research teams in two different countries (Beutler et al., 1991a; Beutler et. al., 1991c).[1] Beutler et al. (1991a) conducted a prospective study of patient resistance and directive versus nondirective therapies among 63 patients with major depression. The results indicated that both initially and one year after treatment ended (Beutler et al., 1993), the results of treatment were predicted by how well the level of patient resistance measures matched with level of therapy directiveness. Highly directive therapies were contraindicated for patients with high trait resistance but indicated for those with low trait resistance, while the reverse was true for self-directed interventions.

Similarly, an analysis of these same variables from the archival data of the Bernese Psychotherapy Research Program (Switzerland) revealed that client-centered therapies were indicated for those patients who scored high on one or more measures of trait resistance but contraindicated for those who measured low on the resistance scales. In contrast, behavioral therapy proved to be most effective among those who scored relatively low on measures of trait resistance and was found to do poorly with those who scored high on measures of trait resistance. Other controlled studies lend further support to this conclusion as applied to problem domains that extend beyond that of depression (e.g., Patterson & Forgatch, 1985).

Behavioral versus Insight-Oriented Treatments

An extensive body of literature has accumulated to support the proposition that behavioral and various nonbehavioral therapies are differentially effective for patients who are high and low on indices of impulsivity and aggressiveness. This body of research suggests that the following conclusion both applies in the narrow domain of depressive spectrum disorders and extends to other problem domains as well.

3. Behavioral strategies are more effective than nonbehavioral ones for patients who are impulsive, and this pattern is reversed for those with well maintained impulse controls.

This conclusion is supported by a large number of investigations, principle among which are the study by Beutler et al. (1991a) previously reviewed and studies by Kadden et al. (1990) and Sloane et al. (1975). In addition to looking at patient resistance, Beutler et al. (1991a) evaluated levels of patient impulsivity and aggressiveness as defined by standard personality inventories. They found that insight-oriented therapies were advantageous over cognitive-behavioral ones among those with low levels of antisocial and aggressive behavioral tendencies, but the reverse pattern occurred among patients with high levels of impulsivity and aggressiveness. These results were further exaggerated one year after treatment (Beutler et al., 1993) when lower relapse rates and the likelihood of continuing improvement was found to be associated with good matches between patient impulsivity and the nature of treatment.

Impetus for the foregoing study was derived from an earlier study of psychotherapy by Sloane et al. (1975). In this study, experienced and widely recognized psycho-

---

[1]Though the first author is the same for these two studies, they are in fact independent investigations, sharing only a collaborative analysis of certain hypotheses.

analytic and behavioral therapists were assigned a mixed group of outpatients for treatment. The insight procedures of analytic therapy proved to be most successful among those whose personality inventories suggested were dysphoric, anxious, and introverted, while the reverse was true among patients who were impulsive, aggressive, and prone to somatization.

Kadden et al. (1990) extended the findings to patients with alcohol dependence. Patients who were well socialized did better in an insight-oriented interpersonal therapy than in a cognitive-behavioral therapy while the reverse was true among those who were poorly socialized and impulsive.

These studies varied somewhat in level of control and prospective design. Both Beutler et al. (1991a) and Kadden et al. (1990) tested a priori hypotheses, using systematic manuals, while Sloane employed a loosely structured therapy model and a post hoc analysis of patient–treatment interactions to reach their conclusions. These results are further supported by a host of other studies, similarly varying in level of control and manualization, including studies on long-term follow-up (Cooney et al., 1991), cross-cultural populations (Beutler et al., 1991c), and psychiatry clinic outpatients (Beutler & Mitchell, 1981; Calvert et al., 1988). The persistent pattern of these results reinforce the conclusion, but with a cautionary note, that the relationship between measures of impulsivity and patient resistance states or traits is still uncertain and the two dimensions are probably not independent.

Conclusions

Managed mental health care generally advocates an eclectic brief treatment philosophy to psychotherapy (Hoyt & Austad, 1992). Treatment manuals mesh well with this philosophy, stressing adherence to specific therapeutic procedures over single theoretical orientations. As therapists become more experienced, they may utilize aspects of various manuals to create highly individualized treatments tailored to the specifics of the presenting problem (Lambert & Bergin, 1994). Treatment manuals promote efficiency, are developed with briefer treatments in mind, and therefore should be attractive to managed care organizations concerned with cost and effect.

The use of prescriptive manualized treatments (i.e., strategic treatment protocols) intended for specific presenting problems could greatly increase treatment efficacy and efficiency. Many manualized treatments have been developed for a wide array of disorders (e.g., Cognitive Therapy of Depression, Beck et al., 1979; Focused Expressive Psychotherapy, Daldrup et al., 1988; Time-Limited Dynamic Psychotherapy, Strupp and Binder, 1984). It is important to note that manualized therapies are not necessarily rigid, inflexible treatments. Indeed, even in application to psychotherapy research, manuals can be developed to be flexible and to allow for divergence based on clinical judgment and patient needs. Manuals of prescriptive interventions are specifically designed to address these issues; however, continuing challenges face the effective use of manuals for the purpose of increasing the effectiveness of managed health care systems.

Chief among the concerns that must still be addressed may be overcoming the ambivalent, if not negative, attitude toward pretreatment assessment that characterizes most MHC systems. Being able to selectively assign treatments requires that relevant patient qualities and traits be assessed (Butcher, 1990). Overcoming this difficulty, in turn, depends on educating MHC programs about the differences and distinctions that exist in different models of psychotherapy and of their selective effects on patient groups whose differences are not reflected in diagnosis alone. An active educational program and sound confirmatory research on MHC populations will be necessary to accomplish these tasks.

A related problem is the need to develop comprehensive but economical assessment procedures. One of the reasons for the hesitancy among MHC programs to authorize assessment is that usually this involves a good deal of patient time and expensive psychological consultation. Time-efficient self-report and computer-generated assessment procedures would make assessment programs more feasible than they are at present (Butcher, 1990, 1995a).

A third challenge is the development of focal treatment programs along with treatment training and monitoring procedures that will ensure that clinicians are in fact providing the assigned treatments and are doing so consistently. This requires the development of multimedia and self-guided instructional resources along with effective but minimally invasive in-treatment monitoring procedures. The advent of computerized instruction and compact disks for infusing these materials with audio and video materials will enhance the development of training programs. Distance learning and monitoring systems will also evolve to economize the contact between trainer and trainee. In the meantime, patient, therapist, and supervisor reports must be developed that will allow unobtrusive, in-treatment monitoring at acceptable levels of reliability. Concomitantly, procedures to identify ineffective clinicians can be developed to aid and supplement tracking procedures that flag those patients whose course of treatment is not producing the desired results.

ACKNOWLEDGMENTS   Grant No. AA 08970 to the second author provided support for this work. Correspondence about this chapter should be addressed to Larry E. Beutler, Department of Education, Counseling/Clinical/School Psychology Program, University of California, Santa Barbara, CA 93106.

References

Austad, C. S., & Hoyt, M. F. (1992). The managed care movement and the future of psychotherapy. *Psychotherapy* 29, 109–118.

Barlow, D. H., & Waddell, M. T. (1985). Agoraphobia. In D. H. Barlow (Ed.), *Clinical handbook of psychological disorders: A step-by-step treatment manual.* New York: Guilford.

Beck, A.T., Ward, C. H., Mendelsohn, M., Mock, J. & Erbaugh, J. (1961). An inventory for measuring depression. *Archives of General Psychiatry* 4, 561–571.

Beck, A. T., Rush, A. J., Shaw, B. F., & Emery, G. (1979). *Cognitive Therapy of Depression.* New York: Guilford Press.

Beutler, L. E. (1979). Toward specific psychological therapies for specific conditions. *Journal of Consulting and Clinical Psychology* 47, 882–897.

Beutler, L. E. (1983). *Eclectic psychotherapy: A systematic approach.* Elmsford, NY: Pergamon Press.

Beutler, L. E. (1991). Have all won and must all have prizes? Revisiting Luborsky et al.'s verdict. *Journal of Consulting and Clinical Psychology* 59, 1–7.

Beutler, L. E., & Clarkin, J. F. (1990). *Systematic Treatment Selection: Toward targeted therapeutic interventions.* New York: Brunner/Mazel.

Beutler, L. E., & Consoli, A. J. (1992). Systematic eclectic psychotherapy. In J. C. Norcross & M. R. Goldfried (Eds.), *Handbook of Psychotherapy Integration.* New York: Basic Books.

Beutler, L. E., & Harwood, T. M. (1995a). Prescriptive psychotherapies. *Applied and Preventive Psychology* 4, 89–100.

Beutler, L. E., & Harwood, T. M. (1995b). How to assess clients in pretreatment planning. In J. N. Butcher (Ed.), *Clinical personality assessment: Practical approaches* (pp. 59–77). New York: Oxford University Press.

Beutler, L. E., & Mitchell, R. (1981). Psychotherapy outcome in depressed and impulsive patients as a function of analytic and experiential treatment procedures. *Psychiatry* 44, 297–306.

Beutler, L. E., Engle, D., Mohr, D., Daldrup, R. J., Bergan, J., Meredith, K., & Merry, W. (1991a). Predictors of differential response to cognitive, experiential, and self-directed psychotherapeutic procedures. *Journal of Consulting and Clinical Psychology* 59, 333–340.

Beutler, L. E., Engle, D., Shoham-Solomon, V., Mohr, D. C., Dean, J. C., & Bernat, E. M. (1991b). University of Arizona: Searching for differential treatments. In L. E. Beutler & M. Crago (Eds.), *Psychotherapy research: An international review of programmatic studies* (pp. 90–97). Washington, D.C., American Psychological Association.

Beutler, L. E., Mohr, D. C., Grawe, K., Engle, D., & MacDonald, R. (1991c). Looking for differential treatment effects: Cross-cultural predictors of differential psychotherapy efficacy. *Journal of Psychotherapy Integration* 1, 121–141.

Beutler, L. E., Machado, P. P. P., Engle, D., & Mohr, D. (1993). Differential patient X treatment maintenance of treatment effects among cognitive, experiential, and self-directed psychotherapies. *Journal of Psychotherapy Integration* 3, 15–31.

Beutler, L. E., Machado, P. P., & Neufeldt, S. A. (1994). Therapist variables. In A. E. Bergin & S. L. Garfield (Eds.), *Handbook of psychotherapy and behavior change* (pp. 229–269). New York: John Wiley & Sons.

Beutler, L. E., Sandowicz, M., Fisher, D., & Albanese, A. L. (1996). Resistance in psychotherapy: What conclusions are supported by research? *In session* 2, 77–86.

Butcher, J. N. (1990). *MMPI-2 in psychological treatment.* New York: Oxford University Press.

Butcher, J. N. (Ed.) (1995a). *Clinical personality assessment.* New York: Oxford University Press.

Butcher, J. N. (1995b). Interpretation of the MMPI-2. In L. E. Beutler & M. Berren (Eds.), *Integrative assessment of adult personality* (pp. 206–239). New York: Guilford.

Calvert, S. J., Beutler, L. E., & Crago, M. (1988). Psychotherapy outcome as a function of therapist–patient matching on selected variables. *Journal of Social and Clinical Psychology* 6, 104–117.

Carson, D. (1993). Managed care: A provider perspective. *Managed Mental Health Care* 59, 81–87.

Castro, J. (1993). What price mental health? *Time* May, 31, 59–60.

Clarkin, J. D., & Hurt, S. W. (1988). Psychological assessment: Tests and rating scales. In J. A. Talbot, R. E. Hales, & S. C. Yudofsky (Eds.), *Textbook of psychiatry*. Washington, D.C.: American Psychiatric Press.

Cooney, N. L., Kadden, R. M., Litt, M. D., & Getter, H. (1991). Matching alcoholics to coping skills or interactional therapies: Two-year follow-up results. *Journal of Consulting and Clinical Psychology* 59, 598–601.

Cummings, N. A. (1995). Impact of managed care on employment and training: A primer for survival. *Professional Psychology: Research and Practice, 26,* 10–15.

Daldrup, R. J., Beutler, L. E., Engle, D., & Greenberg, L. S. (1988). *Focused expressive psychotherapy: Freeing the overcontrolled patient*. New York: Guilford Press.

DeLeon, P. H., VandenBos, G. R., & Bulatao, E. Q. (1991). Managed mental health care: A history of the federal policy initiative. *Professional Psychology: Research and Practice 22*, (1) 15–25.

DeLeon, P. H., Bulatao, E. Q., & VandenBos, G. R. (1994). Federal Government Initiatives in Managed Health Care. In S. A. Shueman, W. G. Troy, & S. L. Mayhugh (Eds.), *Managed behavioral health care: An industry perspective* (pp. 97–112). Springfield, IL: Charles C Thomas.

Derogatis, L. R., Rickels, K., & Rock, A. F. (1976). The SCL-90 and the MMPI: A step in the validation of a new self-report scale. *British Journal of Psychiatry 128*, 280–289.

Dowd, E. T., Milne, C. R., & Wise, S. L. (1991). The therapeutic reactance scale: A measure of psychological reactance. *Journal of Counseling and Development 69*, 541–545.

Elkin, I., Shea, T., Watkins, J. T., Imber, S. D., Sotsky, S. M., Collins, J. F., Glass, D. R., Pilkonis, P. A., Leber, W. R., Docherty, J. P., Feister, S. J., & Parloff, M. B. (1989). National Institute of Mental Health Treatment of Depression Collaborative Research Program: General effectiveness of treatments. *Archives of General Psychiatry 46*, 971–982.

England, M. J. (1994). From fee-for-service to accountable health plans. In R. K. Schreter, S. S. Sharfstein, & C. A. Schreter (Eds.), *Allies and adversaries* (pp. 3–8). Washington, D.C.: American Psychiatric Press.

Francis, A., Clarkin, J. F., & Perry, S. (1984). *Differential therapeutics: A guide to the art and science of treatment planning in psychiatry*. New York: Brunner/Mazel.

Gabbard, G. O. (1994). Inpatient services: The clinician's view. In R. K. Schreter, S. S. Sharfstein, & C. A. Schreter (Eds.), *Allies and adversaries* (pp. 22–30). Washington, D.C.: American Psychiatric Press.

Gaw, K. F., & Beutler, L. E. (1995). Integrating treatment recommendations. In L. E. Beutler & M. R. Berren (Eds.), *Integrative assessment of adult personality* (pp. 280–319). New York: Guilford Press.

Gibson, R. W. (1994). Quality of care guidelines: The clinician's view. In R. K. Schreter, S. S. Sharfstein, & C. A. Schreter (Eds.), *Allies and adversaries*. Washington, D.C.: American Psychiatric Press.

Giles, T. R. (1993). *Managed mental health care: A guide to practitioners, employers, and hospital administrators*. Boston, MA: Allyn & Bacon.

Hamilton, M. (1967). Development of a rating scale for primary depressive illness. *British Journal of Social and Clinical Psychology 6*, 278–296.

Harbin, H. T. (1994). Inpatient services: The managed care view. In R. K. Schreter, S. S. Sharfstein, & C. A. Schreter (Eds.), *Allies and adversaries* (pp. 11–22). Washington, D.C.: American Psychiatric Press.

Henry, W. P., Schacht, T. E., Strupp, H. H., Butler, S. F., & Binder, J. L. (1993). The effects of training in time-limited dynamic psychotherapy. Changes in therapist behavior. *Journal of Consulting and Clinical Psychology 61*, 434–440.

Hersch, L. (1995). Adapting to health care reform and managed care: Three strategies for survival and growth. *Professional Psychology: Research and Practice* 26, 16–26.

Higuchi, S. A. (1994). Recent managed-care legislative and legal issues. In R. L. Lowman & R. J. Resnick (Eds.). *The Mental health professionals guide to managed care* (pp. 83–118). Washington, D.C.: American Psychological Association.

Hillman, A. L. (1988). Financial incentive for physicians in HMOs. *The New England Journal of Medicine* 31, 1743–1748.

Hollister, L. E., & Csernansky, J. G. (1990). Antidepressants. In *Pharmacology of psychotherapeutic drugs* (3rd ed., pp. 59–95). New York: Churchill Livingston.

Hoyt, M. F., & Austad, C. S. (1992). Psychotherapy in a staff model health maintenance organization: Providing and assuring quality care in the future. *Psychotherapy* 29, 119–129.

Janicak, P. C., Davis, J. M., Gibbons, R. D., Ericksen, S., Chang, S., & Gallagher, P. (1985). Efficacy of ECT: A meta-analysis. *American Journal of Psychiatry* 142, 297–302.

Kadden, R. M., Cooney, N. L., Getter, H., & Litt, M. D. (1990). Matching alcoholics to coping skills or interactional therapies: Posttreatment results. *Journal of Consulting and Clinical Psychology* 57, 698–704.

Karon, B. P. (1995). Provision of psychotherapy under managed health care: A growing crisis and national nightmare. *Professional Psychology: Research and Practice* 26, 5–9.

Kazdin, A. E. (1994). Methodology, design, and evaluation in psychotherapy research. In A. E. Bergin & S. L. Garfield (Eds.), *Handbook of psychotherapy and behavior change* (4th edition, pp. 19–71). New York: John Wiley & Sons.

Kernberg, O. F. (1984). *Severe personality disorders: Psychotherapeutic strategies.* New Haven: Yale University Press.

Kielser, C., & Sibulkin, A. (1987). *Mental hospitalization: Myths and facts about a national crisis.* Newbury Park, CA: Sage Publications.

Klerman, G. L., Weissman, M. M., Rounsaville, B. J., & Chevron, E. S. (1984). *Interpersonal psychotherapy of depression.* New York: Basic Books.

Klerman, G. L., Weissman, M. M., Markowitz, J., Glick, I., Wilner, P. J., Mason, B. & Shear, M. K. (1994). Medication and psychotherapy. In A. E. Bergin & S. L. Garfield (Eds.), *Handbook of psychotherapy and behavior change* (4th edition, pp. 734–782). New York: John Wiley & Sons.

Lambert, M. L., & Bergin, A. E. (1994). The effectiveness of psychotherapy. In A. E. Bergin & S. L. Garfield (Eds.), *Handbook of psychotherapy and behavior change* (4th ed.) pp. 72–113. New York: John Wiley & Sons.

Lazarus, A. A. (1967). In support of technical eclecticism. *Psychological Bulletin* 21, 451–416.

Lazarus, A. A. (1992). Multimodal therapy: Technical eclecticism with minimal integration. In J. C. Norcross & M. R. Goldfried (Eds.), *Handbood of psychotherapy integration* (pp. 231–263). New York: Basic Books.

McLean, P., & Taylor, S. (1992). Severity of unipolar depression and choice of treatment. *Behavior Therapy* 30, 443–451.

Nixon, R. M. (1971). Special message to the Congress proposing a National Health Strategy. In *Public papers of the Presidents of the United States* (pp. 170–186). Washington, D.C.: U.S. Government Printing Office.

Norcross, J. C., & Goldfried, M. R. (Eds.) (1992). *Handbook of psychotherapy integration.* New York: Basic Books.

Pallak, M. S., Cummings, N. A., Dorken, H., & Henke, C. J. (1993). Managed mental health, Medicaid, and medical cost offset. *New Directions for Mental Health Services* 59, 27–40.

Patterson, D. Y. (1994). Outpatient services: The managed care view. In R. K. Schreter, S. S. Sharfstein, & C. A. Schreter (Eds.), *Allies and adversaries* (pp. 51–60). Washington, D.C.: American Psychiatric Press.

Patterson, G. R. & Forgatch, M. S. (1985). Therapist behavior as a determinant for client noncompliance: A paradox for the behavior modifier. *Journal of Consulting and Clinical Psychology* 53, 846–851.

Piper, W. E., Azim, H. F. A., McCallum, M., & Joyce, A. S. (1990). Patient suitability and outcome in short-term individual psychotherapy. *Journal of Consulting and Clinical Psychology* 58, 475–481.

Prochaska, J. O. (1984). *Systems of psychotherapy: A transtheoretical analysis* (2nd edition). Homewood, IL: Dorsey Press.

Prochaska, J. O., & DiClemente, C. C. (1992). The transtheoretical approach. In J. C. Norcross & M. R. Goldfried (Eds.), *Handbook of psychotherapy integration* (pp. 300–334). New York: Basic Books.

Prusoff, B. A., Weissman, M. M., Klerman, G. L., & Rounsaville, S. J. (1980). Research diagnostic criteria subtypes of depression: Their role as predictors of differential response to psychotherapy and drug treatment. *Archives of General Psychiatry* 37, 796–801.

Regier, D. A., Boyd, J. H., Burke, J. D., Rae, D. S., Myers, J. K., Kramer, M., Robins, C. N., George, L. K., Karno, M., & Locke, B. Z. (1988). One month prevalence of mental disorders in the U.S. *Archives of General Psychology* 45, 977–986.

Reinhardt, B., & Shepherd, G. L. (1994). Behavioral health case review: Utilization review or case management? One company's view. In S. A. Shueman, W. G. Troy, & S. L. Mayhugh (Eds.), *Managed behavioral health care: An industry perspective* (pp. 76–96). Springfield, IL: Charles C Thomas.

Resnick, R. J., & DeLeon, P. H. (1995). News from Washington, D.C. *Professional Psychology: Research and Practice* 26, 3–4.

Resnick, R. J., Bottinelli, R. W., Puder-York, M., Harris, B., & O'Keefe, B. E. (1994). Basic issues in managed mental health services. In R. L. Lowman & R. J. Resnick (Eds.), *The mental health professionals guide to managed care* (pp. 41–62). Washington, D.C.: American Psychological Association.

Richardson, L. M., & Austad, C. S. (1994). Realities of mental health practice in managed-care settings. In R. L. Lowman & R. J. Resnick (Eds.), *The mental health professional's guide to managed care*. Washington, D.C.: American Psychological Association.

Sackeim, H. A., Portnoy, S., Neeley, P., Steif, B. L., Decina, P., & Malitz, S. (1985). Cognitive consequences of low dosage ECT. In S. Malitz & H. A. Sackeim (Eds.), *Electroconvulsive therapy: Clinical and basic research issues*. Annals of the New York Academy of Science.

Schreter, R. K. (1994). Outpatient services: The clinician's view. In R. K. Schreter, S. S. Sharfstein, & C. A. Schreter (Eds.), *Allies and adversaries*. Washington, D.C.: American Psychiatric Press.

Schreter, R. K., Sharfstein, S. S., & Schreter, C. A. (Eds.) (1994). *Allies and adversaries*. Washington, D.C.: American Psychiatric Press.

Sloane, R. B., Staples, F. R., Cristol, A. H., Yorkston, N. J., & Whipple, K. (1975). *Psychotherapy versus behavior therapy*. Cambridge, MA: Harvard University Press.

Sotsky, S. M., Glass, D. R., Shea, T. M., Pilkonis, P. A., Collins, J. F., Elkin, I., Watkins, J. T., Imber, S. D., Leber, W. R., Moyer, J., & Oliveri, M. E. (1991). Patient predictors of response to psychotherapy and pharmacotherapy: Findings in the NIMH Treatment of Depression Collaborative Research Program. *American Journal of Psychiatry* 148, 997–1008.

Stricker, G., & J. R. Gold (Eds.) (1993). *Comprehensive handbook of psychotherapy integration*. New York: Plenum Press.

Strupp, H. H., & Binder, J. L. (1984). *Psychotherapy in a new key*. New York: Basic Books.

Task Force on Promotion and Dissemination of Psychological Procedures (1995). Training in and dissemination of empirically-validated treatments: Report and recommendations. *Clinical Psychologist* 48(1), 3–23.

Valenstein, E. S. (1980). A prospective study of cingulatomy. In E. S. Valenstein (Ed.), *The psychosurgery debate: scientific, legal, and ethical perspectives*. San Francisco: Freeman.

VandenBos, G. R., & DeLeon, P. H. (1988). The use of psychotherapy to improve physical health. *Psychotherapy* 25, 335–343.

Zimet, C. N. (1994). Psychology's role in a national health program. *Journal of Clinical Psychology* 50, 122–124.

3

Determining the Therapeutic Relationship of Choice in Brief Therapy

John C. Norcross
Larry E. Beutler

The rapid evolution of health care delivery and the encroaching dominance of managed care clamor for time-limited psychological interventions tailored to the individual client. Brief prescriptive therapies, in turn, demand integrative, explicit, and empirically based models of treatment selection. Within 6 or 12 or (perhaps) 26 sessions, the psychotherapy practitioner is required to diagnose discrete behavioral or mental disorders, select specific technical and interpersonal methods to remediate those disorders, apply those methods in sequences or stages over the course of treatment, and then rapidly terminate the efficacious treatment while preventing relapse. Infusing objective psychological assessment and research-informed models of treatment selection into practice are two vital antidotes to the afflictions of managed care.

In this chapter, we offer a treatment selection model, rooted in objective psychological assessment and empirical outcome research, for selecting the therapy relationship of choice in the context of brief psychotherapy. To begin, we review the basics of prescriptive eclecticism and therapeutic relationships of choice, including the question of whether there are any interpersonal stances to be applied universally to all clinical situations. We then review four-plus empirically supported client variables that can guide the psychotherapist in tailoring interpersonal stances to individual patients. We conclude by addressing limitations and alternatives to tailoring therapeutic relationships.

A couple of delimiters are in order regarding the purview of this chapter. First, so that we can manage the topic in the allotted space, we focus on what the psychotherapist offers, not on what the client receives in terms of that relationship. Obviously this is a mutual and bidirectional interaction; in fact, a plethora of studies has demonstrated that the quality of therapeutic relationship depends heavily on the patient's ability to relate comfortably to the therapist. Second, the therapist's stance is an interpersonal posture culminating from a balancing act among therapist variables, patient variables, interactional variables, and treatment setting. We do not mean to imply that the therapeutic relationship should be—or could be— free of the therapist's own values and response dispositions. But for the purpose of this chapter we focus on patient variables and interactional variables. And third, the therapeutic relationship offered is only one component and only one decision of the interactive and cumulative treatment context; it is a part of the general plan of clinical strategies tailored to a given client. In order to ground our discussion, we shall presume individual psychotherapy between 6 and 26 sessions with a client suffering from a nonpsychotic disorder.

Systematic and Prescriptive Eclecticism

The need to match patient and treatment has been recognized from the beginning of psychotherapy. As early as 1919, Freud introduced psychoanalytic psychotherapy as an alternative to classical analysis on the recognition that the more rarified approach lacked universal applicability and that many patients did not possess the requisite psychological-mindedness (Liff, 1992). He referred the majority of so-called "unanalyzable" patients for a psychotherapy based on direct suggestion.

As the field of psychotherapy has matured, the genesis of therapeutic change has been properly recognized as more complex and multifaceted than ever. The identical psychosocial treatment for all patients is now recognized as inappropriate and, in selected cases, even unethical (Norcross, 1991). The efficacy and applicability of psychotherapy will be enhanced by tailoring it to the unique needs of the client, not by imposing a conceptual Procrustean bed onto unwitting consumers of psychological services. Prescriptive matching is embodied in Gordon Paul's (1967) famous question: "*What* treatment, by *whom*, is most effective for *this* individual with *that* specific problem, and under *which* set of circumstances?"

Our respective approaches to psychotherapy closely resemble each other in practice and title: *prescriptive eclectic therapy* (Norcross, 1994), *systematic eclectic psychotherapy* (Beutler, 1983), and *systematic treatment selection* (Beutler & Clarkin, 1990). This form of integrative psychotherapy (Norcross & Goldfried, 1992) attempts to customize psychological treatments and therapeutic relationships to the specific and varied needs of individual patients. It does so by drawing on effective methods from across theoretical camps (eclecticism), by matching those methods to particular cases on the basis of empirically supported guidelines (prescriptionism), and by adhering to an explicit and orderly model of treatment selection (systematic). The result of such a systematic and prescriptive eclecticism is a more efficient and efficacious therapy that fits both the client and the clinician.

On the face of it, virtually every psychotherapist endorses prescriptive match-ing; after all, who can seriously dispute the notion that psychological treatment should be tailored to fit the needs of the individual patient in order to improve the outcome of psychotherapy? Its like endorsing (fat free) apple pie and (a good enough) Mom. However, systematic and prescriptive eclecticism goes beyond this simple acknowledgment in at least four ways. (1) Our basis of prescriptive matching is direct evidence from outcome research, rather than the typical theoretical basis. (2) We adopt an integrative or transtheoretical basis that acknowledges the potential con-tributions of multiple systems of psychotherapy, rather than working from within a single theory. (3) The guidelines for prescriptive matching are culled from mul-tiple diagnostic and nondiagnostic client variables, in contrast to the typical reli-ance on the single, static variable of patient diagnosis. (4) Our aim is the research-informed and practice-tested selection of technical interventions *and* interpersonal stances, whereas most previous prescriptive efforts focused narrowly on the selec-tion of disembodied techniques. Our prescriptive matching, then, applies empiri-cal research from multiple theoretical orientations on both diagnostic and non-diagnostic variables to the task of selecting technical and interpersonal interventions.

Therapeutic Relationships of Choice

The traditional process of prescriptive matching, as we have said, was to diagnose the patient and then to select techniques and interventions for that diagnosis. This was the classical definition of eclecticism, which is now recognized as seriously incomplete (Lazarus, Beutler, & Norcross, 1992).

Psychotherapy will never be so technical and impersonal as to overshadow the power of the therapist's ability to form a therapeutic relationship. Moreover, the predictors and contributors to these interpersonal influences are part of psychological science. The historical neglect of interpersonal stance customized to particular clients is all the more serious in that, with most disorders, the therapeutic relation-ship accounts for as much, if not more, of the psychotherapy outcome variance than does clinical technique (Norcross, 1993).

In what follows we hope to examine and advance the process by which psycho-therapists deliberately customize their interpersonal stance to different patients. One way to conceptualize the matter, paralleling the notion of "treatments of choice" in terms of techniques, is how clinicians determine "therapeutic relationships of choice" in terms of interpersonal stances.

Any Universal Interpersonal Stances?

In his 1957 seminal identification of purportedly "necessary and sufficient condi-tions of therapeutic personality change" Carl Rogers embodied unitary treatment formulation at its best *and* at its worst (Norcross, 1992). At their best, his conten-tions stimulated decades of spirited debate, conceptual improvements, and empirical research. He also forcibly redirected our attention to the curative nature of the real relationship in psychotherapy. At their worst, Rogers' contentions perpetuated simplistic formulations and singular therapeutic relationships for all clinical encounters. Rogers concedes the point in the 1957 article: "As I have worked on this problem I have found myself surprised at the simplicity of what has emerged" (p. 95); and "No other conditions are necessary. If these six conditions exist, and continue over a period of time, this is sufficient" (p. 96). These relationship qualities were to be universally applied to all clients, therapies, and problems; he explicitly declared that these conditions do not apply to one type of client or to client-centered therapy in particular.

An entire generation of psychotherapists grew accustomed to thinking about a single set of relationship stances applied to all therapeutic encounters. The predominant model of imparting relationship skills was to install the capacity to experience and convey (or, at least, mimic) the Rogerian facilitative conditions of accurate empathy, positive regard, and congruence. For better and for worse, this is what most psychotherapists were taught to offer to each and every client.

To illustrate the fallacy of this approach, let us invite you to engage in a provocative "thought experiment" (*Gedankenexperiment*; Shapiro, 1986) we conduct as part of our teaching and workshops. The experiment is this: Are there any universal interpersonal behaviors that you seek to manifest in all clinical encounters and with all patients? No exceptions. If so, write them down.

Most psychotherapists respond initially with a brief list of answers that includes things on the order of "attentiveness," "caring," "establishing a safe haven," "communicating respect," "acceptance," and "empathy." With a little prodding, most of these same psychotherapists can nominate several instances in which they intentionally violated these supposedly universal conditions. Paradoxical techniques, for instance, frequently lead one to respond inattentively. Irreverent communication tactics may occasionally lend themselves to communicating disrespect. Confrontations and interpretations may deliberately produce an unsafe feeling of self-realization.

Consider the case of "empathy," the most frequent response given to our provocative thought experiment. Why not empathy as a universal interpersonal stance? Seasoned psychotherapists immediately conjure up exceptions to the empathic rule: openly paranoid patients who reject attempts at empathic immediacy. Several naturalistic studies and a few controlled investigations have found that suspicious and poorly motivated patients perform relatively poorly with psychotherapists who are particularly empathic, involved, and accepting (Beutler et al., 1986). In certain cases, deeply empathic relationships actually retard rates or magnitudes of improvement.

Of course, you may counter with the argument that the empathic therapist would not be particularly empathic and involved with a paranoid patient. And yes, the evolving client-centered definition of empathy emphasizes the therapist experiencing the world of the client by developing idiosyncratic empathy modes predicated upon the particular client and situation (Bohart, 1995; Prochaska & Norcross, 1994). While this is a conceptual and clinical advancement to be sure, the emergent definition of empathy begins to approach our notion of relational flexibility.

Clinical experience and controlled research convincingly demonstrate the error of applying universal or invariant relationship stances to all patients. In his preface to *Differential Therapeutics in Psychiatry*, Robert Michels (1984, p. xiii) summed it as follows:

The easiest way to practice is to view all patients and problems as basically the same, and to apply one standard therapy for their treatment. Although some may still employ this model, everything we have learned in recent decades tells us that it is wrong—wrong for our patients in that it deprives them of the most effective treatment, and wrong for everyone else in that it wastes scarce resources.

Perhaps the closest we come to a universal relationship stance across all clients is, ironically, a relentless commitment to revise just about any relationship stance when in a patient's best interest. M. Scott Peck (1978, p. 149) put it this way:

> Of all the good and useful rules of psychotherapy that I have been taught, there are very few that I have not chosen to break at one time or another, not out of laziness and lack of discipline but rather in fear and trembling, because my patient's therapy seemed to require that, one way or another, I should step out of the safety of the prescribed (analyst's) role, be different and risk the unconventional.

The thought experiment was intended to demonstrate the therapeutic value of revising or discarding the notion of universal relationship stances, as Rogers and others proposed. For every few patients that a particular relationship helps, there is another patient who is hurt by it. The *Gedankenexperiment* may help free us from stagnant and rigid conceptions of the therapeutic relationship. The clinical upshot is to move toward prescriptive matching and relational flexibility that facilitate change.

Four-Plus Matching Variables

Assuming that psychotherapists want to develop a repertoire of relational styles, the question becomes what criteria are used to match different styles with different clients or with the same client at different points in time. More than 200 client variables have been proposed as potential matchmaking markers (Garfield, 1994), and at least 100 of these have been subjected to empirical scrutiny.

We shall address four-plus client markers that guide the selection of relationship stances to offer to individual clients. These four markers all have empirical support in the research literature, all are readily assessed in clinical practice via objective psychological assessment, and all have been sufficiently operationalized to direct specific dimensions of interpersonal relationships. "Four plus" communicates the idea that we shall cover in some detail four client variables, but current research does not permit confident prescriptions of other, promising variables that most clinicians find useful in some circumstances. For each client marker, we review its definition, its measurement via objective assessment, and its implication for customizing the therapeutic relationships of choice.

Patient Expectancies

If you are *attitudinally* empathic with each client, then you will not be *behaviorally* the same with each client (Bohart, 1995; Greenberg et al., 1993). Genuineness is a ground for a therapist to vary considerably in his or her behavior, from client to client; and with the same client, from moment to moment.

When to be cold, warm, or tepid, when to be active, passive, or in between, and when to be professional, casual, or chummy, then, hinges on the person's expectancies. What does the person expect—or perhaps more specifically, what do they want? These expectations reflect one's historical and demographic background and subsequent experiences with psychotherapy. Beutler and Clarkin (1990) have emphasized the role of both extratherapy and within-therapy expectations deriving from these factors. Extratherapy expectations may be embodied in role preferences for the therapist, expectations about the length of treatment, and the nature of mental health. Expectations derived from prior experiences within psychotherapy may further strengthen expectations about therapist activities, goals, and roles, lending themselves to a global expectation about how successful therapy will be. Beutler and Clarkin have suggested that these expectations, collectively, may have implications for selecting therapists with similar backgrounds and demographics and for adapting the therapist's response during early sessions to combat demoralization and to enhance the therapeutic relationship.

Arnold Lazarus (1989, 1992) has fashioned his notion of the "authentic chameleon" from patient expectancies. He asks clients to describe their expectations regarding therapy on the *Multimodal Life History Inventory*. A person who writes: "The ideal therapist is laid back, quiet, pensive, unobtrusive, an excellent listener who says very little but hears much especially with his or her 'third ear'" is likely to respond negatively to an outspoken, active-directive therapist. Compare the forgoing with another client's perceptions: "I see the ideal therapist as a coach, a trainer, a strict but compassionate teacher, as a person who is not reticent to voice his or her candid opinions, and who is willing to serve as a role model."

The assessment of patient expectancies toward facilitative therapeutic relationship can be undertaken in a variety of ways. Lazarus asks the person directly, in the initial interviews and on the life history questionnaire, about what they experience as most helpful from their friends or previous therapists. A complementary method is to evaluate the interpersonal scales scores on personality inventories—for example, the Minnesota Multiphasic Personality Inventory-2 or the Millon Clinical Multiaxial Inventory-III.

Lazarus (1993) relates an illuminating incident with a Mrs. Healy, a middle-aged woman who indicated she sought an assertive, humorous, and challenging relationship with her therapist. When she first entered the office, she looked Lazarus up and down and asked "Why do you have graves outside your office?" In perfect Rogerian style Lazarus responded, "I have graves outside my office?" "Look out the window, dummy!" she replied. He went to the office window and looked out. Two new flower beds had been installed alongside the front walk on the grass. It was early spring and the shoots had yet to emerge from the soil. "Well, since you ask," Lazarus said, "I have just buried one of my clinical failures in the one grave and the other is earmarked for you Mrs. Healy if you turn out to be an uncooperative client." The twinkle in her eye told Lazarus that the response was an appropriate one. Had he responded in a stodgy or serious way— "Oh, those are merely newly planted flower beds,"—he doubts whether the necessary rapport would have developed, because she strongly valued "people with a sense of humor." Indeed, each session would start with some friendly banter and jesting, followed by attention to the serious issues for which she sought psychotherapy.

Another of his patients, Lazarus discovered, sought a good listener and only a good listener. No interpretations, no advice, no self-disclosure. We all have similar clinical tales in which we met the patient where he or she was.

Does that mean that therapists conducting brief treatment should give patients whatever kind of relationship they desire? Of course not. Transference, clinical, and ethical considerations also operate. It would be naive to assume that patients always know what they want and what is best for them, or that their expectations will remain static over the course of treatment. But if clinicians had more respect for the notion that their client often sense how they can best be served, fewer relational mismatches might result, initially, and therapists would be better able to adapt interventions to accommodate the changing expectations of patients.

People enter therapy with certain expectations. While these expectations often change, it is nonetheless clear that effectiveness of therapy is closely linked to how one responds to these expectations initially. If the therapist's style differs markedly from the patient's ideas about the relationship to which he or she would respond, positive results are less likely to ensue (Lazarus, 1993).

Stages of Change

Individuals who seek our professional assistance do not arrive at the doorstep in the identical stage of change. For most practitioners and programs, patients represent a rather heterogeneous group in terms of readiness to change. What's more, the relationship of choice will probably evolve from the beginning of therapy to the end of therapy.

According to the transtheoretical model (Prochaska & DiClemente, 1984, 1992), change unfolds over a series of at least five stages: precontemplation, contemplation, preparation, action, and maintenance. What follows is a description of each stage and the tasks to be accomplished to progress to the next stage (from Prochaska, DiClemente, & Norcross, 1992).

Precontemplation is the stage at which there is no intention to change behavior in the foreseeable future. Many individuals in this stage are unaware or underaware of their problems. As G. K. Chesterton once said, "It isn't that they can't see the solution. It is that they can't see the problem." Families, friends, neighbors or employees, however, are often well aware that the precontemplators have problems. When precontemplators present for psychotherapy, they often do so because of pressure from others. Usually they feel coerced into changing by a spouse who threatens to leave, an employer who threatens to dismiss them, parents who threaten to disown them, or courts who threaten to punish them. They may even demonstrate change as long as the pressure is on. Once the pressure is off, however, they often quickly return to their old ways. Resistance to recognizing or modifying a problem is the hallmark of precontemplation.

Contemplation is the stage in which people are aware that a problem exists and are seriously thinking about overcoming it but have not yet made a commitment to take action. People can remain stuck in the contemplation stage for long periods.

The essence of the contemplation stage is communicated in an incident related by Alfred Benjamin (1987). He was walking home one evening when a stranger approached him and inquired about the whereabouts of a certain street. Benjamin pointed it out to the stranger and provided specific instructions. After readily understanding and accepting the instructions, the stranger began to walk in the opposite direction. Benjamin said, "You are headed in the wrong direction." The stranger replied, "Yes, I know. I am not quite ready yet." This is contemplation: knowing where you want to go, but not being ready yet to go there.

Preparation is a stage that combines intention and behavioral criteria. Individuals in this stage are intending to take action immediately and report some small behavioral changes. While they have made some reductions in their problem behaviors, individuals in the preparation stage have not yet reached a criterion for effective action, such as abstinence from smoking, alcohol abuse, or heroin use. They are intending, however, to take such action in the very near future.

Action is the stage in which individuals modify their behavior, experiences, and/or environment in order to overcome their problems. Action involves the most overt behavioral changes and requires considerable commitment of time and energy. Modifications of a problem behavior made in the action stage tend to be most visible and receive the greatest external recognition. People, including professionals, often erroneously equate action with change. As a consequence, they overlook the requisite work that prepares changers for action and the important efforts necessary to maintain the changes following action.

Maintenance is the final stage in which people work to prevent relapse and consolidate the gains attained during action. Traditionally, maintenance was viewed as a static stage. However, maintenance is a continuation, not an absence, of change. For chronic problem behaviors, this stage extends from 6 months to an indeterminate period past the initial action. Stabilizing behavior change and avoiding relapse are the hallmarks.

The stages of change can be assessed in clinical practice by three methods. The first is to administer and score a formal questionnaire, the Stages of Change Scale (McConnaughy et al., 1983, 1989). The 32 items measure the precontemplation, contemplation, action, and maintenance stages for a particular disorder or conflict. The second method is to employ a brief algorithm of questions on an intake form or life history form (see Prochaska et al., 1994, for examples). And the third method is to ask a series of crisp questions about the problem behavior: Are you intending to change in the near future? Are you currently changing? Are you changed and working to prevent relapse? These questions, either in the form of the brief algorithm or in the clinical interview, allow for rapid and reliable identifications in clinical practice. Multidisordered patients, however, will probably be in different stages of change for each problem. During a recent intake, one of our new clients put it this way: "I stopped sleeping around and cheating on my wife several months ago and will not go back to it (action or early maintenance stage). Yes, I recognize my depression and will work to change it (contemplation) but not my drinking (precontemplation)."

At least a dozen research studies have examined the clinical utility and predictive validity of the stages of change (Prochaska et al., 1992, 1994). The composite results strongly suggest that tailoring both the clinical intervention and the relationship stance to the person's stage of change can maximize therapeutic outcome. The research and clinical consensus on the therapist's stance at different stages can be characterized as follows.

With precontemplators, often the role is like that of a *nurturing parent* joining with the resistant and defensive youngster who is both drawn to and repelled by the prospects of becoming more independent. With contemplators the role is akin to a *Socratic teacher* who encourages clients to achieve their own insights and ideas into their condition. With clients who are in the preparation stage, the stance is more like that of an *experienced coach* who has been through many crucial matches and can provide a fine game plan or can review the person's own plan. With clients who are progressing into action and maintenance, the psychotherapist becomes more of a *consultant* who is available to provide expert advise and support when action is not progressing as smoothly as expected. As termination approaches in lengthier treatment, the transtheoretical therapist is consulted less and less often as the client experiences greater autonomy and ability to live a life freer from previous disabling problems.

Not coincidentally, if you listen closely to patients discuss their evolving therapeutic relationship during a course of successful psychotherapy, you will probably hear something like this sequence. The therapist was more paternal and active early on; more egalitarian and self-disclosing as treatment progressed. Also not coincidentally, these recommended relationship stances parallel the domain of expertise occupied by the various psychotherapy systems. Psychodynamic and humanistic methods have been found to be most indicated and effective during the precontemplation and contemplation stages, during which the therapist is enjoined to adopt a stance as nurturing parents. Cognitive methods have been found to be most indicated and effective during the preparation stage, when therapists adopt the stance as Socratic teachers. Behavioral methods are most effective during the action and maintenance stages, at which time the therapist becomes coach and consultant.

The integration of stages of change and relationships of choice is an important practical guide for therapists conducting brief treatment. As with patient expectancies, once you know a patient's stage of change, then you will know which relationship stances to apply in order to help him or her progress to the next stage and eventually maintenance. Rather than apply the relationship stances in a haphazard or trial-and-error manner, practitioners can begin to use them in a more systematic and efficient style across the course of psychotherapy.

Resistance Potential

While the nature of the process and the terms used to identify it vary, virtually all theories of psychotherapy acknowledge the frequency with which patients reject the advice and resist the influence of the one from whom they seek help. This self-defeating process is frequently associated with the term "resistance." Therapists generally accept the view that resistance may be manifest as either (a) a transitory, state-like response induced specifically by the therapist and the treatment demands or (b) a trait-like characteristic that guides the manner in which the patient defends him or herself against the threat of external control. Theories differ in the degree to which they concentrate on these two facets of resistance, but most therapists accept the proposition that individuals differ in the level of manifest resistance and the generality of the situations that give rise to it.

Among some people, few events in or outside of therapy itself may give rise to resistance, while others seem to resist the slightest suggestion from the therapist. Some manifest resistance in all or most activities while others constrain their resistant tendencies to certain defined circumstances. At one extreme, patients show a marked tendency to do the opposite of what others suggest. The social psychological concept of "reactance" describes this latter, specific class of resistance in which the patient has a dominant tendency to resist, through oppositional behavior, a threat to their sense of self-control. In prescriptive and eclectic models of psychotherapy, the tendency to react against external influence is considered to be an indicator for a relationship stance along the directive and nondirective continuum.

Within psychotherapy, reactant clients are likely to respond in an oppositional fashion to interventions which threaten their sense of personal control. For example, meta-analytic reviews of research suggest that paradoxical interventions are particularly effective among those whose resistance is manifest in reactance (Hill, 1987; Shoham-Salomon & Rosenthal, 1987). In a corresponding fashion, less extreme cases of resistance may be responsive to a therapeutic stance in which the therapist remains nonauthoritative and nondirective. For example, in a series of studies, Beutler et al. (1991a,d) demonstrated that nondirective and self-directed therapies are uniformly more effective than directive interventions among those whose intake evaluations indicated a high potential for resisting external influence. On the other hand, directive, behavioral interventions were more effective than nondirective and self-directed ones among those patients with low levels of resistant defensiveness. Specifically, low levels of reactance seem to respond best to directive, professionally led interventions.

Clinical acumen and psychological testing are key assessment devices for determining the level of psychological reactance. Clinical acumen will discern high defensiveness or reactance through the patient's life narrative, interpersonal behavior during the interview, and responses to interpretations or homework assignments early in treatment. Formal tests of these tendencies have concentrated either on the specific manifestation of defensiveness in psychotherapy or on identifying a general resistant personality trait (Beutler, Sandowicz, Fisher, & Albanese, 1996). Trait measures like the MMPI have been used with relatively good success to predict the effectiveness of short-term treatments and to indicate the likelihood that directive therapy models, such as cognitive and behavioral therapies, will be successful in removing symptoms of depression and anxiety (e.g., Beutler et al., 1991). Clinicians can monitor transient and situation-specific indicators of resistance (as indexed in their responses to homework assignments, interpretations, and voice qualities), as well as rely on trait-like qualities defined by personality tests, in adjusting the moment-to-moment levels of directiveness.

Consider the case of Jim to illustrate the utility of assessing resistance potential in determining the therapeutic relationships of choice (Gaw & Beutler, 1995). Jim is a 38-year-old divorced white man employed as a laboratory technician who has come to psychotherapy referred by the court following a divorce and custody battle. The court has ordered Jim to attend weekly psychotherapy sessions in order to maintain visitation rights of his three children, who are currently in his ex-wife's custody. Jim has a 20-year history of drug abuse (marijuana, alcohol, and cocaine) but has been sober for the last year, after attending a highly structured, inpatient treatment for 10 days under court stipulation. Jim presents as an angry man who blames his ex-wife for the divorce, the court system for taking his children away, and the court-appointed psychologist for the pathological findings described in his mental health evaluation. This style of accusatory blaming is characteristic of Jim. Although Jim comes across as well socialized, he is socially isolated and without friends and intimate relationships. He is oversensitive and suspicious, presents an interpersonal style of control and manipulation, and feels threatened when his perceived control is in jeopardy. He typically resists control while asking for direction, an ambivalence that typifies a passive–aggressive response to authorities. All of these characteristics suggest a person whose reactance potential is high.

What is the therapeutic relationship of choice for Jim? In terms of his expectations, Jim is likely to benefit most from a therapeutic relationship characterized by warmth, medium activity, and informality. In terms of stage of change, Jim presents in the precontemplation or contemplation stage in which he will seek a nurturing parent and Socratic teacher. In terms of his reactance, Jim's egalitarian expectations and high resistance suggest that he is predisposed to respond negatively to a therapist who is seen as a authoritative expert. He is likely to respond in an oppositional fashion to interventions that threaten his personal and interpersonal control. He is likely to respond to someone exhibiting low directiveness: someone who listens and suggests choice alternatives and who endures the oppositional choices made in situations. Exert little control and work on the establishment of a collaborative relationship in which jointly created exercises are developed.

This case example raises the perennial question of whether to offer therapeutic relationships that patients seek or those in their best long-term interests. Consider a patient with a history of psychological abuse who re-enacts, in conscious and unconscious ways, an unassertive, subservient, perhaps self-denigrating relationship with the more powerful therapist. Is this to be condoned? Certainly not. But one can be more directive in the short-term to work toward more mature and assertive role relationships. The distinction is that between mediating goals and ultimate goals: The mediating goal is to reduce symptomatic distress, and the ultimate goal is to restructure her interpersonal behavior. In the case of Jim, then, we may accede to his high reactance level in the short-run in order to cultivate a therapeutic relationship in which he will examine and modify his anger and hyper-reactance in the long-run.

Personality and Coping Styles

In the psychoanalytic tradition there are two broad configurations of personality style and psychopathology. Anaclitic psychopathologies are disorders primarily preoccupied with issues of interpersonal *relatedness*, such as trust, caring, intimacy, and sexuality. Anaclitic personalities primarily employ avoidant defenses (e.g., denial and repression) to cope with psychological conflict and stress. Anaclitic disorders include dependent personality, anaclitic depression, and hysterical disorders. By contrast, introjective psychopathologies are disorders primarily concerned with establishing and maintaining a viable *self*—that is, a sense of separateness, autonomy, and control. Introjective personalities primarily employ counteractive defenses (e.g., projection, doing and undoing, intellectualizing, reaction formation, and overcompensation). These introjective disorders include paranoia, obsessive–compulsiveness, introjective (guilt-ridden) depression, and narcissism (Blatt & Felsen, 1993).

Blatt (1992) found that these two broad personality styles are differentially related to psychotherapy outcome. He reanalyzed the outcome data from the Menninger Psychotherapy Research Project (Wallerstein, 1986), which compared the effects of psychoanalysis to those of psychodynamic psychotherapy. Despite multiple attempts in the past, research had previously failed to discern any reliable differences in outcome between patients treated with psychoanalysis and those treated with psychodynamic psychotherapy. The Blatt reanalysis indicated that anaclitic patients experienced significantly more positive change in psychodynamic psychotherapy than in psychoanalysis, while introjective patients experienced significantly more positive change in psychoanalysis than in psychodynamic psychotherapy. That is, more dependent, interpersonally oriented patients responded more beneficially to the personal interaction with a psychodynamic therapist, whereas more ideational patients emphasizing separation and autonomy performed better in psychoanalysis. These results are also consistent with the findings of the NIMH Treatment of Depression Collaborative Research Project (Elkin et al., 1989; Imber et al., 1990), which indicated that depressed patients with higher levels of social functioning did better in interpersonal therapy, while depressed patients with higher cognitive functioning did better in brief cognitive-behavioral therapy.

A related set of coping styles, which focuses on behavioral correlates rather than internal conflicts, has been described along an externalizer–internalizer continuum by Beutler (1983; Beutler & Clarkin, 1990). The coping of "Externalizers" reflects a pattern of behavior that includes nurturance-seeking and social extraversion that is behaviorally conceptually similar to Blatt's concept of "introjective" styles. That is, both are characterized, behaviorally, as assertive, gregarious, and acting out. In contrast, Beutler and Clarkin describe "Internalizers" as those who behaviorally are introverted, overcontrolled, and intellectualized, reflecting concepts similar to what Blatt describes as "anaclitic." On such personality measures as the MMPI, these two groups are distinguished by their relative elevations on scales reflecting paranoia and sociopathic deviance (externalization) versus psychasthenia and depression (internalization).

Correspondingly, patients with high scores on measures of externalization tend to respond to behaviorally focused interventions rather than insight-oriented ones, while patients low on externalization tend to respond better to insight-oriented interventions (e.g., Beutler et al., 1991c). For example, in their analysis of the NIMH treatment of Depression Collaborative Research Project (Elkin et al., 1989; Imber et al., 1990), Barber & Muenz (1996) found that obsessively oriented patients (internalizers) did better in Interpersonal Psychotherapy than in Cognitive Therapy while impulsive and avoidant patients (externalizers) did best in Cognitive Therapy compared to Interpersonal Therapy.

Additional Client Markers

As mentioned earlier, at least 200 variables have been proposed as potential sources of relational matchmaking. However, less than half of these have been empirically investigated, and only a precious few have been consistently found to relate to outcome. Moreover, the degree of conceptual distinctiveness among these variables is unknown. Nonetheless, there is research evidence that several other variables may have value as indicators or contraindicators in prescribing the most effective type of relationship to develop with the patient in psychotherapy. That's the meaning of *four plus*. Below we quickly consider some of these additional client markers, bearing in mind that research on them is inconclusive or insufficient to use in all cases.

- *Interpersonal style:* Some interesting work using Benjamin's SASB, Bowlby's attachment types, and Schutz's FIRO-B has emerged in recent years. In general, therapists are advised to adopt a complementary style of interaction. In the Vanderbilt psychotherapy research studies, for instance, Strupp and associates (Henry et al., 1986; Strupp, 1993) found that increasing *anti*complementarity between therapist self-concept and therapists' perceptions of patient behavior is negatively associated with improvement.
- *Fragility:* More fragile, disorganized, and vulnerable patients require a much more supportive, slow therapeutic relationship (Frances, Clarkin, & Perry, 1984).
- *Situational demands* (e.g., the number of sessions allotted): Brief therapy entails a more affiliative, active, and collaborative relationship.
- *Degree of impairment:* The more chronic and functionally impairing the condition, the more intensive and long term the treatment.
- *Problem complexity:* The more complex and repetitive the problem, the more the need to invoke a treatment that is focused on changing the nature of underlying conflicts or dysfunctional systems.
- *Level of distress:* The amount of initial distress should correspond, inversely, with the degree to which the therapist employs procedures that are designed to directly reduce stress or to provide confrontation with feared material.

Conspicuous by their absence are two variables of conventional repute for determining the therapeutic relationship of choice: the patient's primary disorder and the therapist's choice of intervention. The exclusion is based upon the lack of even meager evidence that patient diagnosis is a meaningful contributor to differential treatment decision making. No study to date, to our knowledge, has found that patient diagnosis significantly enters into the equation for differential treatment effects (see Beutler, 1989). Moreover, the best available evidence suggests that therapist acceptance of a theoretical viewpoint, in the absence of specific behavioral adherence to a specific, manualized model of implementation, makes very little contribution to the effectiveness of treatment (Beutler et al., 1994).

Perhaps the limited evidence for the utility of therapist's theoretical orientations can be attributed to a low correspondence between theoretical beliefs and procedural applications. With experience, therapists learn to use interventions in many different ways; with experience, comes flexibility. Clinical experience attests that practically any intervention can be offered in any interpersonal stance. In *Therapeutic Communication*, Wachtel (1993) depicts how classical psychoanalytic interpretations, frequently encountered as harsh and punitive, can be offered in a collaborative therapeutic stance of mutual self-discovery. While specific procedures seem to embody a high degree of flexibility, each theory also proscribes certain interventions. Thus, each single-theory approach is inherently limited in the degree to which it takes advantage of the range of procedures that may and have been used to address issues in psychotherapy. This proscriptive bias may prove to be most limiting to the least experienced and the least skilled therapists who may have difficulty applying a limited number of procedures in the flexible and wide-ranging way needed to affect a breadth of problems and people.

The number of permutations for every possible interaction or matching algorithm among patient, therapist, and relationship is endless without some empirical-driven guidance. The "practicality" of programmatic research can delimit the universe of possible client variables to a manageable number for both research and clinical purposes.

Our point is this: Research has isolated a few readily assessed client features that are reliably associated with differential responses to various styles of therapeutic relating. These four-plus matching variables address separate yet complementary dimensions of the therapeutic relationship: Patient expectancies can guide the degree of warmth, formality, and activity; the stages of change guide the evolution of therapist posture over the course of treatment; reactance level guides the degree of therapist directiveness; and the anaclitic–introjective (or externalizer–internalizer) continuum guides the degree of interpersonal relatedness offered to the patient. With the rapid and reliable assessment afforded by objective psychological testing, all these client characteristics can guide the practitioner in customizing interpersonal stance and thus enhance the efficacy and efficiency of brief psychological treatment.

Limitations and Alternatives

The topic of relationship flexibility is one that conjures up many issues, but three of particular import to practitioners in an era of managed care: the limits of human capacity, the possibility of capricious posturing, and the moral connotations of flexibility (Norcross, 1993; Mahoney & Norcross, 1993).

As Gergen (1991) has aptly argued, the "postmodern self" is literally saturated with social roles and a dizzying diversity of relationships. Although the psychotherapist may, with training and experience, learn to relate in a number of different ways, there are real limits to our human capacity to change relationship stances. It may be difficult to change interaction styles from client to client and session to session, assuming one is both aware and in control of one's styles of relating. The authentic chameleon changes colors and blends in quite naturally in various settings, but no creature has an infinite range of different shades (Lazarus, 1993).

These real limitations on the extent of relational matchmaking should help us guard against grandiose expectations but also help us expand our interpersonal repertoire. We should respect our limitations even while trying to broaden our ability to meet patients' needs. We alternate roles and stances continuously in a day, and practitioners are probably quite capable of altering their therapeutic stances using systematic guidelines. Indeed, several research studies (see Beutler et al., 1994) have demonstrated that therapists can consistently use different treatment models in a discriminative fashion. The question of whether they can shift back and forth between and among the procedures from different models for a given case, within the limits described by prescriptive guidelines, is still an unanswered question. We expect, however, that this is possible. While doing so, we encourage therapists to be careful that the blending of strategies and techniques does not deteriorate into play acting or capricious posturing.

Can one authentically differ from one's preferred or habitual or mood-state-dependent style of relating? There is meager research on this question. What does exist, however, suggests that expert therapists may be capable of more malleability and "mood transcendence" than might be expected. In Gurman's (1973) research, for example, expert therapists appeared to be less handicapped by their own "bad moods" than were their less skilled peers. From the literature on the cognitive psychology of expertise, Schacht (1991) affirms that expert psychotherapists are disciplined improvisationalists who have stronger self-regulating skills and more flexible repertoires than novices. And the extant research on the therapist's level of experience suggests that experience begets heightened attention to the client (less self-preoccupation), an innovative perspective, and, in general, more endorsement of an "eclectic" orientation predicated on client need (Auerbach & Johnson, 1977; Norcross & Newman, 1992).

The moral value aspect of flexibility derives from cultural stereotypes regarding malleability and sincerity. Lazarus's idea of an "*authentic* chameleon" may seem self-contradictory to those who associate authenticity with static notions of experience or self-presentation. However, relational variability in clinical work is not synonymous with either capriciousness or unpredictability. Individual variability may well be the mark of a highly refined "discriminative function," the ability to respond appropriately to subtle changes in patients and situations. It is the talented and seasoned clinician who is able to respond effectively to the unique needs of different clients and settings.

Alternatives to the one-therapist-fits-most-patients perspective are practice limits and differential referral (Andrews, Norcross, & Halgen, 1992; Norcross Beutler et al., 1990). Without a willingness and ability to engage in a range of interpersonal stances, the therapist, by intent of default, may have to limit his or her practice to clients who fit the specific range of behaviors he or she has to offer. These discussions should alert us to the importance of judicious referral. It is not a therapist's cross-client relational consistency—or relational rigidity, in a less positive connotation—per se that is disconcerting, of course. Rather, it is the singular imposition of that preferred relationship stance at the client's expense that raises outcome and ethical concerns (Stricker, 1988).

Concluding Considerations

The use of objective personality assessment and empirically guided treatment selection in determining the therapeutic relationship of choice directly addresses the challenge of brief therapy in an era of managed care. Practitioners are being pressured to "do it quickly and do it well" while preserving their scientific, interpersonal, and ethical standards. Sensitively and scientifically customizing the therapeutic relationship to the singularity of each patient meets these seemingly impossible challenges thrust onto practitioners.

The field of psychotherapy has now reached a stage of development, probably for the first time in its brief history (Lambert & Bergin, 1992), where some empirically driven differential referrals can be consensually made (Beutler & Clarkin, 1990; Norcross & Halgin, 1997; Perry et al., 1990). While consensus is no epistemic warrant and while research will never provide definitive answers to all referral questions, encouraging progress is visible in both training and practice (Mahoney & Norcross, 1993).

Our aim in addressing the "therapeutic relationship of choice" is that it will highlight the benefits of customizing interpersonal stances in enhancing treatment efficacy and efficiency. Perhaps, too, we have assisted you in identifying several of your own beliefs regrading universal or invariant relationship postures that may hamper your clinical effectiveness. And, of course, we hope that this practical review of the research will stimulate you to use these four-plus prescriptive guidelines to improve your clinical work.

Prescriptive and systematic eclecticism posits that many interpersonal stances have a place, a specific and differential place, in the repertoire of the brief therapist. Different folks need different types of interpersonal strokes, and psychotherapy can be enhanced by selecting among extant technical and interpersonal processes in specific circumstances. Herein may ultimately lie the promise of the scientific *and* human enterprise known as brief psychotherapy.

References

Andrews, J. D. W., Norcross, J. C., & Halgin, R. P. (1992). Training in psychotherapy integration. In J. C. Norcross & M. R. Goldfried (Eds.), *Handbook of psychotherapy integration*. New York: Basic.

Auerbach, A. H., & Johnson, M. (1977). In A. S. Gurman & A. M. Razin (Eds.), *Effective psychotherapy: A handbook of research*. New York: Pergamon.

Barber, J., & Muenz, L. R. (1996). The role of avoidance and obsessiveness in matching patients to cognitive and interpersonal psychotherapy: Empirical findings from the Treatment for Depression Collaborative Research Program. *Journal of Consulting and Clinical Psychology*.

Benjamin, A. (1987). *The helping interview*. Boston: Houghton Mifflin.

Beutler, L. E. (1983). *Eclectic psychotherapy: A systematic approach*. New York: Pergamon.

Beutler, L. E. (1989). Differential treatment selection: The role of diagnosis in psychotherapy. *Psychotherapy* 26, 271–281.

Beutler, L. E., & Clarkin, J. (1990). *Systematic treatment selection: Toward targeted thera-peutic interventions.* New York: Brunner/Mazel.

Beutler, L. E., & Consoli, A. J. (1992). Systematic eclectic psychotherapy. In J. C. Norcross & M. R. Goldfried (Eds.), *Handbook of psychotherapy integration.* New York: Basic.

Beutler, L. E., & Consoli, A. J. (1993). Matching the therapist's interpersonal stance to clients' characteristics: Contributions from systematic eclectic psychotherapy. *Psychotherapy* 30, 417–422.

Beutler, L. E., Crago, M., & Arizmendi, T. G. (1986). Therapist variables in psychotherapy process and outcome. In S. L. Garfield & A. E. Bergin (Eds.), *Handbook of psychotherapy and behavioral change* (3rd edition, pp. 257–310). New York: John Wiley & Sons.

Beutler, L. E., Engle, D., Mohr, D., Daldrup, R. J., Bergan, J., Meredith, K., & Merry, W. (1991a). Predictors of differential response to cognitive, experiential and self-directed psychotherapeutic procedures. *Journal of Consulting and Clinical Psychology* 59, 333–340.

Beutler, L. E., Engle, D., Shoham-Salomon, V., Mohr, D. C., Dean, J. C., & Bernat, E. M. (1991b). University of Arizona: Searching for differential treatments. In L. E. Beutler & M. Crago (Eds.), *Psychotherapy research: An international review of pro-grammatic studies.* Washington, DC: American Psychological Association.

Beutler, L. E., Machado, P. P. P., Engle, D., & MacDonald, R. (1991c). Differential pa-tient × treatment maintenance of treatment effects among cognitive, experiential, and self-directed psychotherapies. *Journal of Psychotherapy Integration* 3, 15–31.

Beutler, L. E., Mohr, D. C., Grawe, K., Engle, D., & MacDonald, R. (1991d). Looking for differential effects: Cross-cultural predictors of differential psychotherapy efficacy. *Journal of Psychotherapy Integration* 1, 121–142.

Beutler, L. E., Machado, P. P. P, & Neufeldt, S. (1994). Therapist variables. In A. E. Bergin and S. L. Garfield (Eds.), *Handbook of psychotherapy and behavior change* (4th edi-tion, pp. 229–269). New York: Wiley.

Beutler, L. E., Sandowicz, M., Fisher, D., & Albanese, A. L. (1996). Resistance in psycho-therapy: What can be concluded from empirical research? *In Session: Psychotherapy in Practice,* 2, 77–86.

Blatt, S. J. (1992). The differential effect of psychotherapy and psychoanalysis with anaclitic and introjective patients: The Menninger Psychotherapy Research Project revisited. *Journal of the American Psychoanalytic Association* 40, 691–724.

Blatt, S. J., & Felsen, I. (1993). Different kinds of folks amy need different kinds of strokes: The effect of patients' characteristics on therapeutic process and outcome. *Psychotherapy Research* 3, 245–259.

Bohart, A. (1995). The person-centered therapies. In A. S. Gurman & S. B. Messer (Eds.), *Modern psychotherapies.* New York: Guilford.

Elkin, I. E., Shea, T., Watkins, J. T., Imber, S. D., Stotsky, S. M., Collins, J. F., Glass, D. R., Pilkonis, P. A., Leber, W. R., Docherty, J. P., Fiester, S. J., & Parloff, M. B. (1989). National Institute of Mental Health Treatment of Depression Collaborative Research Program. General effectiveness of treatment. *Archives of General Psychiatry* 46, 974–982.

Frances, A., Clarkin, J., & Perry, S. (1984). *Differential therapeutics in psychiatry.* New York: Brunner/Mazel.

Garfield, S. L. (1994). Research on client variables in psychotherapy. In A. E. Bergin & S. L. Garfield (Eds.), *Handbook of psychotherapy and behavior change* (4th edition, pp. 190–228). New York: John Wiley & Sons.

Gaw, K. F., & Beutler, L. E. (1995). Integrating treatment recommendations. In L. E.

Beutler & M. R. Berren (Eds.), *Integrative assessment of adult personality* (pp. 280–319). New York: Guilford.

Gergen, K. J. (1991). *The saturated self: Dilemmas of identity in contemporary life*. New York: Basic Books.

Greenberg, L., Rice, L., & Elliott, R. (1993). *Facilitating emotional change: The moment by moment process*. New York: Guilford.

Gurman, A. S. (1973). Effects of therapist and patient mood on the therapeutic functioning of high- and low-facilitative therapists. *Journal of Consulting and Clinical Psychology* 40, 48–58.

Henry, W. P., Schacht, T. E., & Strupp. H. H. (1986). Structural analysis of social behavior: Application to a study of interpersonal process in differential psychotherapeutic outcome. *Journal of Consulting and Clinical Psychology* 54, 27–31.

Hill, K. A. (1987). Meta-analysis of paradoxical interventions. *Psychotherapy* 24, 266–270.

Imber, S. D., Pilkonis, P. A., Sotsky, S. M., Elkin, I., Watkins, J. T., Collins, J. F., Shea, T. M., Leber, W., & Glass, D. R. (1990). Mode-specific effects among three treatments of depression. *Journal of Consulting and Clinical Psychology* 58, 353–359.

Lambert, M.J., & Bergin, A.E. (1992). Achievements and limitations of psychotherapy research. In D. K. Freedheim (Ed.), *History of psychotherapy*. Washington, D.C.: American Psychological Association.

Lazarus, A. A. (1989). *The practice of multimodal therapy*. Baltimore: The Johns Hopkins University Press (originally published in 1981 by McGraw-Hill).

Lazarus, A. A. (1992). Multimodal therapy: Technical eclecticism with minimal integration. In J. C. Norcross & M. R. Goldfried (Eds.), *Handbook of psychotherapy integration* (pp. 231–263). New York: Basic.

Lazarus, A. A. (1993). Tailoring the therapeutic relationship, or being an authentic chameleon. *Psychotherapy* 30, 404–407.

Lazarus, A. A., Beutler, L. E., & Norcross, J. C. (1992). The future of technical eclecticism. *Psychotherapy* 29, 11–20.

Liff, , Z. A. (1992). Psychoanalysis and dynamic techniques. In D. K. Freedheim (Ed.), *History of psychotherapy* (pp. 571–586). Washington D.C.: American Psychological Association.

Mahoney, M. J., & Norcross, J. C. (1993). Relationship styles and therapeutic choices: A commentary. *Psychotherapy* 30, 423–426.

McConnaughy, E. A., Prochaska, J., & Velicer, W. (1983). Stages of change in psychotherapy: Measurement and sample profiles. *Psychotherapy: Theory, Research and Practice* 20, 368–375.

McConnaughy, E. A., DiClemente, C. C., Prochaska, W. F., & Velicer, W. F. (1989). Stages of change in psychotherapy: A follow-up report. *Psychotherapy* 26, 494–503.

Michels, R. (1984). Preface. In A. Frances, J. Clarkin, & S. Perry, *Differential therapeutics in psychiatry*. New York: Brunner/Mazel.

Norcross, J. C. (1991). Prescriptive matching in psychotherapy: An introduction. *Psychotherapy* 28, 439–443.

Norcross, J. C. (1992, August). Banishing unitary treatments in psychotherapy: Pluralistic and prescriptive directions. Presented at the 100th annual convention of the American Psychological Association, Washington, D.C.

Norcross, J. C. (1993). The relationship of choice: Matching the therapist's stance to individual clients. *Psychotherapy* 30, 402–403.

Norcross, J. C. (1994). *Prescriptive eclectic therapy*. Videotape in the APA Psychotherapy Videotape Series. Washington, D.C.: American Psychological Association Books.

Norcross, J. C., & Goldfried, M. R. (Eds.) (1992). *Handbook of psychotherapy integration.* New York: Basic.

Norcross, J. C., & Halgin, R. P. (1997). Integrative approaches to psychotherapy supervision. In C. E. Watkins (Ed.), *Handbook of psychotherapy supervision.* New York: John Wiley & Sons.

Norcross, J. C., Beutler, L. E., & Clarkin, J. F. (1990). Training in differential treatment selection. In L. E. Beutler and J. F. Clarkin (Eds.), *Systematic treatment selection: Toward targeted therapeutic intervention* (pp. 289–307). New York: Brunner/Mazel.

Norcross, J. C., & Newman, C. (1992). Psychotherapy integration: Setting the context. In J. C. Norcross & M. R. Goldfried (Eds.), *Handbook of psychotherapy integration* (pp. 3–45). New York: Basic.

Paul, G. L. (1967). Strategy of outcome research in psychotherapy. *Journal of Consulting Psychology* 31, 109–119.

Peck, M. S. (1978). *The road less traveled.* New York: Simon & Schuster.

Perry, S., Frances, A., & Clarkin, J. (1990). *A DSM-III-R casebook of treatment selection.* New York: Brunner/Mazel.

Prochaska, J. O., & DiClemente, C. C. (1984). *The transtheoretical approach: Crossing the traditional boundaries of therapy.* Homewood, IL: Dow Jones-Irwin.

Prochaska, J. O., & DiClemente, C. C. (1992). The transtheoretical approach. In J. C. Norcross & M. R. Goldfried (Eds.), *Handbook of psychotherapy integration.* New York: Basic.

Prochaska, J. O., & Norcross, J. C. (1994). *Systems of psychotherapy: A transtheoretical analysis* (3rd edition). Pacific Grove, CA: Brooks/Cole.

Prochaska, J. C., DiClemente, C. C., & Norcross, J. C. (1992). In search of how people change: Applications to addictive behaviors. *American Psychologist* 47, 1102–1114.

Prochaska, J. O., Norcross, J. C., & DiClemente, C. C. (1994). *Changing for good.* New York: William Morrow.

Rogers, C. R. (1957). The necessary and sufficient conditions of therapeutic personality change. *Journal of Consulting Psychology* 21, 95–103.

Schacht, T. E. (1991). Can psychotherapy education advance psychotherapy integration? *Journal of Psychotherapy Integration* 1, 305–319.

Shapiro, S. I. (1986). Thought experiments for psychotherapists. *International Journal of Eclectic Psychotherapy* 5, 69–70.

Shoham-Salomon, V., & Rosenthal, R. (1987). Paradoxical interventions: A meta-analysis. *Journal of Consulting and Clinical Psychology* 55, 22–28.

Stricker, G. (1988). Supervision of integrative psychotherapy: Discussion. *Journal of Integrative and Eclectic Psychotherapy* 7, 176–180.

Strupp, H. H. (1993). The Vanderbilt Psychotherapy Studies: Synopsis. *Journal of Consulting and Clinical Psychology* 61, 1125–1136.

Wachtel, P. L. (1993). *Therapeutic communication.* New York: Guilford.

Wallerstein, R. S. (1986). *Forty-two lives in treatment.* New York: Guilford.

4

Challenges for Mental Health Service Providers

The Perspective of Managed Care Organizations

Peter A. Ambrose, Jr.

Let us begin this journey by agreeing to some basic assumptions. The premise of this chapter is to help clinicians and students gain a better understanding of how the managed mental health care field has changed in this age of health care reform, determine what they as individuals must do to be better able to provide services for their clients, and compete in a very market-driven professional arena. The purpose of this discussion is not to convince the unbelieving. Most clinicians, depending on educational background and personal preferences, have a repertoire of assessment instruments that they believe to be both clinically relevant and beneficial. This chapter will neither debate the innate qualities of varied assessment tools nor address the merits of counterarguments. It is my intention to outline a series of issues which traditionally act as barriers for professionals who attempt to receive permission or payment for the administration of objective personality assessment instruments.

Few would disagree that in the hands of a qualified clinician, objective personality assessment instruments such as the MMPI-2 contribute to the total understanding of client issues and diagnosis. What I will attempt to illustrate is that the question of whether or not objective personality assessment is valid is no longer the primary question at hand. The question in today's professional managed mental health care environment is whether or not personality assessment is valuable when scrutinized under a cost–benefit analysis paradigm. Simply put, given the finite number of reimbursement resources available to anyone who possesses private health insurance or participates in a managed care organization (MCO) benefit plan, is it a reasonable expenditure of dollars? When one assumes that those dollars might be spent to support a treatment modality rather than an assessment modality, the question's importance becomes more clear. Furthermore, the intent of this chapter is to assist the active clinician to navigate in the somewhat perilous seas of MCOs when attempting to receive reimbursement for what they consider to be valid services provided. As distasteful as it sounds, the question that all health care providers face in this new health care environment is, "Why should managed care pay for these traditional services?" — especially since it is the responsibility of MCOs to ensure that benefits are expended in an appropriate fashion on behalf of the members they serve. While it is fairly easy to document benefits of the extrication of a cancerous tumor from the human body, or the utilization of an advanced radiological technique to identify cerebral malfunction, it is much more difficult to present a uniform cause–effect relationship between the uses of objective personality assessment, and treatment outcomes, given the uniqueness of instrument client–clinician variables.

Definitions of Managed Care

When discussing managed mental health care, people generally assume that we each share the same definition of the icon we are describing. This is not only an elementary mistake, but an expensive one. MCOs are not like homogenized milk. They are a very heterogeneous set of governing bodies, whose goal is to administrate mental health benefits in the most cost-effective manner available. The underlying assumption that each share the same basic premises regarding assessment or treatment to achieve positive outcomes is both simplistic and incorrect. As a clinician, it behooves the individual to identify each of the MCOs they are dealing with and in some ways perform the same basic exercise that we attempt when triaging a client. Each organization will have its own characteristics, a separate set of goals, and, as importantly, a different group of employees involved in the decision-making process. The types of benefits available, the rules and regulations of treatment participation, and the individual education and skill levels of those employees will mitigate each and every decision that the professional attempts to pursue. For example, the following is a list of benefit programs that most clinicians are familiar with:

- PPO   Preferred provider organization
- POS   Point of service
- HMO   Health maintenance organization
- EPO   Exclusive provider organization

For each of the benefit programs listed, a member (any individual who possesses third-party payment reimbursement) will be required to adhere to a different set of rules and regulations in order to receive the highest level of benefit available. For example, in a traditional PPO, a member is allowed to go to any individual provider listed in the organization regardless of specialization, without needing to preauthorize services with anyone in the parent organization. As such, as a member of a PPO, when I decide to access the provider network, my only concern is what percentage of reimbursement I will be required to pay that provider versus what percentage the parent organization will pay. I may go to any participating network provider I choose, when I choose, without any restriction. However, if I belong to an HMO, at the time of initial enrollment in this program, I would have chosen a primary care physician (PCP) who will not only act as my initial resource for every medical condition (regardless of severity), but will also act as gatekeeper to the network of specialists and their services. Thus, if when working in my backyard I drop a brick on my foot, while my initial reaction may be to go to the Emergency Room to have it X-rayed, I am required by program regulation to contact my primary care physician first. It is the primary care physician's obligation to review the severity of my injured foot and then decide whether or not to refer me on for X-rays or, if necessary, an orthopedic specialist. While this may be counterintuitive to me given the intense pain I feel, it is the procedure I am required to adhere to, given the benefit package I purchased. If I fail to adhere to this protocol, I run the risk of receiving no reimbursement for services solicited.

What this means for the typical managed mental health professional is that whenever negotiating with a perspective client, in regard to providing psychological services, it is imperative that both parties recognize that third-party reimbursement is no longer a given, but must be carefully researched so that everyone understands the exact extent of financial liability each party maintains in contracting for services. Therefore, the question of whether the individual clinician is eligible to receive reimbursement from a third-party benefit program needs to be carefully established and verified. Furthermore, even when participation in a mental health care benefit program is verified, the type of service being offered might also need to be verified or "precertified" by the parent health care organization. For example, while most people assume that therapy is the most elementary service rendered by any mental health service provider, the conditions under which particular types of therapy or the duration of this therapy are authorized can be different according to the different MCOs you work with. In particular, one should *not* assume that objective personality assessment instruments or any generic psychological testing is a mandatory reimbursable service, just because you as a participating network provider deem it a viable service alternative. Moreover, while psychological assessment may indeed be a reimbursable benefit according to the benefit plan the client maintains, the limits of payment may be different among different organizations. While one company may pay 80% of psychological services up to a certain dollar maximum, another company may give a flat fee for a generically defined procedure. Thus, while Patient A may pay 80% of a $500 bill, Patient B's company may put a limit of up to $250 annually on the same service.

In summary, a clinician is best served by assuming little about a potential client's level of benefits. In particular, one should never assume that the client fully understands the extent of the mental health benefit package they possess unless they have verified them by reviewing their benefit booklet information or have discussed benefit limits with the parent company Customer Service Department. Traditionally, mental health care benefits are different than the typical medical coverage that is offered within a health care policy benefit program. While all of the medical benefit of a given policy may be reimbursed at a 90% level, it is very likely that services provided for psychiatric or substance abuse care have different dollar limits, visit limits, and, more importantly, participation restrictions.

How do clinicians protect themselves and their clients from misunderstandings or mistakes? The easiest preventive strategy lies in utilizing the Customer Service or Provider Relations Departments that the MCO provides. By reviewing a client's insurance card, which lists a Customer Service number (the number that the client can call to receive information about what benefits actually exist) or Provider Relations number (the number that the clinician calls to discuss extent of benefits available, or any problem that may arise in the course of treatment), problems can be prevented. When contacting the Provider Relations Department, a clinician should record the following:

- Name of the representative with whom they are speaking
- Date and time of day the conversation took place
- Issue discussed
- Information supplied

This information will prove to be invaluable for future reference if a dispute arises. The extent to which the clinician decides it is their responsibility to undertake this investigation, or it is the responsibility of the potential client, is left up to each individual. While this generally relates to the amount of support staff and to the time available given practice parameters, a prudent clinician would be wise to control these preservice issues to as great an extent as possible.

Ultimately, when discussing "managed care," the clinician should avoid generalizing and be specific when identifying the attributes of a specific company and the policies it maintains. The strengths and weaknesses of each company will dictate the tactics and methodologies available to clinicians to gain better access as well as service provision for themselves and their clients. Factors such as geographical differences (is it a local organization or a national conglomerate?), legislative issues (is it an "any willing provider" state or not?), and the impact of statewide professional organizations (does the company have a professional advisory committee which represents the particular clinician?) can affect access to professional services.

Assumptions of Managed Care

It is easy to predict, with some certainty, that MCOs will exist in the foreseeable future. "Managed care," in its most basic form, is a structural arrangement that mitigates treatment decisions that traditionally were the sole responsibility of clinicians and clients, but today require monitoring and approval by the financially responsible third party. As such, it benefits clinicians to learn as much about these organizations as they can, and in particular about the procedures they utilize to achieve their organization goals. In general, MCOs have three simple goals: (1) to demonstrate value, (2) to extend benefits, and (3) to increase treatment outcomes.

When one looks closely at these goals, an inherent question arises: To whom are they attempting to demonstrate value, how are they attempting to extend benefits, and, ultimately, how does one increase treatment outcome opportunities?

Demonstration of value lies in the view of the beholder. Most MCOs recognize that they must satisfy all of the significant players they cater to. This includes the customers that buy their products (this is the employer who buys the product as well as the individual employees who seek services and the providers who treat their customers, and ultimately they must respect the "bottom line" to either an internal corporate structure or a body of shareholders. Demonstrating value generally requires that an MCO provide a set of services or elicit a set of benefits that differentiates them from other health service agencies within a specific marketplace. To the customer, benefits must be seen as being accessible, ubiquitous, and cost effective. It should be recognized, however, that the "value" that the purchasing employer seeks and the treatment-seeking employee expects may be different since the majority of Americans who possess medical coverage do so through either state-funded or employee-driven programs. Their individual ability to negotiate contracts and choose between an endless variety of programs is significantly limited. Therefore, while access to good providers tends to be the single most important provision for most individual clients, doing it at a reasonable cost is an important caveat for the "original" purchasing employer. To the provider, value is determined not only by percentage of reimbursement received for services provided, but also by ease of access into the health care system, resolutions of problems, paperwork requirements, and the degree of respect they feel they obtain from the system. The value of treatment outcomes can be evidenced by quality of service personnel an organization maintains, medical policy administered, and the creativity and flexibility of benefit design products sold. As such, it can be seen that MCOs have a myriad of individuals to please and can only be successful if each of them are respected.

Clinicians must recognize that they will benefit each time they assist the original MCO in solving their problems (meeting these multiple needs). Not only do they increase the opportunity to have their services reimbursed, but also assist their clients in received recommended services. Clinicians improve their ability to being able to provide objective personality assessment services to the extent that it facilitates the MCO goals. A question that clinicians must ask themselves is, How does providing objective personality instruments to a client help the MCO achieve its goals? While most of us never even considered this in our training, it has become a fact of everyday life. As distasteful as it may seem, when communicating our professional opinions, if it can be pointed out how the organization benefits from it, specifically by the individual benefiting from it, you increase the opportunities to have these services approved. While these issues generally are not part of the typical orientation of clinicians, it would appear prudent that if they become more cognizant of these issues and interweave into their negotiation, either verbally or through formal report writing, when discussing benefit management with MCOs.

Ideally, if an objective personality measure can deal with one of the three primary problems the organization has as part of its everyday existence, there is a greater likelihood that the service will be included in the basic overall benefit package that the company offers its customers, and, as such, it will become a given rather than a negotiated service. Furthermore, in a very highly intensive case management environment where individual case managers make decisions in regard to pre-authorization of treatment, a better case can be made when such treatment is valid, necessary, and cost effective.

Provider Assumptions

Typically, when a clinician is asked why should personality assessment measures be paid for by third-party payers, their response generally falls into one of the following categories:

- It improves diagnosis.
- It improves treatment outcomes.
- It shortens treatment.
- I have children in college, and I need the money.

While these responses appear to be logical, there is no conclusive, unequivocal research that demonstrates that objective personality assessment in and of itself does any of the above. Intuitively, we anticipate that the more information we gather about a client, the better likelihood we will be able to improve diagnosis. With a better diagnosis, we can increase treatment outcomes and shorten treatment durations. Yet, most research has never been aimed at a cost benefit analysis of objective personality assessment. Instead, most research is based on a goal of diagnostic or triage verification. This argument, however, does not take place in a vacuum and, as such, is met with a reasonable counterargument. Namely, since there are numerous professionals in the mental health field that generally provide diagnostic services and treatment of a therapeutic nature without the need to implement objective personality measures, why should the MCO pay for such services? If Dr. A can provide the service without assessment tools and get good results, then why should MCOs take a risk that Dr. B will be any more effective with the administration of such an assessment tool? Now, while I recognize that this question is somewhat irritating to the average provider who performs objective personality assessment, it should be recognized that the average MCO does not benefit from playing favorites between the professional organizations that service their clients (M.D., Ph.D., M.S.W., L.P.C., etc.), nor does it approve any treatment modality that has not demonstrated value from a cost–benefit orientation. Therefore, the assumption that all objective personality treatment should be provided for on the simple testimony of a qualified professional tends not to gain either merit or acquiescence.

The justification for objective personality assessment might take several of the following forms:

- In seeking authorization for service approval, the clinician would do well to explain which particular patients are best served by the administration of objective personality measures. The clinician must be able to differentiate between the types of clients they see and the uses of the objective personality measures they administrate. The rationale that objective personality instruments should be given to every patient entering treatment, in order to gain good baseline data, is not only no longer accepted, but has led to the practice of greater scrutiny by MCOs. Utilizing anecdotal information gathered from clients that the clinician and a specific MCO have collaborated on will go a long way in convincing an individual case manager regarding the appropriateness of its particular use at this time.

- What situations generally benefit from objective personality assessment? Beyond diagnostic categories, there are particular sets of circumstances that allow the clinician to gain valuable information that otherwise would not be accessed in a timely fashion. Utilizing objective personality measures in a custody evaluation, for example, would appear to be a logical representation on how such a tool assists in somewhat difficult, if not chaotic, circumstances. Elaborating on the particular situational characteristics that exist and that might contaminate or confuse typical verbal report evaluations will be helpful. If an objective personality measure allows a clinician to prioritize multiple issues in order of importance, this indeed will save valuable time and effort.
- The clinician must address how objective personality assessment will assist a client to resolve his or her own personal issues. What can the clinician expect to share with the individual client that will allow the client to learn and benefit from participating in this endeavor? If an individual has been in long-term treatment with little success, a case can be made that an objective personality assessment tool might provide pertinent information that would lead to greater insight and, thus, greater behavior or characterologic change.
- Finally, what information will the MCO obtain that could be utilized by other providers, possibly offsetting other medical costs. For example, it is not uncommon for individuals to seek treatment for unexplained gastrointestinal problems or migraine headaches. If it can be demonstrated that these issues are most likely due to a particular personality style or life event that can be illuminated by objective personality measure, then the sheer balance of medical expenses offset by the assessment can provide a valuable case for expenditure of mental health dollars.

Assessment Issues for Managed Care Programs

As the Clinical Director of a Department of Managed Mental Health, I have seen several problems related to objective personality assessments. These problems are a product of the clientele served, as well as the variety of testing instruments available. While one could argue that clinicians are the best judge of the assessment instruments to be used, since MCOs hire a variety of professionals themselves with different backgrounds to review treatment plans, a clinician must gain a sense of the level of sophistication, regardless of the policies in place of each organization.

Since the variety of problems that clinicians tackle tends to be endless, and the number of objective personality tools tends to be multiple, MCO case managers lack a simple equation or a rule of thumb that allows them to review client appropriateness for assessment in an expedient fashion. If a benefit policy includes objective personality measures as being a basic reimbursable benefit, then this becomes a moot point. These services need not be preauthorized, nor do results need to be reviewed. However, since MCOs more often review outpatient as well as inpatient services, the likelihood is that objective personality assessment will be one of those services that continue to be reviewed prior to authorization being made. Therefore, the following issues should be recognized when requesting approval for objective personality measures:

No Easy Prescriptions

What instruments should be used, when are they appropriate, and to whom should they be administered are the most critical problems facing a case manager on a day-to-day basis. Confusion between types of psychological testing available, such as cognitive, personality, educational, and projective, often require that a case manager be intimately trained in each, in order to verify whether or not certain procedures are valid. Unlike typical medical precertification where policies are very specific, most clinicians recognize that there is not a uniformly agreed-upon set of standards, nor does the profession lend itself to believe that such standardization is beneficial. Case managers typically struggle with not only what test to give, but who should be giving it. While it is assumed that most psychologists have received training in objective personality assessment, most would admit that geographical differences sometimes influence what set of tests are accepted and are routinely administered. Furthermore, given that MCOs employ professionals who are not psychologists, there is no clear methodology to separate those individuals who should and should not be administered these types of procedures. As one can see, the amount of effort needed to investigate appropriateness of assessments lends itself to a more simplistic rule of thumb: It is easier to exclude testing from a list of benefits available, rationalizing that it is better to allow providers more "treatment time" to get to the heart of the matter and then offer objective personality instrumentation. Again, the issue of professional qualification comes into play: Because it is not uniformly accepted that all mental health providers offer these services, it is easy to conclude that they are not uniformly necessary.

Quality of Information Gathered

Another barrier to the use of objective personality measures lie solely in the court of the clinician. The quality of results and variety of results reported tend to be so individualistic that it is often unclear as to what information should be obtained from these instruments versus what information is actually reported. As such, many times clinicians fail to recall that they not only should be utilizing assessment tools based on the clientele they are administering them to, but should also be tailoring this information to the audience that is reading it. In recent years, the managed care case manager has become a primary member of this audience. Yet, the quality of reports are so variable that, again, the certainty of what value a member is receiving from these tests tends to be ambiguous, thus leading to rejections of future authorizations. The clinician should strive to provide succinct, clearly expressed opinions that not only highlight personality characteristics or issues, but focus squarely on recommendations. A clinician would be best served if they assume that *only* the "Summary" and "Recommendation" portion of their evaluation will be reviewed and, as such, should concentrate on them. Furthermore, the case management "audience" in all likelihood will not at first review be trained in such measures and thus will need to be "educated" in a more collegial fashion. While it is true that every MCO has a panel of peer reviewers who are the clinicians' equivalent, at the point when the evaluation must be reviewed a second time, the variables of individual clinician differences oftentimes work against the submitting clinician. It is usually more beneficial to write a more simple evaluation than anticipate that a peer reviewer will agree with your request or conclusion.

Computer-Assisted Interpretation

Most would agree that the calibration of radiological instrumentation such as X-rays, CAT scans, and MRIs tend to be more uniform when compared to the types of objective personality instruments available to individual clinicians. In an effort to standardize basic objective measurement scoring and interpretation, computer-assisted programs were developed. With the advent of these programs, many clinicians have come to overrely on the computer interpretation of individual results, which devalues their own participation. MCOs have developed a suspicion that they are not getting the full value for the services they are paying for. It is hard to justify paying several hundred dollars for an objective personality measure that is undertaken by a client and takes support staff less than 20 minutes to input into a computer, with a clinician giving little or minimal input. Now while this perception may be an overgeneralization, and indeed may be limited to few cases, when convincing the case manager that such testing is needed, the clinician must deal with the perception that a great deal of effort and individual work may not have gone into the evaluation report. When one considers that the average third-party payer fails to reimburse for "write-up time" (typically all that is reimbursed is the face-to-face contact with the client), then the actual value of the assessment measure is far less than what is typically charged by the average clinician to complete a psychological evaluation. The clinician must be conscientious so as not to overrely on computer-generated aids, thus demonstrating their own value versus that of a computer program.

Influencing Managed Care

The crux of the matter that each clinician faces when discussing objective personality assessment with managed care entities is, How does one convince them to approve services in the present health care environment which typically promote suspicion and mutual mistrust? First and foremost, the relationship that any individual clinician has with a MCO is paramount. Organizations do not tend to rule out specific services (unless specified by benefit contract) of a participating provider if they have an existing relationship that tends to be mutually beneficial. Again, since one of managed care's problems is to demonstrate value to a variety of entities, then allowing its good providers the opportunity to demonstrate their skills, and thus helping their customers, can only provide a "win–win" situation. If a provider has a mutually trusting relationship with an MCO, then it is very likely that they will have the opportunity to at least make a reasonable case for why objective personality assessment on a case-by-case basis is required.

If a clinician does not have an existing relationship with an MCO, an alternative strategy is to have other participating providers within the network vouch for the clinician's services. As much as I have discussed the issue that there are multiple providers who do not utilize personality assessment, it is also true that many other providers, such as psychiatrists and family therapists, value objective personality assessment because of what it adds to their practice and their abilities to treat their patients. Therefore, having other providers vouch for your services and the value of those services tends to be a very important influencing mechanism.

A third methodology which tends to influence MCOs is feedback received from both employers (purchasers of services) and their employees who seek treatment through the MCO's set of plans. As such, whenever an MCO receives feedback from patients or employers indicating that a certain procedure gave a great deal of insight which later led to behavior change, this procedure can only be viewed in the most positive light. Certainly, in a time where violence and drug abuse at work sites tends to be increasing, objective personality assessment instruments which may lead to insight and ultimately to a decrease of these behaviors are viewed not only as individually positive but also as corporatively productive.

Most MCOs are made up of case management professionals whose sole intention is to provide the best available services to their members as is reasonably possible. However, as previously discussed, the educational backgrounds of these case managers tend to be so varied that it is important for a clinician to recognize that they have a duty to educate the MCO case manager as to the benefits of assessment. You should never assume that the case manager has more than the most casual understanding of objective personality assessment, and thus a more simple interpretation prior to delving into the details of the clinical or research aspects of the argument would be very helpful. Supplying examples of the reports, as well as past successes, can only augment an individual clinician's argument, in that anecdotal evidence tends to be very valuable, in particular when it involves another covered member.

If a clinician knows that the case manager they are dealing with is a trained nurse and not a social worker, a different approach may be required. Using a "medical model" versus a social/family relations explanation might better suit their needs. Ultimately, the clinician is faced with the role of educating people in order to convince them that such activities are necessary. Educating the MCO is not only the responsibility of the individual clinician, but also of the local and State Professional Service Organization who may have different inroads to the corporate hierarchy available to them. Soliciting feedback from the Clinical Director, or the head of Provider Relations, can only foster better relationships, thereby reinforcing the required give and take format that is necessary for any healthy professional relationship.

Communicating with the Case Manager

Up until now, I have discussed MCOs as if they were an impersonal icon. The fact of the matter is, on a day-to-day basis, the individual clinician will be dealing with other professionals on a one-to-one basis. The following simple "Do's" and "Don'ts" might assist clinicians in making their points in a more concise and effective manner:

DO: *Educate the case manager.* As previously explained, the level of education each case manager possesses is different. Thus, clinicians will need to utilize their own assessment skills to ascertain how best to share information with the case manager. Discussing agendas such as the appropriateness of assessment, client treatment variables, and types of written explanations will be important. On many occasions, explanations can be brief and verbally informal in the course of day-to-day business. Once a provider has demonstrated to be both effective and cooperative, their reputation tends to become solidified within the organization so that they become a known entity and thus become a resource that requires less scrutiny and maintenance.

DON'T: *Do Not Become Defensive.* Many clinicians oftentimes become very defensive and outraged that they are required to explain what they consider to be an inherent prerogative of their professional capacity. This often leads to a great deal of mistrust and antagonism between both the case manager and the professional. While it was never the intent of the clinician to enter an environment where a majority of their decisions would need to be verified by other professionals (most of whom have much less training than the clinician themselves), the fact of the matter is that the present health care environment is such that such conversations are no longer simply necessary but oftentimes mandatory. Recognizing that you are dealing with an individual who considers himself to be as professional in his capacity as you are in your own, becoming defensive becomes a self-defeating behavior. While it can be time-consuming and troublesome to go through this exercise to educate the case manager, again, if it is done in an orchestrated fashion, it need be repeated only until you have established a professional relationship with the MCO. With the proliferation of MCOs nationally, this exercise will be required with each organization the clinician agrees to sign up as a preferred provider. The value of this positive relationship also goes beyond the issue of clinical decision making to those of problem resolution. Those clinicians who have good relationships with case managers tend to have more of their other issues resolved in an expedient manner simply because they have learned the procedures of the various departments in the MCO.

DO: *The reason for assessment, as well as the results of the assessment instruments. needs to be explained in simple language.* While some clinicians strive to express their opinion in the most complicated manner, simple, common interpretation and recommendations tend to appeal to case managers. Again, because the level of education among case managers differs widely across organizations, succinct and clear discussions and results are better appreciated.

DON'T: *Don't rely on complicated verbiage.* The use of "psychobabble" tends to be viewed as another antagonistic exercise between clinician and professional case manager. While the use of specific psychiatric nomenclature cannot be avoided in some instances, it is oftentimes unnecessary to embellish or elaborate points with clinical jargon as a substitution for clear opinions.

DO: *Solve the case manager's problems.* As discussed earlier, the case manager has certain goals. These include attempting to extend a finite set of benefits, demonstrating value to both providers and customers alike, and increasing treatment outcomes. Fully explaining how an assessment measure may meet these goals may indeed be as convincing as any research available on the subject matter. Again, benefiting the patient and benefiting the MCO should not be viewed as always mutually exclusive.

DON'T: *Threaten.* The rationale for an objective personality measure should not include the threat of an impending lengthy crisis if such an instrument is not administered. Oftentimes, clinicians will argue that if certain treatments or assessments are not utilized, it is very likely that a pending crisis will occur which will lead to either inpatient hospitalization or other, more intrusive or expensive corrective procedures. Since this type of argument may be viewed as a direct threat by calling into question the case manager's intelligence, the clear reasoning behind the exclusion of an objective assessment instrument needs to be highlighted. The threat of crisis or future legal conflict, unless it can be verified that such a benefit actually exists without preauthorization, is both harmful to the member and clinician alike. The member will not receive the treatment the professional deems necessary. The professional will obtain a reputation that will later contaminate the rest of their involvement with other patients. Again, most case managers tend to be rational creatures who rely on concise information clearly communicated by the clinician.

DO: *Send Examples.* Providing the case manager with written examples of previous evaluations will allow the case manager to better judge its value. Written examples can be a powerful tool when attempting to demonstrate the cost-benefit ratio of objective personality assessment. Alternatively, if the evaluation is of poor quality, it can confirm the decision not to authorize the request.

In summary, the best advice I can offer to clinicians attempting to receive authorization for objective personality measures is that they need to utilize those skills which traditionally make them successful in their everyday clinical and personal life. The process clinicians must undertake is to recognize that they are now put into the position of being not only clinicians for their clients, but also advocates for themselves and the profession they represent. While it may gall some clinicians to have to spend time and effort in educating organizations and individuals who may be less trained than they are in a particular area of expertise, the realities of today's managed care environment is such that preauthorization and ongoing reauthorization are becoming the rule rather than the exception. The better educated a case manager becomes, the better off the clinician is. Communication skills, relationship building, and ultimately the capacity to triage an MCO, recognizing its needs and goals, will become paramount in the clinician's ability to remain independent and viable. While most would agree that objective personality assessment has merits of its own, we are now in an environment where, if an MCO agrees, then little effort must be expended. However, if they fail to agree and perceive objective personality assessment as an endeavor that must be reviewed on a case-by-case basis, then the clinician will do well to better understand the MCO prior to fighting it.

5

Psychological Assessment in Capitated Care

Challenges and Opportunities

Cynthia D. Belar

Capitated systems are blossoming in health care and may be the major vehicles for provision of Medicare and Medicaid services in the near future Sullivan (1995).[1] One kind of capitated care plan is the health maintenance organization (HMO), an organized program that takes contractual responsibility for the provision of a specified package of services for a defined group of people who have enrolled voluntarily. Purchasers make a fixed, periodic payment set *prospectively*, and financial risk is shared by the HMO and the service providers for actual cost versus the fixed premium collected in advance.

In the *staff model*, the HMO hires a staff of professionals to deliver services. In the *group model*, the HMO contracts with one or more separately organized professional groups to provide health services. Independent/individual practice association (IPA) *model* HMOs contract directly with service providers in practices or practice associations or with multispecialty group practices.

There are many who believe that capitated care will be the most prevalent model in future health care. The number of HMOs has tripled since 1980, with 591 in operation at the end of 1995. And the number of people cared for by HMOs has increased from 10 million in 1980 to 56 million members nationwide by 1995

---

[1]Parts of this chapter were presented in Belar (1995b).

(Group Health Association of American National Directory of Health Maintenance Organizations).

Market penetration varies by state: In California, 41% of the population is enrolled in an HMO. In three states, more than 25% of the population is enrolled (Massachusetts, Minnesota, Oregon). Although in 1991 the predominant plan model was the IPA, nearly a quarter of all plans were group or staff model HMOs, and these accounted for almost 40% of all HMO enrollees. Group and staff models will most likely dominate the more piecemeal delivery systems common today, because only such integrated systems are capable of providing the comprehensive, seamless care that consumers and major purchasers are demanding.

The Role of Psychological Testing: A Sample Program

To better understand how psychological testing fits into a capitated care model, a brief description of one such service delivery system follows. The Kaiser Permanente Medical Care Program is a group HMO model. It is one of the first HMOs ever established and is perhaps the largest nongovernmental health care system in the country. During my tenure as Chief Psychologist at the Los Angeles Medical Center (1983–1990), this center alone served more than 360,000 members; there are over 6 million Kaiser Health Plan members nationwide.

Within the Kaiser Permanente plan, the Department of Psychiatry was responsible for delivering services related to the mental health benefit; this benefit covered all *psychological counseling* and all *psychological testing* in the health plan contract.[2] Of special note is that there were *no co-payments or limits on any psychological testing service*, which is true to this date. (Other major HMOs also include psychological testing as part of the basic benefit if requested by a clinical practitioner—for example, Group Health Cooperative of Puget Sound).

In the Kaiser Permanente model, professional staff were organized into six general multidisciplinary clinical teams and the Behavioral Medicine Service. Staff included 17 psychiatrists, 13 clinical psychologists, 30 psychiatric social workers, 3 marriage and family counselors, and 3 clinical nurse specialists. A department manual articulated policy and procedures for clinicians, and reflected the overall philosophy of the department. With respect to psychological testing, there were two major sections in this manual. The first had to do with the use of the MMPI.

The MMPI was described as a test which could be ordered by *any* clinician in the department. The manual noted that it could be used to obtain a general picture of patients' personality, symptoms, and treatment suggestions. It also noted that it was to be requested when clinicians had specific questions about the patient's condition (e.g., potential for alcoholism, suicide potential, presence of psychosis)

---

[2]A simplified overview of plans is (a) no charge for consultations to inpatients on medical/surgical units and in the emergency room and (b) outpatient sessions at varying rates, depending upon the plan purchased (e.g., 20 sessions at no charge and $5 per session thereafter; $10 per session for the first 20 sessions followed by private sector rate; $60 per session for the first 20 sessions followed by private sector rates)

or suspected that significant psychological tendencies may be present which are not currently evident. Also recorded was the statement that "Some use the MMPI to provide confirmations for impressions already formulated."

In 7 years with the department, I never once heard of any attempt to limit usage of the MMPI, although we at times debated issues related to format, scoring and report service, and so on. Psychology as a discipline was clearly in charge of the service and ensured that a variety of versions were available to members (e.g., standard booklet, English, Spanish, cassette tape). My colleagues still in the department inform me that this philosophy has been maintained; even in times of constriction, services in this area have not been threatened.

The other form of psychological testing described in the manual was that of test batteries. These were noted as a selection of instruments by a psychologist designed to answer a pertinent clinical question (e.g., intellectual assessment, more detailed personality description, neuropsychological evaluations). The procedure for accessing this form of testing was to first discuss the case in the clinician's team meeting, which occurred on a weekly basis. As noted, these team meetings were multidisciplinary, and always included one or two psychologists. The discussion in the team meeting was for the purpose of clarifying the specific questions which testing might answer and for the psychologist to have input into the appropriateness of the referral. The request was then sent to the Assessment Coordinator, who assigned the case to the psychologist on staff most qualified in that area of practice. Use of psychological testing in this model differed from what I have seen in academic health science centers and independent private practice, where use of sometimes extensive assessment batteries were more routine on intake.

There are some data that illustrate where psychological testing fit in the overall picture of clinical services provided. For example, during one year there were 62,118 total outpatient visits to the department, with 3587 *new* patients seen. Nearly half the visits were for standard one hour adult individual treatment services. Only 764 visits, or 1.23% of total visits, were for psychological testing—and that does not necessarily mean there were 764 different patients. Since testing visits were booked in units of 120 minutes, several visits might be registered if a battery required 4–6 hours, as a neuropsychological evaluation might.

Even more revealing is that in comparison to data from the entire Southern California region during that period, this activity in psychological testing was clearly the *highest* for the region (which served at that time 1.9 million members—now well over 2 million). Other departments ranged from less than 0.2% of total visits for psychological testing, to 1.0% of total visits. And a number of departments provided *no* psychological testing services other than MMPI, month after month!

My interpretation of these differences has been, in part, that the Los Angeles facility had a particularly strong psychology staff with an APA-accredited clinical psychology internship program. In addition, it was a tertiary care medical center that provided specialized medical–surgical (e.g., radiation therapy, complex neurosurgery, organ transplantation) and behavioral medicine services that were not provided elsewhere in the region. For example, over 200 requests for neuropsychological consultation were received each year. And our Behavioral Medicine Service was frequently consulted regarding headache, chronic pain, psychophysiologic disorders, compliance, coping with illness, and others that often involved psychometric procedures in assessment and treatment.

What these data also reflect is that there was in general *little* demand for other types of psychological testing, both in Los Angeles and throughout the region. In my experience, the most frequent consultation requests from mental health professionals were for diagnostic issues in children (especially ADHD); relatively few requests were made for general adult personality evaluations. In fact, more recent information suggests that given the low referral rate, staff sometimes have difficulty finding such assessment cases for interns in training.

It is important to reiterate here that these decisions regarding the delivery of psychological testing services were made *by clinicians*. There was no need for precertification of services; there were no gatekeepers, no insurance carrier case managers, and so on. There were no co-payments and testing was an unlimited benefit (certainly without evidence of overutilization!). These are especially important points because much of what has been written about psychological testing in managed care implies that "they" are the barriers to psychological testing services. Perhaps there are other issues that require attention by our profession if the potential of testing is to be actualized in managed care.

Challenges and Opportunities

There are a variety of challenges facing psychological assessment services in capitated care systems that provide insights into opportunities for psychologists.

Integration of Diagnosis and Treatment

At one time, psychological evaluation and treatment were two separate processes in mental health services. Each patient was seen first for history-taking and then testing as appropriate. At some point after the workup was completed, sometimes long after, the patient was then assigned to still another clinician for treatment. The resulting problems of delay and loss of continuity created unnecessary barriers to effective treatment, and elaborate workups were often of little practical value to the patient.

In the HMO practice model, diagnosis and treatment are not separated but take place concurrently from the outset and are provided by the same clinician, who in fact is often responsible for the whole family. The theoretical underpinning is based on crisis theory and the need to maximize opportunities for intervention at the time of crisis. In addition, over time, HMOs have found that easily accessible outpatient care with timely interventions could significantly reduce the need for more expensive inpatient psychiatric care.

Although this policy promotes promptness, continuity, and coordination of care, it also means that there is no standard "intake battery" for all patients. Clinicians are free at any time to obtain testing or any other diagnostic or therapeutic assistance they may need, but often they do not. To utilize testing, they would need to view it as having "added value" to the basic interview service. Other authors have already noted that currently, in the area of personality assessment, "a major criticism of psychological assessment is the lack of specific, usable recommendations to providers who must practice at an accelerated pace . . ." (Quirk et al., 1995, p. 28). These authors go on to detail a personality feedback consultation model that uses psychological testing to facilitate the work of the therapist. Should this and related models prove effective and useful to other clinicians, there will be more demand for personality testing.

The concept of "added value" in the provision of services has become increasingly important to the major purchasers of health care plans as well as individual clinicians. There are significant challenges for psychology in demonstrating "added value" and, most importantly, in distinguishing between *discretionary* and *necessary* psychological services in health care. There are also great opportunities given psychology's unique strengths as a scientist practitioner profession.

Mind–Body Dualism

Although scientific evidence does not support mind–body dualism in health care, it is still firmly entrenched throughout health policy, even in capitated systems that benefit the most from mind–body integration. For example, as noted previously, all psychological consultation and testing were covered under the *mental* health contract in the Kaiser Health Plan. Thus penile prosthesis surgery could be provided under the basic health plan without additional charge, but the psychological evaluation to determine whether this surgery would be covered under the *mental health* benefit. Although the psychological testing would be without any charge, the consultation interview itself might involve a significant co-payment—which could be a barrier to services or affect the patient's attitude toward the psychological examination itself, perhaps biasing its results.

The kind of mind–body dualism that is reflected in the design of most insurance and health plan benefits will not meet the needs of a truly integrated health care system that recognizes the interface between behavior and health. In addition, it poses special practice problems for clinical health psychologists in the delivery of psychological assessment and intervention services to medical–surgical patients. Psychologists will need to become active in health policy formation in order to contribute to the solution of this kind of problem; working as an independent researcher or service provider will not be sufficient. Testing related to "physical health" problems must not be part of the "mental health" benefit. And behavioral health "carveouts" in general will be especially problematic for this area of practice.

Increased Accountability

Although many have asserted that managed care is "anti-testing," managed health care (and our society in general) is in fact making *increased* demands for (a) measurement of quality of care, (b) assessment of cost-effectiveness, (c) documentation of service needs, and (d) demonstration of value. Psychological measurement is integral to each of these endeavors.

Managed care programs, and the providers within them, will be competing on the basis of quality, not just cost. There are already "report cards" available to purchasers of health care plans, and soon individual service provider information will be available to the consumer. At the present time there are some doctoral programs whose students are comparing their treatment effect sizes to those published in the literature. Valid measurement of treatment outcome will be critical, and this is a task of psychological assessment. Testing will most likely be incorporated throughout treatment in the future, not just at the point of entry. Increased accountability in health care also brings with it an increased emphasis on "quality of life" as an important outcome measure. Clearly, psychological testing could have a bright future in all these arenas.

Role of Psychologists

In the Los Angeles Kaiser Permanente model, psychologists were hired with respect to their special expertise in testing as well as specialized skills in treatment; indeed some psychologists were hired solely for their testing skills (e.g., neuropsychologist). Interestingly, psychologists who presented themselves as generalist psychotherapists were viewed as "expensive social workers" by management, and there was little interest in their employment. A corollary of this was that given the limited demand for psychological testing, there was limited demand for psychologists in some people's view, mostly those who were less informed about other skills that psychologists could contribute to the health care system. Psychologists have also contributed to this lack of awareness.

Of all the behavioral health care professions, psychologists are uniquely trained in research methodology and the measurement of behavior. Needs in health care for the measurement of behavior are numerous, including identification of high-risk individuals in a population, understanding consumer behavior (including over and underutilization of services), adherence to medical regimens, issues in physician–patient relationships, quality of life, quality of service, treatment outcomes, and of course the traditional psychological testing services. Thus there are major contributions that psychology can make using skills in measurement. To take advantage of these opportunities, graduate education needs to incorporate more training in program evaluation research, large sample and epidemiological methods, and cost-effectiveness modeling (Belar, 1989; Belar, 1995a). I predict less need in tomorrow's health care system for psychologists whose skills are primarily as psychotherapists, which is how many have been trained in the past decade.

Ethical Issues

There are also ethical issues with respect to psychological testing in managed health care. First of all, test results should be shared only with those qualified to use them appropriately. This is a potential problem for all providers of psychological testing, and it is no different in managed care.

HMOs do highlight some additional issues, however. For example, with the population-based focus of health maintenance organizations, there are also incentives for early detection of patients in emotional distress so that they can be referred by primary care physicians for psychological treatment. Utilization of psychological testing to facilitate this could be very useful, but an example of potential problems with this approach follows.

Cummings (1985) describes his 1972 Kaiser Permanente study in which 10,000 patients were screened in a multiphasic program including a psychological questionnaire. Patients were randomly assigned to a control group, or one of three experimental groups. In the first experimental group, the information provided the primary care physician was a brief 200- to 300-word description of the assessment findings. The report for the second experimental group provided a more comprehensive description of the patient, and the information provided for the third group was an extensive description not only of the patient's current emotional distress, but also of his or her personality. No information was rendered to the primary care physician on patients in the control group.

Six months later, the number of referrals for psychological services were assessed. As one might expect, all experimental groups generated significantly more referrals than the control group, and each level of information provided generated significantly more referrals. "It was as if the more information, the more compelling the need to refer for psychotherapy." This would seem to be a positive outcome of testing. However, two years later, these patients were followed up and "there was a tabulation of the number of symptoms initially ascribed by the physician to emotional distress or 'no significant abnormality' which were later *rediagnosed* as a physical illness. Using the control group as the baseline for the number of missed diagnoses of physical illness, it was found that the number of missed diagnoses increased significantly in proportion to the amount of psychological assessment information rendered to the primary care provider. It was as if the increasing amount of information not only increased the likelihood of referral for psychotherapy, but it also increased the likelihood that physical illness would be overlooked in the population that was labeled as having emotional distress" (p. 296).

As Cummings has noted, the function of psychological assessment should be to enhance the quality of care, not reduce it. Efficiency is not just in and of itself the criterion for efficacy. To establish the validity and reliability of psychological measures, it is important that the effect of their use on practice also be established.

Summary

Discussions in this chapter have focused on the underutilization of psychological testing in capitated care, even in the absence of administrative or fee barriers to service. Rather than "managed care" not allowing testing, obstacles were identified in the behavior of other clinicians, our own discipline and broad health policy issues. To promote psychological testing realizing its potential in managed care, recommendations are made for psychologists.

1. Utilize testing when it has direct particular clinical problem/decision.
2. Be able to discriminate between necessary and discretionary care.
3. Be able to empirically demonstrate that the use of testing has "added value" to the quality of care.

4. Develop innovative models such as the feedback consultation model.
5. Broaden concepts of testing to measurement of behavior in areas of importance to managed care (quality of life, consumer behavior, risk assessment, etc.)
6. Become involved in health policy development at legislative and corporate levels.
7. Obtain continuing education to develop skills in program evaluation and large sample methods.
8. Consider potential negative "side effects" of developing testing programs.

References

Belar, C. D. (1989). Opportunities for psychologists in health maintenance organizations: Implications for graduate education and training. *Professional Psychology: Research and Practice* 20, 390–394.
Belar, C. D. (1995a). Collaboration in capitated care: Challenges for psychology. *Professional Psychology: Research and Practice* 26, 139–146.
Belar, C. D. (1995b, March). Role of objective personality assessment in managed care. Presented at 30th Annual Symposium on Recent Developments in the Use of the MMPI, MMPI-2 and MMPI-A. St. Petersburg Beach, Florida.
Cummings, N. A. (1985). Assessing the computer's impact: Professional concerns. *Computers in Human Behavior* 4, 293–300.
Quirk, M. P., Strosahl, K., Kreilkamp, T., & Erdberg, P. (1995). Personality feedback consultation to families in a managed mental health care practice. *Professional Psychology: Research and Practice* 26, 27–32.
Sullivan, M. J. (1995). Medicaid's quiet revolution: Merging the public & private sectors of care. *Professional Psychology: Research and Practice, 26*, 229–234.

6

Incorporations of Objective Assessment in Mental Health Care Provision

An Important Role for Practice of Psychology

Ralph H. Earle
Roxanne R. Witte

As working psychologists in the areas of marriage, family, and sex therapy, assessment has become an essential task for us in developing diagnostic and treatment plans. We cover a range of services, such as individual therapy, marital therapy, family therapy, assessments for courts, assessment for addictions, domestic violence, the seriousness of affective disorders, challenges to families and systems, and parenting issues—just to name a few.

One of the most important requirements for success in independent practice has always been networking—that is, developing a consistent and effective referral base (Beisel, Earle, Fleischman, & D'Andrea, 1990). Developing a strong network of practitioners and referral sources is fundamental in clinical practice, but it is even more essential in this era of managed health care. Now included in the family system of networking are the gatekeepers and decision makers in managed care. A working understanding of the client's needs by the therapist, patient, and managed care person is essential. Early reliable assessment information is the key to the clinical intervention. Thus appropriate and adequate assessment has become essential to understanding and facilitating briefer solution-based therapy.

It is no secret that independent practice requires a diversity of skills and ability to deal with more severe problems and extreme psychopathology. It has never been appropriate for the independent practitioner to "play God" and try to be the end all for all cases. Thus, assessment testing has provided an independent understanding of clinical issues and needs to make appropriate dispositions. Clearly at the inception of treatment, it is essential to have a map for treatment, which includes boundaries for the therapists, therapeutic skills to provide the treatment, and a determination of whether medication is likely to be needed or not. We obtain substantial information from the MMPI-2 to help us plan our "staffing," our treatment strategy, and our interpretation for the managed care consultant. The instrument also provides a "shared language" for therapists, the managed care person, and the patient, which facilitates communication about the client's problems. As psychiatric hospitals quickly become crisis and stabilization facilities, independent practitioners are now asked to deal with more seriously disturbed cases in fewer sessions. We have found the MMPI-2 to be the most useful instrument in our practice for this purpose.

Utilizing the MMPI-2

The MMPI has been a part of our treatment and evaluation for 25 years. This has included evaluations for marital therapy, family therapy, and individual diagnoses. Literally thousands of MMPIs were administered to prospective employees of a nuclear facility near Phoenix to aid in making a "fit for duty" assessment. The MMPI has also been an important assessment component to most of our custody evaluations. There have been some cases where testing was not needed; however, our experience has been that we have never regretted giving the MMPI-2. And there have been times when we wished that we had given an MMPI or MMPI-2 and did it later in the treatment process, when a situation emerged which we had missed without the testing. For example, sometimes in working with sex offenders, we have not given an MMPI to the offender's spouse and have discovered issues which might have been more quickly understood if we had given an MMPI to both partners initially. We have learned the lesson that a thorough assessment is necessary the "hard way." We are also continually reminded that it makes sense to give an MMPI to each person in the relationship in order to avoid communicating the wrong message to clients.

The MMPI-2 is particularly useful with severe cases. "Severe" in our practice means that an individual, couple, or family spends a minimum of a week to a maximum of five weeks doing individual, family, marital, or group therapy at least five days a week. An MMPI-2 is given to each adult (and adolescent) who is part of this intensive process, since having the clearest map at the inception of the intensive treatment is important. The MMPI is a nonnegotiable part of that process—everyone gets it.

When working with children and their families, objective assessment of Attention Deficit Disorders and behavioral problems can be obtained by using an Achenbach or a Connors Behavioral Assessment. Or a more standardized battery using the Weschler Intelligence Scales, Revised, as well as the Roberts Apperception Test and other projectives, may be utilized. With children in general, objective assessment is helpful in identifying and developing issues that may be contributing to the child's emotional or behavioral problem. The assessment allows one to obtain observable, measurable data to which the parents can relate and helps create criteria to help set up measurable, achievable goals within the family.

Sometimes this assessment still does not solve the problem. As we work systemically, we will always be looking at the family system, as well as the child's functioning. Sometimes at this point we will give an MMPI-2 to one or both of the parents. Often we have found that there may be a significant personality disorder or severe psychopathology present, which is interfering with that parent's ability to utilize and follow through on treatment goals that we have been setting for the child and family. Once we have this information, then we can usually work with that particular parent, either individually or within the marital dyad to help facilitate the understanding and changes needed to assist the system in dealing with the child and parenting issues.

Couples usually come in with communication or sexual issues as the identified problem. What we often find is that the "real" issues are very different and can include infidelity, sexual addictions, alcoholism, domestic violence, and a severe personality disorder. More often than not, what we see is a combination of the above. Again, the MMPI-2 can help quickly clarify any personality characteristics or psychopathology that is coexisting along with the identified behaviors. If this information is not obtained, one can spend a lot of time trying to change a family system, a marital system, or behavior that proves to be ineffective or not maintained over time, due to not identifying underlying psychological factors that need to be addressed. In addition to the utilization of clinical scales, the validity scales may be very helpful to gauge levels of denial and minimization or attempts to appear better or worse than they are. Frequently, when these issues are addressed, other "secrets" are disclosed which are impacting on intra- and interpersonal functioning.

When clients reveal a severe history of sexual trauma or physical abuse, or both, we usually need an accurate, minimally intrusive assessment of their ego strength and general functioning. If one does not have this information, the client can be inadvertently harmed by the type of treatment in which they are placed. If they are not ready for a group treatment or a particular intensive type of intervention, but need a more supportive, slower pace, one can inadvertently trigger a decompensating process which could be avoided in having this information before treatment goals are set.

Three examples might be useful to make this point.

A client undergoing individual therapy was also involved in a group treatment situation in which there was some intense confrontation and some very deep probing into potential abuse issues. Because this client was not emotionally able to tolerate this kind of work, due to a personality structure, he decompensated and we saw an increase in his level of paranoia and confusion. Had the therapists paid attention to information revealed in the MMPI-2, they would have known that this type of therapy was inappropriate for this client.

A second scenario involved a client who was placed in a group for incest survivors. Her primary therapist was not involved with the group, and she appeared to be doing quite well. She had not been given the MMPI-2; and due to this oversight, what became apparent after several months of working is that she was not benefitting from the group treatment and eventually dropped out. When her primary therapist did eventually give her an MMPI-2, we were able to see the high level of passive-aggressiveness and the loose thinking, accompanied with anxiety, that she was experiencing. Had we had this information sooner and addressed these issues more directly, there is no doubt that the group experience would have been more meaningful for her, and she would not have left therapy prematurely.

A third case involved intensively focused brief therapy. The MMPI-2 provides a guideline to understand our limits in working with patients, including how hard to "push a patient." The worst-case scenario would be to cause harm to the client during patient care. The MMPI-2 can provide information about how severe the psychological disorder is or how tenuous the individual's adjustment is; for example, one would not employ stiff confrontation with individuals who are unable to cope with it.

The chief complaint of many clients who come in with a personality disorder is that some type of interpersonal disruption, whether its violence, chronic marital discord, job-related personnel issues, or social isolation, is occurring on a fairly regular basis. An MMPI-2 helps us accurately diagnose the type of personality disorder they may be experiencing, as well as any concomitant affective disorder that often accompanies this. It is important for us to see the level of mood disorder, so that appropriate referrals can be made to a psychiatrist for a medical evaluation and appropriate psychopharmacological intervention, if necessary. In one case, a 36-year-old male client, who had been in therapy for several years, became our client and was asked to take the MMPI-2. In going over the MMPI-2 with him, we noted a significant elevation in the depression and anxiety scales. He revealed for the first time that he was experiencing a significant level of depression and had been for many years, but had never brought this up in therapy before. He was referred for an appropriate medical evaluation, and therapy is now progressing at a rate that was not possible prior to this intervention.

At this point, it would be helpful to present a case in some detail to illustrate how the MMPI-2 contributes to our understanding of clients in the initial stages of therapy.

Case Illustration

A Caucasian male in his mid-forties was referred to us by the court for treatment issues surrounding his sexual abuse of his daughter. The MMPI-2 provided us with multiple levels of information for use in developing an individual treatment plan for this patient (see Figure 6.1 for the father's MMPI-2 and Figure 6.2 for the daughter's profile information), as well as a plan for family therapy which was to be started at a later date. In assessing the validity scales, his profile was within acceptable parameters, indicating that he was as honest and open as he could be at this time. His clinical elevations were as follows: Scale 2 (T-85), Scale 5 (T-75), and Scale 7 (T-73).

The test indicated that he was in many ways a depressed and frightened person and that pattern has been chronic. His reported history supported this as we questioned him about the results from the MMPI. He had always had fears about leav-

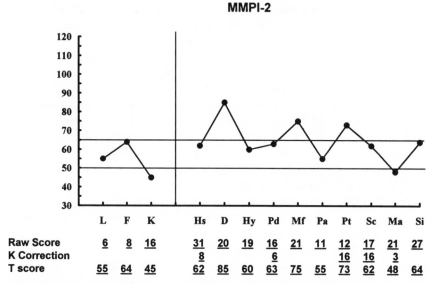

Fig. 6.1 MMPI-2 profile of a 40-year-old father evaluated at the clinic (incest perpetrator)

ing home, fears about going to kindergarten and first grade, fears about going to college, fears about support, and fears about academics in general. Even when he did well, he would still have a negative feeling about himself. The eventual sexual abuse of his daughter only served to increase his feelings of worthlessness and low self-esteem. The test results also indicated an inherent shyness that kept him from

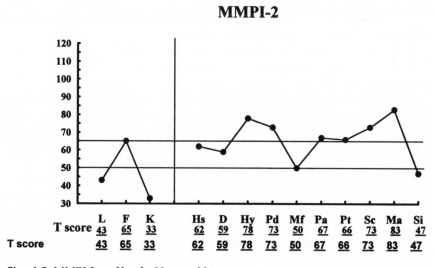

Fig. 6.2 MMPI-2 profile of a 23-year-old incest victim.

going outside of his immediate family to express his sexual and social interests. The test also indicated that he was a very sensitive person, who was easily hurt by others, particularly if he had perceived any type of criticism.

His MMPI profile had a "neurotic slope," with his primary elevations running highest on the left side of the profile. His history supported the old term of psychasthenia, literally meaning the low flows of nervous energy, now more frequently thought of as an individual who is chronically a worrier with strong depressive tendencies. Again, his history showed that he had an ulcer when he was in school as a child, and he had a teacher he perceived as being a "mean" person. Concerning treatment, this client worried about financial and legal matters and about his family breaking up, as well as about his inappropriate sexual behaviors and the impact that they were having on his daughter.

His subclinical elevation on Scale 0 (Social Introversion scale) indicated his innate shyness, even though he initially presented as self-confident and had to interact with many people at his work. His low score on Scale 9 indicated that in spite of his long working hours and having a long history of carrying more than one job at a time, he still had a low level of energy. This subclinical information was helpful to interpret, because it allowed us to see that he had developed a professional facade that hid his social introversion, as well as his chronic sense of physical and emotional exhaustion. In this case, the MMPI-2 raised areas of concern that may not have been discussed or explored until further into therapy.

Even though psychopathology was present in his test pattern, nothing on the MMPI test results indicated that he could not make changes. He came in with a high motivation for change and not just because of his legal situation. He was ready to take responsibility for what had happened and to do whatever was possible to heal himself and his family.

Several months after we began working with the father, we began working with the client's daughter who was 23 years of age. She came in primarily because of family pressures to have a session with her father, who was ready to make amends and wanted to apologize directly to her for his past actions.

During the initial session, it became clear that while father was ready to begin making his amends, his daughter was not ready to hear them nor did she want to interact with him directly. During the session, she was disengaged from both her father and the therapist and unable to respond to either one of them. At that point, the session was stopped, and the daughter was seen by the therapist alone. She reported that she was not ready to speak with her father about the past, but she felt unable to say no to the family pressures to do so. She agreed to take the MMPI-2 and to continue with some individual sessions.

During the first few sessions with her, she was often experienced as scattered, emotionally labile, and very susceptible to outside pressures, particularly from her family. She also appeared to be somewhat impulsive when frightened and exhibited a self-referenced view of the world. In addition, she often came up with idiosyncratic perceptions of events and other people's behaviors. What was confusing about this client was that she would vacillate in the following manner: Initially she would seem quite strong, capable, and able to understand the multiple events happening to her, yet within a few minutes (within the same session) she could decompensate to the behaviors previously discussed.

Our concern became what would be the best choice of treatment for her because whenever she became stressed during a session, she quickly defocused and shut down. In staffing her case, it was felt that supportive therapy, as opposed to uncovering or more in depth-type therapy, would be beneficial. The results of the MMPI-2 were helpful in clarifying this clinical picture by identifying the specific vulnerabilities she was predisposed to experiencing.

She was a 9–3' code type with a T score of 83 on Scale 9 and a T score of 78 on Scale 3. Scale 4 (T-73), Scale 8 (T-73), Scale 6 (T-67), and Scale 7 (T-66) were also clinically elevated. As indicated by the MMPI-2 interpretive text (Greene, 1991), she was indeed gregarious and outgoing. She also had great difficulty looking at her own psychological factors that were contributing to her stress. She mainly wanted to focus on situational factors such as her family or boyfriend. Also as indicated by her elevation on Scales 3 and 4, she had difficulty discharging her hostility directly and was overtly very quiet and conforming. Her past history supported this in that she was a straight A student at school and was reported to have no behavior problems at school or at home.

Of most help in understanding this client was her elevation on Scale 8 (T-73), because this helped clarify what was interfering with her decision making and her inability to concentrate during our sessions. The MMPI-2 confirmed the therapist's clinical impressions that, indeed, she was more vulnerable and susceptible to cognitive decompensation than she let on and not able to set some of the strong boundaries necessary for her independence and maturity. She could also easily be manipulated by others.

The results of the MMPI helped us take a strong, supportive, therapeutic stance to progress slowly with her, even though there was a great deal of family pressure to move more quickly, because others tended to see her much less emotionally vulnerable than she was in reality.

Oftentimes, when we are working systemically, we will have family members who have radically different personality styles and/or needs in the present. Understanding how each of these personality styles and particular defense mechanisms and/or vulnerabilities interact with each other helps us in supporting the needs of each family member while maintaining the appropriate support and protection of family members who are most vulnerable or who have already been victimized in the past.

With this particular family, we were able to help them see how each of them were functioning differently in an emotional sense. This was helpful in allowing the daughter the time and support she needed to work through many of her intrapsychic, as well as interpersonal, issues before trying father/daughter sessions again. We also encouraged the father's therapist to support him to continue his own work and to move forward, even though he was unable to start the process with his daughter as he had wanted to. This was helpful within this family because it was already extremely enmeshed, with poor boundaries and the propensity for each of the family members to misunderstand and blame each other for the breakdown in communication.

The final result, after having worked with this family in family and individual sessions, is that the father was given "lifetime probation" when usually that particular offense would have led to some period of incarceration. The judge decided that his treatment program, which he had participated in rigorously for three years, led to "lifetime probation"—the decision which would make the most sense in the best interest of the child and family, including the sex offender. This individual remains in self-help groups, continuing with a sponsor, and doing therapy as needed. The MMPI-2 helped us to understand the parameters for the treatment, from the point of view of both (a) the issues that led to the sex offense and (b) the prognosis for his being able to make the changes in himself to be safe for him and others around him. He is a person who has, over time, developed clear boundaries in terms of what is okay and not okay, worked out by therapists, probation officers, his family, and his own desire to remain safe.

His daughter has also continued to do her own individual and group therapy, as well as participating in family therapy. Through her own growth and understanding of herself and the hard work that she put forth in therapy, she has continued to mature and develop in healthy ways. She has gone on to get married and is currently pursuing a college degree.

Further Factors to Consider in Using the MMPI-2 in Independent Practice

The MMPI-2 not only provides accurate diagnostic and relevant treatment information, but also can be used to educate the clients about themselves. The information given during the feedback session can help them understand who they are and how they function. It is frequently helpful to patients to go through the critical items as a way of understanding dimensions that require attention as part of the patient's care. Clients often feel more understood and free to talk about frightening issues or disturbing subjects that come up because the interpretive information from the MMPI-2 lends itself toward those kinds of discussions. Clients also like objective feedback in addition to what a therapist might tell them. It also helps build a collaborative relationship between client and therapist in which they are helping identify problems through their honest test-taking behaviors and then the collaborative feedback session that follows.

It is not always appropriate to give an MMPI-2. Like any assessment, we need a reason for doing so. We usually have one or more questions that we have not been able to answer during the initial clinical interview. Because we no longer have the luxury of assessment over time and getting to know our client over an extended number of sessions, many of the questions that would eventually be answered through traditional long-term therapy cannot be answered in a brief period of time without some objective assessment being utilized.

Sometimes we have very specific concerns we believe need to be addressed before we specify the type and duration of treatment. Some examples of these issues would be suicidal ideation, the level of depression or anxiety, the person's thought processes and connection to reality, their level of paranoia, and/or how they are dealing with their anger and feelings in general. These are all things that will clearly impact the therapeutic relationship and subsequent treatment of the client. The sooner we have information about this which can be provided by the MMPI-2, the more effective we can facilitate therapy.

Sometimes a case seems simple and clear-cut in initial presentation, and then a problem will suddenly come up unexpectedly. For example, we did a family therapy session with a mother, father, and a young daughter who had attention deficit disorder. During one of the initial sessions with the family, we noted that the mother dissociated during the session. This issue of mother's dissociation needed to be addressed immediately, and understanding what was happening to her had to be clarified before it made sense to continue family therapy. Again, in giving her the MMPI-2, it was helpful to see the level of anxiety and cognitive distortions she was experiencing. Seeing this aspect of her personality allowed us to refer her out for appropriate medication to facilitate the work that we were doing with the family.

Lastly, sometimes a case just seems to get stuck without much movement; and if we haven't given an MMPI-2, we will do so at that time to help clarify if there are any personality characteristics and/or psychopathology that we have missed or that have been well-hidden by the client and yet are getting in the way of progress.

Having a clear conceptualization and rationale for why we use the MMPI-2 or any testing procedure then helps clinicians in facilitating our work with gatekeepers and managed care staff. We keep regular contact with managed care providers. Discussing treatment with "gatekeepers" has proven to be beneficial in educating both gatekeepers and ourselves, because at times gatekeepers have some very helpful suggestions to make because of the volume of cases in which they are involved. Our approach has always been that we are part of a team in treatment, and the gatekeepers are a part of that treatment team—not adversaries to our process. Since all of us can benefit from learning to work in the framework of managed care, we need to view this collaborative relationship as positive instead of negative. More cooperation between the therapist and case manager is called for and is helpful to prevent ulcers for the therapists.

Clearly, the utilization of the MMPI-2 is a part of a "practice audit" to do our best to prevent potential litigation. It is essential to have the best diagnostic tools at our disposal and to demonstrate that we have used them when "under fire." Over the years, there have been many cases where it has been extremely helpful to be able to state that, as clinicians, we believe certain strategies and treatment were important, and part of our belief was validated or strategy changed because of information from the MMPI-2. We tell patients that the MMPI-2 is not a god and that we're not gods, and the MMPI-2 becomes a part of the team to help us to work together in the patient's best interest. It is also our belief that the MMPI-2 is cost effective in cases where it is needed. Moreover, it helps to clarify treatment needs— an efficient and needed strategy for busy practitioners. Finally, we have found it useful for enhancing brief therapy.

At times, when flexibility is essential, the MMPI-2 provides the practitioner with more options. It is a fact that the MMPI-2 is helpful in clinical care in the office, but it can also be useful in personnel selection in the corporate world. It can be used for risk assessment and in other arenas. Our job is to think creatively to be able to provide the right tools at the right time.

References

Beigel, J. K., Earle, R. H., Fleischman, L., & D'Andrea, R. (1990). *Successful private practice in the 1990's*. New York: Brunner/Mazel.

Greene, R. L. (1991). *MMPI-2/MMPI: An interpretive manual*. Boston: Allyn & Bacon.

Part II

THE ROLE OF OBJECTIVE PERSONALITY ASSESSMENT IN TREATMENT PLANNING

The MMPI-2 in Practice

7

Psychological Tests in Treatment Planning

The Importance of Objective Assessment

Kelly Klump

James N. Butcher

Psychological treatment is often begun in darkness and proceeds in the confusion of low illumination for some time. Many therapists begin the complex process of psychological therapy without sufficiently understanding either of the nature or extent of problems the patient experiences. This is analogous to beginning a journey through unknown territory without the benefit of maps, knowledge of the terrain to be traversed, or the makeup of our fellow traveler(s) who share the journey. The outcome is often similar: The sojourners get lost or bogged down in thickets and find themselves going in circles. Therapists who begin a therapeutic journey without sufficiently surveying the problems and the patient's resources through psychological assessment procedures (whether the approach is behavioral, analytic, or some other) are not providing the unwary client the service they expect and need when they consult a mental health professional—that is, *professional expertise* which includes a scientific understanding of the person's problems and strengths.

Effective psychological assessment in pretreatment planning can accomplish a number of important goals:

1. A psychological assessment can forearm the therapist with important, indeed essential, patient information as to the client's motivation for treatment, likely sources of resistance, extent of problems, diagnostic considerations that assist the therapist in developing a framework for selecting a therapeutic approach, and clues to possible long-term personality characteristics that could undermine treatment.

2. Conducting an objective psychological assessment communicates to the patient that the therapist is making efforts to understand the individual's problems and personality.

3. An assessment study provides a source of valuable personality information that can serve as a *baseline* for later treatment evaluations during therapy or at treatment termination. In this context a personality test evaluation can be an essential ingredient to understanding the therapy process.

4. A not-insignificant matter facing psychologists today involves the possibility that the therapist will need to document (from a legal perspective) that the therapy was an "appropriate psychological practice" which was conducted in a competent manner. Should the treatment become problematic from a legal standpoint, it is important for the therapist to be able to ensure that the failing did not result from actions of the therapist. There have been several cases in which pretreatment or "on course" MMPIs have been used in legal cases to document therapeutic decisions and outcomes.

5. An initial testing can provide the therapist with important personality information that can be used to bring about behavioral change (Finn and Tonsager, 1993). (See Chapter 8 of this volume for further discussion of the model describing the use of psychological test feedback in bringing about treatment change.)

In *Dyer's Hand*, W. H. Auden, (1962) observed: "Almost all of our relationships begin and most of them continue as forms of mutual exploitation, a mental or physical barter, to be terminated when one or both parties run out of goods."

As in any important relationship, therapists who fail to understand their patient's problems in a timely manner and develop effective treatment plans to deal with them "run out of goods" rather quickly. There are several possible consequences to a failed assessment in psychotherapy. One of the tragic consequences of inadequate assessment in pretreatment planning is *early dropout* from therapy. Many therapeutic contracts end early—often as a result of the patient's dissatisfaction with the course of therapy. Therapists often misread the nature and extent of the patient's problems, failing to meet the individual's expectations in entering therapy. Even when therapy proceeds, without clear personality information, therapeutic progress is often plagued by *unfocused goals*. Without clear practical treatment goals, therapy is most often without direction and often without progress. Lack of pertinent personality and symptom information also results in using *inefficient treatment strategies* and failed or off-mark interpretations. Failure to recognize treatment-destructive personality problems such as obsessional traits or acting out behavior can lead to ineffective treatment goals or strategies.

Many therapies fail because the therapist does not gain a clear understanding of the patient before the patient runs out of motivation and the therapist runs out of therapeutic leverage. Therapists fail to fully assess their patients for a number of reasons: (a) bad training and lack of assessment skills, or (b) negative attitudes toward psychological assessment. Moreover, some therapists hold an antiquated and misguided view that having psychological assessment information might bias them and cause them to reject their patients. Some therapists subscribe to a limited treatment model that has not incorporated adequate assessment methods.

The MMPI-2 in Treatment Planning

The MMPI-2 can provide the practitioner with an objective outside opinion of the individual's problems and motivations and can provide "summaries" of problems in the patient's own words when one uses content scale measures. The MMPI-2 validity patterns can provide the practitioner with information as to likely forms of treatment resistance. There are a number of test indices that provide the practitioner with an appraisal of the individual's treatment motivation. The traditional clinical scales, with their extensive research and contemporary normative base, can reflect the extent to which the client is in "need" for therapy. Finally, the MMPI-2 scores and indices, when shared with the client, can give the practitioner an excellent mechanism for providing test feedback (see the discussion of "assessment therapy" by Finn and Martin in Chapter 8). We will next summarize the MMPI-2 measures and provide an overview of their uses in treatment planning.

Assessment of Treatment Readiness and Accessibility to Change

The MMPI-2 can be extremely useful in assessing those client attitudes and beliefs that can affect the psychological treatment process. The MMPI-2 validity scales, clinical scales, and content scales can provide the clinician with hypotheses regarding the accessibility of the client to psychological treatment and the change process.

MMPI-2-Based Validity Scales   The ?, *L*, *K*, and *F* scales can provide valuable information regarding how patients view the present clinical situation, how well they have cooperated with the assessment, and how accessible they are to treatment. This information can be obtained both from the interpretation of the individual validity scales and from the interpretation of the validity scale configuration.

Cannot Say Score (?) The Cannot Say Score is useful in treatment planning because it reflects the client's cooperativeness with the psychological evaluation. Clients taking the test in a pretreatment situation are assumed to be seeking help and understanding from the therapist; such persons would not be expected to omit many items, for fear of being misunderstood. Therefore, those clients who fail to reply to 8 to 10 items within the first 370 questions (the MMPI-2 validity and clinical scales are scorable from the first 370 items) are being more evasive and cautious than would be expected in a pretreatment setting. Clients with 11 to 19 omissions likely have considerable difficulty discussing personal problems. Profiles with 20 or more omitted items likely indicate a lack of a treatment-readiness attitude. Individuals with these profiles tend to have resistance issues that should be addressed early in the treatment process.

Lie Scale (L). Individuals with a T score of 55–65 on the Lie scale are likely to engage in overly virtuous self-presentations that could be counterproductive in therapy. These people often perceive themselves as being highly principled, virtuous, and above fault; consequently, frank, open and direct communication with the therapist is often difficult. If the L scale is elevated above 65, then therapy is unlikely to proceed well, little progress will be made, and premature termination is likely. Clients with virtuous self-perceptions are too rigid and "perfect" to change their behavior or views about themselves. These individuals often do not see a need to discuss their problems or difficulties with anyone.

F Scale (F). The F scale is used in psychological treatment planning to assess the level of psychological distress the client is experiencing. The lower the scale elevation, the less discomfort or distress the client is experiencing (or reporting). Without recognized symptoms, there is little intrinsic motivation for seeking help. Such clients would not be expected to seek out counseling. When the F scale is between 51 and 59 T-score points, then the individual may be reporting symptoms of distress that could require psychological treatment. The level of distress, however, is considerably below that of most people who seek help. But, if a slight elevation on the F scale is higher than both the L and K scales, a problem-oriented self-review can be assumed to be present. When the F-scale range is between 60 and 79 the individual is engaging in appropriate symptom expression, particularly if F is greater than L and K.

If the F-scale range is between 80 and 90, the person is expressing a great deal of distress, confusion, and a broad range of psychological symptoms. This range indicates that the patient is reporting a multiproblem situation and a lack of resources to deal with the problems. This is the fairly common "plea for help pattern" seen in emergency settings or crisis contacts. Immediate attention to an individual with such an elevation is recommended. MMPI-2 profiles with F elevations above 91 indicate that the person has grossly exaggerated his/her symptom picture. This exaggeration may be present for a multitude of reasons, including disorientation, psychoticism, or a desire to appear "disturbed." Presence of such exaggeration can be a negative treatment factor, because it may indicate that the person is interested in treatment only for the secondary gains it may provide.

K Scale. The K scale can be used as an indicator of treatment readiness because it assesses an individual's willingness to disclose personal information. When the K scale is in the lower ranges (below 40–45), an openness to emotional expression is indicated. In its upper ranges (above $T = 70$), the K scale suggests a resistance toward problem expression and the discussion of emotions. The K scale is a little more complicated than this, however, and must usually be interpreted in conjunction with information about socioeconomic status and education level. As discussed elsewhere (Butcher, 1990), the K-scale elevation can vary depending upon these two variables. Consequently, SES and education level should always be taken into account when interpreting the K score.

Validity Scale Configuration   Much of the information that the validity scales can provide about treatment readiness comes from the interpretation of the validity scale profile. A few prominent configurations and their relationship to treatment will be reviewed briefly.

1. *The highly virtuous or unwilling patient*. This validity pattern of "naive" defensiveness is characterized by relatively high elevations on both L and K (above 60), as well as by L and K elevations that are above the F elevation (which is below

60). In this validity pattern, L is greater than K. Individuals with this validity pattern tend to be difficult to engage in the therapy process. They often maintain attitudes of perfectionistic thinking and a reluctance or refusal to engage in self-criticism. They feel little need for discussing problems, often viewing their psychological adjustment as "good." These clients often appear distant, unrealistic, and uninvolved in their own problems.

2. *The reluctant, defended, and hesitant participant.* These individuals are less moralistic and virtuous than those described above but are, nonetheless, reluctant to discuss their problems in therapy. This profile is dominated by an elevated K score and is thus marked by denial and presentation of positive mental health. Individuals with this configuration often view themselves quite positively and are reluctant to disclose personal weaknesses.

3. *Exaggerated symptom expression—the need for attention to problems.* This "plea for help" pattern is marked by relatively high elevations on the F scale and low elevations on L and K. This configuration is found frequently among individuals seeking psychological help. One implication of this pattern for treatment is the fact that, in the extreme ranges, the problems being presented tend to be nonspecific and involve several life areas. As a consequence, clients with this pattern may be unable to focus on specific issues in treatment sessions. These individuals appear prone to develop "crises" that seem to consume all of their energy and adaptive resources.

4. *Open, frank problem expression.* A problem-oriented approach to self review is reflected in an MMPI-2 profile with a moderate elevation on the F scale in conjunction with lower L and K scores. Clients with this configuration are relatively easy to engage in psychological treatment and are more inclined to discuss their problems.

Openness to Treatment as Reflected by the MMPI-2 Clinical Scales

Scale 1: Hypochondriasis (Hs) individuals whose highest scale elevation is on the Hs scale typically do not view their problems as psychological in origin. They report numerous somatic complaints and attempt to obtain physical explanations for their symptoms. They typically have low motivation for behavioral change and usually tolerate considerable psychological strain before change is considered. Noncompliance with treatment and early termination are frequent problems with these individuals.

Scale 2: Depression. Individuals with this peak score have taken the test with a problem-oriented approach and are open to discussing their problems. They typically are experiencing much psychological distress; as a consequence, their motivation for relief is high. A positive response to therapy has been well-documented in the research. Good treatment prognosis in people with adequate verbal skills is expected since these individuals tend to become engaged in therapy and remain in treatment; these individuals typically show improvement at follow-up.

Scale 3: Hysteria. High hysteria (Hy) individuals do not usually seek psychological help for their problems; instead, they view themselves as physically ill and will frequently seek medical solutions for their problems, even though actual organic findings are minimal. These individuals typically possess characteristics that interfere with the therapeutic process, including defensiveness, naiveté, and low psychological mindedness. They tend to minimize personal weaknesses and are often unmotivated for change. Although significant improvement may only come through long-term treatment, these individuals tend to terminate therapy prematurely.

Scale 4: Psychopathic Deviate. Individuals with high psychopathic deviate (Pd) elevations are typically uninterested in treatment or changing their behavior. They seldom seek treatment for themselves; instead, they often choose therapy in response to the demands of others, such as a spouse, family, or the court. They typically fail to see a need for changes in their behavior. Interpersonally, these individuals tend to be manipulative, aggressive, deceptive, exhibitionistic, and self-oriented; as therapy takes place in an interpersonal domain, these characteristics can often thwart treatment efforts. Premature termination with little significant improvement is often present with high Pd individuals.

Scale 5: Masculinity–Femininity. The masculinity–femininity (Mf) scale reflects a person's level of cultural awareness and openness to new ideas. The Mf scale has different interpretive significance depending upon the level of elevation and the gender of the client.

In men:

1. *The man with a score below T = 45* may be viewed as a poor candidate for insight-oriented psychotherapy. Individuals with this pattern tend to show a lack of interest in discussing their problems with others. They typically lack psychological mindedness, are uninsightful, and are usually uninterested in psychological matters or treatment.
2. *The man with a score of T = 65–70* possesses characteristics such as sensitivity and insightfulness that suggest openness to experience and amenability to treatment.
3. *The man with a score above T = 75* may have difficulties with relationships due to possible passivity and heterosexual adjustment problems. These individuals often have problems dealing with anger, which could prove difficult in treatment. Passivity and an impractical approach to life may prevent him from trying new roles and alternative behaviors that might emerge out of therapy.

In women:

1. *The woman with a score below T = 40* has an ultrapassive lifestyle suggestive of low treatment potential. These individuals may show masochistic, self-deprecating, and self-defeating behavior that may be hard to alter in therapy.
2. *The woman with a score above T = 70* tends to be aggressive, dominant, rebellious, and cynical in her interactions with others. These individuals generally have difficulties expressing emotions and tend not to be very introspective nor insightful. Verbal psychotherapy may be contraindicated in women with this Mf pattern.

Scale 6: Paranoia. The paranoia (Pa) scale can be very valuable in treatment planning because it assesses the client's trust in interpersonal relationships, attitudes toward authority figures, and flexibility toward change. High Pa clients are generally not viewed as good candidates for psychological treatment because of their tendency to blame others for their problems. They tend to be argumentative, resentful, and cynical. Aloofness and defensiveness are typically present, along with a reluctance to confide in the therapist. Many of the aforementioned characteristics make the development of a therapeutic relationship characterized by mutual respect, warmth, and empathic feeling difficult, if not impossible. Early termination of therapy is common; many clients do not return after the first visit because they believe the therapist does not understand them.

Scale 7: Psychasthenia. High psychasthenia (Pt) clients generally express a great need for help and appear to be quite motivated for symptom relief because they are quite anxious. They may also seek medical solutions for their physical problems which are probably associated with intense anxiety. High Pt clients tend to remain in therapy longer than most patients, generally making slow but steady progress. Clients with extremely high elevations on this scale (T > 90) may show considerable interpersonal rigidity and unproductive rumination that may interfere with the implementation of therapeutic changes. The high Pt individual is often so self-critical that he or she engages in a degree of perfectionistic behavior that impedes progress in treatment.

Scale 8: Schizophrenia. Individuals with peak scale elevations on the schizophrenia (Sc) scale generally present with a problem-oriented focus in initial treatment sessions. However, it is useful for the therapist to evaluate the severity of potentially relevant information in this scale as shown in the following way.

1. A *score of T= 65–75* suggests the presence of disorganized life circumstances and a chaotic lifestyle that may produce a multiproblem situation that is difficult to pinpoint in therapy. Interpersonal difficulties may interfere with the establishment of rapport. Psychological treatment may be undermined by a preoccupation with the occult or superstitious beliefs. Such clients may avoid emotional commitments and may not respond well to therapy. Because they may feel that no one understands them, their prognosis for therapy tends to be poor. Their problems tend to be chronic and long-term; consequently, lengthy treatment is anticipated.
2. *Scores of T = 76* and above suggest the presence of severe confusion and disorganization. Withdrawal and bizarre thought processes may deter psychological treatment.

Scale 9: Mania. In order to appraise client motivation for and accessibility to treatment, the range of scores on the Ma scale must be examined.

1. *Scores below T = 45.* Clients with scores in this range tend to have difficulty in psychological treatment. They often feel unmotivated, inadequate, depressed, hopeless, and pessimistic about the future. They may be experiencing multiproblem situations and have difficulty getting mobilized to work on these various problems.
2. *Scores of T= 46–69.* This range of scores reflects self-assurance and self-confidence. If the Ma score is the highest peak in the profile, then the client is denying problems and reporting feelings of self-assurance. Individuals with this profile typically do not seek treatment. For all practical purposes, this should be considered a normal range profile.
3. *Scores above T = 70.* Clients scoring in this range typically prove to be difficult and uncooperative, due to their distractibility and overactivity. These clients are inclined to be narcissistic and manipulative and often disregard therapy times. They tend to use denial to avoid self-examination. These clients often consider therapy unnecessary and thus tend to attend sessions irregularly and terminate therapy prematurely.

Si Scale: Social Introversion–Extroversion. The Si scale is one of the most useful scales in pretreatment planning because it assesses several aspects of interpersonal functioning. The level of elevation provides valuable clues to an individual's capacity to form social relationships as well as readiness to become engaged in the process of self-disclosure.

1. Low Si (scores below T = 45) clients may not see the need for treatment. They tend to feel little or no anxiety and do not feel uncomfortable enough to change. They usually are too superficial and glib to form deep emotional relationships. They are neither reflective nor interested in inward scrutiny; consequently, they are typically viewed as poor candidates for therapy.
2. Moderate Si elevations (scores of T = 60–69) reflect difficulty in forming personal relationships. These clients tend to be shy and inhibited and may have great difficulty articulating their feelings. They are quite insecure and nonconforming; thus, they may expect the therapist to be directive and dominant in the sessions.
3. High Si elevations (scores of T = 70 or greater) suggest probable difficulty in developing an effective therapeutic relationship. These clients are quite inhibited and may have difficulties expressing their feelings. They are very slow to trust the therapist. Such clients may appear unmotivated and passive, yet quite anxious and distressed. These clients have great difficulty making changes in their social behavior or putting into practice new modes of responding outside of the treatment setting.

Treatment Planning with the MMPI-2 Content Scales   The MMPI-2 content scales, as expected from content-based MMPI-2 measures, address significant content themes that the client is willing and open to confide through the items in the assessment context. That is, the items endorsed can reflect direct communications between the patient and the therapist. For example, patients who are feeling depressed approach the MMPI-2 items with a frank and open response attitude and will share information about this through their endorsement of the content of the items.

Two of the MMPI-2 content scales are particularly useful in pretreatment planning: the Negative Treatment Indicators scale (TRT) and the Negative Work Attitudes scale (WRK). These scales summarize maladaptive attitudes and negative views related to accepting help or changing behavior.

Negative Treatment Indicators Scale (TRT). The TRT scale was developed as a means of assessing the client's potential to cooperate with treatment and to detect the presence of personality factors or attitudes that may reflect an unwillingness or inability to change. High scorers on this scale are presenting the view that they are unwilling or unable to change their life situation at this time, and that they are pessimistic about the future. Such individuals often have negative attitudes toward physicians and mental health professionals and feel that nobody can understand or help them. Because these clients often prefer to give up rather than face a crisis or difficulty, they are difficult to engage in psychotherapy.

Negative Work Attitudes Scale (WRK). The WRK scale was developed to assess attitudes or habits that would be counterproductive to rehabilitative efforts. Clients who score high on this scale are presenting the view that they have many problems that prevent them from being successful at work. These clients may have difficulty getting started on things and may give up quickly when problems mount. Therapists should be aware that work-related problems are, or could become, central problems in any person's life situation. Therefore, people with high scores on this scale may have a poor prognosis for achieving treatment success since their environmental pressures are likely to absorb most of their energies.

Client–Therapist Matching

The interpretation of MMPI-2 scores in treatment planning best proceeds with the inclusion of pertinent background or demographic factors. We will examine several pertinent factors and their notable impact on personality test interpretation. The idea that appropriate client–therapist "matches" enhance the effectiveness of psychological treatment has been around a long time (Parloff et al., 1978; Whitehorn & Betz, 1960). Researchers and clinicians alike have often speculated that therapists who are compatible with their clients on a number of important variables will be better able to understand and empathize with them than will those therapists who are not compatible with their clients. This interesting idea has led to vigorous research efforts aimed at identifying client-therapist combinations that are optimal for therapeutic change. As can be imagined, several different client and therapist characteristics have been hypothesized to be important for these combinations, including demographic variables, relationship variables, and extratherapy variables. Due to the vastness of this research, we are unable to review all of the relevant findings here. However, it is possible to review and discuss a few variables that appear to be important for clinicians to consider during pretreatment assessment. These variables include demographic characteristics, treatment expectations, personality, and type of client problem. As discussed below, it appears as though paying attention to these few variables early in the treatment process will often lead to enhanced therapeutic change and enhanced treatment outcomes.

In addition to a general review of the literature surrounding these characteristics, client matching strategies with the MMPI-2 will also be discussed. The MMPI-2 has the potential to be an extremely valuable tool for optimizing client–therapist matches, particularly in the areas of expectations, personality, and type of client problem. Information obtained from the MMPI-2 can aid the clinician in identifying those clients he/she is most likely to work well with, ensuring that the needs of each client are met and that limited resources are not unwisely used.

Demographic Variables

Ethnicity   A great number of studies and reviews have emerged looking at the effects of client-therapist racial matching on the process and outcome of psychotherapy (Abramowitz & Murray, 1983; Barrett & Wright, 1984; Costello et al., 1979; Gardner, 1972; Griffith & Jones, 1978; Heffernon & Bruehl, 1971; Jones, 1978; Krebs, 1971; Niemeyer & Gonzales, 1983; Proctor & Rosen, 1981; Sattler, 1977;

Terrell & Terrell, 1984; Williams, 1984). In general, evidence for an effect of racial matching on treatment outcome has not been obtained (Beutler et al., 1986; Dembo et al., 1983). When differences have emerged, an insensitivity to ethnic issues and a lack of understanding of racial differences have characterized the dissimilar dyads (Turner & Armstrong, 1981; Yamamoto et al., 1967). For example, Yamamoto et. al. (1967) found that white therapists scoring high on a measure of ethnocentricity were less likely to see their black clients for six or more sessions than they were to see their white clients that often.

Although positive effects on treatment outcome have generally not been obtained, ethnic matching has been found to be beneficial for enhancing communication and feelings of satisfaction within the therapeutic relationship (Abramowitz & Murray, 1983). Patient participation in the early stages of therapy may even be enhanced by ethnic similarity, and patient dropout rates may be decreased (Banks, 1972; Bryson & Cody, 1973; Carkhuff & Pierce, 1967; Grantham, 1973; Proctor & Rosen, 1981).

In summary, it appears as though ethnicity is not as important for optimal therapist–client matching as are attitudinal variables such as cultural openness and sensitivity to ethnic differences. While ethnic-matching may enhance the therapeutic relationship, at least in the beginning, it appears as though culturally minded therapists have the potential to be successful with any clients, regardless of the clients' and/or therapist's ethnicity.

Age   As Beutler et al. (1986) correctly point out, there are two methodological difficulties with looking at the effects of age matching on treatment outcome. The first is that age is often confounded with experience; the older the therapist, the more training and expertise he/she likely has. Because of this, caution must be exercised when comparing age-similar and age-dissimilar dyads, especially for older clients. The second difficulty involves the fact that age is not "unidirectional" (Beutler et al., 1986); that is, age differences can exert a different effect when a therapist is the older member of a dyad as opposed to when a client is the older member. Therefore, both *actual* and *relative* age need to be investigated in studies of age compatibility (Beutler et al., 1986). Unfortunately, few studies to date have examined age in this optimal way. Consequently, many of the results summarized below are limited by the aforementioned confounds and should be interpreted with appropriate caution.

In general, age matching appears to exert only a mild effect on treatment outcome (Morgan et al., 1982). The little effect it does have appears to be mediated by the fact that age similarity appears to enhance the development of a helping treatment relationship, especially in younger clients (Dembo et al., 1983; Getz & Miles, 1978; Karasu et al., 1979; Lasky & Solomone, 1977; Luborsky et al., 1983). For example, Karasu et al. (1979) found that patients and therapists of comparable ages engaged in more effective treatment processes than those of dissimilar ages. In addition, Lasky & Solomone (1977) observed that adolescents prefer and become more attached to age-similar counselors when discussing personal problems.

The influence of age matching on outcome may also be mediated by other variables, including patient gender, patient age, and type of patient problem (Beutler et al., 1986). Patient gender appears particularly salient for female patients, since regardless of their own age, female patients have been shown to prefer older therapists over younger ones (Donnan & Mitchell, 1979; Simons & Helms, 1976). In addition, patient age may be an important variable for older clients, because studies have indicated that older patients tend to view young therapists as "insufficiently wise and too immature to be maximally helpful" (Beutler et al., 1986). Type of problem may also influence the effectiveness of age matching. For example, adolescents have been found to prefer older therapists for discussing career-related concerns but prefer younger therapists for discussing personal problems (Getz & Miles, 1978).

In general, it appears as though age-matching has a mildly positive effect on treatment outcome, most likely through its ability to enhance the development of a helping therapeutic relationship. However, it is uncertain whether these effects are caused by age congruency per se or are instead caused by a plethora of other variables, including therapist experience and skill level, type of problem, patient age, and/or patient gender. Only when the effects of these confounding variables are partialled out through systematic research studies will a true understanding of the effects of age similarity on treatment outcome be attained.

Social Class   Questions regarding whether middle or upper class therapists are able to understand, communicate and empathize with lower-class clients have been a concern of both clinicians and researchers alike (Parloff et al., 1978). This concern may be well-founded, since most professional therapists tend to fall within the middle to upper strata of society, while many of their clients may not. However, attempts to study the effects of client–therapist socioeconomic status (SES) dissimilarity on treatment outcome have been hindered by disagreements as to how best to study SES. Should current status be considered, or should the SES of origin be the focus of investigation? Many researchers feel that the SES of origin matters most; this belief is based on the assumption that therapists who have had backgrounds and experiences similar to those of lower-class patients would be more responsive to them and more able to understand them, and thus more able to help them (Parloff et al., 1978).

Research findings, however, are scarce in this area. Few studies to date have directly related SES (either current status or SES of origin) congruency with treatment outcome (Beutler et al., 1986). Of the few that have, inconsistent results have been obtained. For example, Luborsky et al. (1980) found that sociodemographic variables were not related to outcome in their study of patient and therapist variables that predict improvement rates. By contrast, Holzman (1962) observed in his patient and therapist sample that similarity of sociodemographic background and attitudes did relate positively with therapeutic improvement. This observed relationship between *attitudes* and treatment outcome has been discussed by other researchers as being more important for improvement than actual SES status; as with ethnicity, the general consensus is that therapists who treat low-SES clients in an "egalitarian" manner are able to bring about improvement, regardless of the degree of client–therapist SES "match" (Beutler et al., 1986; Howard et al., 1970; Lerner, 1972, 1973).

In summary, more research is needed in this area before it can be determined for certain whether SES matching is beneficial for therapeutic outcomes. It seems likely that attitudinal factors play at least a moderate role in this relationship; hence, these factors should be routinely taken into consideration when examining the effects of SES similarity on treatment outcome.

Gender   Since the advent of the Women's Movement, a great deal of research into the effects of gender matching on therapeutic outcomes has been conducted. There basically have been three types of investigations in this area: (1) investigations looking at the effects of biological gender; (2) studies examining the effects of sexual attitudes and role identities; and (3) investigations looking at sex role flexibility and sex role acceptance (Beutler et al., 1986). Although these gender dimensions may appear similar, they each have been found to affect therapeutic outcomes differently for both males and females alike.

With regard to biological gender, most studies have found gender matching to have a moderately positive effect on therapeutic outcomes (Blase, 1979; Jones & Zoppel, 1982; Kaschak, 1978; Kirshner et al., 1978; Orlinsky & Howard, 1976). For example, Kaschak (1978) found that same-sex dyads obtained estimates of change that were more favorable than those of opposite-sex dyads. Similarly, Jones & Zoppel (1982) reported that both males and females found same-sex dyads to be more helpful than opposite-sex dyads. Although helpful for treatment outcome, gender similarity has not been shown to relate to dropout or rehospitalization rates, marital satisfaction, length of time in psychotherapy, or clinician's estimates of prognosis (Beutler et al., 1986).

In general, evidence for an effect of similar role identity on therapeutic outcome has been inconclusive; of the five studies conducted, two obtained nonsignificant results (Andrews, 1976; Morrow, 1980), while three suggested that sexual role identity *similarity* facilitated therapeutic change (Beutler et al., 1978; Brooks, 1981; Hart, 1981). Adding to the confusion, Feldstein (1979) found that patients whose therapists held a view of sexual roles that was *opposite* of the traditional, normative views of one's gender mates judged their therapists as more understanding and accepting and also were more engaged in the therapy process. As evidenced above, inconsistent findings in this area make it impossible to determine for certain whether similarity of role identity actually enhances or hinders therapeutic improvement.

As with ethnicity and social class, it appears as though sex role flexibility and an atmosphere of acceptance are both important for therapeutic change (Beutler et al., 1986). For example, Beutler et al. (1978) found that improvement in treatment was enhanced if both members of a dyad were accepting of the other's sexual attitudes and roles. Similarly, it has been found that patients are more comfortable disclosing to nontraditional, "egalitarian" therapists of both sexes. Likewise, women have been found to be better able to develop a positive treatment relationship with "egalitarian" male therapists as opposed to more traditional ones (Beutler et al., 1986).

In summary, it appears as though both client–therapist gender similarity and therapist role flexibility may enhance therapeutic outcomes. At this time, it is unclear whether similar sexual role identity facilitates improvement in psychotherapy.

However, what does appear clear is that egalitarian, accepting therapists have the potential to work well with any client, regardless of client or therapist gender or role identities.

Use of the MMPI-2 for Client-Therapist Matching

The MMPI-2 has many potential uses for enhancing client–therapist compatibility. Employed as a pretreatment assessment tool, client matching with the MMPI-2 can potentially shorten the length of the treatment process and enhance the therapeutic effects. There are basically three main areas in which the MMPI-2 can be utilized for client–therapist matching: (1) expectations, (2) personality, and (3) types of client problems. Unfortunately, research in these areas has been relatively sparse; personality is the only domain in which empirical studies have actually been conducted. Therefore, the purpose of this section is twofold: first, to inform the clinician of the different strategies for maximizing client–therapist compatibility with the MMPI-2, and, second, to generate further research in this important use of the MMPI-2 in pretreatment assessment.

Expectations

One way in which the MMPI-2 can be helpful in increasing client–therapist compatibility is in the area of expectations. Studies of the relationship between expectation similarity and improvement in psychotherapy have been based on the assumption that treatment outcome will be enhanced if the client and therapist are congruent in their attitudes, beliefs, and expectations about the treatment process (Parloff et al., 1978). In general, studies testing this assumption have shown that clients who hold expectations for therapy similar to those valued by psychotherapists do tend to reap the most therapeutic benefit (Childress & Gillis, 1977; Curran, 1976; Hoehn-Saric et al., 1964; Holliday, 1979; Jacobs et al., 1972; Sloane et al., 1970; Strupp & Bloxom, 1973; Truax & Wargo, 1969; Warren & Rice, 1972). These studies have looked at induced expectation similarity in clients who have been "prepared" for psychotherapy; that is, these clients have been helped to understand their "role" and their therapist's "role" in the treatment process and have been aided in assimilating treatment expectations similar to those valued by psychotherapists. For these individuals, an orientation to the nature of psychotherapy and their role in it helped them to become more engaged in their treatment and enabled them to experience greater therapeutic change (Mayerson, 1984; Parloff et al., 1978; Turkat, 1979; Wilson, 1985; Zwick & Attkisson, 1985).

The MMPI-2 can be a valuable tool in pretreatment assessment for identifying clients that may be good candidates for such therapy "preparation." In particular, the Negative Treatment Indicator scale (TRT) and the Work Attitude scale (WRK) can be extremely helpful in determining whether the client possesses attitudes contraindicating positive change expectations. For example, high scorers on the TRT scale typically hold attitudes that reflect an unwillingness or inability to change. Their pessimistic view about the future tends to lead to low expectations for treatment and the belief that their life situation is unchangeable. These low expectations for change are often bolstered by negative attitudes toward physicians and mental health professionals. Early identification of such attitudes and expectations provides the clinician with the option of employing some "preparatory" strategies in order to enhance the treatment process and increase the chances for a positive outcome. One recent study (Clark, 1996) reported that the TRT scale was a significant predictor of treatment-related change.

Similarly, individuals with elevations on the WRK scale often possess attitudes or habits that would be counterproductive to rehabilitative efforts. These clients may have difficulty getting started on things and may give up quickly when problems mount. These attitudes, while destructive by themselves, likely also lead to negative expectations for treatment. Consequently, clinicians may want to consider employing some form of "preparatory" strategy with these clients in order to increase their chances of experiencing therapeutic improvement.

In summary, the MMPI-2 can be an extremely useful tool for "matching" client and therapist expectations during pretreatment assessment. Through its ability to identify those clients most likely to have incongruent beliefs and attitudes early on, the MMPI-2 can help clinicians bring greater therapeutic change to clients who might otherwise reap few positive benefits from psychological treatment.

Personality

It is in the area of personality assessment that the MMPI-2 has been most widely utilized for client–therapist matching. Within this area, there have been many ideas about what degree of similarity, dissimilarity, and compatibility is optimal for therapeutic change (Parloff et al., 1978). Some feel that clients who are substantially similar to their therapist will experience the most therapeutic change; these individuals feel that rapport and understanding will be enhanced if the client and therapist share some "important" personality attributes (Parloff et al., 1978). Others believe that client–therapist *dissimilarity* will enhance therapeutic outcomes. Proponents of this theory feel that a therapist must be appropriately dissimilar from the client in order to maintain objectivity (Parloff et al., 1978). Still others feel that a curvilinear relationship exists between personality similarity and outcome. These individuals believe that an appropriate amount of similarity is necessary for positive outcomes because it enables the clinician to become " in tune" with the client (Parloff et al., 1978). However, too much similarity is believed to lead to "overidentification" with the client and a decline in therapeutic effectiveness (Parloff et al., 1978). Finally, there are those that feel that personality similarity per se is not what's important; it's *compatibility* on *dissimilar* attributes that matters most. These individuals feel that effective client–therapist dyads are those that are compatible on the few or several personality attributes that the dyad does not share. An example of this type of dyad would be one in which the client is dependent, submissive, and inhibited, while the therapist is autonomous, oriented, and dominant (Parloff et al., 1978).

In general, studies looking at personality matching with personality measures have been inconclusive; about an equal number of studies have found evidence for a similarity effect as have found evidence for a negative effect and a curvilinear relationship (Bare, 1967; Berzins, 1977; Mendelsohn & Geller, 1967; Snyder & Snyder, 1961; Swenson, 1967). Some studies have even failed to show any influence of personality matching on treatment outcome (Antonuccio et al., 1982; Carson & Llewellyn, 1966; Lichenstein, 1966; Vogel, 1961).

Examples of the aforementioned inconsistencies can be found in the MMPI literature. In the first study to examine personality similarity with the MMPI, Carson and Heine (1962) found a curvilinear relationship between personality similarity (as measured by MMPI profile shape) and treatment outcome. They found that dyads with medium similarity experienced significantly more therapeutic change than dyads of either low or high similarity. However, Lichtenstein (1966) and Carson and Llewellyn (1966) used methodologies similar to the above in an attempt to replicate this earlier finding; however, neither set of researchers was successful.

In contrast, Wogan (1970) used pretreatment MMPI-derived factor scores to match client and therapist and found that increasing personality similarity was negatively related to outcome in terms of decreased patient ratings of progress and likability of therapist. He interpreted these findings as showing that if the patient and therapist have similar ways of dealing with psychological problems, then the therapist has little to offer the client outside of theoretical knowledge. However, if the patient and therapist have opposing defense strategies, then the therapist may be able to provide a new perspective on the patient's difficulties and may be able to suggest fresh solutions or approaches to the patient that he/she may be able to benefit from. Wogan (1970) concurred with Carson & Heine's (1962) and Carson & Llewellyn's (1966) conclusion that global personality dimensions appear to be inappropriate for client–therapist matching. He surmises that such global measures may obscure significant findings for specific, individual personality dimensions.

Finally, Swenson (1967) matched client and therapist on Leary's (1957) dominance–submission and love–hate dimensions using the scoring system he developed for the MMPI. He found that therapeutic progress was enhanced when the client and therapist were opposite (complementary) on the dominance submission dimension and similar on the love-hate dimension.

It appears as though evidence pertaining to the best personality "match" for effective client–therapist dyads is inconclusive at this time. Beutler et al. (1986) concluded from their review that "the best matching studies available suggest that dissimilarity in certain interpersonal and cognitive styles may facilitate treatment process and outcome." They go on to caution, however, that this finding has not been a particularly strong or reliable one. They further suggest that client–therapist personality matching likely does not exert a very significant influence in psychotherapy outcome.

Clearly, what is needed is additional research into the effects of client–therapist personality matching using specific dimensions of personality. In particular, studies utilizing the MMPI-2 are needed to determine if this revised instrument is more effective at determining optimal personality matches than its predecessor, the MMPI. It is believed that the addition of the MMPI-2 content scales (viewed as direct communications between client and therapist) and several new supplementary scales likely enhance the MMPI-2's ability to identify matching characteristics most likely to lead to positive treatment outcomes.

Type of Client Problem

The MMPI-2 can also be useful in pretreatment assessment for identifying types of client problems a therapist knows he/she can't work with. Beutler & Harwood (1994) point out that "Dissimilarity in any single demographic or interpersonal response characteristic does not preclude successful therapeutic outcome; however, dissimilarities among several characteristics may prove problematic. Therapists should be aware of any potential conflicts and adjust themselves accordingly." Merbaum & Butcher (1982) found that therapists who like their patients rate them as more likely to gain from therapy than patients they do not like.

Obviously, an awareness of such conflicts must precede actions to rectify them. Hence, pretreatment planning should always include an assessment of personality and interpersonal characteristics that may lead to conflicts between the client and the therapist. Because of its many empirically validated clinical, content, and supplementary scales, the MMPI-2 is an ideal instrument for such an assessment. The MMPI-2's ability to measure personality characteristics, response styles, interpersonal skills, and lifestyle characteristics make it a perfect tool for identifying incompatible characteristics among therapists and clients. For example, if a clinician is aware that he/she has difficulties working with clients with addictive disorders, then the MMPI-2 MacAndrew Alcoholism Scale (MAC-R), Addiction Potential Scale (APS), and Addiction Acknowledgment Scale (AAS) can all provide clues to the clinician that he/she may need to refer the client elsewhere. Similarly, the Anger (ANG) and Cynicism (CYN) content scales can provide useful information to the clinician who may have difficulties working with hostile and/or cynical clients. In such a situation, the clinician may want to either refer the client elsewhere or adjust himself or herself accordingly.

Early identification by the MMPI-2 of such conflicting characteristics increases the client's chances that his/her needs will be met and that therapeutic change will occur. Such assessment also decreases the chances that resources will be unwisely used in a treatment setting in which positive change is unlikely to occur. This optimization of resources is likely to be a welcome benefit for clients, therapists, and researchers alike.

Assessment and Mode of Intervention

An unfortunate reality of the mental health field is that not all clients respond well to all treatments; in fact, depending upon the severity and type of client problem, some clients can actually be harmed by poorly planned interventions. Hence, it is increasingly important that pretreatment assessment include an evaluation of client characteristics that are likely to suggest one treatment approach over another. Psychological assessment with the MMPI-2 can aid the clinician in determining the appropriate treatment approach for each individual client. Information regarding effective treatment settings and effective treatment modalities is readily available through an examination of the MMPI-2 clinical scale elevations and MMPI-2 code types. Information obtained from these sources can prove invaluable during pretreatment assessment when the clinician is faced with the often arduous task of planning the most effective and the most efficient treatment for his/her clients.

As mentioned above, both the MMPI-2 clinical scales and MMPI-2 code types can be extremely useful for determining optimal modes of intervention for clients. Many pertinent hypotheses that can be generated from MMPI-2 scores are summarized in references such as Butcher (1990), Butcher & Williams (1992), and Graham (1993).

Patient Personality Patterns

Potential Treatment Destructive Characteristics of Some Clients

The MMPI-2 can also be used to assess client characteristics that can prove destructive to the treatment process. Prior knowledge of such attributes enables the clinician to organize treatment in such a way as to circumvent problems or difficulties that may arise as a result of these attributes. Without this prior knowledge, unforeseen problems can occur that may be damaging to the client-therapist relationship. The following is a sample of potentially destructive personal attributes assessed by the MMPI-2 that may be found to disrupt psychological treatment.

Social Perceptions and Styles of Interacting   Information obtained from the MMPI-2 about a client's social relationships and typical style of interacting can be useful in forewarning a therapist that a person's interpersonal difficulties could become problematic. Particularly useful in the beginning stages of therapy are clues to the presence of crippling lack of confidence in social relationships and feelings of isolation and alienation. Such problems in developing interpersonal relations often make relationship-oriented psychotherapy difficult. Therapists who are aware of these problems in their clients are forewarned that difficulties in the development of a therapeutic alliance may occur; armed with such information, therapists can work to avert these difficulties by structuring the sessions in such a way as to accommodate or counter feelings of isolation. By doing this, a therapist is likely to avoid further withdrawal and possible early termination of treatment.

Unrecognized Substance Abuse Problems   Substance abuse problems are a prominent problem in modern society today. The pervasiveness of addiction disorders has resulted in situations in which clients referred to therapists for very specific, non-substance-related problems will often end up having prominent substance abuse problems also. Failures to detect such problems when they are present can be extremely detrimental to the treatment process; addictive disorders are difficult enough to handle in settings where they are expected and in clinics that are equipped to handle them. The MMPI-2 at initial assessment can help determine if alcohol or drugs are likely to be a problem for the client. Given the frequency of these problems, clinicians are well advised to routinely consider addiction disorders as potential problems and to assess this possibility during pretreatment evaluations.

Acting-Out Behavior   Other forms of acting-out behavior assessed by the MMPI-2 can be detrimental to psychotherapy as well. For example, individuals with high Pd elevations, high Ma elevations, or the 49 profile type have the capacity to act out in very destructive ways. Their impulsivity and poor judgment often make these clients vulnerable to engage in such antisocial acts as violence toward family members and reckless sexual behavior. Therapists working with these individuals need to be cognizant of these potentially destructive characteristics in order to avert disaster before it strikes.

Other Personality Characteristics   Pathological distrust and unproductive rumination are two other personality characteristics assessed by the MMPI-2 that can be detrimental to the treatment process. Individuals exhibiting pathological distrust tend to be hostile, resentful, defensive, and argumentative. Because of their guardedness, these individuals typically do not like to talk about their emotional problems and often have difficulty establishing rapport with the therapist. These difficulties with relationship-building can interfere with the treatment process; premature termination can result if these trust issues are not dealt with appropriately during early sessions.

Individuals with prominent Pt elevations often exhibit unproductive rumination that can interfere with the treatment process. These individuals are likely to be obsessive, overly ideational, and rigid to the point of being unable to implement new behaviors or view themselves or their situations in different ways.

Assessment and Outcome

The MMPI-2 has also been used in psychological treatment for assessing therapeutic outcomes. There have basically been two ways in which the MMPI-2 has been used within this context: (1) for the prediction of outcomes and (2) for the assessment of change following interventions (Greene & Clopton, 1994). When used for prediction, the ability of MMPI-2 profiles and code types to predict treatment outcomes in specific client populations is assessed. The prediction of both treatment successes and treatment failures (i.e., treatment dropouts) have been examined. Therapeutic change or improvement following treatment is typically assessed through the administration of the MMPI-2 at the start of treatment and then again at post-treatment. Changes in scale elevations are then evaluated in order to determine whether therapeutic improvement has occurred.

The vastness of the literature in this area (over 1000 research publications) makes it difficult to review them all in any single chapter. Instead, a brief overview is provided. In addition, only the general findings relating to alcohol dependence/abuse and chronic pain will be reviewed because these two diagnostic groups have received the most attention and the results are relevant to a number of different clinical groups. For a more comprehensive review of the findings in this area, the interested reader is referred to the annotated bibliography by Rouse et al. (Chapter 10, this volume), the review article by Hollon & Mandell (1979), and the summaries provided by Dahlstrom et al. (1975).

Assessment of Change

As briefly noted above, the MMPI-2 can be a valuable tool for monitoring change both during the treatment process and after treatment has been terminated. When employed during the therapy process, the MMPI-2 can highlight areas that still need to be addressed and inform the client and therapist about improvement in areas previously targeted. Following treatment, the MMPI-2 can provide the clinician with information regarding the effectiveness of the treatment and the level of improvement the client has attained as a result of the intervention. Knowledge of the effectiveness of different types of treatment can be important both for the monitoring of current clients and for planning interventions with future clients. In addition, administering the MMPI-2 following treatment enables the client and therapist to gain insight into problems the client may encounter as therapy ends, as well as resources the client can rely on to meet such problems. As a result of end-of-treatment testing, clients can get a sense of their progress and gain the confidence that comes from being more in control of their personal life than when treatment began.

Before beginning a review of the research findings relating the MMPI-2 to treatment effects, a few caveats need to be borne in mind. First, clinicians should be cognizant of the fact that some of the MMPI-2 scales (Hypochondriasis [Hy], Psychopathic Deviate [Pd], Schizophrenia [Sc],and Social Introversion [Si]) and items are designed to assess characterological qualities, qualities that are not expected to change much over time (Greene & Clopton, 1994; Hollon & Mandell, 1979). Other scales (Depression [D], Psychasthenia [Pt], and Anxiety [A]) are more reactive and would be expected to reflect changes in the client's state. Consequently, clinicians should not expect to see global changes across all of the scales following treatment (Greene & Clopton, 1994).

Second, it should be kept in mind that the MMPI-2 is designed as an initial screening instrument to measure the types of psychopathology that are being expressed by a particular client, and the norms reflect the typical amount of defensiveness that is to be expected during initial testing (Greene & Clopton, 1994). Consequently, when the MMPI-2 is used to measure changes across the course of treatment, clinicians and researchers should examine profile changes relative to the *client's previous scores* rather than to a set of norms (Greene & Clopton, 1994). For example, it is probably more accurate to say that the patient's score on Scale 7 decreased 19 points across treatment than to say that the patient's score of 58 is now within normal limits following treatment (Greene & Clopton, 1994).

Finally, it should be noted that the MMPI-2's sensitivity to changes in the client's state may be limited because some items are worded in the past tense and inquire about past behaviors (Greene & Clopton, 1994). As Greene & Clopton (1994) note, "clients would not be expected to change their response to the item," and "I have used alcohol excessively, regardless of how effective their alcohol treatment had been" (p. 149). Greene & Clopton (1994) go on to speculate that the finding that the MacAndrew Alcoholism scale (MAC-R) does not change over the course of treatment (Gallucci et al., 1989; Huber & Danahy, 1975; Rohan et al., 1969) may reflect the wording of its items and their ultimate focus on past behaviors.

Alcohol Abuse   An excellent review of the MMPI alcohol abuse/dependence treatment effects literature prior to 1976 was provided by Hollon & Mandell (1979). These authors reviewed 12 outcome studies assessing change in the MMPI profiles of alcoholics following the completion of various forms of substance abuse treatment. In general, they found consistent decreases in scales D and Pt following completion of treatment across all studies. Although these findings are significant, the authors noted that decreases in these scales may be due to hospitalization alone, given that the D and Pt scales are the two MMPI scales most sensitive to change. This possibility brings up the question of whether the MMPI-2 is detecting generalized treatment effects or treatment effects related to alcohol rehabilitation. As Hollon & Mandell (1979, p. 282) point out, decreases in dysphoria and psychological distress may not necessarily parallel decreases in alcohol abuse. The authors conceded that in order to answer the question of generalized versus specific treatment effects, "standardized and generally accepted criteria for successful treatment of alcoholism must first be established."

Another consistent pattern evident across studies is the lack of a reduction in the MacAndrew scale (MAC) following treatment. Hollon & Mandell (1979) discuss many possible explanations for this stability, including the MAC's assessment of current *and* past drinking patterns and the possibility that the MAC measures a characterological trait of addictiveness. The authors concluded that the utility of the MAC scale for assessing treatment effects needs to be explored further before using it for outcome evaluation in clinical contexts.

Many methodological difficulties were noted by the authors as limiting factors in this area of research. The first is the confounding of outcome studies by the heterogeneity of alcoholic populations. The authors note that most alcoholic populations are not homogeneous; indeed, they cite many researchers that have attempted to subtype and categorize this diverse group of clients, some to no avail. Second, the treatment programs employed with these patients are typically as diverse and mixed as the population itself. The authors point out that research on specific treatment techniques and methods are rare. Third, few studies have employed a "no-treatment control groups condition" for a point of comparison. And finally, the authors note that the empirically derived clinical scales of the original MMPI are not content homogeneous.

Hollon & Mandell (1979) concluded from their review that it was unknown whether changes in pre- and posttreatment MMPI scores reflect treatment effects from substance abuse interventions. They stated that these changes need to be cross-validated against independent, standardized outcome criteria before any conclusions can be made. The authors made the point that "Completion of an alcoholism rehabilitation program in and of itself does not constitute a valid indication of treatment success. Thus lower MMPI scores between admission and discharge do not necessarily indicate a corresponding recovery from alcohol addiction" (p. 284).

Research since 1976 has been relatively limited in this area; only about eight outcome studies evaluating treatment effects with the MMPI have been conducted over this two decade time span. In general, findings from these newer studies have not been entirely consistent with the findings of those discussed above. For example, while consistent decreases following treatment have continued to be found for scale D (Bobrov et al., 1993; Krupitskii et al., 1993; Moran et al., 1978; Pena-Ramos & Hornberger, 1979), such decreases have not been consistently found for Pt (Bobrov et al., 1993; Krupitskii et al., 1993; McWilliams & Brown, 1977; Passini et al., 1977). Adding to this discrepancy is the fact that some researchers have failed to find any Pt scale changes in studies in which scores on other anxiety measures, such as the Taylor Anxiety Scale and the State/Trait Anxiety Inventory (STAI; Spielberger et al., 1968), have exhibited significant changes following treatment (Krupitskii et al., 1993; Passini et al., 1977). One possible explanation for this finding is that the Pt scale may be less sensitive to changes in the psychological state of alcoholics than was previously believed.

One methodological improvement that many of the newer studies have made is the inclusion of a no-treatment control group. Findings from studies that have included such a comparison group indicate that changes in MMPI and MMPI-2 profiles do seem to indicate treatment effects; little or no changes on the MMPI have been observed for the majority of the control groups, while significant changes have been observed for the experimental groups (Bobrov et al., 1993; Krupitskii et al., 1993; Passini et al., 1977; Moran et al., 1978; Poulos, 1981).

Although the above finding appears promising for clinicians and researchers hoping to use the MMPI-2 for the evaluation of treatment effects, a study conducted by McWilliams and Brown (1977) brings into question the usefulness of the MMPI-2 for this purpose. These investigators examined the relationship between changes in MMPI scores following treatment and the frequency of relapse in three groups of alcoholics: (1) 49 patients who completed an alcoholism rehabilitation program and received a problem-free discharge, (2) 27 patients who had less than perfect participation in and completion of the program (although they stayed in the program for the required minimum of six weeks) and who did not receive a "clean" discharge because they engaged in prohibited behaviors such as a drinking episode, illicit drug taking, refusal of medication, or disciplinary violations, and (3) 35 patients who left the program before the sixth week. Unfortunately, MMPI data were only available for groups 1 and 2. However, findings indicated that the pre- and posttreatment MMPI scores of groups 1 and 2 showed similar decreases following treatment; no differences were found between the two groups on any MMPI scale. This finding was contradictory to what the investigators expected, because they had believed that group 1 (the completers) would exhibit more thera-peutic change on the MMPI than group 2 (the individuals with disciplinary prob-lems). Paradoxically, relapse rates following treatment did differentiate between the two groups; 63% of group 2 had one or more readmissions within 18 months, while only 31% of group 1 had similar readmissions. The investigators noted that group 2 was actually more similar to group 3 (the noncompleters) than to group 1 in terms of relapse, even though groups 1 and 2 had very similar MMPI profile changes following treatment. The authors interpreted this contradictory finding as an indication that "the success of treatment cannot be evaluated from MMPI change scores" (p. 485).

Although this finding appears somber for those wishing to use the MMPI for the evaluation of treatment effects, it must be kept in mind that relapse in terms of hospital readmission may not be the best outcome measure for alcoholics undergoing substance abuse treatment. As McWilliams and Brown (1977) readily admit, there are several possible reasons why an alcoholic may or may not be readmitted to a hospital, including "death, movement from catchment area, jailing, and hospitalization for reasons other than drinking" (p. 482). Because many of these reasons have nothing to do with the success of an alcoholism treatment program, relapse rates are likely not the best criterion for evaluating treatment success. As discussed above, knowledge regarding the usefulness of the MMPI for measuring treatment effects awaits the development of "standardized and generally accepted criteria for successful treatment of alcoholism . . . " (Hollon & Mandell, 1979, p. 282).

Unfortunately, the new studies in this area have not improved upon many of the other methodological difficulties limiting the pre-1976 research. As before, several of these newer studies are confounded by the heterogeneity of both the alcoholic populations studied and the treatment methods employed. In addition, few studies included outcome measures other than treatment completion or post-treatment MMPI scores, and none included an objective measure of such treatment outcome. Therefore, as concluded before, knowledge regarding the true nature of MMPI changes following alcohol rehabilitation and their relationship to treatment outcome awaits studies devoid of the above limitations.

Chronic Pain   The number of studies investigating the ability of the MMPI or MMPI-2 to detect treatment effects in chronic pain patients has been relatively small; indeed, the majority of studies conducted in this area focus on the ability of the inventory to predict treatment outcome, a topic that will be discussed at some length in the next section. For the few studies that have been conducted in this area, however, there do seem to be some consistent findings. For example, consistent decreases in the D scale across studies has been found for a variety of chronic pain interventions (Brena et al., 1980; Dolce et al., 1986; Moore et al., 1986; Naliboff et al., 1988; Peniston et al., 1986; Roberts & Reinhardt, 1980). Likewise, Ma scale scores have been shown to be relatively resistant to change in many of the studies conducted thus far (Brena et al., 1980; Moore et al., 1986; Naliboff et al., 1988; Peniston et al., 1986; Roberts & Reinhardt, 1980). A possible explanation for this resistance can be found in the fact that the Ma scale has not been shown to be a regularly elevated score in the profiles of chronic pain patients, and thus would not be expected to change much following treatment.

As will be outlined below, profiles exhibiting the "neurotic triad"—that is, elevations on scales Hy, D, and Hs—have been shown to be quite common among chronic pain patients. A pertinent question regarding this triad of scores might be whether there is any evidence that chronic pain treatment decreases the elevations on these scales. Although evidence suggesting that D scale scores often decrease is currently available, the question is whether there is any evidence indicating that the other scores constituting the "triad," namely Hy and Hs, are also reduced following treatment. In general, it appears as though the answer to this question is "yes"; chronic pain interventions have been shown to result in a reduction of the symptoms reflected in these scales (Dolce et al., 1986; Moore et al., 1986; Naliboff et al., 1988; Roberts & Reinhardt, 1980). However, at least one study has shown that although these scores are reduced, they are still relatively elevated following treatment (Brena et al., 1980). In addition, several studies have found relative reductions on many, if not all, of the MMPI scales (except Ma) following chronic pain interventions, not only reductions on the "neurotic triad" scales (Dolce et al., 1986; McArthur et al., 1987; Moore et al., 1986; Naliboff et al., 1988). This finding begs the question of whether the MMPI is detecting generalized treatment effects or treatment effects related to chronic pain rehabilitation.

Fortunately, this question can be answered because many researchers in this area have applied outcome measures other than treatment completion or MMPI change scores, such as pain severity ratings, work status, medication use, exercise levels, and so on, in order to cross-validate outcome findings obtained from the MMPI (Dolce et al., 1986; McArthur et al., 1987; Moore et al., 1986; Naliboff et al., 1988; Peniston et al., 1986). The majority of these researchers have found that changes in MMPI profiles following treatment are paralleled by changes in pain-related behaviors and by changes in psychological functioning (as measured by other psychological indices, such as the Beck Depression Inventory (BDI) and the Profile of Mood States (POMS) (Dolce et al., 1986; Moore et al., 1986; Naliboff et al., 1988; Peniston et al., 1986). This consistent finding of improvement across several areas of functioning provides some support to the view that the MMPI is measuring the specific effects of the chronic pain intervention. Complete support of this view, however, comes only from the knowledge that a no treatment control group of chronic pain patients does not exhibit MMPI changes similar to those exhibited by patients who did receive treatment. This type of evidence would add credence to the view that the MMPI is detecting changes in the patient's state directly related to the effects of the *treatment* and not to the nonspecific effects of time.

Only two studies have attempted to gain this type of evidence, both with positive results (Moore et al., 1986; Peniston et al., 1986). Specifically, both studies failed to find any changes in their control groups' MMPI profiles or pain-related behaviors, while they did find such changes in their experimental groups. Clearly, replication of these results is needed before it can be concluded for certain that the MMPI-2 is able to detect treatment-specific changes; however, the above findings do appear promising for those hoping to use the MMPI-2 in this context.

Based on the limited research conducted thus far, it appears as though the MMPI-2 has the potential to be extremely useful for assessing treatment outcome in chronic pain patients. It is hoped that future studies in this area will take into account the discussion above and include both a variety of outcome measures and a no-treatment control group. Only through such developments will the exact nature of MMPI-2 changes following chronic pain treatment be recognized.

Prediction of Outcome

The MMPI-2 can provide important information regarding the likelihood that a particular client will respond well to psychological treatment. Research examining the predictive utility of various MMPI-2 scales has begun to delineate within diagnostic groupings specific scales and profile types that are associated with positive outcomes. Likewise, this research has also provided information regarding personality characteristics that may predict poor outcome or premature termination of therapy.

Before reviewing the use of the MMPI-2 for predicting treatment outcome, there are a few general conclusions that can be drawn based on research with the original MMPI. First, environmental and nonpersonality variables (e.g., demographics, education, socioeconomic status, age, and prior drinking status) have been shown to contribute more to the prediction than personality variables (Greene & Clopton, 1994; Nathan & Skinstad, 1987). For example, Keithly et al. (1980) found that patient motivation was a significant predictor of both the therapist's and the clinician's ratings of overall patient improvement. Findings such as these highlight the importance of using multiple criteria in assessing outcome.

Second, the original MMPI may be useful for outcome prediction in those studies in which specific subgroups are identified within particular patient populations, but these findings have not been replicated consistently across investigations (Greene & Clopton, 1994). Related to the above, the original MMPI has not been shown to be related to treatment outcome in studies in which heterogeneous patient populations have been examined. A frequent assumption in this literature is that there is a typical, prototype patient within a particular diagnostic group or setting; this assumption does not allow for the possibility that interactions between type of patient or treatment and outcome of therapy might exist (Greene & Clopton, 1994).

Outcome prediction with the MMPI and MMPI-2 has been examined in a number of different ways. Prediction from single scales, from profile code types, and from "subgroups" have all been explored. Likewise, positive and negative outcomes (including treatment dropouts) have also been examined. In an attempt to gain a clear understanding of the nature of outcome prediction with the MMPI and MMPI-2, research involving single scales, profile types, positive and negative outcomes, and treatment dropouts, where pertinent, will all be reviewed.

Alcohol Abuse   A number of investigators have examined the MMPI and MMPI-2 profiles of alcoholics to determine whether certain scales predict treatment outcome in this patient population. Greene & Clopton (1994) concisely summarized this extensive research, finding much inconsistency. For example, they cite many studies that have found that alcoholics who have profiles involving elevations on Scales 4 (Psychopathic Deviate) and 9 (Hypomania) are more likely to drop out of treatment or have poorer outcomes than alcoholics with other profile types. They note, however, that there have been numerous investigators that have failed to find such an association.

Greene & Clopton (1994) also report that alcoholics exhibiting denial and minimization on the MMPI are more likely to drop out of treatment. Again, however, several other researchers were unable to replicate this finding. Finally, Greene & Clopton (1994) note that a number of studies have reported that alcoholics with the highest profile elevations are more likely to terminate treatment prematurely or experience poor treatment response. As pointed out by Greene & Clopton (1994), however, it is uncertain whether the higher elevations in these profiles reflect the presence of more psychopathology and/or an exaggeration of symptoms. Greene & Clopton (1994, p. 151) note that "It is important to delineate which of these alternative explanations is accurate, because they would have different implications for treatment."

Questions surrounding the usefulness of the MAC scale for treatment outcome prediction led one group of researchers (Hoffmann et al., 1974; Kammeier et al., 1973; Loper et al., 1973) to examine the MAC scales' effectiveness at differentiating alcoholics from nonalcoholics. The findings from these investigations, which compared alcoholics' MAC scores upon admission to college and admission to treatment to the MAC scores of a control group of students entering college at the same time, were summarized by Greene & Clopton (1994). For the alcoholics, an average time span of 13 years had elapsed between college admission and entrance into alcoholism treatment. Findings from this study indicate that the alcoholic students had significantly higher MAC scores than the control group both at college admission and at treatment admission. The MAC scores (using a cutoff score of 26) correctly classified 72% of the alcoholic group both at entrance into college and treatment admission. Greene & Clopton (1994) note that the consistency of the MAC scores across such an extensive time span suggests that the MAC scale is measuring an aspect of behavior that is resistant to change. They point out that this finding is consistent with research showing that MAC scores in alcoholics remain elevated following treatment, as discussed above.

Methodological limitations in this research are similar to those found in the alcoholism treatment effects literature. Often the alcoholic populations are extremely heterogeneous; subtyping alcoholics into homogeneous groups may yield more consistent findings. In addition, the treatment methods employed are quite diverse. Research examining the outcomes of specific treatments and specific techniques may reveal the existence of significant associations not yet observed.

In general, it appears as though clinicians working in substance abuse settings should be aware that clients exhibiting psychopathic tendencies or denial and minimization may be more likely to drop out of treatment; thus, these issues should be dealt with directly (Greene & Clopton, 1994). In addition, clinicians should be cognizant of the fact that clients with the most elevated MMPI-2 profiles are more likely to experience poorer outcomes. It is important for clinicians to assess whether these high-ranging profiles are the result of severe psychopathology or an overreporting of symptoms and then plan treatment accordingly (Greene & Clopton, 1994).

Chronic Pain   A number of reviews have recently emerged looking at the prediction of treatment outcome from MMPI-2 profiles for chronic pain patients (Greene & Clopton, 1994; Keller & Butcher, 1991; Love & Peck, 1987; Snyder, 1990). The majority of these reviews have examined outcome studies aiming to predict client response to either (a) invasive medical procedures such as surgery, chemonucleosis, or epidural stimulation or (b) pain management programs.

Beginning with medical interventions, some general results include the finding that greater elevations on Hs and Hy are related to poorer outcome (Greene & Clopton, 1994; Keller & Butcher, 1991; Love & Peck, 1987). This negative treatment response has been interpreted by some as "evidence of rigid defenses and use of somatization to avoid psychological and life problems" (Keller & Butcher, 1991). However, this finding has been rather inconsistent, because a number of investigators have not found elevated Hs and Hy scores to be predictive of treatment failure (Greene & Clopton, 1994; Keller & Butcher, 1991). On the contrary, Keller & Butcher (1991) report that some have found D alone or in combination with elevated Hs and Hy scores to be better predictors of poor outcome. As Keller & Butcher (1991, p. 31) point out, however, "the literature tends to support the view that high elevations on the neurotic-triad scales, particularly on Hs, are associated with poor response to invasive treatments." On the positive side, Greene & Clopton report that some investigators have found that chronic pain clients with profiles within normal limits (no clinical scale at or above a T score of 70 on the MMPI) have better outcomes.

Studies attempting to predict client response to pain management programs have not uniformly found neurotic-triad scores to be associated with negative outcomes (Keller & Butcher, 1991; Love & Peck, 1987). Love & Peck (1987) concluded that these types of management programs appeared to be less sensitive to MMPI scale elevations than some types of medical treatments. While a degree of somatic preoccupation and an avoidance of psychological and life problems (elevated conversion-V profiles) were quite common in clients with a negative response to treatment, the presence of such a profile did not rule out success (Keller & Butcher, 1991; Love & Peck, 1987). However, Love & Peck (1987) report that other MMPI scales did appear to be related to outcome, namely the Ego Strength scale, the Pa scale, and the Sc scale. These authors report that low Ego Strength scores and elevated Pa and Sc scores tended to indicate poor prognosis.

Methodological difficulties also limit the findings in this area. As with the treatment effects alcoholism research, therapeutic methods and outcome measures are extremely heterogeneous across studies, as are the patient populations being assessed (Keller & Butcher, 1991). Keller & Butcher (1991) note that findings from many studies have suggested that the performance of predictors may vary with characteristics of both the patient population and the treatment modality and that different predictors may be more accurate with certain aspects of outcome than others. They further stress that outcome prediction within complex pain management programs must go beyond searching for elevated neurotic-triad profiles, which are exceedingly common in this population and are not necessarily predictive of treatment response. Keller & Butcher (1991) agree with Love & Peck's (1987) recommendation that other scale elevations, such as Pa and Sc, need to be taken into account and that "subgroup analysis" may have important implications for outcome prediction in multimodal treatment programs.

In addition to the above limitations, Keller & Butcher (1991) question the usefulness of the aforementioned associations for prediction at the individual level. They note that a large overlap often exists between successful and unsuccessful groups when sorted by MMPI elevations. In addition, they report studies indicating that neurotic-triad scores may not be stable, premorbid predictors of vulnerability to chronic pain, but instead tend to change with the chronicity of the problem. They conclude that the MMPI's usefulness for predicting response to chronic pain treatment likely lies in its ability to indicate the degree of functional impairment already present. They speculate that it is this level of impairment that predicts poor response to a single-modality treatment such as surgery.

Response to Psychotropic Medication

The MMPI has been used extensively in psychotropic medication research. It has been employed in a variety of ways within this context, including (1) assessment of residual symptoms following pharmacological treatment, (2) as a screening tool to determine if a particular client is appropriate for psychotropic drug treatment (Nathan et al., 1986), and (3) as a monitoring device during pharmacological treatment to track improvement and progress.

One of the most interesting ways in which the MMPI has been used in this area is for the prediction of client response to psychotropic medication treatment. For most drug classes (e.g., benzodiazepines, antidepressants, stimulants, etc.), the bulk of the prediction research was conducted over two decades ago and appears rather extensive. This extensiveness makes a review of this literature beyond the scope of any single chapter [interested readers are referred to Cleveland (1989), Yehuda (1976), and Zubin & Katz (1964)]. However, lithium carbonate has experienced a rather recent resurgence of interest by MMPI researchers. These researchers have attempted to delineate specific MMPI scales and indices that predict client response to lithium treatment. To follow is a concise review of this literature that we hope will act to highlight issues and findings that are relevant for other psychotropic medications and other diagnostic groups.

The ability of the MMPI to predict treatment response to lithium has been examined both with the standard MMPI scales and with the Lithium Response Scale. Findings relating to the standard scales have appeared rather inconsistent. For example, Ananth et al. (1979, 1980) found that manic–depressive patients and psychiatric patients with high scores on the Pd and Pa clinical scales showed a poor response to lithium. Conversely, House & Martin (1975) found that severely depressed inpatients with low scores on the D and Pt scales were the poorest responders.

Equally discrepant are the findings related to positive responders. Here, although both Ananth et al. (1980) and House & Martin (1975) found high scores on the Pt scale to be related to a positive response, Ananth et al. found high Hs and Si scorers to be good responders while House & Martin found high D scorers to be the better responders.

Although seemingly discrepant, the findings cited above may be a reflection of the different patient populations being examined. A plausible explanation for this inconsistency might be that the predictive utility of the MMPI-2 scales for lithium treatment varies across diagnostic groupings. Because different diagnostic categories often produce different elevations on the MMPI-2, MMPI-2 scales are likely to have differential predictive ability depending upon the disorder being assessed. If this is the case, one would not expect to find a scale or set of scales that consistently predicts lithium response across all patient types. Instead, you would find that some scales predict well with some disorders, while other scales predict well with other disorders, as the findings above would suggest.

Findings relating to the ability of the Lithium Response Scale to differentiate lithium responders from nonresponders have also been inconsistent. For example, Donnelly et al. (1978) found that this scale successfully discriminated depressed female treatment responders from depressed female nonresponders with relatively high accuracy (approximately 89%). However, Burdick & Holmes (1980) found in their small sample of outpatients that the female and male versions of the Lithium Response Scale were not successful at predicting lithium response. These authors concluded that the two scales should be used with caution because their predictive ability appeared to be low. Finally, Garvey et al. (1983) found that the Lithium Response Scale performed at no better than chance level for predicting response to lithium treatment in depressed patients. In general, it appears as though there is currently more support for the use of the standard scales in the prediction of lithium response than there is for the Lithium Response Scale. Relatively few studies have been conducted, however, and thus definite conclusions cannot yet be made. In order to clarify the relationship between MMPI-2 scores and lithium response, future research should examine more closely the differential predictive ability of the MMPI-2 scales across diagnostic groupings; it is felt that this type of a research effort might yield more consistent results than have previously been obtained.

Cost–Benefit Aspects of Assessment in Treatment Planning

Now that the many uses of the MMPI-2 for treatment planning have been reviewed and discussed in some detail, one might ask what the benefits are of such psychological assessment during pretreatment evaluation. Assessment psychologists have been somewhat remiss in not developing the necessary documentation and addressing the appropriate concerns with respect to cost–benefit aspects of psychological assessment. Several pertinent questions at this point might be, "Can we safely say that the benefits of using the MMPI-2 during pretreatment assessment far outweigh the costs of such an endeavor?" and "Is the client better off clinically from such an assessment?" Unfortunately, research studies evaluating the costs and benefits of psychological assessment, including use of the MMPI-2, in treatment planning are not currently available. Consequently, it is as yet unknown whether the benefits of pretreatment assessment with the MMPI-2 can be *empirically* shown to outweigh the costs. *Clinically*, many therapists would argue, the benefits do appear to outweigh the costs. The problem, however, is that in order for clinicians to be able to justify their use of psychological assessment to clients and third party coverers, empirical evidence verifying its effectiveness needs to be available in a more user-friendly form than has been available in the past.

A similar situation as that described above exists in the psychotherapy literature as a whole. A recent article by Yates (1994) discusses and carefully outlines the need for clinical researchers to incorporate costs, cost-effectiveness, and cost–benefit analysis into their psychotherapy research. He notes that most research in this area currently does not include such an assessment, although its importance can be clearly recognized in that "By focusing scientific scrutiny on only the outcomes of treatment, investigators may be making mistakes that could become serious as budgets dwindle and clients become more sophisticated consumers of health services" (p.729).

The importance of cost–benefit analyses in psychotherapy investigations can be clearly evidenced by reviewing the findings from the limited research that has been conducted thus far. For example, Yates (1994) presents data showing that costs, as experienced by the clients, can be significantly related to treatment outcomes: One study cited found that client compliance with treatment was related to the client's perceptions of the benefits of treatment relative to the time costs and "hassle" required. In addition, Yates (1994) presents empirical evidence showing that costs and outcomes can be inversely related rather than directly related; for example, clients may benefit most from treatments that cost less than from other, more expensive viable alternatives. Yates (1994) points to these findings, among others, as indicators of the importance of including of cost–benefit analysis in psychotherapy research. He encourages clinical researchers to study the relationships between "(a) monetary and other costs, (b) treatment techniques and treatment deliver systems, and (c) psychological and economic outcomes" (p. 729). Yates (1994) feels that such investigation will make it easier for clinicians and researchers to become "better scientist-manager-practitioners" (p. 735).

The relevance of the above findings and conclusions for assessment psychologists can be readily seen. It is likely that a cost–benefit analysis of psychological assessment would produce similar results. For example, clients who perceive assessment as more "beneficial" than "costly" may invest more time and energy into both the assessment process and the treatment that logically follows from the assessment. In this sense, clients who feel their therapists are attempting to gain a greater understanding of them through psychological assessment may be more likely to feel that the benefits accrued from such an understanding far outweigh the costs involved in the assessment process.

We will next present a framework for contrasting the potential costs and benefits of using the MMPI-2 for treatment planning (see Table 7.1). This list is probably not exhaustive but might serve as a "first approximation" of the factors involved. This listing, being theoretically derived, is thus open to expansion or reduction as pertinent research develops. It is hoped that this list will serve as a catalyst for research efforts aimed at empirically validating the benefits of the MMPI-2 in treatment planning that have already been observed and appreciated in clinical settings.

Costs

1. *Client's time.* A small proportion of client therapy time is needed for the administration of the MMPI-2. This time commitment is typically minimal, however, equaling only 1–2 hours.

2. *Therapist's time.* The therapist's time involvement in the assessment process includes the administration, scoring, and the interpretation of the MMPI-2. However, as above, the time commitment is often minimal, given the ease and quickness of MMPI-2 administration and scoring. Administration (and even hand scoring) are often delegated to trained clinical personnel. Depending on the therapist, interpretation of MMPI-2 test results may be somewhat more time consuming.

Table 7.1. Costs and Benefits of Using the MMPI-2 for Treatment Planning.

Costs	Benefits
Administrative resources (space, materials)	Increased understanding of patients problems
Therapist's time to introduce the test	An objective summary of the clients personality and problems
Clerical/computer scoring	
Professional time to interpret the results	Identification of problems not apparent in interview
	Enhanced rapport
	Information regarding treatment need
	A mechanism for providing personality feedback
	Decreased therapy time
	Establishes a baseline of symptoms for later treatment evaluation
	Can aid in the maximization of limited resources

However, with the aid of computer-generated reports (see Chapter 9, this volume), interpretation time can often be considerably reduced without any loss of clinical accuracy.

3. *Resources.* Some resources will be expended for the purchase of test booklets, scoring systems, and possibly computerized interpretations. As before, however, this expenditure is typically minimal.

4. *Facilities for testing.* It is important to conduct psychological assessment in a professional context. Tests need to be administered in a comfortable, quiet office under monitored conditions. It is not appropriate for psychologists to allow patients to take tests home with them to fill out.

Benefits

1. *Increased understanding.* One of the main benefits of using the MMPI-2 in pretreatment assessment is the increased understanding of the client that the clinician is likely to be gained. Information regarding the client's personality characteristics, interpersonal functioning, treatment accessibility, and typical response styles are all readily available to both the clinician and the client from the MMPI-2. This vast amount of important information is rarely available from initial clinical interviews alone.

2. *Provision of an objective viewpoint.* Using the MMPI-2 for treatment planning can also provide the clinician and the client with an objective "outside opinion" about the client and his/her problems. People in treatment need to have pertinent, objective information about themselves if they are to know what behaviors need to be changed. Clinicians also need this type of objective information in order to focus treatment on the main issues and problems causing the client difficulties. The MMPI-2 test results provide a valuable framework from which clients and clinicians can obtain important information about the client.

3. *Identification of problems not apparent from the clinical interview.* During pretreatment assessment, MMPI-2 test results might reveal issues or problems that the therapist and client did not discuss in initial interviews. This function of the MMPI-2 seems particularly important, given that without the aid of the MMPI-2, such "hidden" difficulties might not have surfaced until well into the treatment process.

4. *Enhanced rapport.* Employing the MMPI-2 in pretreatment assessment can often help to enhance rapport between client and therapist. People who seek help feel the need to be understood by the therapist; they usually appreciate the therapist's effort to know them. Consequently, when a therapist communicates the need for pretreatment assessment to gain a better understanding of a client, the client will generally recognize the therapist's purpose and respond positively. In addition, sensitive, tactful test interpretation can often be shared with clients early in therapy and can actually improve the treatment relationship because it reassures the clients that they are not going to be embarrassed or harmed by the process of self-discovery with the therapist. This evaluation stage of treatment can often serve to teach clients that disclosing "secrets" about themselves is important and that the treatment situation is a safe place in which to discuss their private thoughts.

5. *Information regarding the need for treatment.* One of the most important benefits of the MMPI-2 in treatment planning is that it provides the therapist with a perspective on the extent and nature of the patient's symptom pattern. The MMPI-2 scale scores provide summaries of symptoms and attitudes that indicate the relative strength or magnitude of the problems experienced. These scale scores can also provide information about the general quality of the individual's adjustment as well as the prevalence of long-term problems versus more situationally based difficulties. All of the above information can prove invaluable to the clinician when assessing an individual's need for treatment, as well as when setting treatment goals and attempting to project a course of therapy.

6. *Provides a mechanism for providing patient feedback early in the therapy.* The provision of test feedback, as noted earlier, serves to focus the therapy on productive issues.

7. *Decreased therapy time.* Another possible benefit of the MMPI-2 in treatment planning is the reduced therapy time that may result from its use. If the therapist is able to gain a clear understanding from the MMPI-2 of the client's problems, adjustment level, interpersonal functioning, and accessibility to treatment early in therapy, then it stands to reason that the treatment process will proceed in an organized, efficient manner. In essence, the therapist will be able to make informed decisions regarding the treatment situation, planning the most effective and the most time-efficient treatment for each individual client. Such thoughtful planning will often reduce the chances of "hidden" problems emerging in the middle of therapy. As a result, therapy is more likely to proceed without interruption and is more likely to lead to expedient positive outcomes.

8. *Establishes baseline information which can serve as a record of progress*—a record by which later behavior change can be evaluated.

9. *Maximization of limited resources.* A final benefit of the MMPI-2 in pretreatment assessment is the maximization of resources that results from careful, informed

treatment planning. As discussed above, treatment planning with the MMPI-2 can help ensure that resources will not be unwisely used in treatment contexts in which therapeutic change is unlikely to occur. Efficient planning increases the chances that clients will have access to psychological treatment by maximizing the limited resources currently available from third-party coverers. Treatment planning with the MMPI-2 can help ensure that clients' needs are met and that new clients will have the opportunity to benefit from psychological services in the future.

Conclusions

The purpose of this chapter has been to highlight the importance of objective assessment in treatment planning. In line with this, a further aim was to demonstrate the utility of an empirically validated psychological instrument, the MMPI-2, for use in pretreatment assessment. A number of different ways in which the treatment planning process can be enhanced through the use of the MMPI-2 have been discussed. It is hoped that the many strategies and techniques presented in this chapter will aid both researchers and clinicians alike in their attempts to improve the treatment planning process and the interventions that naturally flow from this process.

Although much research on the MMPI-2 in pretreatment evaluation has already been conducted, there are still many unanswered questions. As such, a secondary purpose of this chapter has been to spark research interest into the uses of the MMPI-2 that have not yet been adequately assessed within this domain. For example, it is hoped that the discussion of client–therapist matching with the MMPI-2 will lead researchers to explore this potentially valuable use of the instrument in pretreatment assessment.

One area of treatment planning that has been undoubtedly ignored is the area of cost–benefits analysis. We are astounded by the lack of research in this most pertinent area. It would seem that in this day of limited resources and financial crises in mental health care delivery, psychologists would be eagerly collecting data supportive of the value of their services. Puzzling as it may be, such documentation is currently missing from the literature. To quote Yates (1994, p. 729) again at this time seems appropriate, because his point is well-taken: "By focusing scientific scrutiny on only the outcomes of treatment, investigators may be making mistakes that could become serious as budgets dwindle and clients become more sophisticated consumers of health services." It is hoped that the framework presented in this chapter for conceptualizing cost–benefits analyses will serve to stimulate needed research in this important area of investigation. It is increasingly important for assessment psychologists to provide evidence of empirical validation and clinical utility. Thus, it is likely that the future of these procedures use of psychological assessment instruments will depend upon the accumulation of empirical support verifying its effectiveness.

In summation, using the MMPI-2 in pretreatment assessment is likely to benefit the most important party concerned — the client. As clinicians we must remember that it is the client who relies on our knowledge and skills as "experts" to deliver the most effective and efficient interventions. We must also remember that it is the client who has the most to gain or lose from our planned interventions.

References

Abramowitz, S. I., & Murray, J. (1983) Race effects in psychotherapy. In J. Murray & P. R. Abramson (Eds.), *Bias in psychotherapy* (pp. 215–255). New York: Praeger.

Ananth, J., Engelsmann, F., Kiriakos, R., & Kovlivakis, T. (1979). Prediction of lithium response. *Acta Psychiatrica Scandinavia* 60, 279–286.

Ananth, J., Engelsmann, F., & Kiriakos, R. (1980). Evaluation of lithium response: Psychometric findings. *Canadian Journal of Psychiatry* 25, 151–154.

Andrews, S. B. (1976). The effect of sex of therapist and sex of client on termination from psychotherapy. *Dissertation Abstracts International* 36, 4143B.

Antonuccio, D. D., Lewinsohn, P. M., & Steinmetz, J. L. (1982). Identification of therapist differences in group treatment for depression. *Journal of Consulting and Clinical Psychology* 50, 433– 435.

Auden, W. H. (1962). *Dyer's hand*. New York: Random House.

Banks, W. M. (1972). The differential effects of race and social class in helping. *Journal of Clinical Psychology* 28, 90–92.

Bare, C. E. (1967). Relationship of counselor personality and counselor-client similarity to selected counseling success criteria. *Journal of Counseling Psychology* 14, 4419–4425.

Barrett, C. L., & Wright, J. H. (1984). Therapist variables. In M. Hersen, L. Michelson, & A. S. Bellack (Eds.), *Issues in psychotherapy research* (pp. 361–391). New York: Plenum.

Berzins, J. I. (1977). Therapist–patient matching. In A. S. Gurman & A. M. Razin (Eds.), *Effective psychotherapy: A handbook of research*. New York: Pergamon Press.

Beutler, L. E., & Harwood, M. T. (1994). How to assess clients in pretreatment planning. In J. N. Butcher (Ed.), *Clinical personality assessment: Practical approaches* (pp. 59–77). New York: Oxford University Press.

Beutler, L. E., Pollack, S., & Jobe, A. M. (1978). "Acceptance," values and therapeutic change. *Journal of Consulting and Clinical Psychology* 46, 198–199.

Beutler, L. E., Crago, M., & Arizmedi, T. G. (1986). Therapist variables in psychotherapy process and outcome. In S. L. Garfield & A. E. Bergin (Eds.), *Handbook of psychotherapy and behavior change* (3rd edition, pp. 257–301). New York: John Wiley & Sons.

Blase, J. J. (1979). A study of the effects of sex of the client and sex of the therapist on clients' satisfaction with psychotherapy. *Dissertation Abstracts International* 39, 6107B–6107BB.

Bobrov, A. E., Shurygin, A. N., & Krasil'nikov, S. V. (1993). Study of the effectiveness of combined use of monoaminoxidase inhibitors and psychotherapy in the treatment of chronic alcoholism. *Journal of Russian and East European Psychiatry* 26, 3–11.

Brena, S. F., Wolf, S. L., Chapman, S. L., & Hammonds, W. D. (1980). Chronic low back pain: Electromyographic, motion and behavioral assessments following sympathetic nerve blocks and placebos. *Pain* 8, 1–10.

Brooks, V. R. (1981). Sex and sexual orientation as variables in therapist's biases and therapy outcomes. *Clinical Social Work Journal* 9, 198–210.

Bryson, S., & Cody, J. (1973). Relationship of race and level of understanding between counselor and client. *Journal of Counseling Psychology* 40, 495–498.

Burdick, B. M., & Holmes, C. B. (1980). Use of the lithium scale with an outpatient psychiatric sample. *Psychological Reports* 47, 69–70.

Butcher, J. N. (1990). *MMPI-2 in psychological treatment*. New York: Oxford University Press.

Butcher, J. N., & Williams, C. L. (1992). *Essentials of the MMPI-2 and MMPI-a interpretation*. Minneapolis, MN: University of Minnesota Press.

Carkhoff, R. R., & Pierce, R. (1967). Differential effects of therapist race and social class upon patient depth of self-exploration in the initial clinical interview. *Journal of Consulting Psychology* 31, 632–634.

Carson, R. C., & Heine, R. W. (1962). Similarity and success in therapeutic dyads. *Journal of Consulting Psychology* 26, 38–43.

Carson, R. C., & Llewellyn, C. E. (1966). Similarity in therapeutic dyads. *Journal of Consulting Psychology* 26, 38–43.

Childress, R., & Gillis, J. S. (1977). A study of pretherapy role induction as an influence process. *Journal of Clinical Psychology* 33, 540–544.

Clark, M. E. (1996). MMPI-2 negative treatment indicators, content and content component scales: Clinical correlates and outcome prediction for men with chronic pain. *Psychological Assessment*, 8, 32–38.

Cleveland, S. E. (1989). Personality factors in the mediation of drug response. In S. Fisher and R. P. Greenberg (Eds.), *The limits of biological treatments for psychological distress* (pp. 235–262). Hillsdale, NJ: Lawrence Erlbaum Associates.

Costello, R. M., Baillargeon, J. G., Biever, P., & Bennett, R. (1979). Second-year alcoholism treatment outcome evaluation with a focus on Mexican American patients. *American Journal of Drug and Alcohol Abuse* 6, 97–108.

Curran, T. F. (1976). Anxiety reduction as a preliminary to group treatment. *Psychotherapy: Theory, Research, and Practice* 13, 354–360.

Dahlstrom, W. G., Welsh, G. S., & Dahlstrom, L. E. (1975). *An MMPI handbook*, Vol. II: *Research applications* (revised edition). Minneapolis, MN: University of Minnesota Press.

Dembo, R., Ikle, D. N., & Ciarlo, J. A. (1983). The influence of client-clinician demographic match on client outcomes. *Journal of Psychiatric Treatment and Evaluation* 5, 45–53.

Dolce, J. J., Crocker, M. F., & Doleys, D. M. (1986). Prediction of outcome among chronic pain patients. *Behavior Research and Therapy* 24, 313–319.

Donnan, H. H., & Mitchell, H. D., Jr. (1979). Preferences for older versus younger counselors among a group of elderly persons. *Journal of Counseling Psychology* 26, 514–518.

Donnelly, E. F., Goodwin, F. K., Waldman, I. N., & Murphy, D. L. (1978). Prediction of antidepressant response to lithium. *American Journal of Psychiatry* 135, 552–556.

Feldstein, J. C. (1979). Effects of counselor sex and sex role and client sex on client's perceptions and self-disclosure in a counseling analogue study. *Journal of Counseling Psychology* 26, 437–443.

Finn, S., & Tonsager, (1992). Therapeutic effects of providing MMPI-2 test feedback to college students awaiting therapy. *Psychological Assessment*, 4, 278–287.

Gallucci, N. T., Kay, D. C., & Thornby, J. I. (1989). The sensitivity of 11 substance abuse scales from the MMPI to change in clinical status. *Psychology of Addictive Behaviors* 3, 29–33.

Gardner, W. E. (1972). The differential effects of race, education and experience in helping. *Journal of Clinical Psychology* 28, 87–89.

Garvey, M. J., Johnson, R. A., Valentine, R. H., & Schuster, V. (1983). Use of an MMPI scale to predict antidepressant response to lithium. *Psychiatry Research* 10, 17–20.

Getz, H. G., & Miles, J. H. (1978). Women and peers as counselors: A look at client preferences. *Journal of College Student Personnel* 19, 37–41.

Graham, J. R. (1993). *MMPI-2: Assessing personality and psychopathology*. Second Edition. New York: Oxford University Press.

Grantham, R. J. (1973). Effects of counselor sex, race, and language style on black students in initial interviews. *Journal of Counseling Psychology* 20, 553–559.

Greene, R. L., & Clopton, J. R. (1994). Minnesota Multiphasic Personality Inventory-2. In M. E. Maruish (Ed.), *The use of psychological testing for treatment planning and outcome assessment* (pp. 137–159). Hillsdale, NJ: Lawrence Erlbaum Associates.

Griffith, M. S., & Jones, E. E. (1978). Race and psychotherapy: Changing perspectives. In J. H. Masserman (Ed.), *Current psychiatric therapies*, Vol. 18 (pp. 225–235). New York: Grune and Stratton.

Hart, L. E. (1981). An investigation of the effect of male therapists' views of women on the process and outcome of therapy with women. *Dissertation Abstracts International 42*, 2529B.

Heffernon, A., & Bruehl, D. (1971). Some effects of race of inexperienced lay counselors on black junior high students. *Journal of School Psychology 9*, 35–37.

Hoehn-Saric, R., Frank, J. D., Imber, S. D., Nash, E. H., Stone, A. R., & Battle, C. C. (1964). Systematic preparation of patients for psychotherapy: I. Effects on therapy behavior and outcome. *Journal of Psychiatric Research 2*, 267–281.

Hoffman, N. H., Loper, R. G., & Kammeier, M. L. (1974). Identifying future alcoholics with MMPI alcoholism scales. *Quarterly Journal of Studies on Alcohol 35*, 490–498.

Holliday, P. B. (1979). Effects of preparation for therapy on client expectations and participation. *Dissertation Abstracts International 39*, 35517B.

Hollon, S., & Mandell, M. (1979). Use of the MMPI in the evaluation of treatment effects. In James N. Butcher (Ed.), *New developments in the use of the MMPI* (pp. 241–302). Minneapolis: University of Minnesota Press.

Holzman, M. S. (1962). The significance of the value systems of patient and therapist for the outcome of psychotherapy. *Dissertation Abstracts 22*, 4073.

House, K. M., & Martin, R. L. (1975). MMPI delineation of a subgroup of depressed patients refractory to lithium carbonate therapy. *American Journal of Psychiatry 132*, 644–646.

Howard, K., Rikels, K., Mock, J. E., Lipman, R. S., Covi, L., & Baumm, N. C. (1970). Therapeutic style and attrition rate from psychiatric drug treatment. *Journal of Nervous and Mental Disease 150*, 102–110.

Huber, N. A., & Danahy, S. (1975). Use of the MMPI in predicting completion and evaluating changes in a long-term alcoholism treatment program. *Journal of Studies on Alcohol 36*, 1230–1237.

Jacobs, D., Charles, E., Jacobs, T., Weinstein, H., & Mann, D. (1972). Preparation for treatment of the disadvantaged patient: Effects on disposition and outcome. *American Journal of Orthopsychiatry 42*, 666–674.

Jones, E. E. (1978). Effects of race on psychotherapy process and outcome: An exploratory investigation. *Psychotherapy: Theory, Research, and Practice 50*, 226–236.

Jones, E. E., & Zoppel, C. L. (1982). Impact of client and therapist gender on psychotherapy process and outcome. *Journal of Consulting and Clinical Psychology 50*, 259–272.

Kammeier, M. L., Hoffmann, H., & Loper, R. G. (1973). Personality characteristics of alcoholics as college freshmen and at time of treatment. *Quarterly Journal of Studies on Alcohol 34*, 390–399.

Karasu, T., Stein, S. P., & Charles, E. (1979). Age factors in patient–therapist relationship. *Journal of Nervous and Mental Disease 167*, 100–104.

Kaschak, E. (1978). Therapist and client: Two views of the process and outcome of psychotherapy. *Professional Psychology 9*, 271–277.

Keithly. L. J., Samples, S. J., & Strupp, H. H. (1980). Patient motivation as a predictor of process and outcome in psychotherapy. *Psychotherapy and Psychosomatics 33*, 87–97.

Keller, L. S., & Butcher, J. N. (1991). *Assessment of Chronic Pain Patients with the MMPI-2*. Minneapolis, MN: University of Minnesota Press.

Kirshner, L. A., Genack, A., & Hauser, S. T. (1978). Effects of gender on short-term psychotherapy. *Psychotherapy: Theory, Research, and Practice* 15, 158–167.

Krebs, R. L. (1971). Some effects of a white institution on black psychiatric outpatients. *American Journal of Orthopsychiatry* 41, 589–596.

Krupitskii, E. M., Burakov, A. M., Karandashova, G. F., Lebedev, V. B., Katsnel'son, I. S., Nikitina, Z. S., Grinenko, A. I., & Borodkin, I. S. (1993). A method of treating affective disorders in alcoholics. *Journal of Russian and East European Psychiatry* 26, 26–37.

Lasky, R. G., & Solomone, P. R. (1977). Attraction to psychotherapy: Influences of therapist status and therapist-patient age similarity. *Journal of Clinical Psychology* 33, 511–516.

Leary, T. (1957). *The interpersonal diagnosis of personality*. New York: Ronald Press.

Lerner, B. (1972). *Therapy in the ghetto: Political impotence and personal disintegration*. Baltimore: Johns Hopkins University Press.

Lerner, B. (1973). Democratic values and therapeutic efficacy: A construct validity study. *Journal of Abnormal Psychology* 82, 491–498.

Lichenstein, E. (1966). Personality similarity and therapeutic success: A failure to replicate. *Journal of Consulting Psychology* 30, 282.

Loper, R. G., Kammeier, M. L., & Hoffmann, H. (1973). MMPI characteristics of college freshman males who later became alcoholics. *Journal of Abnormal Psychology* 82, 159–162.

Love, A. W., & Peck, C. L. (1987). The MMPI and psychological factors in chronic low back pain: A review. *Pain* 28, 159–162.

Luborsky, L., Mintz, J. Auerbach, A., Christoph, P., Bachrach, H., Todd, T., Johnson, M., Cohen, M., & O'Brien, C. P. (1980). Predicting the outcome of psychotherapy: Findings of the Penn Psychotherapy Project. *Archives of General Psychiatry* 37, 471–481.

Luborsky, L., Crits-Cristoph, P., Alexander, L., Margolis, M., & Cohen, M. (1983). Two helping alliance methods for predicting outcomes of psychotherapy: A counting signs vs. a global rating method. *Journal of Nervous and Mental Disease* 171, 480–491.

Mayerson, N. H. (1984). Preparing clients for therapy: A critical review and theoretical formulation. *Clinical Psychology Review* 4, 191–213.

McArthur, D. L., Cohen, M. J., Gottlieb, H. J., Naliboff, B. D., & Schandler, S. L. (1987). Treating chronic low back pain: I. Admissions to initial follow-up. *Pain* 29, 1–22.

McWilliams, J., & Brown, C. C. (1977). Treatment termination variables, MMPI scores and frequencies of relapse in alcoholics. *Journal of Studies on Alcohol* 38, 477–486.

Mendelsohn, G. A., & Geller, M. H. (1967). Similarity, missed sessions, and early termination. *Journal of Counseling Psychology* 14, 210–215.

Merbaum, M. & Butcher, J. N. (1982). Therapists' liking of their psychotherapy patients: Some issues related to severity of disorder and treatability. *Psychotherapy, Research and Practice*, 19, 69–76.

Moore, J. E., Armentrout, D. P., Parker, J. C., & Kivlahan, D. R. (1986). Empirically derived pain-patient MMPI subgroups: Prediction of treatment outcome. *Journal of Behavioral Medicine* 9, 51–63.

Moran, M. Watson. C. G., Brown, J., White, C., & Jacobs, L. (1978). Systems releasing action therapy with alcoholics: An experimental evaluation. *Journal of Clinical Psychology* 34, 769–774.

Morgan, R., Luborsky, L., Crits-Christoph, P., Curtis, H., & Solomon, J. (1982). Predicting the outcomes of psychotherapy by the Penn Helping Alliance Rating Method. *Archives of General Psychiatry* 39, 397–402.

Morrow, C. (1980). The effect of matching sex role attitude of client and therapist on therapy outcome. *Dissertation Abstracts International* 41, 1120B.

Naliboff, B. D., McCreary, C. P., McArthur, D. L., Cohen, M. J., & Gottlieb, H. J. (1988). MMPI changes following behavioral treatment of chronic low back pain. *Pain* 35, 271–277.

Nathan, P. E., & Skinstad, A. H. (1987). Outcomes of treatment for alcohol problems: Current methods, problems, and results. *Journal of Consulting and Clinical Psychology* 55, 332–340.

Nathan, R. G., Robinson, D., Cherek, D. R., & Sebastian, C. S. (1986). Alternative treatments for withdrawing the long-term benzodiazepine user: A pilot study. *International Journal of the Addictions* 21, 195–211.

Niemeyer, G. J., & Gonzales, M. (1983). Duration, satisfaction, and perceived effectiveness of cross-cultural counseling. *Journal of Counseling Psychology* 30, 91–95.

Orlinsky, D. E., & Howard, K. I. (1976). The effect of sex of therapist on the therapeutic experiences of women. *Psychotherapy: Theory, Research, and Practice* 13, 82–88.

Parloff, M. B., Waskow, I. E., & Wolfe, B. E. (1978). Research on therapist variables in relation to process and outcome. In S. L. Garfield and A. E. Bergin (Eds.), *Handbook of psychotherapy and behavior change* (pp. 233–282). Toronto: John Wiley & Sons.

Passini, F. T., Watson, C. G., Dehnel, L., & Herder, J. (1977). Alpha wave biofeedback training therapy in alcoholics. *Journal of Clinical Psychology* 33, 292–299.

Pena-Ramos, A., & Hornberger, R. (1979). MMPI and drug treatment in alcohol withdrawal. *Journal of Clinical Psychiatry* 40, 361–364.

Peniston, E. G., Hughes, R. B., & Kulkosky, P. J. (1986). EMG biofeedback-assisted relaxation training in the treatment of reactive depression in chronic pain patients. *The Psychological Record* 36, 471–481.

Poulos, C. J. (1981). What effects do corrective nutritional practices have on alcoholics? *Journal of Orthomolecular Psychiatry* 10, 61–64.

Proctor, E. K., & Rosen, A. (1981). Expectations and preferences for counselor race and their relation to intermediate treatment outcomes. *Journal of Counseling Psychology* 28, 40–46.

Roberts, A. H., & Reinhardt, L. (1980). The behavioral management of chronic pain: Long-term follow-up with comparison groups. *Pain* 8, 151–162.

Rohan, W. P., Tatro, R. L., & Rotman, S. R. (1969). MMPI changes in alcoholics during hospitalization. *Quarterly Journal of Studies on Alcohol* 30, 389–400.

Sattler, J. M. (1977). The effects of therapist–client racial similarity. In A. S. Gurman and A. M. Razin (Eds.), *Effective psychotherapy: A handbook of research* (pp. 252–290). New York: Pergamon.

Simons, J. A., & Helms, J. E. (1976). Influence of counselor's marital status, sex, and age on college and noncollege women's counselor preferences. *Journal of Counseling Psychology* 23, 380–386.

Sloane, R. B., Cristol, A. H., Pepernik, M. C., & Staples, F. R. (1970). Role preparation and expectation of improvement in psychotherapy. *Journal of Nervous and Mental Disease* 150, 18–26.

Snyder, D. K. (1990). Assessing chronic pain with the MMPI. In T. W. Miller (Ed.), *Chronic pain* (pp. 215–257). Madison, CT: International Universities Press.

Snyder, W. U., & Snyder, B. J. (1961). *The psychotherapy relationship*. New York: Macmillan.

Spielberger, C. D., Gorsuch, R. L., & Lushene, R. (1968). *Self-Evaluation Questionnaire*. Palo Alto, CA: Consulting Psychologists Press.

Strupp, H. H., & Bloxom, A. L. (1973). Preparing lower-class patients for group psychotherapy: Development and evaluation of a role-induction film. *Journal of Consulting and Clinical Psychology* 41, 373–384.

Swenson, C. H. (1967). Psychotherapy as a special case of dyadic interaction: Some suggestions for theory and research. *Psychotherapy: Theory, Research and Practice* 4, 7–13.

Terrell, F., & Terrell, S. (1984). Race of counselor, client sex, cultural mistrust level, and premature termination from counseling among black clients. *Journal of Counseling Psychology* 31, 371–375.

Truax, C. B., & Wargo, D. G. (1969). Effects of vicarious therapy pretraining and alternate sessions on outcome in group psychotherapy with outpatients. *Journal of Consulting and Clinical Psychology* 33, 440–447.

Turkat, D. M. (1979). Psychotherapy prepatory communications: Influences upon patient role expectations. *Dissertation Abstracts International* 39, 4059B.

Turner, S., & Armstrong, S. (1981). Cross-racial psychotherapy: What the therapists say. *Psychotherapy: Theory, Research, and Practice* 18, 375–378.

Vogel, J. L. (1961). Authoritarianism in the therapeutic relationship. *Journal of Consulting Psychology* 25, 102–108.

Warren, N. C., & Rice, L. N. (1972). Structuring and stabilizing of psychotherapy for low-prognostic clients. *Journal of Consulting and Clinical Psychology* 39, 173–181.

Whitehorn, J. C., & Betz, B. J. (1960). Further studies of the doctor as a crucial variable in the outcome of treatment with schizophrenic patients. *American Journal of Psychiatry*, 117, 215–223.

Williams, B. M. (1984). Psychotherapy: The powerful placebo. *Journal of Consulting and Clinical Psychology* 52, 570–573.

Wilson, D. O. (1985). The effects of systematic client preparation, severity and treatment setting on drop out rate in short-term psychotherapy. *Journal of Social and Clinical Psychology* 3, 62–70.

Wogan, M. (1970). Effect of therapist-patient personality variables on therapeutic outcome. *Journal of Consulting and Clinical Psychology* 35, 356–361.

Yamamoto, J., James, Q., Bloombaum, M., & Hattem, J. (1967). Racial factors in patient selection. *American Journal of Psychiatry* 124, 630–636.

Yates, B. T. (1994). Toward the incorporation of costs, cost-effectiveness analysis, and cost–benefit analysis into clinical research. *Journal of Consulting and Clinical Psychology* 62, 729–736.

Yehuda, S. (1976). The influence of behavioral and environmental factors on drug effects. In D. I. Mostofsky (Ed.), *Behavior control and modification of physiological activity* (pp. 297–313). Englewood Cliffs, NJ: Prentice-Hall.

Zubin, J., & Katz, M. M. (1964). Psychopharmacology and Personality. In P. Worchel and D. Byrne (Eds.), *Personality change* (pp. 367–395). New York: John Wiley & Sons.

Zwick, R., & Attkisson, C. C. (1985). Effectiveness of a client pretherapy orientation on videotape. *Journal of Counseling Psychology* 32, 514–524.

8

Therapeutic Assessment with the MMPI-2 in Managed Health Care

Stephen E. Finn
Hale Martin

The Current Crisis in Psychological Assessment

The role of psychological assessment in mental health care has been declining over recent years, especially because managed care systems have been on the rise. This decline is multiply determined, but is based in part on perceptions of assessment among mental health professionals and in part on pressures from managed health care systems. Perhaps the most important reason behind this decline is the faltering interest in assessment by psychologists, those most directly trained in psychological testing. Reasons for this weakened interest include perceptions that assessment requires less skill and provides less personal satisfaction than psychotherapy, beliefs that assessment is dehumanizing of clients, questions about the incremental validity of assessment, and economic pressures.

Many professionals believe that psychological assessment is a distant second to psychotherapy in challenging their talents and skills as a psychologist. They find more fulfillment and prestige in the provision of psychotherapy than in that of assessment. This attitude may be an unfortunate outgrowth of the traditional approach to psychological assessment. Typically, training in psychological assessment emphasizes the use of standard techniques and rigid protocols to collect "sterile" data. Test data are then mechanically pieced together into a report that is—at best— glanced at by others who often read only the summary statements. The resulting report is then placed in the client's file for some nebulous future reference. As is to be expected with this approach, traditional psychological assessment is often viewed as a semiskilled technical enterprise that is not personally fulfilling for a doctoral-level psychologist. Generally, as soon as one is able, the task of test administration is delegated to lesser-trained mental health professionals, and doctoral-level psychologists then focus on interpretation of data or supervision of those learning assessment, if they continue to do psychological assessment at all (Moreland et al., 1994; Finn & Tonsager, in preparation).

This traditional approach to psychological assessment is unappealing to many psychologists in that it does not require the creative and adaptive application of the knowledge and skills acquired through training and experience. Even when the interpretation of test data does provide a challenge, it is removed from the interpersonal interaction that lured many into the mental health field in the first place. Holt (1968, p. 29) notes that "All in all, diagnostic testing is not an emotionally and motivationally satisfying activity for the full-time endeavors of the kind of person who is likely to be best at it." The clinician is often left to paperwork—that is, the sometimes grueling process of writing a report for those who requested the testing. Perhaps most significantly, the clinician is often left feeling as though she/he had little impact on the client. Although she/he may have carefully collected (or had someone else collect) test data from the client and correctly analyzed the findings, the resulting report is often only understood by fellow professionals, and it is they who are left to use (or not use) the results of the testing for the benefit of the client. Thus, just as traditional assessment is based upon sterile data, the process often tends to feel sterile as well and it holds little allure for the humanistic professional.

The perceptions that psychological assessment requires less skill, generates more paperwork, and provides less stimulation and fulfillment than psychotherapy all contribute to psychologists holding psychological testing in less esteem. This decline in prestige further decreases the appeal of assessment for the competent professional. This generally diminished regard for the work of psychological assessment may contribute to its not being as well compensated on an hour-for-hour basis as other endeavors of the psychologist. This even further diminishes the appeal of assessment for the newly trained clinician. In the increasingly difficult economic environment, a professional can often be better rewarded financially for work other than psychological assessment.

In addition to these personal factors that may cause psychologists to gravitate away from psychological assessment, some professionals believe that psychological assessment is not in the best interest of the client. Many view traditional assessment as dehumanizing those assessed in both purpose and effect. Traditionally, assessment has served a diagnostic function—where a label or judgment is applied that the client often does not understand. Such judgments have been used to deny clients privileges such as custody of a child, employment, or even freedom to walk the streets. Rightly or wrongly, a diagnostic label can follow a person throughout her/his life, regardless of its accuracy. As Korchin and Schuldberg (1981) note, "assessment became identified with . . . labeling and has been criticized as useless, if not harmful."

Some professionals argue that the process of psychological assessment is inherently demeaning, disrespectful, and abusive of clients. Unfortunately, such critics do not have to look far to find clients who complain of feeling manipulated, invaded, unappreciated, and ignored after an assessment. Such feelings are heightened when assessments are conducted without test procedures being adequately explained to clients or without test results being shared after an assessment is completed. Fortunately, recent legal advances in clients' right to be informed (Brodsky, 1972) and ethical stipulations that clients be given feedback about test results in language they can understand (American Psychological Association, 1992) have worked to diminish the abuse clients have sometimes felt at the hands of psychologists who misuse the traditional approach to assessment.

From a more technical perspective, psychological assessment is subject to questions of incremental validity and utility. First, does it actually provide more accurate information than can be obtained through other, perhaps less costly methods; and second, if it does provide additional data, is that added information useful? More generally, is psychological assessment worth the time and effort it requires? Parsimony is a quality sought by good clinicians and by managed care systems who seek to limit costs. Many professionals believe that after a few psychotherapy sessions a competent clinician will know the information necessary for treatment without resorting to expensive, time-consuming psychological assessment. A recent survey of nine of the largest managed care firms reflected the belief that an interview is sufficient to clarify diagnosis (Griffith, 1995). For these reasons some clinicians reserve assessment for those few clients who are puzzling, even after many psychotherapy sessions, or for those patients who are uncooperative.

So the issue remains, When is psychological assessment warranted as an effort to gain further information? It seems likely that assessment can be a useful data-gathering tool in many situations, but it may not be so efficient as to warrant being a routine standing order on psychiatric units as it has been in the recent past (Meier, 1994). If additional useful information is needed, one should consider carefully the most effective means of data collection in light of the specific circumstances of a case. Although psychological testing may play an important role at times in information gathering, it may not always be the approach of choice when all factors are considered.

Finally, concerns about dehumanizing the patient and questions of incremental validity fuel the debate that psychological assessment is undesirable and an unnecessary expense to those who are paying the bills. Managed care systems see little need for the information provided by extensive assessment. The aforementioned survey of large managed care firms confirmed that reimbursement of psychological assessment is tightly restricted. All nine companies contacted required precertification of testing, and many reported suspicion of any request for testing. Their preferences were against full batteries due to cost and against projective testing due to validity concerns (Griffith, 1995).

Managed care is interested in helping those they ensure for the lowest cost possible. They have fixed financial resources based on the rates they charge for coverage. In order to be competitive with other companies, they must offer rates that are attractive to those seeking health insurance. Their hope for profit and economic survival comes from their ability to hold costs down as low as possible while still meeting the obligations to those they cover. Many insurance companies believe they are doing a service to those they insure by maximizing the mental health benefit squeezed from generally low limits of coverage for mental health services. To administrators of these managed care systems, the basic questions are, Why spend this amount of money for psychological assessment? What will our subscribers receive in return? What is the value of psychological assessment in relation to other ways limited resources might be allocated? Approached from the perspective of traditional assessment, the answers to these questions may make assessment difficult or impossible to justify.

Therapeutic Assessment

Fortunately, the field of psychological assessment is evolving in response to many of the same observations, issues, and concerns that have motivated the evolution of self-psychological, interpersonal, intersubjective, social constructivist, and feminist philosophies and approaches to psychological treatment. Meier (1994) notes that psychological assessment has historically striven to be relevant and to respond to the changing demands made on it and opportunities open to it. Therapeutic Assessment is a new paradigm for psychological assessment that addresses many of the limitations, reservations, and concerns related to traditional assessment (Finn & Tonsager, in preparation). It is collaborative, interpersonal, focused, time-limited, and flexible. It is an approach to assessment that is very interactive and requires the greatest of clinical skills in a challenging role for the clinician. It is unsurpassed in its respectfulness for clients: collaborating with them to address *their* concerns (around which the work revolves), acknowledging them as experts on themselves and recognizing their contributions as essential, and providing to them usable answers to their questions in a therapeutic manner (Finn & Tonsager, in preparation). When practiced correctly, Therapeutic Assessment is of enormous impact and benefit to clients, providing them with a sense of efficacy in co-directing the process, self-worth in being accurately seen and valued, and hope in exploring new ways of addressing difficult problems. Therapeutic Assessment promises to be an economically efficient approach in helping clients grapple with difficulties they are having.

Goals and Principles

The ultimate goal of Therapeutic Assessment is to provide an experience for the client that will allow her/him to take steps toward greater psychological health and a more fulfilling life. This is done (a) by recognizing the client's characteristic ways of being, (b) understanding in a meaningful, idiographic way the problems the client faces, (c) providing a safe environment for the client to explore change, and (d) providing the opportunity for the client to experience new ways of being in a supportive environment (Finn, 1996; Finn & Tonsager, in preparation). The general principles underlying Therapeutic Assessment work to increase the likelihood of reaching the goal of a transforming experience.

Therapeutic Assessment recognizes that assessment is a vulnerable experience for the client. It involves giving personal information of an uncertain significance to a stranger who will use that information to draw conclusions that will be used to either help or harm the client. Therapeutic Assessment requires that clients be assessed only after they fully understand the kind of information that can be derived from the assessment procedures and how that information will be used after the assessment. In accordance with current ethical standards, Therapeutic Assessment acknowledges that the assessor has the responsibility of clarifying with the client the goals and purpose of the assessment (American Psychological Association, 1992).

Therapeutic Assessment advances the belief that clients become most engaged in an assessment and are most likely to give accurate information when they are treated as collaborators whose ideas and cooperation are essential to the assessment. Additionally, they become most invested in an assessment when the results will be used to address their personal questions and goals. When clients understand the nature of an assessment and voluntarily agree to participate, they are often looking for emotional support and for new information that will help them address life's problems. By giving clients feedback about assessment results in an emotionally supportive manner, the assessor helps clients feel affirmed, less anxious, and more hopeful and to better understand and manage life's problems.

Research on Therapeutic Assessment with the MMPI-2

Research has just begun to investigate the effects of Therapeutic Assessment, but early results suggest that it can have a substantial beneficial impact on clients. The seminal study of Therapeutic Assessment (Finn & Tonsager, 1992) demonstrated that clients from a university counseling center who received feedback about MMPI-2 results showed a significant decrease in psychological distress, an increase in self-esteem, and increased hopefulness. In this study, students in the experimental group ($n = 32$) were interviewed, took the MMPI-2, and received feedback of results in a session with the assessor. Students in the control group ($n = 29$) were interviewed and did not take the MMPI-2, but they were given "therapeutic attention" by the assessor in the final session.

In comparison to the control group, the experimental group showed clinically significant decreases in psychiatric symptomatology. This change in psychic distress continued to grow over the two-week follow-up period of the study. Relative to the control group, the experimental group also showed significantly increased hopefulness about their problems and a significant increase in self-esteem. These effects were also maintained, and even slightly increased, at the end of the two-week follow-up period. In addition, those who received MMPI-2 feedback had an overwhelmingly positive impression of the assessment experience. The effect of test feedback on self-esteem is particularly noteworthy in that psychotherapy outcome studies rarely document any change in self-esteem after psychotherapy. Subsequent research has confirmed the significant therapeutic effects of MMPI-2 assessments done from a collaborative approach (Newman, 1996).

In a related study (Finn & Bunner, 1993), feedback of assessment results had a significant impact on psychiatric inpatients' satisfaction with clinical services. Most of the subjects were hospitalized for affective disorders or substance abuse. Thirty-four patients completed The Assessment Questionnaire-2 (Finn et al., 1995), a measure of client satisfaction with assessment. Patients who received verbal feedback about their assessment results ($n = 14$) were more satisfied with their assessment experiences than were those who did not receive feedback ($n = 20$). Those who received feedback rated themselves as having learned more about themselves, feeling more understood, and having more positive feelings about the assessor. This study is important in that client satisfaction is an important outcome variable itself, with obvious implications for client's future use of mental health services.

Factors That May Contribute to Therapeutic Effects of MMPI-2 Assessments

How can assessment with the MMPI-2 have such beneficial impact on the client? One can speculate many possible reasons for the therapeutic effects, some of which have been postulated earlier by Finn and Butcher (1991). Receiving self-verifying information about oneself can have an affirming effect (Swann, 1983). Providing words that describe experiences and feelings of which one is only vaguely aware can aid self-understanding and provide a sense of mastery that is empowering to an individual. Merely openly expressing one's concerns can have a cathartic effect, and when those concerns are understood by a person in some position of authority, one would likely feel less isolated and more hopeful about dealing with their problems. The experience of feeling accurately seen and attended to by another person (mirroring) can be a powerful stimulus to growth of the self.

The experience of connecting in a meaningful way with another person can decrease feelings of alienation and provide a sense of more control in the world through enhanced self-image and feelings of self-efficacy. Feeling respected and valued during the testing situation can be internalized to positively impact self-esteem. It can revive hope and trust and instill confidence that other relationships can be improved. Many people have had little positive experience when in a one-down position so that feeling respected in their vulnerability can have a significant impact on self-esteem and increase hope for relationships.

Finally, the MMPI-2 assessment process can provide a good model for relationships by providing an experience of mutual respect, of being seen for who one is, and of saying good-bye and grieving loss. This model could instill greater confidence in one's ability to manage other relationships in life. Further research is needed to increase our understanding of the therapeutic mechanisms involved in Therapeutic Assessment. Results of such studies could contribute to refinements that further enhance the efficacy and efficiency of psychological assessment.

A Model for Conducting Therapeutic MMPI-2 Assessments

Therapeutic Assessment is flexible in its procedure because it tries to accommodate the questions and needs of clients. However, a general model of MMPI-2 assessment that has proved effective in previous research (Finn & Tonsager, 1992; Newman, 1996) can provide useful guidelines. The following flow chart is a condensation and modification of that described by Finn (1996):

Step 1. Initial interview with client. A 60- to 90-minute interview allows the client and assessor to build rapport, identify personal questions the client wishes the MMPI-2 to address, review relevant history about the questions, and make a clear contract about the logistics of the assessment, including cost, duration, and timing of the feedback session.

Step 2. Administration of the MMPI-2. The MMPI-2 is administered, scored, and interpreted to gain insight into answers to the client's questions.

Step 3. Assessment intervention session. In this 60–minute session, the assessor uses "softer" tests, such as the Thematic Apperception Tests, to explore findings from the MMPI-2 and engage the client as an observer of her/his behavior *in vivo* (Fischer, 1994). The target behavior is generally one that provides an important insight into an assessment question. For example, a client who has asked, "Why am I so depressed lately?" may produce a 2–4 code type on the MMPI-2, suggesting that her/his depression may be related to feelings of being "trapped." During an assessment intervention, this client may be given cards from the TAT that pull for depressive themes. The client's stories may then be discussed with the MMPI-2 results in mind, with the assessor asking whether characters in the stories have a way out of their predicaments. Parallels may then be explicitly drawn from the story to the client's own situation and to her/his question posed at the beginning of the assessment. Finally, new alternatives can be suggested by the assessor and "tried on" by the client by integrating them into the story. To continue the example, the assessor might suggest that the client needs to be assertive when first noticing twinges of resentment and that this option might prevent a buildup of resentment and help short-circuit the client's depression. The client then retells the TAT story — integrating some aspect of assertiveness — to see how it feels as a potential new way of being. Such a new alternative may provide a small but pivotal step in the client's personal growth and may trigger other therapeutic effects, such as renewed hopefulness.

Step 4. Construct a feedback outline. The assessor uses knowledge of the client and of the feedback process to arrange the answers to the questions asked by the client in such a way as to maximize the impact of the feedback session.

Step 5. Feedback session with client. The assessor communicates the MMPI-2 findings in response to the client's questions and solicits input from the client to refine the findings. MMPI-2 results are presented to the client in such a way that she/he can most likely accept them. Clients may choose to audiotape the feedback session.

Step 6. Written report to client. Following the feedback session, the assessor mails a written report to the client summarizing the assessment results and answers to the client's assessment questions and asks the client for written feedback about the assessment.

Therapeutic Assessment with Managed Care Clients

Educating Managed Care Staff about Therapeutic Assessment

Therapeutic Assessment can be done within a managed care environment, but it typically is necessary to educate staff with whom one has contact about the differences between this approach and traditional assessment. We have found several ways of doing this, depending on the openness of managed care staff and the number of questions they have about the procedures of Therapeutic Assessment. In increasing order of effort, these are the methods we have found effective for educating managed care staff:

1. *Discuss the principles of Therapeutic Assessment with managed care "gatekeepers."* Because gatekeepers are responsible for ensuring that members of a managed care plan receive only necessary treatments, it is important that they understand the distinction between a traditional assessment and an assessment conducted according to the principles of Therapeutic Assessment. Often it is possible to discuss these differences when approaching the gatekeeper for preauthorization for the assessment. Relevant points to mention are that the psychological testing is being done as a brief form of psychotherapy, the client will be asked to collaborate in the assessment and will receive feedback about the test results, and the client will receive a short report about the testing. Such information also helps the gatekeeper understand the various charges for which one is seeking preauthorization.

One particular point of information that may be useful to share with gatekeepers involves the policies of the American Psychological Association (1985, 1992) regarding feedback about psychological testing. Both the *Standards for Educational and Psychological Testing* (1985) and the *Revised Ethical Principles for Psychologists* (1992) explicitly state that psychologists are responsible for providing feedback to clients about psychological testing. These policies may be important in explaining to gatekeepers why one is conducting and charging for test feedback sessions, and they provide justification that one is not simply seeking to "pad" the number of hours for which one bills.

2. *Send written information about Therapeutic Assessment.* We have found it very effective to follow up phone conversations with gatekeepers by sending them written information about Therapeutic Assessment. For example, we have a brief information sheet for referring professionals that summarizes the principles and procedures of Therapeutic Assessment (see Table 8.1) Managed care gatekeepers have found this information sheet to be useful in understanding how we conduct our assessments. Often, we will also send a copy of relevant research articles (e.g., Finn & Tonsager, 1992) that document the beneficial effects of Therapeutic Assessment. A short note may be included, asking the gatekeeper to share the enclosed information with other colleagues, thereby maximizing the possibility of reaching other professionals in the managed care organization.

3. *Ask if you may visit and conduct a staffing on Therapeutic Assessment.* Several years ago, we repeatedly faced difficulties getting preauthorizations for assessments from one large managed care organization that contracts with our clinic. At that time, one of us (SEF) asked if it would be possible to visit the organization to discuss Therapeutic Assessment. The offer was enthusiastically accepted and a staffing was held in which Therapeutic Assessment was discussed and gatekeepers got to view videotaped excerpts of actual client–assessor interactions. The response from the managed care staff was overwhelmingly positive and, for quite a while afterwards, not only did we easily receive assessment preauthorizations, we also got a number of referrals from the organization for assessments.

Table 8.1.   Information Sheet for Referring Professionals

What Is Therapeutic Assessment?

Therapeutic Assessment is an approach developed by Stephen Finn, Constance Fischer, and others. It uses psychological tests and a collaborative assessment method to help clients reconceptualize their lives and move forward in their healing. Research has demonstrated that after a therapeutic assessment, many clients exhibit less distress and have higher self-esteem. In addition, valid and usable test data are collected, which may be used for diagnosis, treatment planning, or documentation of change after treatment.

How Is Therapeutic Assessment Different from Traditional Assessment?

In the Therapeutic Assessment model, psychological testing is seen as a potential intervention and a method of gathering information about a client. We involve clients and referring persons in all stages of the assessment process, as collaborators, co-observers, and co-interpreters of certain test results. We always give verbal feedback to clients about test results and provide a written report when it is desired. At the end of an assessment we solicit written feedback from clients about their experience of the assessment.

When Should I Refer for a Therapeutic Assessment?

We welcome referrals for psychological assessment when you feel this process will be useful to you and your client. Common times for making such a referral are (1) at the beginning of therapy to help in treatment planning, (2) when you and/or your client are puzzled about the client's history or experience, (3) when therapy is "stuck" and you wish an outside event to move it forward, (4) when you feel a client is planning to terminate therapy prematurely, and (5) as part of the termination process to document change and plan for the future. Our collaborative assessment methods are often particularly better than traditional procedures for clients who have strong reservations about being tested. We never proceed with an assessment until we have a client's cooperation.

What Types of Assessment Do You Do?

We accept referrals for outpatient individual assessments, including intellectual testing, learning disability evaluations, personality testing, diagnosis and treatment planning, and neuropsychological screening with clients 4 years of age and above. If we determine that more extensive neuropsychological testing or educational testing is needed, we will make a referral to an allied professional. We also perform innovative evaluations of couples and families, which include the production and analysis of a consensual Rorschach protocol. Except in rare instances we do not accept referrals for forensic evaluations.

What Can I Expect from You, the Assessor?

We will address the questions you and your client pose for the assessment, or let you know beforehand if the assessment is unlikely to provide the information you seek. We will keep in contact with you during the assessment and discuss findings with you before they are shared with the client. We will provide you and your client with a written report, if desired. We will remain in contact with you and/or your client until the assessment results have been fully explored and integrated into your work. We are available to meet with your client months or even years after an assessment to again discuss test results. All assessments done by our clinic staff are closely supervised by our Director, Stephen E. Finn, Ph.D.

What Will You Expect of Me as a Referring Professional?

We ask that you prepare your client for the assessment by discussing the specific questions you would like answered by the assessment and helping the client to form his/her own questions. Early

(continued)

Table 8.1.   *(continued)*

in the assessment, we will contact you to get background information on the client. While the assessment is taking place, your client may need emotional support and/or help describing the experiences of the assessment. If you notice a change in your client's behavior in or outside of therapy during an assessment, please let the assessor know as soon as possible. If possible, we ask that you attend the feedback session where the assessment results will be presented to the client, and we welcome your suggestions before the feedback session about how to best discuss the assessment findings with your client. If we can, we will come to your office for the feedback session, because your client is likely to feel most comfortable in this setting. After the assessment is completed, we will ask you for feedback about our work, so that we may better serve you and other referring professionals in the future.

How Much Does an Assessment Cost?

The fees for a therapeutic assessment vary depending on the complexity of the referral questions and whether a verbal summary or written report is desired. After the initial interview with a client, we quote a fee for the entire assessment, including interviews, testing sessions, test scoring and interpretations, written reports, and feedback sessions. We ask that, if possible, your client pay half this fee at the beginning of the assessment and half at the completion. Typically, we can fairly accurately estimate our fees from talking with you about your client.

How Long Will It Take to Have My Client Assessed?

Because of the high demand for our assessments, we generally have a 3 to 5 week waiting period between the date of a referral and the beginning of an assessment. Once an assessment has begun, we typically provide the feedback session within 4 weeks, except in very complicated assessments. Although we prefer to test clients over 2–3 weeks to allow us to see them in different contexts, we can perform assessments within short periods of time (e.g., 3–5 days) if you so desire.

How Do I Refer My Client?

Please contact Stephen Finn, Ph.D. at (512) 329–5090 to discuss your particular client or if you would like more information about our approach to psychological assessment.

Getting Preauthorization for an MMPI-2 Assessment

Obviously, the procedures a psychologist must follow in seeking preauthorization for a therapeutic MMPI-2 assessment will vary from region to region and according to the specific contract the provider has signed with a managed care organization. Typically in our area, we are allowed to see a client for one hour of initial diagnostic interview (CPT code 90801) before we must seek further approval from a gatekeeper for an MMPI-2 assessment. We use the initial interview, as described earlier, to gather specific goals and questions that the client wishes to have addressed by the assessment. Then, when we approach the gatekeeper, we have the rationale for the assessment in hand. When discussing the client with the gatekeeper, we find it expedient to address the following points:

1. *Presenting issues of the client and initial diagnostic impressions.* For example, a client may seek an assessment due to worrying and difficulties sleeping. We might share with the gatekeeper our impression that the client seemed clinically depressed.

2. *Specific questions to be addressed by the MMPI-2.* For the aforementioned

client these might include such questions as, "Why am I having difficulty sleeping?" "Why am I worrying so much about my business?"

3. *A rationale for the use of the MMPI-2 to address the specific assessment questions.* Some explanation must typically be given for why the MMPI-2 is an appropriate assessment instrument to address the referral questions. For example, in the current example one might explain that the MMPI-2 is a good measure of anxiety and depression, both of which are suspected as underlying the client's stated difficulties.

4. *Clarification of how to bill the assessment intervention session, the MMPI-2 scoring charges, and the MMPI-2 feedback session.* Different managed care carriers prefer to have us bill the assessment intervention session and feedback session under CPT code 90830 (psychological testing) or as psychotherapy (CPT code 90844). Similarly, some organizations have a specific fee they will cover for the MMPI-2 scoring expenses. Such issues should be openly discussed with the gatekeeper when applying for preauthorization, so that billing can proceed without complications.

Billing for an MMPI-2 Intervention

Table 8.2 shows a sample bill for an MMPI-2 intervention. In this instance, the assessment intervention session has been billed under CPT code 90830 (psychological testing) and the MMPI-2 feedback session has been billed under CPT code 90844 (psychotherapy). Again, because the procedures of Therapeutic Assessment constitute test-based psychotherapy, the provider has some flexibility in how to list these charges and should consult the gatekeeper when seeking preauthorization.

Occasionally we work with a managed care organization that does not require preauthorization before bills are submitted. In such an instance, an explanation of

Table 8.2   Sample Bill for Therapeutic MMPI-2 Assessment

Bill for Psychological Services

Client: Ms. S
Identification No.: 999–99–9999
Date of Birth: XX-XX-XX
Diagnosis: 301.9

Date	Service	Time	CPT	Charge
XX-XX-XX	Initial interview	1 hour	90801	$100.00
XX-XX-XX	Psych. testing	1 hour	90830	$90.00
XX-XX-XX	Psych. testing	1 hour	90830	$90.00
XX-XX-XX	Psychotherapy	1 hour	90844	$80.00

Total Charges $350.00

Stephen E. Finn
Stephen E. Finn
Licensed Psychologist
TX license #2–3064
Tax ID #—xxx-xx-xxxx

the bill for an MMPI-2 intervention is often in order, since the procedures of Therapeutic Assessment differ from those of traditional assessment. Table 8.3 shows a sample letter we have drafted for such purposes.

Enlisting Clients as Advocates of Therapeutic Assessment

Infrequently, we run across an insurer that balks at paying for any psychological testing or—more frequently—that wishes to severely limit the number of hours of psychological testing in such a manner that a Therapeutic Assessment cannot realistically be performed. (For example, one company refused to pay for more than one hour of psychological testing for an MMPI-2 assessment.) Obviously, we first attempt to work with such an insurer by providing them with information about Therapeutic Assessment, as detailed above. In the few instances where this strategy has failed, we have found it useful to involve clients in the preassessment process,

---

Table 8.3   Letter to Insurance Company Regarding Billing for MMPI-2 Intervention

[Date]
[Insurance Company]
[Street Address]
[City], [State] [Zipcode]

Dear colleagues:
This letter accompanies a bill for my client, [Client Name], and will explain some of the charges. [Client Name] recently participated in a brief psychotherapeutic intervention at our clinic. This intervention is called "Therapeutic Assessment" and has been developed by myself and other colleagues at the University of Texas at Austin and the Center for Therapeutic Assessment. The enclosed article by Finn and Tonsager (1992) documents the efficacy of one version of this therapy—using only the MMPI-2—on clients' distress and self-esteem. [Client Name] participated in a longer version, involving [Total hours] total contact hours and the following psychological test instruments: [Tests Used]. Because this intervention combines both elements of assessment and psychotherapy, the total contact hours have been billed as follows: Diagnostic Interview = [Int Hours] hours, Psychological Testing (and Report) = [Testing Hours] hours, Psychotherapy = [Therapy Hours] hours. This breakdown reflects the hours spent with the client in the various activities.

   If you would like further information about Therapeutic Assessment or about the billing on [Client Name], please feel free to contact me at the number above. We look forward to continuing to work with your clients at our clinic.

Sincerely,

Stephen E. Finn
Director and Licensed Psychologist

as advocates of Therapeutic Assessment. A few well-placed phone calls from a client or—even more effective—from the client's employer can do wonders in influencing an insurer to look more favorably on Therapeutic Assessment.

Another important strategy—especially when working with a new carrier—is to ask satisfied clients to call or write a brief letter to their insurance carrier after an assessment expressing their satisfaction with Therapeutic Assessment and detailing how it helped them. We have done this on several occasions and have received feedback that the clients' letters had a positive impact on the insurance carriers to which they were sent.

One indirect way to use client feedback with insurance carriers is to collect information regarding client satisfaction with assessment services and to share this information with gatekeepers when discussing Therapeutic Assessment. We routinely ask clients to fill out a standardized evaluation form, the Assessment Questionnaire-2 (Finn et al., 1995), following a psychological assessment. On several occasions, we have been able to use such data to demonstrate that most of our clients are highly satisfied with their assessment experiences.

Case Example

Referral   Ms. S was a 35-year-old woman referred for a personality assessment by her psychotherapist, Dr. B, who felt that she and Ms. S had reached an impasse in their treatment. Ms. S had sought psychotherapy 8 months earlier complaining of being "angry all the time" and concerned about how frequently she yelled at her two young children (ages 6 and 4). While both women felt that they had made progress in understanding the source of Ms. S's anger (i.e., physical abuse in childhood and marital problems), Ms. S felt she had made little progress in controlling her anger. Ms. S was now contemplating terminating psychotherapy due to her frustration with its slow pace; Dr. B hoped the assessment would provide information that would rescue and reorient the stalled treatment.

Initial Contact with Insurer   Dr. B had already made contact with Ms. S's insurer to let them know that she had referred Ms. S for an assessment. Thus, when the assessor (SEF) called for preauthorization, he requested and was granted approval to conduct and bill for an initial interview (CPT 90801) with Ms. S.

Initial Interview with Ms. S   Ms. S arrived 10 minutes late for the initial interview but claimed to be enthusiastic about the assessment. She confirmed Dr. B's referral and explained that she wanted therapy to help "get rid of her anger," especially with her husband. She described him as a disabled Vietnam veteran "with PTSD" who abused prescription medications and left all household duties to her. She said that she had worked extensively in therapy on confronting her husband with her anger toward him, but still found herself "stuck" when it came time to talk with him. To date, he had refused to attend sessions with Dr. B. Ms. S also puzzled aloud about her continuing feelings of anger at her parents, explaining that she had "cut them off" six months earlier. She described her mother as a "controlled alcoholic" who drank every day to "get numb." She said her father was a World War II combat veteran and told of his beating her "until she urinated in her pants" when she was a child. Ms. S had discontinued contact with her parents after her younger sister revealed that she had been sexually abused by her father as a child. Ms. S had expected that her anger toward her parents would subside because she no longer talked with them, but said that she still "dug her nails into her palms" whenever she thought of them.

Ms. S posed the following questions for the assessment:

1. Why am I so angry all the time?
2. What can I do to better manage my anger and express it?
3. Is this a good time for m]e to stop therapy?

Ms. S agreed to complete an MMPI-2 to address these questions, and she contracted to meet with the assessor two more times—once after the MMPI-2 to further explore her questions (i.e., the assessment intervention session) and once after that with Dr. B to go over the assessment results. The assessor also promised Ms. S a brief written report addressing her questions. It was made clear that this plan was contingent upon our clinic's getting preauthorization for the assessment.

Steve's initial impressions of Ms. S were that she was an intelligent, capable woman who had made a good adaptation to a difficult past. He was struck by her stated desire to "get rid of her anger," as if it were an offensive trait that she wished to have removed. Steve noted that Ms. S seemed disappointed with Dr. B in discussing her psychotherapy, and he hypothesized that her desire to stop psychotherapy was an expression of anger, similar to her "cutting off" her parents. The MMPI-2 seemed to be an excellent instrument to explore Ms. S's questions, because of the great deal of information it provides about the management and expression of anger.

Second Contact with Insurer   After the initial interview with Ms. S, Steve called her insurer again to seek preauthorization for the assessment. At this point, because of his earlier contact, Steve simply needed to give his initial impressions of Ms. S, relate their mutually developed assessment questions, and give a rationale for the proposed sessions. The gatekeeper approved three additional service hours beyond the diagnostic interview: two hours of psychological testing (CPT 90830)—to cover the assessment intervention session, the scoring and interpretation of the MMPI-2, and the writing of the brief report—and one hour of psychotherapy (CPT 90844) for the assessment feedback session. (The actual bill for Ms. S's assessment was presented earlier, in Table 8.3.)

Analysis of MMPI-2 Results   Figure 8.1 presents the main graph of Ms. S's MMPI-2 results. The profile is valid and it appears that Ms. S responded to the items in a consistent manner (TRIN = 10; VRIN = 5). The configuration of L, F, and K suggests that she answered the test items candidly, without any significant attempt to influence her self-presentation. The profile reveals little emotional distress, although there were indications of family problems (FAM = 62T) as reported by her in the interview.

The major difficulties indicated by the profile are—not surprisingly—characterological issues concerning the expression of anger. To quote Butcher and

MMPI-2

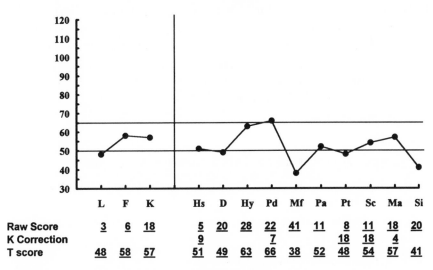

Figure 8.1. Ms. S's basic K-corrected MMPI-2 profile.

Williams (1992, pp. 116–117), people with Ms. S's code type (4–3) typically demonstrate:

> "... chronic, intense anger. ... Individuals with this clinical profile may harbor hostile and aggressive impulses but cannot express them appropriately. ... Usually somewhat overcontrolled, they tend to experience occasional brief episodes of assaultive, violent acting-out. They tend to lack insight into the origins and consequences of their aggressive behavior. ... Individuals with this code type show long-term and ingrained feelings of hostility toward family members. They tend to demand attention and approval from others. They are overly sensitive to rejection and are usually hostile when criticized. They may be outwardly conforming but inwardly rebellious."

From this information it was possible to formulate initial answers to Ms. S's assessment questions: She probably felt angry all the time because she tended to overcontrol her anger until she "boiled over." Managing her anger better would require her to be aware of her anger earlier and to express it directly while she could still do so in a controlled fashion. This strategy would likely be especially difficult because of her need for approval and her intense fears of rejection, and she would be most likely to defer to men (low 5). It would seem unwise to end therapy until she made more progress on these issues, and perhaps her current plans to terminate were an indirect way of expressing anger toward Dr. B.

Assessment Intervention Session   While discussing the above information with Ms. S would, by itself, most likely have been of therapeutic benefit, Steve decided to conduct an assessment intervention session with Ms. S to further explore her questions. As described earlier, one goal of this session was to create *in vivo* examples of

Ms. S's presenting problems, so that these could be discussed in light of the MMPI-2 results. Steve selected the Thematic Apperception Test (TAT) for the intervention session and began by giving Ms. S the first card (picturing the boy with the violin) along with the standard instructions. Ms. S told the following story:

> MS. S: "It's a little boy whose parents make him play the violin. He doesn't really want to practice. He's sitting there looking at it, going 'Why do I have to do this? I've already put in my work today.' He begrudgingly picks it up and begins to practice."
>
> SEF: "What is he feeling?"
>
> MS. S: "Tired."

Below is the dialogue that Steve and Ms. S had following this story:

> SEF: "That seems like the kind of situation where a child might feel frustrated. I noticed you said 'tired.'"
>
> MS. S: "You're right, maybe this boy could say 'Listen mom, I don't like the violin,' but he doesn't."
>
> SEF: "And he's tired. Is that at all like you?"
>
> MS. S: "I do a lot of things in my life and I would probably choose to cut back, but that's what I really get a kick out of so I won't . . . . When I'm frustrated I really go gung ho and clean house, etc. As Dr. B puts it, I 'stuff it.'"
>
> SEF: "This little boy does too. How about telling the story over again with the little boy being more assertive?"

Ms. S then told the following story to Card I:

> "Okay, the beginning's the same. He comes home and his mother tells him to go practice the violin. He sits there and looks at the violin, thinking 'I don't really want to do this. What I really want to do is get on my bike and go play with Billy down the road and go to our fort in the woods.' Finally, he looks at the violin long enough and turns and tells him mom, 'I want to go play.'"
>
> SEF: "What happens then?"
>
> MS. S: "His mom tells him, 'Okay, but you'll have to practice when you get home.'"
>
> SEF: "How does he feel?"
>
> MS. S: "Relieved that he got out of it and he goes and plays with Billy at the fort."

Again, Steve led Ms. S in a discussion:

> SEF: "How did it feel to tell that?"
>
> MS. S: "Well, I noticed my nails in my palm again. It's difficult, although it makes so much more sense. For some reason it doesn't set well with me. It's not my style. . . ."
>
> SEF: "You said 'it doesn't set well.' What about it?"
>
> MS. S: "It just feels uncomfortable. I think it's a good thing. It just feels wrong."
>
> SEF: "Can you describe the discomfort?"
>
> MS. S: "I'm not terribly assertive. It's intimidating to go up against people."

Notice how these responses provide rich examples of the difficulties described in the MMPI-2 code book. With Steve's guidance, Ms. S is "discovering" on her own the results of the standardized testing.

The assessment intervention session continued with Steve asking Ms. S to tell an "assertive story" to Card 4 (a picture of a woman with her hand on the arm of a determined looking man):

> MS. S: "It appears to be like this 1930s kind of picture. He's a rugged blue-collar working man and she's a stay-at-home housewife. In my mind there's not much assertive about that. The only story that comes to mind is her hanging on to him and saying, 'Don't go—stay with me.'
>
> ... He's gotten up this morning and he's getting ready to go do a fairly dangerous job. His wife has been concerned about it. She tries to grab hold of him and tell him not to go. He basically pushes her aside and goes on to work."

Once again, the ensuing discussion confirmed the results of the MMPI-2:

> MS. S: "I just couldn't think of an assertive story."
>
> SEF: "Well it sounds like the man's being assertive."
>
> MS. S: "Oh, I didn't think about that. I thought I had to make the woman assertive."
>
> SEF: "It was easier to picture him assertive?"
>
> MS. S: "Yeah, I don't know why."
>
> SEF: "Is that similar to you—that you have more experience with men being assertive than women?"
>
> MS. S: "It's similar to my growing-up life. . . . My mom was not very verbally assertive . . ."

Here we see the expression of Ms. S's internalized stereotypes of men and women, shown in her low score on Scale 5 of the MMPI-2.

Because of her difficulties telling an assertive story to Card 4, Steve then modeled an assertive story by telling about a woman confronting her husband about an affair. Ms. S enthusiastically claimed to like the story.

> MS. S: "That was great. I like the way she did that."
>
> SEF: "What gets in the way of your imagining stories like that?"
>
> MS. S: "I get so angry some of the time that I don't want to say things that are hurtful and I might be sorry for. I know grudges build up in me, then sometimes I blindside my husband over some small thing."
>
> SEF: "So you're afraid of hurting others with your anger?"
>
> MS. S: "And not making sense. It'll sound like the babbling of a crazy woman."

The final insight came when Steve asked Ms. S to tell an "angry or assertive story" to Card 18GF, a picture of a younger woman supporting an older woman on a staircase:

> MS. S: "It looks like a woman strangling somebody. The older woman is maybe the mother. She [the younger woman] has never had a very good relationship with her mother and her

mother is ailing. She's been taking care of her for years. The mother's continued to treat her bad even though the daughter's become her caretaker. The mother said one thing too many and she [the daughter] just turned her around and backed her up and put her hand around her neck and said, 'If you don't knock it off I'm going to choke you.' . . ."

This story provided the crucial piece for Steve to make a summary interpretation:

SEF: "How does that feel?"

MS. S: "God awful! I never thought I would make up a story about choking somebody. That wasn't confrontation either."

SEF: "Well what I'm wondering is if you don't stuff your anger for so long, like the boy with the violin, that you build up huge grudges. Then when it all comes tumbling out it's pretty explosive—even violent. Then you might feel foolish and ashamed and start holding it all in again."

MS. S: "I think that's right. I think of my father and I never wanted to do that to some-body else. He could get so out of control. But are you saying that because I won't be angry that I end up acting like him?"

SEF: "Perhaps so. Things might work better if you could give yourself more permis-sion to be angry in small doses. Then you might not explode so much at your children."

Feedback Session   As might be expected, the assessment intervention session had well prepared Ms. S for the MMPI-2 feedback. Ms. S's first two questions were easily addressed in the first part of the feedback session. Steve was able to use another well-known characteristic of persons with the 4–3 profile to confront Ms. S about her plans to terminate psychotherapy. The following excerpt is from the last third of the feedback session:

SEF: "There is one other characteristic of people with your test scores that I'd like to discuss. I think it might have to do with your last question."

MS. S: "Okay."

SEF: "People with test scores like yours have a strong desire to be taken care of, often because they didn't get much nurturing while growing up—which certainly sounds like it's true for you. Unfortunately, these people were also taught that they should basically take care of themselves. Thus, they usually find it very hard to ask for things from people. This typically leads to a lot of frustration inside that others aren't reading their minds and doing more for them. There's a real Catch-22 going on, of wanting a lot and being frustrated that others aren't picking up on it. Do you think that fits for you?"

MS. S: "Oh yes. I'm always wanting my husband to do more things around the house, but I never ask him to. I just get furious about it."

SEF: "Of course, because you're afraid to say something for fear of being unreason-able like your father."

MS. S: "Exactly."

SEF: "I'm wondering, do you ever get frustrated with Dr. B and wish that she were doing more for you?"

MS. S: (looking tense) "I'm not sure what you mean."

SEF: "I'm thinking that sometimes you might want her to take better care of you — to read your mind — but that she might not pick up on it and that this could be frustrating for you."

MS. S: "Well now that you mention it, I do wish that she would come out more and tell me what I should do with my husband and my children. (She turns to Dr. B.) You're usually so noncommittal."

DR. B: "And does that make you angry?"

MS. S: "It's annoying. Because I feel I need more direction."

SEF: "Good for you. You see right now you're changing your pattern and being assertive. Can you tell Dr. B more about what you want from her?"

MS. S: "Well I've been wondering . . . I mean . . . we've been talking for some time about my husband coming in to our sessions. I have a really hard time asking him. I keep thinking that maybe if you asked him. . . ."

DR. B: "Is that something that you want?"

MS. S: "Well I think he might listen better if you ask."

DR. B: "I think I can do that. Let's talk about it more in our next session."

SEF: (to Ms. S) "Again, I think this is just great what you're doing — saying exactly what you want. I've been wondering . . . Do you think your plans to leave therapy had anything to do with these types of frustrations?"

MS. S: "Well, I guess so. I've been feeling so stuck. . . ."

SEF: "I'm thinking that if you can learn to express your anger and frustrations more, then you'll have other options besides breaking off relationships."

Written Report   Following the feedback session, Steve sent a brief written report to Ms. S, shown in Table 8.4. As described earlier, the purpose of this report was to summarize the answers to Ms. S's assessment questions.

Comments from Ms. S   As described in Finn (1996), we typically ask clients for written feedback following a Therapeutic Assessment. Ms. S responded to this request by writing a letter to Steve after she received his report. Below is an excerpt:

> The assessment was much more helpful than I ever imagined. I still can't believe that the MMPI told so much about me . . . and those story cards were absolutely amazing. . . . I never knew why I was so afraid of being angry. The way we put it together really made sense. . . . I've been thinking a lot about what you said about me not asking Dr. B for what I want and I've decided to stay in therapy for now. She agreed to call my husband and ask him to come in for some couples' sessions and yesterday we had our first one. It was hard but I did manage to tell him some of the things I've been furious about. . . . I didn't act too unreasonable and felt better afterwards. I'm starting to have hope again. . . . Thanks again for all your help.

Table 8.4 Written Report to Ms. S

MMPI-2 Report
Client: Ms. S   Age: 35
Referred by: Dr. B   Date: XX/XX/XX

1. Why am I so angry all the time?

Your scores on the MMPI-2 suggest that you tend to harbor frustration and resentments for fear of losing control and being unreasonable with your anger (like your father was). Thus, you feel angry all the time because you are holding in your anger. Unfortunately, because you don't express your anger in small doses, it tends to build up and then boil over in explosions—thereby confirming your worst fears and setting you up to try to suppress it all over again. The harder you try to hold in your anger, the angrier you'll feel.

2. What can I do to better manage my anger and express it?

I think the first key is to realize that you can't simply get rid of the part of you that feels anger. If you don't express it early on, it won't go away. Rather, the longer you hold it in, the more likely it is that your anger will pop out in ways that hurt someone or are embarrassing to you. I suggest you make a resolution to say something about your frustrations *as soon as you can* after realizing they are there. You may need to use Dr. B for support in doing this, but it should get easier as you practice and let out some of the old built-up anger. I also suggest you practice by expressing any frustration you have with Dr. B. She is paid to not take your anger personally, even if you do act like your father and get out of hand.

3. Is this a good time for me to stop therapy?

As we explored in the feedback session, I suspect that you've been thinking of stopping therapy because you've wanted more direction and help from Dr. B than you've been getting. If you can't express your frustrations about such things, it's understandable that you would see no option but to end a relationship. Unfortunately, this solution just perpetuates that problems you have with anger.

Instead of stopping therapy, I want to encourage you to keep telling Dr. B what you want from her (as you did in the feedback session) and how frustrating it is not to get what you want. I know that this will be scary, because the MMPI-2 suggests that you weren't allowed to ask for what you wanted as a child. In fact, you will know you are doing a good job at this if you think you are being unreasonably demanding with Dr. B. Again, remember that it is her job to help you sort this all out and that it is safer to practice with her than with your best friends or children.

Ms. S., thank you again for letting me get to know you. Feel free to contact me if you have any questions about this report. Also, enclosed you'll find the form I told you about, for you to give me feedback about the assessment. It will help me if you will fill this out and return it in the enclosed stamped envelope.

Best wishes,
Steve Finn
Stephen E. Finn, Ph.D.

Summary and Conclusions

Many psychologists feel the increased scrutiny of psychological assessment by managed care companies is unwarranted and represents professional harassment. We understand how frustrating it is for busy clinicians to respond to requests for paperwork and demands that they justify their work. Nevertheless, might the requirement of increased accountability be an opportunity for us psychologists to reexamine our assessment practices and raise our standards of care? Perhaps the increased scrutiny of managed care companies can lead us to better articulate the value of the MMPI-2 and other assessment instruments and to demonstrate through controlled research the benefits that psychological assessment can have on clients.

In this chapter, we have outlined a model of psychological assessment—Therapeutic Assessment—which collaboratively involves clients in framing assessment questions, interpreting test results, and tying test findings to their problems in living. While still in its early stages of development, Therapeutic Assessment with the MMPI-2 has been shown in controlled research to be highly beneficial to clients. Managed care companies have responded very favorably to our approach. At our clinic, we remain committed to training other professionals in Therapeutic Assessment and to researching its powerful effects.

ACKNOWLEDGMENTS   We wish to thank Mary E. Tonsager for her comments on an earlier draft of this chapter.

References

American Psychological Association. (1985). *Standards for educational and psychological testing*. Washington, D.C.: APA.

American Psychological Association. (1992). *Revised ethical principles for psychologists*. Washington, D.C.: APA.

Butcher, J. N., & Williams, C. L. (1992). *Essentials of MMPI-2 and MMPI-A interpretation*. Minneapolis, MN: University of Minnesota Press.

Finn, S. E. (1996). *A manual for using the MMPI-2 as a therapeutic intervention*. Minneapolis, MN: University of Minnesota Press.

Finn, S. E., & Bunner, M. (1993, March). Impact of test feedback on psychiatric inpatients' satisfaction with assessment. Presented at the 28th Annual Symposium on Recent Developments in the Use of the MMPI, St. Petersburg Beach, FL.

Finn, S. E., & Butcher, J. N. (1991). Clinical objective personality assessment. In M. Hersen, A. E. Kazdin, & A. S. Bellack (Eds.), *The clinical psychology handbook* (2nd edition, pp. 362–373). New York: Pergamon Press.

Finn , S. E., & Tonsager, M. E. (1992). Therapeutic effects of providing MMPI-2 test feedback to college students awaiting therapy. *Psychological Assessment 4*, 278–287.

Finn, S. E., & Tonsager, M. E. (in preparation). *Therapeutic Assessment: Using psychological testing to help clients change*.

Finn, S. E., Schroeder, D. G., & Tonsager, M. E. (1995). The Assessment Questionnaire-2 (AQ-2): A measure of clients' experiences with psychological assessment. Unpublished manuscript, Center for Therapeutic Assessment, Austin, TX.

Fischer, C. T. (1994). *Individualizing psychological assessment*. Hillsdale, NJ: Lawrence Erlbaum Associates. (Originally published in 1985).

Griffith, L. F. (1995). "Surviving no-frills mental health care: The future of psychological assessment". Unpublished manuscript, The Fielding Institute.

Holt, R. (1968). Editor's foreword. In D. Rapaport, M. M. Gill, & R. Schafer (Eds.), *Diagnostic psychological testing* (revised edition, pp. 1–44). New York: International Universities Press.

Korchin, S. J., & Schuldberg, D. (1981). The future of psychological assessment. *American Psychologist 36*, 1147–1158.

Meier, S. T. (1994). *The chronic crisis in psychological measurement and assessment*. San Diego: Academic Press.

Moreland, K. L., Fowler, R. D., & Honaker, L. M. (1994). Future directions in the use of psychological assessment for treatment planning and outcome assessment: Predictions and recommendations. In M. Maruish (Ed.), *The use of psychological testing in treatment planning and outcome assessment* (pp. 581–602). Hillsdale, NJ: Lawrence Erlbaum Associates.

Newman, M. (1996, March). Therapeutic effects of providing MMPI-2 assessment feedback to clients at a university counseling service: A collaborative approach. Presented at the 15th International Conference on Personality Assessment, Melbourne, Australia.

Swann, W. B., Jr. (1983). Self-verification: Bringing social reality into harmony with the self. In J. Suls & A. G. Greenwald (Eds.) *Social psychological perspectives on the self*, Vol. 2. Hillsdale, NJ: Lawrence Erlbaum Associates.

9

Use of Computer-Based Personality Test Reports in Treatment Planning

James N. Butcher

Psychological treatment proceeds more rapidly and effectively if objective personality information—from a comprehensive personality assessment instrument like the MMPI-2—can be incorporated early in the process. Great efforts have been made in the past toward speedy and reliable test processing so that results may be incorporated in the early stages of treatment. Consider the following scenario:

> The patient, a 48-year-old business executive, came to the medical facility for unexplained chest pains that he was experiencing. Following a thorough medical examination in which his physician was unable to determine a physical basis to his problem, his doctor, considering the possibility of an anxiety-based disorder, referred him for a psychological evaluation. His physician indicated that he would like for him to take the MMPI-2 before the appointment with the psychologist later in the day. Reluctantly, the patient consented to the testing. He was administered the MMPI-2 and shortly afterward was ushered into the psychologist's office by the nursing staff. The psychologist, after establishing a friendly and concerned rapport, began inquiring about the patient's current life stressors and how he attempted to deal with them. As the session proceeded the psychologist introduced a computer output of the client's MMPI-2 scores and discussed with him what the objective evaluation suggested—that in all likelihood the client was experiencing a great deal of anxiety and depression and was feeling panicked over his life circumstances or at least the way that he was perceiving them. What initially began as a diagnostic interview evolved into a treatment session, with a client now feeling more receptive to what the psychologist had to say!

The MMPI and MMPI-2 have a long tradition in clinical assessment and have been used extensively in assessing patients in pretreatment psychological evaluation (Rouse, et al, in press). This chapter is devoted to describing the use of automated interpretation and the impact of computer-based personality description can have in clinical assessment and treatment planning.

Computer-based test interpretation has a long tradition in psychological assessment going back to 1961 when John Pearson and Wendell Swenson programmed a computer to provide an interpretation of the original version of the MMPI at the Mayo Clinic (Rome et al., 1962). Computers have now become an indispensable standard for processing psychological assessment results in many health care, forensic, mental health, and other settings. The psychological practitioner can employ a computer in a number of ways in the clinical evaluation to administer test items, to score and profile test results, and even to interpret test scores and generate a comprehensive narrative report on the client.

The use of the electronic computers in assessment allows the psychologist to synthesize vast amounts of information and provide interpretations that can be incorporated in clinical tasks such as determining prognosis and treatment planning. This chapter will address the use of computer-based psychological test reports in treatment planning and evaluation as follows. First, the rationale and value of using computer-based reports will be explored. Next, the clinical use of one computer-based test report, the Minnesota Report for the MMPI-2, will be described, and illustrated with clients in psychological treatment. After a practical case example is described, this chapter will conclude with a discussion of potential problems with computer-based psychological test reports and remedies for avoiding problems.

Computer-Based Psychological Tests in Treatment Planning

Computer-based objective test interpretation can be an enormous aid to the practitioner in the early stages of psychological treatment.

1. The use of computer-based interpretation provides a more comprehensive and objective summary of relevant test-based hypotheses than the practitioner is usually able to obtain in the time available for assessment. The computer interpretive report can incorporate more relevant scores in the assessment and will not ignore or fail to consider important information that many human interpreters do in more subjective assessment or that is customarily found in the rushed setting of an active clinical practice. Computer-assisted test interpretations are usually more comprehensive and more substantially documented than reports developed by individual interpreters.

2. The use of computer-based test reports avoids or minimizes subjectivity in describing the patient's problems. The objective approach to interpretation provides agreed upon interpretations that are keyed to standard test variables.

3. Computer interpretation systems are more reliable than interpretations of individual practitioners on the same set of scores; also, a computer report will produce the same report whereas clinician's interpretation will vary, depending upon situational circumstances.

4. Computer-based psychological test reports are cost-effective and can be available for the clinician very quickly—even in the first session. For example, as noted in the example above, a test report can be available within minutes after the client has completed the inventory. The cost of having computer based reports available in the clinical situation is relatively low and determined, in part, on the volume of tests administered in the practice. For example, if the clinic uses 10 MMPI-2s in a month, the cost for mail-in processing is $25 for each case; the cost for a protocol scored by computer in office would be about $24 each. If the clinic uses 20 or more administrations in a month, the cost for mail in processing is $23 for each; the cost for computer interpretation in-house would be $22 for each protocol.

MMPI-2 Processing Formats

Several methods for data entry and computer-based test processing are available for practitioners to consider depending on their available computer hardware and whether or not they need immediate processing.

Mail-in Service   The oldest method of test-based scoring and interpretation that became commercially available was the mail-in test processing option. Mail-in scoring continues to be a viable effective format for practitioners because it is an easy means of test processing if clinic volume is low or when rapid processing is not required. For example, for clients who are seen on a weekly basis, test results could be processed between visits. This approach is limited by the speed of the mail so if immediate results are required, other options should be considered. In the mail-in mode, tests are administered to the clients using a paper and pencil form and then mailed to the testing service for processing. This format is usually efficient and relatively low cost.

In-office computer processing   There are also several "in-house" test processing options available for computer interpretation. If the practitioner or clinic has a computer available, a software program is available that can *administer MMPI-2 test items on-line*. In this option, the client is presented the items on a computer screen and responds to them by typing his or her answers on the computer keyboard. This format is attractive because it is usually faster and liked by many patients today because it is faster. However, this processing option requires that the clinician have available a computer on which the patients can be administered the items—a task that will tie up the machine for about 1 to 1–1½ hours.

Key-Entry Option   Another scoring option involves administering the items by a paper and pencil format and having a clerical assistant key-enter the items on a computer file—a procedure that usually takes about 10 minutes. Patients typically do not mind this approach, but staff time commitments might not allow this option to work optimally.

Optical scanning   A third widely used method of test processing involves administering the items with the paper and pencil version and then *optically reading* the answer form. An optical scanner, a type of copier that reads blackened marks directly into a computer, can be tied into most computers. The optical scanner usually costs an additional three or four thousand dollars, but is very cost-effective (requiring little staff time for processing) and will quickly pay for itself in time savings if about eight or more tests are processed a week.

Data Telephone Transmission   MMPI-2 responses can also be submitted for scoring by transmitting them electronically to the scoring service computer. The test answers are transmitted by modem to the test interpretation service for processing, and the scored results and interpretations are usually returned to the user immediately by modem.

Fax Processing Option   With the broad availability of fax machines it has become possible to transmit answer sheets to the scoring service by fax. Test processing by fax is relatively fast. In using the fax machine as a test processing option, the practitioner does not need a computer and modem. The practitioner administers a paper and pencil form of the test and faxes the answer sheet to the test scoring company for processing.

The Computerized Report

The MMPI-2 is used in this chapter to illustrate computer-based interpretation because the MMPI and its derivatives have been the most widely used clinical instruments in most settings (Lubin, Larsen, Matarazzo, 1984; Piotrowski & Keller, 1989). Computer-based MMPI-2 (MMPI) interpretation is derived from the line of research that demonstrated that tests can be more effectively interpreted in an objective (actuarial) manner than through clinical interpretation strategies (see Meehl, 1954). A psychological report comprised of objectively applied personality and clinical symptom descriptions that have been established for the test scales or patterns can be more accurately combined by machine than reports derived by clinical means.

A computer-based test interpretation program for the MMPI-2 is essentially an electronic textbook or resource database. Computer-generated clinical reports can be conceptualized as structured or "canned" statements that can be applied to individuals who score in particular ranges on psychological tests. The interpretive paragraphs in the computerized report are stored in computer memory and automatically retrieved when the profile matches particular scale elevations, profile types, or scale indices. The behavioral correlate information on which reports are based can be found in several sources (see Butcher & Williams, 1992; Graham, 1993; Graham, Ben-Porath, and McNulty, in press; Butcher et al., 1990; Gilberstadt & Duker, 1963; Lewandowski & Graham, 1972; Marks et al., 1975).

The actuarial description of personality from the original MMPI scales is very well established; however, the empirical research on any psychological test does not sufficiently describe all possible MMPI-2 scale combinations. Some interpretations are based upon expert conclusions about the meaning of scale scores. Fowler (1969) suggested the term "automated clinician" to more accurately describe computer-based interpretive systems since reports are generally based on clinical judgment in addition to the empirical actuarial data. The validity and utility of the computerized systems will depend, in great part, upon how closely the developer has relied upon to the actuarial data and whether clearly established correlates have been used to develop narrative descriptions.

Case Illustration

The client was a 37-year-old Asian American male who was referred to therapy by his employer after an incident in which he allegedly threatened a fellow employee who filed a complaint against him. A psychological assessment was undertaken in an effort to determine if there were possible personality factors present that might need to be addressed in psychological treatment planning. The therapist was concerned over the possibility that the client's behavior problems at work might be related to an underlying personality disorder. In addition, the therapist was concerned that the client might be experiencing other symptoms of mental disorder that might require further attention in therapy. The diagnostic questions centered around whether the client was depressed and experiencing post-traumatic stress symptoms.

The patient, a somewhat quiet and reticent man, had been an hourly employee of the company in a manufacturing job (on the production line) for about 5 years. The fellow employee, a woman, who filed the complaint against the patient has complained about the patient's aggressive behavior to her supervisor in the past. On this occasion she felt that he was physically threatening her and she was afraid for her safety. The patient, originally from Southeast Asia, has had one year of college and has lived in the United States since he was 5 years old. His therapist reported that the client seemed to have low self-esteem and thought that his communication skills needed to be improved. The therapist also indicated that the client has a tendency to openly and uncontrollably express anger toward others.

In the initial therapy interview the patient reported that he was experiencing sleep and appetite problems and indicated that he was not experiencing much pleasure in life at this time. The patient indicated that he was depressed and was having some family problems, particularly with his daughter. He reported that he was also feeling guilty about the problem at work and felt that others might think he was a "bad person." He impressed the therapist as a troubled man who may have been severely affected as a result of his having been severely physically abused as a child.

The therapist administered the MMPI-2 in order to determine if there were significant personality or mental health problems or long-standing personality problems that might affect the treatment. See the Appendix at the end of this chapter.

Hypotheses About the Client's Amenability to Treatment from the Minnesota Report

The Minnesota Report pointed out a number of problems with the patient's performance on the testing that questioned his cooperation with the evaluation. First, he omitted five items on the test. This number is not sufficient to invalidate the test, however, any item omissions in a pretreatment planning situation is suspect—indicating that the client is not fully cooperating with the symptom review and disclosing information to the clinician. Second, the client produced a relatively high TRIN (T) score. This suggests that he has been somewhat inconsistent with responding to questions and has tended to endorse similar content in different directions. This situation suggests that he has not been fully cooperative with the evaluation in sharing personal information. The therapist should be aware that the client may not be very open to disclosing personal information in a reliable and consistent manner in therapy. If possible, the treatment should be structured as soon as possible to confront the possibility of noncompliance before it results in a failed treatment situation.

The clinical and content scales of the MMPI-2 reflect a number of problems that the practitioner needs to consider in beginning psychological treatment. First, the prominent MMPI-2 scores of Pd and Ma reflect a strong possibility of an underlying personality disorder that could result in early termination from therapy. Problems of impulsivity and aggressiveness appear to be more salient than anxiety or depression, which appear to be minimal. Individuals with this pattern typically do not fare well in verbal psychotherapy in that they often do not see a reason to change their behavior but instead tend to project and externalize blame. They tend to avoid responsibility for their own actions and may engage in acting out behavior of an aggressive quality. Consequently, the prognosis for this individual modifying his pattern of thinking and behavior is poor. The possibility that he would not be a serious candidate for remediation should be considered by the therapist. He also shows some signs of anger control problems and potential substance abuse problems that require further attention. Any psychological treatment considered with this client should consider anger-control management and substance abuse potential as primary goals.

The psychological assessment was valuable in this case because it forewarned the therapist that the prognosis for the patient to alter his personality in any substantial way through brief verbal psychotherapy was generally low given the long-standing personality characteristics of interpersonal manipulatation and persistent self-oriented behavior that he manifested. In all likelihood the client's irresponsible behavior and reluctance to engage in treatment would contribute to strong treatment resistance in treatment, and his low impulse control would likely continue to present problems if he became angry. In this case it is unlikely that a brief psychotherapeutic intervention would bring about the desired effect and that firmer administrative and supervisory involvement to modifiy his behavior might be required. Treatment would most effectively center around a behaviorally oriented program aimed at anger control possibly in the context of a substance abuse evaluation and treatment.

Clinical Use of a Computerized MMPI-2 Report: Providing Client Feedback in Therapy

A suggested approach for using computer-based test reports in pretreatment planning will be described and illustrated. The utility of having MMPI-based information for giving the client personality information he or she can use in therapy has been clearly established (Finn, 1990; Finn & Tonsager, 1992; Newman, 1996).

Therapy patients are administered the MMPI-2 early in the treatment process or prior to the beginning of therapy. It is recommended that the practitioner, evaluating the client in pretreatment planning, also conduct a test-feedback session with the client. In the test feedback session, the individual's test-taking attitudes and their implication for appraising treatment motivation and readiness for therapy can be discussed. The extent and description of the individual's problems, symptoms, and so on can be described. Finally, recommendations and predictions about prognosis for resolving problems can be explored with potential strategies for problem resolution suggested. This approach to providing MMPI-2 feedback in pretreatment planning can be found in more detail (Butcher, 1990; Erdberg, 1979; Quirk et al., 1995; Finn & Tonsager, 1992; Chapter 8, this volume).

Several factors need to be taken into account in conducting a test-feedback session. The current psychological status of the person receiving the feedback information needs to be carefully considered. In providing test information to clients, the clinician needs to assess the capacity of the client to understand and utilize the information available. For example, effective feedback provision requires that the client have sufficient reality contact and a "receptive" attitude toward the session in order to be able to understand and integrate the test information accurately. The client's current cognitive functioning and fund of information (educational background) also need to be considered. For example, if the client is intelligent and well educated, more specific and detailed information can be discussed than if the individual is less well educated or less capable intellectually. The presentation should be varied to suit the individual's general ability to comprehend and integrate information. The type of setting in which the test was given is an important variable to take into account. Published sources such as Butcher & Williams (1992), Graham (1993), and Greene (1991) can be consulted to obtain more specific information about relevant MMPI-2 scale descriptors for various patient groups.

Value of Computer-Based Report Feedback

Providing test feedback in therapy has been found to be a valuable treatment strategy.

1. Test-based feedback provides an objective, "outside" opinion. The therapist can raise hypotheses for the client to explore without being faulted for raising a sensitive topic or for "criticizing" the patient. For example, when a particular client is suspected of having a substance abuse problem that might be a factor in the case, this fact can be introduced early without the therapist being "blamed" for raising it. The clinician can introduce such problems by stating "The computer report suggests that you are having a problem with. . . ." Having difficult topics directly introduced from an outside source early in therapy can give the therapist and client some issues or problem areas to explore together rather than pitting them against each other in the early stages of therapy.

2. The computer report lays out a great deal of personality-based information up front in the session. Problem areas brought out may be dealt with on a continuing basis: The computer report can serve as an archive to be referred to from time

to time. Once introduced, a topic becomes part of the material that needs to be addressed as therapy proceeds.

Steps in Providing Test Feedback to Clients

The following strategy for providing test feedback to clients in pretreatment planning, described by Butcher (1990), is an effective means of incorporating feedback into therapy.

Step 1. It is usually a valuable strategy to first provide the client with information about the MMPI-2 in order to give them a basis for appreciating the credibility and objectivity of the test. It is often useful to point out to the client that the MMPI has been used for over 55 years in mental health settings and is the most widely used clinical test in the United States today (Lubin et al., 1984, Piotrowski & Keller, 1989). The MMPI/MMPI-2 is also the most widely used personality instrument in other countries as well, with over 150 translations of the original MMPI and over 25 for MMPI-2 (see Butcher, 1996).

Step 2. Describe the extensive research basis of the MMPI-2 by briefly explaining the way in which the scales were developed. It may be helpful to use the client's own test scores and profiles as the test scales are being described. Clients can usually gain an understanding of the clinical importance of scales by viewing their own scores in comparison with other people or clinical problem groups.

Step 3. Explain how the validity indicators operate on the MMPI-2 to provide a picture of the person's general approach to the testing. The validity section of the report can be employed to summarize the client's current treatment accessibility. Describe how the client might have presented himself or herself and how he or she appears to be viewing the problem situation at this time. Perhaps they were defensive and inaccessible on the testing or were exaggerating their symptoms. The individual's motivation for being understood by the therapist—his or her accessibility to therapy—can be effectively explored through examining their approach to the validity measures. This discussion often leads to unveiling potentially destructive antitreatment attitudes on the part of some clients.

Step 4. Discuss the likely interpretations of the client's highest ranging clinical scores in terms of what prevailing personality factors, attitudes, symptoms, problem areas, and so forth, are important. Try to avoid using psychological jargon by translating technical words into language the person can understand. The extent to which the client's problems can be placed in a normative perspective can be described. For example, it is useful to point out how frequent the client's problems are in comparison with other patients in therapy and with persons in other different settings.

Step 5. Describe important content themes that the client has endorsed through the items. Discuss the clinically significant scale elevations on the MMPI-2 Content Scale descriptions (see Butcher et al., 1990) and how they can be used to summarize problem areas. The Content Scales are particularly valuable in giving test feedback to clients because they are viewed as summarizing "messages" or communication between the client and therapist. The Content Scale scores represent direct self-disclosures of problems, attitudes, beliefs, or symptoms. The meanings of these scale elevations are usually readily accepted by the client because he or she has openly endorsed them in the inventory.

Step 6. The therapist–client dialogue during the feedback process is an extremely valuable therapeutic interchange. It is important to encourage the client to ask questions about his or her scores on the test in order to clear up any questions or concerns that he or she might have about the meanings of the test. Some clients might become fixated on an inconsequential, trivial, or incorrect point. Therefore, it is important to detect these and deal with them in the session. The practitioner needs to correct any erroneous beliefs about the testing that the client might have acquired in receiving feedback.

Step 7. Discuss with the client how he or she feels the test has described his or her problems and behaviors. This discussion can help to summarize the feedback that has been given to him or her and can also help the clinician evaluate whether there are elements of the test interpretation that were particularly surprising or misunderstood by the client. Finally, this session will provide the therapist with clues about the client's openness to insight and amenability to changing his or her behavior.

Points a Therapist Needs to Consider in Using Computerized Psychological Reports

Several issues concerning using computer-based personality test evaluations in treatment planning need to be addressed. It is important to ensure that the particular interpretation in the computer-based report is an appropriate match for the patient's test scores. The therapist needs to ensure that the particular interpretations in the computer-based report are appropriate for the client. The closer the match between the client's scores and those of the prototype pattern on which the personality descriptions are based, the more relevant and appropriate the report will be. The best way of ensuring a good match of the report with the client is for the therapist to have a good working knowledge of the instrument by studying one of the basic texts (Butcher & Williams, 1992; Graham, 1993) or keeping up to date through continuing professional education workshops. The computer-based clinical report is a summary of the most likely patient characteristics and problems for the particular set of test scores.

To effectively use computer-based reports a clinician must be alert to and avoid the following potential problems:

Computerized results are considered to be an aid to assessment and should not be considered a substitute for clinical observation and astute integration of pertinent information. The clinician needs to be aware that computer-derived reports can produce a complacent attitude about the assessment. Computerized assessments can engender an overly passive stance toward clinical assessment. Much can be learned about a patient by carefully observing and keeping in close touch with the test situation, as well as through thoughtful summarizing and integrating the results.

Computer report interpretations may contain general descriptions which may not be specific enough to provide useful descriptions to some clients. Although they may sound useful, insightful, and descriptive, some reports may contain some overly generalized statements that are not very useful in making clinical decisions. Vague or general statements that might emerge in a computer-based report may be so nonspecific that they apply to virtually anyone. Try to employ only those descriptions that can lead to good therapeutic interaction.

Be aware that computer-based reports are protypic descriptions that are pertinent to a class of scores that the patient's profile matches. As noted above, not all information included in a computer-based assessment report matches every patient. Some correlates for a particular scale pattern that are obtained from research articles or textbooks and included in the report might not apply for any and all cases that have the test pattern. The clinician needs to determine if the test hypotheses from the report are relevant and appropriate for the client. Review the patient's report in advance and determine if there are potentially useful points that can be made and select the major points to be discussed carefully. Any interpretations or hypotheses that are not appropriate, based upon what we know about the client from other sources of information, should be ignored or presented as tentative. An interesting situation that sometimes occurs in conducting feedback with computer-based reports is that some piece of information may, according to the patient, not fit. It is not unusual for therapists in therapy to make slightly or even greatly "off track" interpretations in the process of providing test feedback to clients. Therapists usually learn how to deal with off-target interpretations during their training. For example, the client's view that a particular interpretation does not fit him or her may not be accurate—it may be that the interpretation does not "sit well" with the client at the time it was introduced but may need to be explored further or at a later time in therapy to determine its relevance.

The psychotherapists, in providing test feedback to the client, may choose to use some of the profile graphs or parts of the narrative to explain the results to the client. The graphs are particularly valuable in showing the client how his or her score on a particular scale compares with "normals" or other clinical patients. Practitioners need to ensure that computer-derived test reports are appropriately controlled and are not misused (Pope et al., 1993). Clients should not be given their report to keep. Computer-based psychological reports, as usually noted on the narrative, were developed for professional use. Computer printouts that become a part of a patient's file should be properly labeled to prevent them from being mistaken for the final report on the patient. We need to keep in mind that the computerized test reports are *raw test data* not final products. They are not recommended to stand alone as a psychological report. If a computer printout is kept in a patient's file, it should contain language as to how the information was used in the final report (Butcher & Williams, 1992) to assure that future users of the file will not mistake the computer-based hypotheses for the clinician's final report. The clinician therapist should assure that the information on the computerized report is properly labelled.

Accuracy of Computer-Based Systems in Describing Personality

Computer interpretation systems that are based closely on research validated indexes tend to have similar outputs. However, some research has shown that different test interpretation services may differ with respect to the amount of information and accuracy of the interpretations (Eyde et al., 1991). Practitioners using an automated interpretation system should be familiar with the issues of computerized test interpretation generally and the validity research on the particular system used (see Eyde, 1993; Eyde et al. 1991; Moreland, 1987). Several studies depicting the accuracy of the Minnesota Report have been conducted. In one study, computer-based reports were compared with clinician ratings of MMPI profiles. The Minnesota Personnel Adjustment Rating Report was empirically evaluated as follows. Butcher (1988) conducted a study in which 262 airline-pilot applicants who were evaluated by use of computer-based decision rules and were also rated by expert clinicians. The applicants were rated in terms of their "overall level of adjustment." Clinicians, using the MMPI profile, rated applicants according to whether their adjustment was viewed as "Adequate," "Problems Possible," or "Problems Likely." The cases were processed by the Minnesota Personnel Report Adjustment Rating Rules. The results of the study showed that the computer decisions and the clinical ratings were congruent in the majority of cases, indicating that computer-derived decisions are highly consistent with the decisions that expert clinicians make on the same profiles, however, the amount of time savings for the computer-based decisions was substantially greater than that for the clinical judgments.

Several studies have demonstrated the validity of the MMPI Minnesota Clinical Report in clinical contexts. Moreland and Onstad (1985), for example, demonstrated that the Minnesota Report accurately described personality characteristics and problems in clinical settings. They had clinicians rate Minnesota Report narratives compared with a control (random) report and found that actual reports were viewed as more accurate than the control report. In a more comprehensive comparative study, Eyde et al. (1987) and Fishburne et al. (1988) evaluated the accuracy of seven computer-based MMPI reports. The MMPI answer sheets for several patients were submitted to seven commercial computer-reporting services for processing. The computer-based reports from each were then compared for accuracy by (a) initially separating the reports into component statements and coded, (b) submitting the separate statements (with statements from the various reports intermixed) to clinicians familiar with the case, and (c) asking the clinicians to rate the accuracy of the statement. The Minnesota Report was rated consistently as the most accurate of the seven MMPI clinical reports studied. In addition to this research, two recent studies explored the accuracy of the Minnesota Report in assessing clients in mental health settings in other countries. Berah et al. (1993) in Australia and Gillet et al. (1996) in France found high degrees of rated accuracy in therapists' ratings of computer-based MMPI-2 reports.

Summary

Computer-based psychological test reports can add significantly to the practitioner's clinical evaluations in terms of providing valuable, thorough, accurate information that is processed in a timely manner. Computer-based test interpretations are an objective and comprehensive means of interpreting psychological tests; they can be rapidly processed and made available early in the treatment session; and they have a high degree of reliability in describing patient problems and are formatted to serve as a user-friendly feedback mode.

This chapter provided a discussion of how clinicians can incorporate computer-based information into their clinical practice. A case example was included to illustrate the types of information available and the ways it can be incorporated into treatment planning. Several possible problems that could arise with the use of computer-based psychological tests were noted, and suggestions for minimizing them were discussed. It is important for practitioners to be aware of and avoid the potential problems that can occur with the use of automated assessment into one's clinical practice.

Appendix

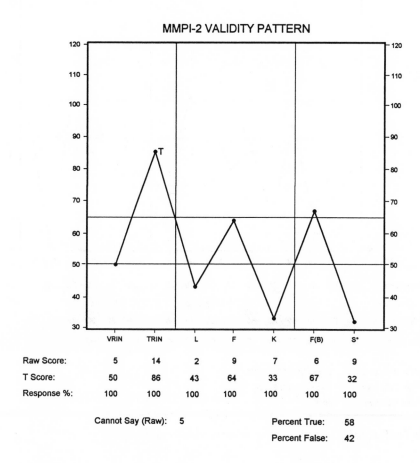

MMPI-2 VALIDITY PATTERN

	VRIN	TRIN	L	F	K	F(B)	S*
Raw Score:	5	14	2	9	7	6	9
T Score:	50	86	43	64	33	67	32
Response %:	100	100	100	100	100	100	100

Cannot Say (Raw): 5

Percent True: 58
Percent False: 42

*Experimental

Figure 9.1. MMPI-2 validity pattern.

MMPI-2 BASIC AND SUPPLEMENTARY SCALES PROFILE

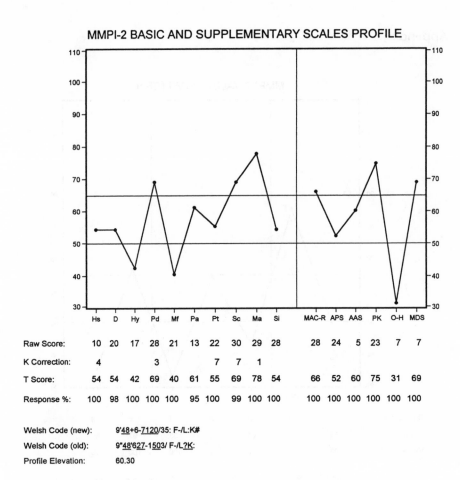

	Hs	D	Hy	Pd	Mf	Pa	Pt	Sc	Ma	Si		MAC-R	APS	AAS	PK	O-H	MDS
Raw Score:	10	20	17	28	21	13	22	30	29	28		28	24	5	23	7	7
K Correction:	4			3			7	7	1								
T Score:	54	54	42	69	40	61	55	69	78	54		66	52	60	75	31	69
Response %:	100	98	100	100	100	95	100	99	100	100		100	100	100	100	100	100

Welsh Code (new):   9'48+6-7120/35: F-/L:K#
Welsh Code (old):   9"48'627-1503/ F-/L?K:
Profile Elevation: 60.30

Figure 9.2. MMPI-2 basic and supplementary scales profile.

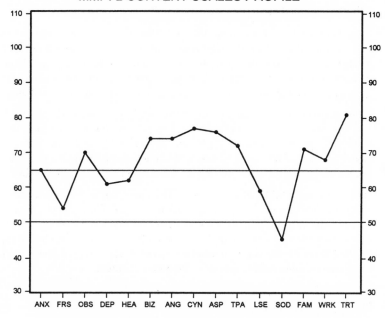

MMPI-2 CONTENT SCALES PROFILE

	ANX	FRS	OBS	DEP	HEA	BIZ	ANG	CYN	ASP	TPA	LSE	SOD	FAM	WRK	TRT
Raw Score:	12	5	11	10	10	9	13	21	17	15	8	5	13	17	17
T Score:	65	54	70	61	62	74	74	77	76	72	59	45	71	68	81
Response %:	100	100	100	100	100	100	100	100	100	100	100	100	100	97	100

Figure 9.3. MMPI-2 content scales profile.

Figure 9.4. Minnesota Report Narrative.

PROFILE VALIDITY

The client omitted 5 items on the MMPI-2. Although this is not enough to invalidate the resulting MMPI-2 clinical profile, some of his scale scores may be lower than expected because of these omissions. It may be helpful to talk with him to determine the reasons for his omissions. Many clinicians prefer to readminister the omitted items (listed at the end of this report) to ensure the most accurate interpretation possible.

The pattern of his item omissions should be carefully evaluated. He omitted from 10 to 15 percent of the items on Scale Pa2. Omitting items may result in an underestimate of the problems measured by the affected scales. Of course, any scale elevations above a T score of 60 should be interpreted, but it should be understood that if there are omitted items, the score probably underestimates problems reflected by the scale.

This is a valid MMPI-2 clinical profile. The client was quite cooperative with the evaluation and appears to be willing to disclose personal information. There may be some tendency on the part of the client to be overly frank and to exaggerate his symptoms in an effort to obtain help. In addition, please note that the client's approach to the MMPI-2 items was somewhat inconsistent. He endorsed items in a pattern that suggests some carelessness or inattention to content.

SYMPTOMATIC PATTERNS

This report was developed using the Pd and Ma scales as the prototype. This MMPI-2 clinical profile suggests that the client does not view his problems as extreme or unmanageable. However, he appears to be rather extroverted, enthusiastic, verbal, spontaneous, and uninhibited. With a high need for stimulation, he engages in many activities, but he may become so involved in them that he ignores important aspects of life. Individuals with this profile tend to be somewhat self-indulgent, hedonistic, and manipulative in order to gratify their wishes. The client shows a lack of impulse control and poor social judgment at times, appearing rather irresponsible.

He may become easily bored and will go on to other things even if some projects or tasks are left incomplete. Such clients tend to ignore or deny problems rather than confront them directly.

The client has a low Mf score, suggesting that he has a rather limited range of interests and tends to prefer stereotyped masculine activities over literary and artistic pursuits or introspective experiences. He tends to be somewhat competitive and needs to see himself as masculine. He probably prefers to view women in subservient roles. Interpersonally, he is likely to be intolerant and insensitive, and others may find him rather crude, coarse, or narrow-minded.

In addition, the following description is suggested by the content of the client's item responses. The client's recent thinking is likely to be characterized by obsessiveness and indecision. He may feel somewhat estranged and alienated from people. He is suspicious of the actions of others, and he may tend to blame them for his negative frame of mind. He has endorsed a number of items reflecting a high degree of anger.

He appears to have a high potential for explosive behavior at times. He reports some antisocial beliefs and attitudes, admits to rule violations, and acknowledges antisocial behavior in the past. He has endorsed a number of unusual, bizarre ideas that suggest some difficulties with his thinking. He seems to be highly manipulative and self-indulgent. He seems to have had much past conflict with authority and is quite resentful of societal standards of conduct. He shows some competitive and possibly hostile behavior at times. He endorses statements that show some inability to control his anger. He may physically or verbally attack others when he is angry.

PROFILE FREQUENCY

It is usually valuable in MMPI-2 clinical profile interpretation to take into consideration the relative frequency of a given profile pattern in various settings. The client's MMPI-2 high-point clinical scale score (Ma), the highest scale score peak in his profile, is found in 15.2% of the MMPI-2 normative sample of men. Moreover, 8.3% of the sample have Ma as the peak score at or above a T score of 65, and 6.3% have well-defined Ma spikes. This elevated MMPI-2 profile configuration (4–9/9–4) is very rare in samples of normals, occurring in less than 1% of the MMPI-2 normative sample of men. His MMPI-2 high-point clinical scale score (Ma) peak is the most frequent high-point score in the sample of active-duty military men, occurring in 33.3% of the sample (Butcher, Jeffrey, et al., 1990). Furthermore, 18.5% of the sample have the Ma scale at or over a T score of 65, and 15.9% of these are well-defined Ma spikes at that level of elevation.

He scored relatively high on MAC-R, suggesting the possibility of a drug- or alcohol-abuse problem. The base rate data on his profile type among residents in alcohol and drug programs should also be evaluated. His MMPI-2 profile configuration contains one of the most frequent high points, the Ma score, among alcohol- and drug-abusing populations. Over 19% of the men in substance-abuse treatment programs have this pattern (McKenna & Butcher, 1987).

PROFILE STABILITY

The relative elevation of his clinical scale scores suggests that his profile is not as well defined as many other profiles. There was no difference between the profile type used to develop the present report and the next highest scale in the profile code. Therefore, behavioral elements related to elevations on Sc should be considered as well. For example, emotional alienation, unusual thinking, bizarre perceptions of others, and strong tendency to engage in extreme fantasy could be important in his symptom pattern.

INTERPERSONAL RELATIONS

He usually makes a very good impression and is effective at persuading and engaging others in conversation readily, but his relationships tend to be somewhat superficial.

(continued)

169

Figure 9.4. (*continued*)

His high score on the Marital Distress Scale suggests that his marital situation is problematic at this time. He has reported a number of problems with his marriage that are possibly important to understanding his current psychological symptoms.

The content of this client's MMPI-2 responses suggests the following additional information concerning his interpersonal relations. He appears to be an individual who has rather cynical views about life. Any efforts to initiate new behaviors may be colored by his negativism. He may view relationships with others as threatening and harmful. He views his home situation as unpleasant and lacking in love and understanding. He feels like leaving home to escape a quarrelsome, critical situation and to be free of family domination. He feels intensely angry, hostile, and resentful of others, and he would like to get back at them. He is competitive and uncooperative, tending to be very critical of others.

DIAGNOSTIC CONSIDERATIONS

Any clinical diagnostic formulation should take into consideration his manipulative and impulsive personality features. His response content is consistent with the antisocial features in his history. These factors should be taken into consideration in arriving at a clinical diagnosis. His unusual thinking and bizarre ideas need to be taken into consideration in any diagnostic formulation.

He appears to have a number of personality characteristics that have been associated with substance abuse or substance use problems. His scores on the addiction proneness indicators suggest that there is a possibility of his developing an addictive disorder. Further evaluation for the likelihood of a substance use or abuse disorder is indicated. In his responses to the MMPI-2, he has acknowledged some problems with excessive use or abuse of addictive substances.

TREATMENT CONSIDERATIONS

Individuals with this MMPI-2 clinical profile typically report feeling "great," have little anxiety, and usually do not seek psychotherapy on their own. They tend to deny that they have problems and are not very introspective. If they are somehow brought into psychotherapeutic treatment at the insistence of others, they may at first appear agreeable and cooperative and seemingly enjoy therapy. However, they soon become bored or diverted by other activities and terminate treatment early.

The client endorsed item content that seems to indicate low potential for change. He may feel that his problems are not addressable through therapy and that he is not likely to benefit much from psychological treatment at this time. His apparently negative treatment attitudes may need to be explored early in therapy if treatment is to be successful.

Examination of item content reveals a considerable number of problems with his home life. He feels extremely unhappy and alienated from his family. He reports that his home life is unpleasant and that he does not expect it to improve. Any psychological intervention will need to focus on his negative family feelings if progress is to be made.

He harbors many negative work attitudes that could limit his adaptability in the work-place. His low morale and lack of interest in work could impair future adjustment to employment, a factor that should be taken into consideration in treatment.

His acknowledged problems with alcohol or drug use should be addressed in therapy.

NOTE: This MMPI-2 interpretation can serve as a useful source of hypotheses about clients. This report is based on objectively derived scale indices and scale interpretations that have been developed in diverse groups of patients. The personality descriptions, inferences, and recommendations contained herein need to be verified by other sources of clinical information because individual clients may not fully match the prototype. The information in this report should most appropriately be used by a trained, qualified test interpreter. The information contained in this report should be considered confidential.

References

American Psychological Association (1986). *American Psychological Association Guidelines for Computer-Based Tests and Interpretations*. Washington, D.C.: American Psychological Association.

Berah, E., Butcher, J., Miach, P., Bolza, J., Colman, S. & McAsey, P. (1993). Computer-based interpretation of the MMPI-2: An Australian evaluation of the Minnesota Report. Presented at the Australian Psychological Association Meetings, Melbourne, October.

Butcher, J. N. (1988). Use of the MMPI in personnel screening. Presented at the 23rd Annual Symposium on Recent Developments in the Use of the MMPI, St. Petersburg, FL.

Butcher, J. N. (1990). *Use of the MMPI-2 in treatment planning*. New York: Oxford University Press.

Butcher, J. N. (Ed.) (1996). *International adaptations of the MMPI-2*. Minneapolis, MN: University of Minnesota Press.

Butcher, J. N., & Williams, C. L. (1992). *MMPI-2 and MMPI-A: Essentials of clinical interpretation*. Minneapolis, MN: University of Minnesota Press.

Butcher, J. N., Graham, J. R., Williams, C. L., & Ben-Porath, Y. S. (1990). *Development and use of the MMPI-2 Content Scales*. Minneapolis, MN: University of Minnesota Press.

Erdberg, P. (1979). A systematic approach to providing feedback from the MMPI. In C. S. Newmark (Ed.). *MMPI: Clinical and research trends* (pp. 328–342). New York: Praeger.

Eyde, L. (1993). Tips for clinicians using computer based test interpretations (CBTIs). In B. Schlosser and K. Moreland (Eds.), *Taming technology: Issues strategies and resources for the mental health practitioner* (pp. 97–99). Washington, D.C.: American Psychological Association.

Eyde, L., Kowal, D., & Fishburne, F. J. (1991). In T. B. Gutkin & S. L. Wise (Eds.), *The computer and the decision making process* (pp. 75–123). Hillsdale, NJ: LEA Press.

Finn, S. E. (1990, June). *A model for providing test feedback with the MMPI and MMPI-2.*

Presented at the 25th Annual Symposium on Recent Developments in the Use of the MMPI (MMPI-2), Minneapolis, MN.

Finn, S. and Tonsager, M. (1992). Therapeutic effects of providing MMPI-2 test feedback to college students awaiting therapy. *Psychological Assessment* 4, 278–287.

Fishburne, J., Eyde, L., & Kowal, D. (1988). Computer-based test interpretations of the MMPI with neurologically impaired patients. Paper given at the *Annual Meeting of the American Psychological Association*, Atlanta, Georgia.

Fowler, R. D. (1969). Automated interpretation of personality test data. In J.N. Butcher (Ed.), *MMPI: Research developments and clinical applications* (pp. 105–125). New York: McGraw-Hill.

Gilberstadt, H., & Duker, J. (1963). *A handbook of clinical and actuarial MMPI interpretations*. Philadelphia: Saunders.

Gillet, I., Simon, M., Guelfi, J., Brun-Eberentz, A., Monier, C., Seuvenel, F., & Svarna, L. (1996). The MMPI-2 in France. In J. N. Butcher (Ed.), *International adaptations of the MMPI-2* (pp. 395–425). Minneapolis: University of Minnesota Press.

Graham, J. R. (1993). *MMPI-2: Assessing personality and psychopathology* (2nd edition). New York: Oxford University Press.

Graham, J. R., Ben-Porath, Y. S., & McNulty, J. (In press). *Using the MMPI-2 in outpatient mental health settings*. Minneapolis, MN: University of Minnesota Press.

Greene, R. (1991). *The MMPI-2/MMPI: An interpretive manual*. Needham Heights, MA: Allyn & Bacon.

Lewandowski, D., & Graham, J. R. (1972). Empirical correlates of frequently occurring two-point code types: A replicated study. *Journal of Clinical Psychology* 39, 467–472.

Lubin, B., Larsen, R., & Matarazzo, J. D. (1984). Patterns of psychological test usage in the United States: 1935–1982. *American Psychologist* 39, 451–454.

Marks, P. A., Seeman, W., & Haller, (1975). *The actuarial use of the MMPI with adolescents and adults*. Baltimore: Williams & Wilkins.

Meehl, P. E. (1954). *Clinical versus statistical prediction: A theoretical analysis and a review of the evidence*. Minneapolis, MN: University of Minnesota Press.

Moreland, K. (1987). Computerized psychological assessment. What's available. In J. N. Butcher (Ed.), *Computerized psychological assessment* (pp. 26–49). New York: Basic Books.

Moreland, K. L., & Onstad, J. (1985, March). *Validity of the Minnesota Clinical Report I: Mental health outpatients*. Presented at the 20th Annual Symposium on Recent Developments in the Use of the MMPI, Honolulu.

Newman, M. L. (1996). Therapeutic Effects of Providing MMPI-2 Assessment Feedback to Clients at a University Counseling Service: A Collaborative Approach. Presented at the 15th Conference on Personality Assessment, Melbourne, Australia.

Piotrowski, C., & Keller, J. W. (1989). Psychological testing in outpatient mental health facilities: A national study. *Professional Psychology: Research and Practice* 20, 423–425.

Pope, K., Butcher, J. N. & Seelen, J. (1993). *The MMPI/MMPI-2/MMPI-A in court: Assessment, testimony, and cross-examination for expert witnesses and attorneys*. Washington, D.C.: American Psychological Association.

Quirk, M. P., Strosahl, K., Kreilkamp, T. & Erdberg, P. (1995). Personality feedback consultation to families in a managed mental health care practice. *Professional Psychology: Research and Practice* 26, 27–32.

Rome, H. P., Swenson, W. M. Mataya, P. McCarthy, C. E., Pearson, J. S., Keating, F. R. & Hathaway, S. R. (1962). Symposium on automation technics in personality assessment. *Proceedings of the Staff Meetings of the Mayo Clinic* 37, 61–82

10

Treatment-Oriented
MMPI/MMPI-2 Studies

Steven Vay Rouse
Jill Sullivan
Jeanette Taylor

According to recent reviews, the MMPI/MMPI-2 continues to be listed as the personality assessment instrument most frequently used both in research and in clinical practice. Clinicians have found it to be invaluable in the identification of psychological difficulties, in the formulation of treatment plans, and in the evaluation of treatment progress. In addition, researchers have used it to evaluate the relative effectiveness of several theoretical modalities and therapy variables in the treatment of a wide range of psychological disorders and conditions.

In the preparation of this bibliography, nearly 1000 references were collected in which the MMPI/MMPI-2 was utilized for some aspect of treatment planning or treatment evaluation. To provide some structure for this intimidating quantity of research, an attempt was made to group articles according to similar themes and subject areas which may be of interest to both the practicing clinician and the researcher. Short reviews of each area of literature are included in order to highlight recent emphases in that area.

A few provisos must be noted. First, although an attempt was made to collect as many relevant references as possible, this bibliography should not be assumed to be a comprehensive collection of all research relevant to psychological treatment issues. Since it could be argued that any research which enhances our understanding of an assessment tool is relevant to its use in psychological treatment, it is likely that many articles which would be of interest have not been included. Only articles which used the MMPI/MMPI-2 explicitly for treatment planning and evaluation have been included.

Second, although the references included in this bibliography span 50 years of MMPI/MMPI-2 research, the annotations emphasize documents published in the past 20 years. This decision was made because the recent research reflects topics and issues which are of more immediate concern to the contemporary clinician or researcher. In addition, the research published more than two decades ago was reviewed in a superb annotated bibliography by Dahlstrom, Welsh, and Dahlstrom (1975), so there was no need to duplicate their effort. Any readers with interest in historical research on the MMPI will find their resource to be invaluable.

The compilers of this bibliography hope that this will be a useful resource to both clinicians and researchers interested in the use of the MMPI/MMPI-2 in treatment planning and treatment evaluation.

Types of Psychotherapy

Cognitive-Behavioral

Literature on the use of the MMPI in evaluating behavioral and cognitive-behavioral therapies and techniques suggests that the test is widely respected among behavioral clinicians. It has been used to evaluate behavioral and cognitive treatments of a variety of disorders and complaints including obesity (Fardan & Tyson, 1985; Molinari et al., 1991), irritable bowel syndrome (Blanchard et al., 1992), chronic pain and chronic headaches (Blanchard, 1985; Naliboff et al., 1988; Sweet, 1981; Wojciechowski, 1984), and substance abuse (Beasley et al., 1991; Mabli et al., 1985; Miller, 1978).

The evaluation of the treatment of depression has been one of the most frequent applications of the MMPI in this area (Azrin & Besalel, 1981; Matson, 1982; Mirabel-Sarron et al., 1993; Rehm, 1981; Rush & Watkins, 1981). One theme observed in much of this research is that while cognitive-behavioral and behavioral techniques appear to be effective in the reduction of depressive indicators, the format of the therapy appears to be less important. For example, Schmidt and Miller (1983) examined the effectiveness of a multidimensional program for the treatment of depression that included behavioral management components, cognitive restructuring components, and assertiveness training components. Regardless of whether the participants were assigned to individual therapy, small groups, large groups, or bibliotherapy, MMPI scores showed significant symptom reduction when compared with a waiting-list control sample. Little difference was observed, however, between participants assigned to individual therapy, group therapy, or bibliotherapy. Other research suggests that cognitive-behavioral marital therapy is also effective in reducing MMPI scores among couples in which one of the spouses is depressed (Sher et al., 1990).

Williams (1982) demonstrated that the MMPI can be easily and usefully incorporated during several stages of behavior therapy. Presenting the case of a female client with complaints of anger and anxiety, Williams described how the

MMPI administered at pretreatment assisted the therapist in the selection of an appropriate treatment, in the development of a therapeutic relationship, and in explaining the treatment rationale to the client. In addition, the MMPI was administered at post-treatment and six-month follow-up to help the client perceive the improvements.

> Al-Issa & Kraft, 1967; Andrews, 1973; Azrin & Besalel, 1981; Balson, 1971; Ban et al., 1969; Barrett, 1969; Beasley et al., 1991; Birk et al., 1971; Blanchard, 1985; Blanchard et al., 1992; Cionini & Giovannoni, 1984; Collet et al., 1987; Edelman, 1969, 1971; Fardan & Tyson, 1985; Fazio, 1972; Firestone & Witt, 1982; Fox & Di Scipio, 1968; Fry, 1984; Fuchs & Rehm, 1977; Geer, 1964; Goldstein et al., 1982; Goorney, 1970; Joanning, 1976; Kraft, 1969; Kraft & Wijesignhe, 1970; Lanyon et al., 1972; Levis & Carrera, 1967; Lewinsohn et al., 1970; Linder, 1981; Lomont et al., 1969; Mabli et al., 1985; Matson, 1982; McNamara & Andrasik, 1982; Miller, 1978; Miller & Gottlieb, 1974; Mirabel-Sarron et al., 1993; Molinari et al., 1991; Munjack, 1976; Naliboff et al., 1988; Nawas, 1971; L. Pancheri et al., 1988; Perez-Solera, 1992; Pickens, 1979; Rehm, 1979, 1981; Rehm & Marston, 1968; Rosenthal, 1967; Rush & Watkins, 1981; Schmidt & Miller, 1983; Sher et al., 1990; Shrauger & Katkin, 1970; Silver, 1976; Solyom et al., 1969, 1971; Stampfl & Levis, 1973; Sweet, 1981; Tanner, 1971, 1973, 1974; Valliant & Antonowicz, 1992; Wadden, 1984; Williams, 1982; Wojciechowski, 1984; Zeisset, 1968.

Marriage and Family Systems

Early studies of marital maladjustment have focused on profile differences between distressed and nondistressed couples. For example, Floyd (1974) noted the relationship between marital happiness and scores on the Pt scale; findings were presented that related problems of emotional dependence, sociability, and the struggle for dominance in marriage to specific MMPI profiles. This study noted the shortcomings of such research, including the need for studies of specific scales as indices of marital adjustment.

While it has been found that the Pd scale and the MMPI-2 Content Scale FAM tend to be associated with family problems in general (Butcher & Williams, 1992), neither was developed specifically in relation to marital distress. Hjemboe et al. (1992) have developed the Marital Distress Scale (MDS), which contains items with content related to marital problems and relationship difficulties. This scale provides the best possible measure of marital functioning and distress.

The MMPI has been used not only as an objective measure of marital adjustment, but also as a therapeutic tool. In a study by Dorr (1981), a battery of personality tests, including the MMPI, was administered to married couples who later participated in an interpretative feedback session. A psychologist presented the partners with test results and aided them in making their own interpretations. Such an approach allows the partners to engage in problem-solving by deciding whether or not the interpretation applies to him or her, opens discussion of personality features of importance to other family members, and provides a strategy for building rapport between the therapist and the couple.

Although emphasis on the marital dyad is essential, it is often important to include other members of the family constellation as well. The MMPI can serve as a measure of the appropriateness of fit between specific client populations and therapy types. Chaffin (1992) followed the treatment progress of 36 intrafamilial sexual abusers and found that subjects with higher degrees of personality disturbance showed lower rates of both attainment of empathy for the victim and treatment program completion. Firestone and Witt (1982) investigated the characteristics of families with hyperactive children who completed or prematurely discontinued a behavioral parent-training program. Several differences in MMPI profiles were found between parents who completed the program and those who dropped out. Both studies stress the need for careful pretreatment personality assessment.

The MMPI most frequently is used as a measure of the success of family therapy. Croake and Hinckle (1983) administered the MMPI and two child-rearing scales as pre- and post-therapy measures to subjects participating in Adlerian family counseling. Each session began with a statement of a family problem. After sketching the family constellation and making an estimate of present difficulty, the counselor engaged family members in discussions about their feelings and elicited suggestions for problem-solving. Results showed that all subjects improved their test scores in a favorable direction (e.g., exhibiting more favorable interpersonal behavior and improved family interactions) as a result of their participation.

The MMPI is also useful as measure of the success of family therapy with specific populations. For example, in a study of a family-centered, behavioral approach to chronic pain, family members were taught techniques that rewarded nonpain behavior in the patient (Hudgens, 1979). Goals of the treatment included improving family relationships, regaining occupational roles, reducing use of pain medication, increasing tolerance for exercise, and reducing use of the health care system. Subjects' level of functioning, MMPI profiles before and after treatment, and a description of work with the family system were reported.

Chaffin, 1992; Croake & Hinckle, 1983; Dorr, 1981; Firestone & Witt, 1982; Floyd, 1974; Hjemboe et al., 1992; Hudgens, 1979; Johnson et al., 1970; McClellan & Stieper, 1971; Pearce, 1970; Rittenhouse, 1970; Sher et al., 1990; Smith, 1963, 1967.

Psychodynamics and Hypnotherapy

The MMPI is a useful measure of the appropriateness of fit between clients and various types of therapy. Havik (1982) studied three groups of patients accepted for short-term psychotherapy. MMPI results revealed that two-thirds of the patients evaluated as appropriate candidates had profiles that were different from those of subjects who had been judged as inappropriate candidates for insight-oriented therapy. In a study of patient characteristics and outcome in both psychotherapy and behavior therapy, Sloane (1976) found that greater success with psychotherapy was associated with higher socioeconomic status and less overall psychopathology on the MMPI. Psychotherapy was least effective for clients with high elevations on the Hy and Pd scales. There was a strong trend for more improvement with subjects who were younger, female, married, later born, more intelligent, and from smaller families. When a particular form of short-term dynamic psychotherapy is selected according to subjects' ego resources and motivation for therapeutic change, subjects will attain substantial symptom relief and changes in adaptive functioning as confirmed by changes on the MMPI (Barth et al., 1988).

In addition to determining whether a client is an appropriate candidate for psychotherapy, MMPI scores are useful in predicting persistence of compliance with therapeutic regimens. An investigation by Koss (1980) revealed that scores on the D and Si scales added to the prediction of length of stay in private practice psychotherapy. In an examination of MMPI and psychotherapy attendance data, Walters et al. (1982) found that male persisters tended to be less defensive though experiencing greater distress; female persisters tended to be more introverted and less impulsive than their low-persisting counterparts.

Other ingredients that are effective in predicting psychotherapeutic outcome are patient motivation and the ability to become involved in a therapeutic relationship. Strupp (1980) reported a comparison of therapeutic success and failure. Results showed that therapy outcome was a function of the subjects' ability to work within the framework provided by the therapist and to become involved in a therapeutic relationship, as measured by the MMPI, the Global Change scale, and clinical study of all tape-recorded therapy sessions. Keithly et al. (1980) examined the effect of patient motivation on process and outcome in short-term psychotherapy. Analyses suggested that motivation was a good predictor of the subject's behavior in therapy and also may influence the therapist's behavior during treatment. Ratings of motivation significantly predicted the therapist's subjective ratings of overall improvement, but not subjects' ratings of overall improvement or residual maladjustment scores derived from the MMPI.

Nichols (1974) confirmed the effectiveness of emotive psychotherapy in producing catharses which lead to therapeutic improvement, as validated by changes in MMPI profiles and other outcome data. Bierenbaum et al. (1976) examined the role of emotional catharsis in brief emotive psychotherapy sessions of varying length and frequency. Outcome was assessed using the sum of MMPI scales D, Pt, and Sc, a personal satisfaction interview, and behavioral complaints. Patients participating in half-hour sessions twice a week improved the most on the MMPI scales, irrespective of the amount of catharsis produced.

The MMPI has also been used as an outcome measure with various therapeutic techniques, including hypnotherapy. Objective measurements, including the MMPI, have shown increases in self-control, improved self-concept, elimination of pathological symptoms, and cessation of panic attacks following directed hypnotherapy (Der and Lewington, 1990). Similar findings showing substantive changes in thoughts, feelings, bodily responses, and behavior have been reported for patients suffering from migraine headaches (Howard et al., 1982), chronic myofibrositis pain (Elkins, 1984), and anxiety neurosis (Tosi et al., 1982).

Adams, 1962; Albert, 1970; Alexander, 1968; Alpher, 1992; Ashby et al., 1957; Barron, 1953a, b; Barron & Leary, 1955; Barth et al., 1988; Baughman et al., 1959; Bellak & Rosenberg, 1966; Bergin, 1966; Bergin & Garfield, 1971; Bergin & Jasper, 1969; Bergin & Strupp, 1972; Bierenbaum et al., 1976; Black & Petty, 1977; Blank, 1965;

Bobrov et al., 1993; Borghi, 1965; Campbell & Sinha, 1983; Canter, 1971; Cartwright, 1956; Cartwright et al., 1963; Dahlstrom, 1975; Danet, 1968a, b; Decourcy, 1971; Deforest & Johnson, 1981; Der & Lewington, 1990; Devlin, 1953; Dymond, 1955; Elkins, 1984; Endicott & Endicott, 1964; Epstein & Deyoub, 1981; Fairweather et al., 1960; Ford, 1959; Forsyth & Fairweather, 1961; Fox & Di Scipio, 1968; Garfield, 1971a, b; Gendlin, Beebe, Cassens, & Oberlander, 1968; Gendlin & Rychlak, 1970; Gomes-Schwartz, 1978; Gomes-Schwartz & Schwartz, 1978; Gordon et al., 1954; Greenfield, 1958; Grof et al., 1973; Harris & Christiansen, 1946; Havik, 1982; Hecht & Kroeber, 1955; Helweg, 1971; Holmes & Heckel, 1970; Horowitz, 1970; Howard et al., 1982; Johnston, 1993; Kahn, 1953; Keithly et al., 1980; Kellner, 1967; Kiesler, 1971; Kline, 1952; Koss, 1980; Malan et al., 1968; Manos & Vasilopoulou, 1984; Meehl, 1955; Meltzoff & Kornreich, 1970; Mick, 1956; Monroe & Hill, 1958; Monsen et al., 1989a, b; Mowrer, 1953; Nacev, 1980; Newburger, 1963; Newmark et al., 1974; Nichols, 1974; Nielsen, 1982, 1984; Nielsen et al., 1988, 1989; Persons, 1965, 1966; Prager & Garfield, 1972; Reardon et al., 1977; Rogers, 1967; Schoenberg & Carr, 1963; Schofield, 1964, 1966; Schonfield & Donner, 1972; Schork et al., 1994; Shands et al., 1959; Shapiro et al., 1976; Shapiro, 1969; Sifneos, 1969; Simonsen, 1985; Slawson, 1965; Sloane, 1976; Snyder & Snyder, 1961; Soskin, 1973; Stava, 1984; Stewart & Cole, 1968; Stieper & Wiener, 1959; Stieper & Wiener, 1965; Stoddard et al., 1988; Strupp, 1980; Strupp & Bloxom, 1975; Strupp & Hadley, 1979; Sullivan et al., 1958; Szalanski, 1975; Taulbee, 1958, 1961; Tibilova & Tsytsareva, 1988; Tosi et al., 1982; Uhlenhuth et al., 1969; Van der Veen, 1967; Volsky et al., 1965; Walters et al., 1982; Wiener & Phillips, 1948; Williams & Baron, 1982; Yensen, 1976.

Biofeedback and Relaxation Training

The MMPI has been used to evaluate the effectiveness of biofeedback and relaxation training for concerns including insomnia (Coursey et al., 1980; Lick & Heffler, 1977), anxiety (Crebelli et al., 1983; Delle-Chiaie et al., 1981; Pancheri, 1982), impotence (Cionini & Giovannoni, 1984), depression (De Piano et al., 1984; Peniston et al., 1986), post-traumatic stress disorder (Hickling et al., 1986), and substance abuse (Cernovsky, 1984; Nathan et al., 1986; Passini, 1977).

Within this field, a significant quantity of research has been conducted on the efficacy of biofeedback and relaxation training in the treatment of chronic headaches (Blanchard, 1983, 1985; Delzotti et al., 1983; Ellertson, 1988; Grazzi et al., 1988). One issue which has raised debate is whether or not the MMPI can be used to identify headache-sufferers who are likely to benefit from these procedures (Blanchard, 1982; Diamond & Montrose, 1984; Onorato & Tsushima, 1983). Collet (1987) argued that the MMPI does serve as a prognostic indicator for improvement and that depression, as indicated by an elevation on the D scale, is a negative prognostic factor for treatment of headaches. Jacob et al. (1983), however, did not support this argument; while scores on the Beck Depression Inventory were negatively correlated with improvement, no such correlation was observed for the D scale.

Discussion has also examined whether or not biofeedback serves merely as a placebo. Plotkin and Rice (1981) trained anxious college students to control their levels of EEG alpha activity. Although some participants were instructed to increase the level of alpha activity and others were taught to decrease the level, anxiety reductions were correlated with the participants' ratings of their success at the feedback task, not the direction of instructed change. While this evidence suggests a placebo effect, other evidence suggests that the improvement gained through biofeedback is greater than that gained through a placebo activity. Wojciechowski (1984) trained subjects to use either relaxation or a credible-sounding concentration placebo in the reduction of tension headaches. Although subjective ratings made by both groups after treatment were not significantly different, diary records of headache frequency and severity indicated that relaxation was more effective than the placebo task at reducing headaches. Therefore, while biofeedback and relaxation training are not merely placebos, subjective ratings of the effectiveness of biofeedback may not be reliable; this underscores the utility of an objective measure, such as the MMPI, in treatment evaluation.

Baiocco, 1991; Blanchard, 1982, 1983, 1985; Burke et al., 1985; Cernovsky, 1984; Cionini & Giovannoni, 1984; Collet, 1987; Coursey et al., 1980; Crebelli et al., 1983; Delle et al., 1981; Delzotti et al., 1983; DePiano et al., 1984; DeShazo & Kissiah, 1971; Diamond & Montrose, 1984; Dolce et al., 1986; Edelman, 1970; Ellertson, 1988; Evans & Blanchard, 1988; Ford et al., 1982, 1983; Frankel, 1978; Freeman et al., 1980; Goldstein et al., 1982; Grazzi et al., 1988; Guthrie et al., 1983; Hickling et al., 1986; Howard et al., 1982; Jacob et al., 1983; Johnson & Spielberger, 1968; Lacroix et al., 1986; Lick & Heffler, 1977; McFarlane et al., 1982; Miller & DiPilato, 1983; Nathan et al., 1986; Nigl & Jackson, 1979; Onorato & Tsushima, 1983; Pancheri, 1982; Passini, 1977, Peniston et al., 1986; Perez-Solera, 1992; Plotkin & Rice, 1981; Scita et al., 1988; Stoudenmire, 1972; Sweet, 1981; Tanner, 1971; Tsushima et al., 1987; Tsushima & Stoddard; 1990; Tsushima et al., 1991; Tyre et al., 1987; Wadden, 1983, 1984; Wojciechowski, 1984; Zeisset, 1968.

Group Therapy

An essential component in the effectiveness of group therapy is identification amongst group members. Using pre- and post-test MMPI profiles and self-report of the incidence of identification, Jeske (1973) found that the incidence of identification was significantly higher for group members showing positive change in therapy than for those who did not. An additional positive correlation was found between the frequency of identification and changes in therapy.

MMPI profiles are frequently used as a measure of treatment outcome. Joanning (1976) found significant increases in the frequency and quality of assertive behavior but found decreases in feelings and manifestations of social anxiety for students participating in a behavioral rehearsal group. Koch (1983) investigated changes in personal constructs for members of psychotherapy groups versus waiting-list controls. Individualized and general predictions of possible therapeutic changes were made; data indicated significant improvement within each therapy group and confirmed more individualized than general predictions. In addition, Koch outlined a model for the further evaluation of personal construct methodology within group settings. Coche and Flick (1975) conducted small groups aimed at improving interpersonal problem-solving skills for 41 psychiatric inpatients. Subjects' levels of psychological disturbance were measured using the MMPI. Subjects' functioning on a test of problem-solving improved as a result of hospitalization alone, but significantly greater advancement was achieved for those participating in the problem-solving training groups. Furthermore, greater gains were made by more disturbed patients than by the less disturbed.

Profile changes also have been examined for specific patient populations. Ross et al. (1974) examined the effectiveness of marathon group psychotherapy for female narcotic addicts. Subjects participated in either one 17-hour marathon group session or 2-hour group psychotherapy sessions for two weeks. Both groups showed reduced post-test scores on the "neurotic triad" of the MMPI (scales Hs, D, and Hy), though the marathon group also showed a significant change toward internal control and changes in specific attitudes toward criminal and drug subcultures. Profile changes following experiences with group therapy have also been studied for alcoholics (Flores, 1982), cancer patients (Florez, 1979), agoraphobics (Linder, 1981), and men with sexual dysfunctions (Reynolds, 1981).

Anderson, 1959; Bozzetti, 1972; Cabeen & Coleman, 1961; Coche & Flick, 1975; Danet, 1968a,b; Davis, 1968; Ends & Page, 1957, 1959; Flores, 1982; Florez, 1979; Fryrear & Stephens, 1988; Gerstein & Hotelling, 1987; Giedt, 1961; Hess, 1992; Hisli, 1987; Jacobson & Wirt, 1969; Jeske, 1973; Joanning, 1976; Johnsgard & Muench, 1965; Kelly, 1966; Klett, 1965; Koch, 1983; Koch & Greger, 1985; Kraus, 1959; Leak, 1980; Leary & Coffey, 1955; Lewinsohn & Shaw, 1969; Liederman et al., 1967; Linder, 1981; Lomont et al., 1969; Mathias & Sindberg, 1986; McCall, 1974; McClellan & Stieper, 1971; Melson, 1982; Metzen, 1971; Newburger & Schauer, 1953; Peake, 1979; Price, 1981; Rashkis & Shaskan, 1946; Reynolds, 1981; Roback & Strassberg, 1975; Rosen & Golden, 1975; Ross et al., 1974; Russell & Bennett, 1972; Speer, 1970; Spielberger et al., 1962; Stockey, 1961; Straus & Hess, 1993; Taylor, 1966; Teitelbaum & Suinn, 1964; Truax & Carkhuff, 1965; Truax et al., 1965, 1968; Truax & Wargo, 1969; Vernallis et al., 1970; Welkowitz, 1960.

Types of Medical Therapy

Lithium

The past two decades of research on lithium and the MMPI has focused largely on the instrument's ability to discriminate patients who respond from those who do not respond to the therapeutic effects of the drug. The relevant research is equally divided between studies which examine the predictive ability of the standard MMPI scales and those which examine a Lithium Response Scale of the MMPI.

Three studies examined MMPI standard scale differences between patients who responded and those who did not respond to lithium treatment. In a sample of 54 manic–depressive patients, Ananth et al. (1979) found that patients with higher scores on the Pd and Pa clinical scales showed poor response to lithium treatment. Ananth et al. (1980) obtained similar results in a sample of 59 psychiatric patients, with poor responders to lithium treatment scoring higher on scales Pd, Pa, and Ma than treatment responders. Conversely, responders to lithium treatment scored higher than nonresponders on the Hs, Pt, and Si scales. Finally, House and Martin (1975) examined 26 severely depressed inpatients and found that those who responded to lithium treatment scored high on the D and Pt scales while non-responders scored low on those two scales.

The three studies examining lithium response and the MMPI Lithium Response Scale vary widely in their findings and conclusions. Donnelly et al. (1978) found that a lithium response scale derived from the MMPI discriminated female treatment responders from female nonresponders with high accuracy. Burdick and Holmes (1980) found the Lithium Response Scale-Female and -Male to predict lithium responders from nonresponders with low accuracy in a small sample of outpatients. The authors concluded that the scale had low predictive ability. Finally et al. (1983) used the Lithium Response Scale to preselect depressed patients for lithium treatment. The scale performed at about chance level.

Ananth et al., 1979, 1980; Burdick & Holmes, 1980; Campbell & Kimball, 1985; Cutler & Heiser, 1978; Donnelly et al., 1978; Garvey et al., 1983; House & Martin, 1975; Steinbook & Chapman, 1970

Benzodiazepines and Other Sedative-Hypnotics

The majority of the research on benzodiazepines and other sedative-hypnotics using the MMPI was conducted prior to 1975. Recent investigations of this drug class have used the MMPI as a screening tool to select appropriate subjects (e.g., Nathan et al., 1986) or as a measure of depression or anxiety (e.g., Overall et al., 1973; Pancheria et al., 1988b; Schweizer et al., 1990). The MMPI has not been used as a tool for treatment outcome prediction with this class of drugs in the past two decades.

Abse et al., 1960; Brick et al., 1966; Cogswell, 1960; Dimascio et al., 1969; Fleeson et al., 1958; Goldstein & Weer, 1970; Goldstein et al., 1970; Haertzen & Hill, 1959; Hankoff et al., 1964; Hanlon et al., 1965; Janecek et al., 1966; Kelly et al., 1958; Lorr et al., 1961; Nathan et al., 1986; Overall et al., 1962, 1973; Pancheri et al., 1988a; Pennington, 1964; Prange et al., 1963; Raab et al., 1964; Reznikoff & Toomey, 1965; Rickels et al., 1959; Rosen et al., 1971; Ross & Priest, 1970; Schweizer et al., 1990; Shaffer, 1963; Sulzer, 1959; Toms, 1961; Vestre et al., 1969; Wiener et al., 1963.

Antidepressants

Although a majority of the research on antidepressant drugs using the MMPI was conducted over two decades ago, recent research on antidepressant drugs has used the MMPI in a variety of roles. In two investigations, the MMPI was administered following a period of treatment with antidepressant drugs (Faravelli & Sacchetti, 1984; Overall et al., 1973). The MMPI was used as one measure of anxiety in an investigation of the efficacy of an antidepressant versus antihypertensive drug for the treatment of panic disorder with and without agoraphobia.

At least one study on antidepressant drugs utilized the MMPI for it's predictive properties. Donnelly et al. (1979) examined the association between pretreatment responses to the MMPI and response to imipramine. Responders to the drug were distinguished from nonresponders with great accuracy using male and female versions of an empirically derived Imipramine Response Scale, though the traditional MMPI scales failed to differentiate responders from nonresponders. More recent research with the MMPI has not focused on the instrument's ability to predict response to other specific antidepressant drugs.

Bellak & Rosenberg, 1966; Brick et al., 1962, 1965; Destounis et al., 1965; Dimascio et al., 1968; Donnelly et al., 1979; Faravelli & Sacchetti, 1984; Friedman et al., 1961; Fryer & Timberlake, 1963; Habrat & Walecka, 1991; Heller et al., 1971; Hollister & Overall, 1965; Hollister et al., 1963; Janecek et al., 1963; Khanna et al., 1963; Kline & Schacter, 1965; Kurland et al., 1967a; Lafave et al., 1965; McDonald et al., 1966; Mena et al., 1964; Munjack, 1985; Olson, 1962; Overall et al., 1962, 1964, 1966, 1973; Roulet et al., 1962; Sandifer et al., 1965; Shaffer et al., 1964a; Stanley & Fleming, 1962; Sulzer & Schiele, 1962; Tredici et al., 1966; Uhlenhuth & Park, 1963; Vestre et al., 1969; Wilson et al., 1964, 1966, 1967; Wittenborn et al., 1973.

Anti-Substance Abuse Medications

The MMPI has been used extensively in research on alcoholism and drug abuse. It has also been used in the investigation of drugs which help combat substance abuse. One of the six studies conducted in the past two decades on this topic relates to drug treatment for alcoholism while the other five are concerned with the treatment of heroin addiction.

In their examination of male inpatient alcoholics, O'Neil et al. (1983) used the MMPI to differentiate those who accepted versus those who rejected disulfiram (Antabuse) therapy following detoxification. A significant difference was found between groups on scale Mf; higher scale scores were obtained for individuals who accepted the drug.

The research related to drug therapy for heroin addicts consists largely of studies of methadone treatment programs and related treatment variables. For example, research has been conducted which uses the MMPI to evaluate personal characteristics of effective counselors at a methadone treatment program (e.g., Snowden & Cotler, 1974). Other investigations focused the use of the MMPI on differentiating heroin addicts who would remain in a methadone maintenance program for at least one year from those addicts who would drop out (e.g., Krakowski & Smart, 1974).

Two investigations used the MMPI to classify heroin addicts into various treatment or demographic categories. Ottomanelli (1977) used the MMPI and a measure of psychopathy to accurately classify about half of the sampled methadone-treated patients into employment, arrest, and attrition categories using discriminant function analysis. Similarly, Ottomanelli et al. (1978) used the MMPI in a discriminant analysis of 148 new admissions to a methadone treatment program. The analysis showed that individuals with stable MMPI profiles at intake had more favorable treatment outcomes.

Bobrov et al., 1993; Denson & Sydiaha, 1970; Ditman et al., 1970; Krakowski & Smart, 1974; Kurland et al., 1967b; Ochoa Mangado et al., 1992; O'Neil et al., 1983; Ottomanelli, 1977; Ottomanelli et al., 1978; Shaffer et al., 1962, 1964b; Simopoulos et al., 1968; Snowden & Cotler, 1974; Soskin, 1970.

Miscellaneous Drug Research

Research on drug treatment utilizing the MMPI is not always easily categorized because the MMPI has been used in research on a diverse list of drug treatments. Recent MMPI research has covered topics from actuarial prediction of drug choice in treatment (Henry et al., 1976) to assessment of differences between elderly male patients on various numbers of psychotropic medications (Fracchia et al., 1974). Additionally, Cleveland (1989) contributed a book chapter which reviews and critiques research on drug response and the relationship to personality factors.

Burish, 1981; Cleveland, 1989; Fracchia et al., 1974a, b; Hanlon et al., 1969; Henry et al., 1976; O'Neil et al., 1983; Stein et al., 1978; Weintraub & Aronson, 1963.

Surgery

Prior to 1975, the research relating the MMPI to surgical outcome focused almost exclusively on the lobotomy procedure. As one might expect, the research on the relationship between personality factors and surgery in the past two decades has focused on a variety of other surgical procedures.

At least one investigation using the MMPI has been done on both the thalamotomy and the hysterectomy. Jurko et al. (1974) administered the MMPI to eight patients before and after thalamotomy. A significant long-term decrease from pre- to postsurgery was seen in scale Ma scores, while a significant short-term decrease was found for scores on scale Pt. Tsoi et al. (1984) examined 20 patients before and after hysterectomy using the Hs. The authors reported mixed findings and called for further research into the relationship between personality factors and perceived hysterectomy outcome.

Finally, three studies were conducted using the MMPI as part of the investigation of surgery to alleviate lower back pain, each taking a different approach in its use of the MMPI to evaluate treatment efficacy. Oostdam and Duivenvoorden (1983) used six scales of the Dutch version of the MMPI (in addition to other measures) to predict outcome of surgery for lower back pain. The discriminating variables among satisfactory, moderate, and unsatisfactory outcomes were somatic complaints, hypochondriasis, and hysteria. Turner et al. (1986) examined the efficacy of the Pain Assessment Index (PAI) of the MMPI to predict outcome following lumbar surgery. The PAI had good predictive ability, though Hs and Hy performed almost as well on the same task. Finally, Uomoto et al. (1988) pitted the MMPI against the Millon Clinical Multiaxial Inventory (MCMI) in a test of outcome prediction for lumbar laminectomy. Both instruments showed moderate predictive ability.

Andersen, 1949; Ferreira, 1953; Fleming, 1981; Hunt & Hampson, 1980; Hutzler et al., 1981; Jurko et al., 1974; Oostdam & Duivenvoorden, 1983; Ruja, 1951; Tsoi et al., 1984; Turner et al., 1986; Uomoto et al., 1988; Vidor, 1951; Witton & Ellsworth, 1962.

The Treatment of Psychological Disorders

Schizophrenia

A review of the most recent literature on the use of the MMPI with schizophrenic populations shows that the MMPI has been used for the evaluation of treatment effects, the prediction of treatment outcome, and the measurement of follow-up success.

Butter and Dutil (1985) reported on the assessment of psychosocial treatment with chronic schizophrenics using neuropsychopharmacological indices. Neuroleptic availability with genotypic and phenotypic typology of introversion, extroversion, and ambiversion characterized the personality structure of the schizophrenic patients. However, clinical, psychometric, and psychophysiological results failed to differentiate between the psychosocially treated and control patients.

Burkovsky et al. (1988) examined the prognostic significance of clinical, personality, and psychosocial characteristics of schizophrenic patients in rehabilitative therapy. Of the 487 characteristics that were analyzed, 209 were linked with remission type at a statistically significant level.

In a follow-up study of former ECT therapy and drug-treated schizophrenic patients, Exner and Murillo (1977) found that the two groups did not differ significantly from each other on a battery of tests, including the MMPI. Both groups, however, continued to differ from controls, who performed better in several intellectual operations, had better reality testing on the Rorschach, and gave fewer pathological answers to MMPI questions. In spite of these differences in performance, the functional effectiveness of both the ECT- and drug-treated schizophrenics is emphasized.

Anger-Diaz, 1987; Burkovsky et al., 1988; Butter & Dutil, 1985; Distler, 1964; Exner & Murillo, 1977; Fischer et al., 1969; Gendlin, 1962; Grace, 1964; Hennessy, 1971; Jenkins, 1952; Kiesler, 1971; Kiesler et al., 1967; Luckey & Schiele, 1967; Marks et al., 1963; May, 1968; May & Distler, 1968; McKeever et al. 1965; Mena, 1965; Murillo & Exner, 1973; Overall et al., 1964; L. Pancheri et al., 1988; Pearson, 1950; Reznikoff & Toomey, 1965; Ritchey, 1968; Rogers, 1967; Ruja, 1951; Schiele et al., 1969; Schofield et al., 1954; Simon et al., 1958; Truaz, 1971; Vestre et al., 1969; Weiss, 1957; Wirt & Simon, 1959.

Anxiety Disorders

Recent research in the MMPI treatment evaluation literature has addressed the treatment of anxiety disorders, including phobias (Delzotti et al., 1983; Dubois,

1983; Levitt, 1975), obsessive–compulsive disorder (Fals Stewart & Schafer, 1993), panic disorder/agoraphobia (Der & Lewington, 1990; Faravelli & Albanesi, 1987; Linder, 1981, Munjack, 1985; Pancheri et al., 1988a), and post-traumatic stress disorder (Hickling et al., 1986; Munley et al., 1994; Peniston & Kulkosky, 1991; Perconte & Griger, 1991). These disorders have been treated from a variety of approaches, including biofeedback (Crebelli et al., 1983; Hardt & Kamiya, 1978; Lavellee et al., 1982; Plotkin & Rice, 1981), pharmacotherapy (Munjack, 1985; Overall et al., 1973; Stein et al., 1978), cognitive therapy (Fals-Stewart & Schafer, 1993; Linder, 1981), systematic desensitization (Levitt, 1975), stress inoculation (Holcomb, 1986), and hypnosis (Der & Lewington, 1990; Elkins, 1984; Tosi et al., 1982).

Aitken et al., 1971; Andrews, 1973; Archibald, & Tuddenham, 1965; Brick et al., 1962, 1965, 1966; Crebelli et al., 1983; Delle Chiaie et al., 1981; Delzotti et al., 1983; Der & Lewington, 1990; DeShazo, & Kissiah, 1971; Dubois, 1983; Elkins, 1984; Fals Stewart & Schafer, 1993; Faravelli & Albanesi, 1987; Gallagher, 1953b; Goorney, 1970; Hardt & Kamiya, 1978; Hickling et al., 1986; Holcomb, 1986; Horowitz, 1970; Jacobs et al., 1971; Johnson & Spielberger, 1968; Kaplan, 1966; Kraft & Wijesinghe, 1970; Lavellee et al., 1982; Lebo et al., 1958; Levitt, 1975; Linder, 1981; Lorr et al., 1961; McReynolds, 1969; Metzen, 1971; Munjack, 1985; Munley et al., 1994; Nawas, 1971; Newburger, 1963; Overall et al., 1973; Pancheri, 1982; L. Pancheri et al., 1988; Peniston & Kulkosky, 1991; Perconte & Griger, 1991; Plotkin & Rice, 1981; Raab et al., 1964; Rehm & Marston, 1968; Rosenthal, 1967; Schroeder & Craine, 1971; Sherman, 1972; Shrauger & Katkin, 1970; Sifneos, 1969; Simono, 1968; Solyom et al., 1969, 1971; Stein et al., 1978; Stoudenmire, 1972; Tanner, 1971; Tosi et al., 1982; Watkins, 1967.

Mood Disorders

During the past two decades, the MMPI has been frequently used to assess treatment effectiveness for major depression, depressive symptoms, and depressive disorders in a wide variety of populations, including maritally distressed couples (Sher et al., 1990), the elderly (Fry, 1984; Tibilova & Tsytsareva, 1988), alcohol abusers (Donovan & O'Leary, 1979; Shaw et al., 1975), mentally retarded individuals (Matson, 1982), and clinically-depressed individuals (Collet et al., 1987; Horton & Johnson, 1980; Rush & Watkins, 1981). Although research on unipolar mood disorders has been vigorous in the MMPI literature, few MMPI studies have focused on participants diagnosed with a bipolar mood disorder (Ananth et al., 1979; Vein & Airapetov, 1986; L. Pancheri et al., 1988; Tibilova & Tsytsareva, 1988).

Among depressive clients, behavioral approaches (Azrin & Besalel, 1981; Matson, 1982) and cognitive approaches (Mirabel-Sarron et al., 1993; Nezu, 1986; Shipley & Fazio, 1973) to therapy have been extensively evaluated by MMPI research. For example, Rehm's Self-Control Therapy program has been evaluated by examining improvement in scores on the D scale of the MMPI, as well as the overall reduction in psychopathology as measured by a variety of MMPI scales (Fuchs & Rehm, 1977; Rehm, 1979, 1981).

Pharmacotherapeutic approaches to the treatment of depression have also been extensively evaluated in the recent MMPI literature, specifically focusing on the effects of clomipramine (Faravelli & Sacchetti, 1984), fluoxetine (Fava et al., 1993), imipramine (Donnelly et al., 1979), and lithium (Ananth et al., 1979; Donnelly et al., 1978; Garvey et al., 1983; House & Martin, 1975). One question which has generated research in this area is whether or not the MMPI may be used as a prognostic tool for predicting which depressed clients will respond positively to pharmacotherapy (Garvey et al., 1983; Habrat & Walecka, 1991). Although House and Martin (1975) concluded that the D and Pt scales of the MMPI could be used to identify those clients likely to respond to pharmacotherapy, Donnelly et al. (1978, 1979) were unable to predict response using any of the standard clinical scales. However, using empirically derived MMPI scales, they obtained accuracy rates in the range of 90% for the identification of those likely to respond positively to both lithium and imipramine.

Ananth et al., 1979; Azrin & Besalel, 1981; Ban et al., 1969; Bellak & Rosenberg, 1966; Brick et al., 1962, 1965, 1966; Cole et al., 1959; Collet et al., 1987; De Piano et al., 1984; Dimascio et al., 1968; Donnelly et al., 1978, 1979; Donovan & O'Leary, 1979; Faravelli & Sacchetti, 1984; Fava et al., 1993; Flemenbaum & Schiele, 1971; Friedman et al., 1961; Fry, 1984; Fryer & Timberlake, 1963; Fuchs & Rehm, 1977; Fullerton et al., 1968; Garvey et al., 1983; Goldstein & Brauzer, 1971; Gomes-Schwartz, 1978; Habrat & Walecka, 1991; Hankoff et al., 1964; Heller et al., 1971; Hollister & Overall, 1965; Hollister et al., 1963; Horton & Johnson, 1980; House & Martin, 1975; Jacob et al., 1983; Janecek et al., 1963; Khanna et al., 1963; Kurland et al., 1967a, b, 1968; Lewinsohn & Shaw, 1969; Lewinsohn et al., 1970; Matson, 1982; Mirabel-Sarron et al., 1993; Nelson-Gray et al., 1989; Nezu, 1986; Nussbaum & Michaux, 1963; Nussbaum et al., 1963; Olson, 1962; Overall et al., 1962, 1964, 1966, 1973; L. Pancheri et al., 1988; Peniston et al., 1986; Reardon et al., 1977; Rehm, 1979, 1981; Robin & Wiseberg, 1958; Roulet et al., 1962; Rush & Watkins, 1981; Sanchez et al., 1980; Sandifer et al., 1965; Santucci, 1963; Schmidt & Miller, 1983; Shaffer et al., 1964a; Shaw et al., 1975; Sher et al., 1990; Shipley & Fazio, 1973; Simopoulos et al., 1968; Stanley & Fleming, 1962; Stein et al., 1978; Tibilova & Tsytsareva, 1988; Tredici et al., 1966; Truax, 1971; Uhlenhuth & Park, 1963; Vein & Airapetov, 1986; Weckowicz et al., 1971; Wilson et al., 1963, 1966, 1967; Wittenborn & Plante, 1963; Wittenborn et al., 1961, 1973.

Substance Use Disorders

Substance abuse is perhaps the largest mental health problem facing clinicians today. Clients can be addicted to any number of available substances, and this often impacts the type of treatment they need. Moreover, substance abuse may be just one of several comorbid disorders found in clients. The research into substance abuse has been both prolific and varied. The research using the MMPI to investigate substance abuse issues is no exception. Considering the quantity and breadth of research in this area, only selected investigations using the MMPI in substance abuse treatment evaluation and prediction will be described.

Several investigations have focused their use of the MMPI on evaluating scale score differences between groups after treatment for substance abuse; the findings have not always been consistent. For example, Beasley et al. (1991) examined MMPI differences among individuals completing 12 months of biobehavioral treatment for alcoholism. Outcome was predicted by elevations on scales F, Hs, and Ma. In an investigation of alcoholism treatment facilities, Schroeder and Piercy (1979) found equally high prevalence rates of the 2-4/4-2 MMPI code type. This finding was interpreted as an indication of an alcohol-specific personality type.

Research on nonalcohol substance abuse has uncovered inconsistent patterns of MMPI scale scores for successful treatment. Biasco et al. (1983) examined the personalities of individuals in a therapeutic community drug abuse program. Successful males had higher scores on scales Hs, Hy, and Mf; successful females had high Si scale scores and low Mf scale scores. Code types for successfully and unsuccessfully treated individuals were also identified: 4-9/9-4 code types were not successful, whereas 4-8/8-4 code types enjoyed treatment success. Unlike the female drug users in Beasley et al. (1991), female narcotic addicts gave lower scores on MMPI scales Hs, D, and Hy after treatment (Ross et al., 1974). Williams and Baron (1982) also found lower scores on scales Hs and D among a group of youthful substance abusers receiving short-term hospital treatment. However, they also reported decreased scores on scales Pa and Rare Answers. Finally, heroin addicts successfully treated with a multimodal program were characterized by lower scale Pt scores and higher scale Es and L scores than those of unsuccessfully treated addicts (Sutker et al., 1976).

Another area of research using the MMPI has focused on the prediction or delineation of groups of substance abusers who will complete from those who will prematurely terminate treatment with limited consistency among the findings. Huber and Danahy (1975) found no differences on either the MacAndrew Alcoholism Scale or the Unitary Alcoholism Scale between completers and noncompleters in a 90-day alcoholism treatment program. In an investigation of treatment termination variables, McWilliams and Brown (1977) found no differences in MMPI scale scores among three groups of alcoholics in treatment (treatment completers, those prematurely discharged by the program, and those who prematurely withdrew from the program). All three groups of alcoholics had elevated scores on scales D, Pd, and Sc. Sladen and Mozdzierz (1985) found consistent differences on validity and Sc scales among inpatient alcohol treatment completers and noncompleters. Additionally, they developed the Against Medical Advice (AMA) Scale from MMPI items which differentiated completers from noncompleters and was found to have moderately high predictive ability.

Finally, at least two investigations have focused on MMPI code type differences between substance abuse treatment program completers and noncompleters. Zuckerman et al. (1975) compared completers and noncompleters of therapeutic communities for drug abuse. A higher prevalence of code type 4-9/9-4 was found among completers; noncompleters had higher rates of two-point codes containing psychotic scales. This somewhat contradicts the finding of Biasco et al. (1983) mentioned earlier wherein unsuccessfully treated drug abusers had a high rate of the 4-9/9-4 code types and successful clients had a higher rate of the 4-8/8-4 code type. Sheppard et al. (1988) examined MMPI code types among completers and noncompleters of a residential alcoholism treatment program. Three types of clients emerged: those with code type 4-2-8 and additional psychopathology, those with code type 4-9/9-4, and those with code type 2-4/4-2. Again, in direct contrast to the findings of Zuckerman et al. (1975) with drug abusers, Sheppard et. al. (1988) found the 4-9/9-4 code type to be most prevalent among noncompleters.

Amini et al., 1982; Bean & Karasievich, 1975; Beasley et al., 1991; Biasco et al., 1983; Blum et al., 1988; Bobrov et al., 1993; Bozzetti, 1972; Cernovsky, 1984; Clemens & Kahn, 1990; Craig, 1984a, b; Curlee, 1971; DeLeon & Jainchill, 1982; Denson & Sydiaha, 1970; Ditman et al., 1970; Donovan & O'Leary, 1979; Dunlap, 1961; Edwards et al., 1977; Ends & Page, 1957; Filstead et al., 1983; Flores, 1982; Fowler et al., 1967; Frankel & Murphy, 1974; Grof et al., 1973; Guenther, 1983; Haertzen et al., 1968; Heilbrun, 1971; Huber & Danahy, 1975; Hutzell, 1984; Kahn et al., 1979; Kaplan, 1972; Keegan & Lachar, 1979; Kennedy & Minami, 1993; Knapp et al., 1991; Kraft, 1970; Kraft & Wijesinghe, 1970; Krakowski & Smart, 1974; Krasnoff, 1976; Krupitskii et al., 1993; Kurland et al., 1967b; Lanyon et al., 1972; Lerner, 1953; Levinson & McLachlan, 1973; Lowe & Thomas, 1976; Mabli et al., 1985; Mascia, 1969; McWilliams & Brown, 1977; Miller, 1978; Monroe & Hill, 1958; Moran, 1978; Muzekari, 1965; Nathan et al., 1986; O'Neil et al., 1983; Ochoa Mangado et al., 1992; Ottomanelli et al., 1978; Ottomanelli, 1976, 1977; Overall et al., 1973; Passini, 1977; Pekarik et al., 1986; Pena-Ramos & Hornberger, 1979; Poulos, 1981; Price & Curlee-Salisbury, 1975; Rae, 1972; Robinson & Little, 1982; Ross et al., 1974; Russell & Bennett, 1972; Schroeder & Piercy, 1979; Shaffer et al., 1964b; Shaffer et al., 1962; Shaw et al., 1975; Sheppard et al., 1988; Sherer et al., 1984; Sikes et al., 1965; Simopoulos et al., 1970; Sinnett, 1961; Skolnick & Zuckerman, 1979; Sladen & Mozdzierz, 1985; Smith et al., 1971; Snowden, 1984; Snowden & Cotler, 1974; Soskin, 1970; Sutker et al., 1976; Svanum & Dallas, 1981; Svanum & McAdoo, 1989; Thurstin et al., 1986; Tosi et al., 1993; Viaille, 1964; Walfish et al., 1990a, b; Weiss & Russakoff, 1977; Wesson et al., 1974; Wilkinson et al., 1971; Williams & Baron, 1982; Wilson & Kennard, 1978; Zuckerman et al., 1975.

Eating Disorders

Recent literature has investigated the influence of personality on treatment effectiveness with eating disorders, particularly anorexia nervosa. It has been suggested that better prognostic outcomes are offered by lower general profiles on the MMPI, especially lower scores on the Sc scale (Pierloot et al., 1975). A follow-up study by Schork et al. (1994) found a substantial relationship between the severity of eating disorder symptomatology and the severity of comorbid general psychopathology. Women who had no residual eating disorder showed essentially no psychopathology on the MMPI, while those still suffering from a severe eating disorder displayed clinically significant levels of comorbid general psychopathology. Rank order correlations were significant between levels of eating disorder symptom severity and 7 MMPI clinical scales.

The MMPI also can be utilized as a measure of treatment effectiveness. Skoog et al. (1984) compared pre- and post-treatment profiles and found that Hs, D, and Si scores decreased significantly after treatment. Gerstein and Hotelling (1987) found post-treatment changes in MMPI profiles that indicated fewer feelings of inferiority and insecurity and the ability to implement changes learned in therapy.

The MMPI is further useful in the prediction of treatment outcomes for particular subtypes of anorexia nervosa. A study by Edwin et al. (1988) found that prediction of the ability to maintain improvement after inpatient treatment was enhanced by the classification of anorexic subjects into clinical subtypes. Results showed that 49% of the restricting subtype subjects maintained improvement at follow-up, compared with 29% of the bulimic subtype subjects. While successful subjects of the restricting subtype were more distressed and dramatic, MMPI profiles that were elevated in distress, depression, and impulsivity predicted failure among subjects of the bulimic subtype.

Colligan et al., 1983; Edwin et al., 1988; Gerstein & Hotelling, 1987; McFarlane et al., 1982; Pierloot et al., 1975; Schork et al., 1994; Skoog et al., 1984.

Sexual Disorders

The MMPI often serves as a measure of the effectiveness of treatment of sexual disorders. In a study of orgasmic dysfunction, Munjack (1976) noted significant improvement on the MMPI and other objective measures, lending support to a behavioral treatment approach. Price (1981) noted improvement over waiting-list controls for men with secondary erectile dysfunction who participated in group therapy. Cionini and Giovannoni (1984) presented a case of sexual impotence that was successfully treated with EMG biofeedback. Subsequent MMPI profiles were improved for the Mf and Si scales. Although broader cognitive-behavioral intervention is desirable in cases of impotence connected with more general problems, EMG biofeedback is presented as the treatment of choice given this particular personality profile.

The MMPI is also useful for treatment planning with pre- and postsurgery transsexuals. Hunt and Hampson (1980) followed 17 biological males who had undergone sex-reassignment surgery, finding no changes in levels of psychopathology and only modest gains in overall functioning and interpersonal relationships. It is concluded that an individual's presurgery adjustment is one of the best indicators of success in coping with the stress of surgery. Fleming (1981) examined assessment issues concerning transsexualism and found significant differences in mean raw scores attributable to both sex and surgical status. Postsurgical subjects were found to have higher levels of psychological adjustment.

Cionini & Giovannoni, 1984; Fleming, 1981; Hunt & Hampson, 1980; Munjack, 1976; Price, 1981; Reynolds, 1981.

The Treatment of Medical Disorders

Neuropsychological Injury

In A compendium of neuropsychological tests: Administration, norms, and commentary, Spreen and Strauss (1991) provided thorough descriptions of a wide range of commonly used neuropsychological and personality tests (including the MMPI). Emphasis was placed on clinically useful means for making inferences about the functional integrity of brain regions. The authors included instructions for administration, scoring procedures, sample score sheets, normative data, and information on reliability and validity.

Recent literature shows that personality measures not only serve as aides for making inferences and diagnoses, but also assist in predicting of neuropsychological results. Walker et al. (1987) evaluated the effects of brain injury on premorbid personality and subsequent problematic behavioral manifestations in adults with closed-head injuries. Comparisons were made between nonrecovered patients and recovered patients who had returned to work, school, or sheltered workshops. Results showed that nonrecovered patients were significantly higher on the Pd scale. Kuperman et al. (1979b) examined the role of the MMPI in predicting the outcome of neurosurgery for patients with one or more disrupted discs. Their findings showed that even in cases with a well-documented need for surgery, psychological factors can significantly influence outcome. The authors suggested presurgery psychological interventions that may increase the likelihood of a good outcome.

Amini et al., 1982; Andersen, 1949; Anker, 1961; Archer, 1994; Bell, 1961; Ferreira, 1953; Johnston & McNeal, 1964, 1967; Jurko et al., 1974; Kuperman et al., 1979b; Ruble, 1961; Ruja, 1951; Schoenberg & Carr, 1963; Vidor, 1951; Walker et al., 1987; Witton & Ellsworth, 1962; Wood et al., 1976.

Chronic Pain

Within the MMPI literature on chronic pain and headaches, researchers have vigorously attempted to identify MMPI scales which are predictive of treatment success or failure. The results of this line of research, however, have been inconclusive and, at times, contradictory. While some studies have concluded that the Hs and Hy scales are significant predictors (e.g., Akerlind et al., 1992), others fail to support their effectiveness (e.g., Aronoff & Evans, 1982). Of those studies which have found support for the predictive use of the Hs scale, some studies conclude that high scores are predictive of success (e.g., Brandwin & Kewman, 1982), while others conclude that high scores are predictive of poor treatment outcome (e.g., Kuperman et al., 1979a; McCreary et al., 1979). Disagreement also exists concerning whether or not the D scale is predictive (Jacob et al., 1983; Sweet, 1985), as well as whether a high score on the D scale is predictive of desirable or undesireable treatment outcome (Brandwin & Kewman, 1982; Kleinke & Spangler, 1988). Similarly, the predictive value of Smith and Duerksen's (1979) Pain Assessment Index, which is a weighted combination of six MMPI scales, has been supported by some research (Turner et al., 1986), but other research has failed to support it (Guck et al., 1987).

The inconclusive nature of the research described above may be explained by the heterogeneous nature of the chronic pain population. Costello et al., (1987) addressed this possibility by developing a four-cluster typology system: P-A-I-N. In this system, Type P patients have multiple scale elevations, Type N patients have no scale elevations, and Type A patients are intermediate to both Type P and Type N. Type I patients have primary elevations on scales Hs, D, and Hy. While this typology has been proposed for use by pain clinics in matching treatment to the type of client (Costello et al., 1989), it has been criticized for being too restrictive for use; in one clinical sample, the classification algorithm failed to classify 69% of the MMPI profiles (Robinson et al., 1989). Research is needed to determine whether treatment by type interactions affect treatment outcome, as well as whether the interactions affect the predictive value of the MMPI scales.

The MMPI has been used to assess the effectiveness of a wide range of treatments, including behavior therapy (Blanchard, 1985; Hudgens, 1979), surgery (Oostdam & Duivenvoorden, 1983; Uomoto et al., 1988), accupuncture (Tavola et al., 1992; Toomey et al., 1977), hypnotherapy (Howard et al., 1982), and biofeedback (Baiocco, 1991; Lacroix et al., 1986).

Akerlind et al., 1992; Aronoff & Evans, 1982; Baiocco, 1991; Beausoleil & Rioux, 1983; Blanchard, 1982; Blanchard, 1983; Blanchard, 1985; Brandwin & Kewman, 1982; Brennan et al., 1987; Collet, 1987; Costello et al., 1987, 1989; Delzotti et al., 1983; Diamond & Montrose, 1984; Dolce et al., 1986; Ellertson, 1988; Evans & Blanchard, 1988; Ford et al., 1983; Freeman et al., 1980; Grazzi et al., 1988; Guck et al., 1987, 1988; Howard, Reardon, & Tosi, 1982; Hudgens, 1979; Jacob et al., 1983; King & Snow, 1989; Kleinke & Spangler, 1988; Kuperman et al., 1979a; Lacroix et al., 1986; Love & Peck, 1987; McArthur et al., 1987; McCreary et al., 1979; Miller, 1990; Moore et al., 1986; Naliboff et al., 1988; Onorato & Tsushima, 1983; Oostdam & Duivenvoorden, 1983; Peniston et al., 1986; Reich et al., 1985; Robinson et al., 1989; Seltzer et al., 1983; Smith & Duerksen, 1979; Snyder, 1990; Sweet, 1981, 1985; Tavola et al., 1992; Toomey et al., 1977; Tsushima & Stoddard, 1990; Tsushima et al., 1987, 1991; Turner et al., 1986; Uomoto et al., 1988; Williams, 1987; Williams et al., 1986; Wojciechowski, 1984.

Hypertension

A handful of studies have been conducted which investigate treatment for hypertension. Generally, the role of the MMPI in these investigations has been one of a number of administered psychological tests. In each of the studies, the primary focus was on testing the effectiveness of one treatment versus another.

Frankel, 1978; Goldstein et al., 1982; Scita et al., 1988; Wadden, 1983, 1984.

Research with Special Populations

Criminal Justice Populations

Sex Offenders   The MMPI has often been administered before and after treatment as a measure of treatment efficacy for sex offenders. Various types of treatments have been tested with the MMPI. For example, Whitaker and Wodarski (1988) used the MMPI to test the efficacy of a time-limited outpatient treatment program for a sample of eight male sex offenders. Stava (1984) used a test battery which included the MMPI, measures of penile tumescence, and other instruments to assess treatment effects of hypnotically induced dreams in a sample of pedophiles. Miner et al. (1990) used the MMPI to show improvement in life circumstances of 50 men released by the California Sex Offender Treatment and Evaluation Project. Silver (1976) utilized the MMPI to assess an outpatient treatment program based on group interaction and behavior therapy principles for adult sex offenders. Finally, Valliant and Antonowicz (1992) found no significant MMPI profile differences between a group of male sex offenders and a group of offenders imprisoned for assault-related crimes.

Additional research on sex offenders using the MMPI has focused on specific types of sex offenders. Chaffin (1992) used the MMPI to assess personality disturbance in 23 father–daughter/stepdaughter sexual abusers prior to their completion of a two-year outpatient treatment program. Pretreatment personality assessment was related to treatment outcome. Similarly, Kalichman et al. (1990) found a significant relationship between pretreatment MMPI profile type and subsequent treatment participation. Attendance at group meetings and ratings of client participation by clinicians were predicted by certain MMPI scales. Finally, Davis and Hoffman (1991) administered the MMPI before and after a group treatment program for 61 incarcerated child molesters. Scales L, D, Hy, Pt, and Si decreased significantly after treatment.

Cabeen & Coleman, 1961; Chaffin, 1992; Davis & Hoffman, 1991; Kalichman et al., 1990; Miner, Marques, Day, & Nelson, 1990; Silver, 1976; Stava, 1984; Valliant & Antonowicz, 1992; Whitaker & Wodarski, 1988.

Other Offender Types   In addition to the work done with sex offender samples, the MMPI has been used with a wide variety of offenders, institution types, and research designs. The MMPI has been used most frequently as a measure of treatment effectiveness among various types of offenders.

Edwards and Roundtree (1981) found no significant difference on scale Es of the MMPI between first offender shoplifters who received and those who did not receive eight weeks of group therapy. In another investigation of first offenders, Panton (1979) used the MMPI to assess the effectiveness of an intensive psychotherapeutic program versus the effect of not receiving therapy. Control subjects showed no significant scale differences at posttest. Subjects completing the therapy improved significantly on several clinical and supplemental scales.

Ziegler et al. (1978) found significant MMPI scale score changes in a group of incarcerated alcoholics having completed six months of a multimodal milieu treatment program. Positive changes were found for scales F, Pt, Es, L, K, D, Si, and A. The authors noted the Pd scale as an exception: The increase in that scale score was not viewed as a positive finding.

Finally, the MMPI has also been used in a predictive capacity with criminal populations. McNamara and Andrasik (1982) investigated recidivism risk in a sample of 64 adult males paroled from an institutional behavior modification program. Recidivism was not predictable from MMPI scores. Villanueva et al. (1988) administered the MMPI to 98 male offenders in a residential treatment center in an investigation of personality characteristics in offenders. Discriminant analysis was used to differentiate successful from unsuccessful offenders in the program. Four scales (Prison Adjustment, O-H, Hs, and Mf) combined to differentiate 70% of the cases.

Amini et al., 1982; Brick et al., 1962, 1965, 1966; Caditz, 1961; Deforest & Johnson, 1981; Edwards & Roundtree, 1981; Forman, 1960; Haertzen et al., 1968; Heilbrun, 1971; Jacobson & Wirt, 1969; Leak, 1980; Lebo et al., 1958; Lerner, 1953; Mabli et al., 1985; Mathias & Sindberg, 1986; McNamara & Andrasik, 1982; Panton, 1979; Persons, 1965; Persons & Marks, 1970; Scapinello & Blanchard, 1987; Sowles & Gill, 1970; Veldhuizen, 1972; Villanueva et al., 1988; Watt, 1949; Weiss, 1957; Ziegler et al., 1978.

Obesity and Weight Control Clients

Efforts have been made to determine whether the MMPI may be used to identify obese individuals who are likely to succeed in weight loss programs. Research thus far has been inconclusive (Bradley et al., 1980; Sanso, 1984). Wadden and Lucas (1980) observed a positive correlation between weight loss and the Es scale, along with negative correlations between weight loss and scores on scales Hs and Hy, suggesting the possibility that certain profile configurations could be used prognostically. In addition, a panic–fear scale has been related to weight loss; individuals with lower scores were more likely to succeed in a calorie-restriction diet program (Flanagan & Wagner, 1991). Despite findings such as these which suggest that certain MMPI scales may be useful in predicting the likilhood of success, other research has failed to support this claim. Keegan, Dewey, and Lucas (1987) observed no correlations between weight loss and MMPI scores; however, several scales, including Es, Si, and Do, were correlated with compliant behavior and program attendance. Although the research to date has been inconclusive, it should be noted that it is unrealistic to discuss a population of obese individuals as a homogeneous group. No efforts have been made to date to identify subgroups of obese individuals and to determine if different scales are predictive of success among differing subgroups.

The MMPI also has been used to identify psychological changes which occur during the weight loss process (McCall, 1974). Prior to weight loss, a higher level of general psychopathology has been observed in obese samples (Hutzler et al., 1981), while a sample of successful weight losers had significantly lower mean scores than a sample of unsuccessful attempters for almost all of the MMPI clinical scales (McCall, 1973).

Biggers, 1966; Bradley et al., 1980; Fardan & Tyson, 1985; Flanagan & Wagner, 1991; Hutzler et al., 1981; Keegan et al., 1987; McCall, 1973, 1974; Molinari et al., 1991; Sanso, 1984; Wadden & Lucas, 1980.

Adolescents

Before the publication of the MMPI-A, clinicians who used the MMPI with adolescent populations frequently discovered problems with accuracy of interpretations based on adult norms. Williams (1986) described differences between adolescent and adult profiles, including case examples. Guidelines were presented for interpretative strategies, the use of the MMPI during treatment, and use with significant others. The need for a more appropriate measure for use with young people was noted. Archer (1994) presented information on the MMPI-A, designed specifically to include adolescent themes such as peer-group influences, family relations, and school issues. A number of recommendations for the use of the MMPI-A in treatment planning and for treatment outcome evaluation are included. Meyer (1993) offered practical help for diagnosing and treating emotional disorders in late adolescents, including specific assessment and test data and recommended intervention procedures.

The MMPI is often used with adolescents as a measure of treatment effectiveness. In Knapp et al.'s (1991) investigation of the variables that predicted success of adolescent inpatient drug treatment, favorable outcome was associated with gender, having fewer legal difficulties, fewer neurological risk factors, less pathology on the MMPI, high verbal IQ, and lower performance IQ. Knapp et al. stated that more emotionally disturbed children may benefit from augmentation or modification of available treatment programs. Kennedy and Minami (1993) found that relapse among adolescents with chemical dependencies was more likely for subjects with severe drug use and psychopathology, as measured by the MMPI. Abstinence from substance use, participation in self-help programs, and improved interpersonal functioning and family relationships were associated with treatment success.

The MMPI also has been used to assess the utility of novel treatment programs. For example, Trulson (1986) followed juvenile delinquents who received training under one of three martial arts programs. Group 1 received training in traditional Tae Kwon Do, Group 2 received training in a modern version that did not emphasize the psychological/philosophical aspects of the sport, and Group 3 served as a control group. Group 1 showed decreased aggressiveness, lowered anxiety, increased self-esteem and social facility, and an increased value in orthodoxy. Group 2 exhibited a greater tendency toward delinquency on the MMPI than they did at the beginning of the study and a large increase in aggressiveness. Lorandos (1990) evaluated the effectiveness of a Teen Ranch treatment program for adolescent boys. Intellectual and personality variables were compared to describe changes following treatment; nine of each were significant and decreases in pathological processes were noted. Positive change in intellectual assessments and decreases in depression over time indicated the effectiveness of the program.

Caditz, 1961; Capwell, 1945; Chabot, 1969; Colligan et al., 1983; Horton & Kriauciunas, 1970; Kennedy & Minami, 1993; Klinge et al., 1982; Knapp et al., 1991; Lorandos, 1990; Meyer, 1993; Persons, 1966; Shea, 1972; Sowles & Gill, 1970; Stockey, 1961; Szalanski, 1975; Trulson, 1986; Veldhuizen, 1972; Watt, 1949; Westendorp & Brink, 1982; C. L. Williams, 1986; Williams & Baron, 1982.

College Students

One of the most active areas of MMPI research with college clients in the past two decades has been the attempt to identify the "effective ingredients" necessary for therapeutic success. Recent research suggests that the availability of feedback from the MMPI is a vital ingredient for therapuetic success. Finn and Tonsager (1992) selected a sample of students who were on a college counseling center's waiting list, and then they divided the sample into two groups; one group completed the MMPI-2 and received test feedback, while the other group received examiner attention. The group that received test feedback reported a diminished degree of symptoms that was maintained through a 2-week follow-up. It should be noted that the mere administration of the MMPI does not appear to result in the reduction of symptoms (Glenwick & Arata, 1977), but the provision of feedback from the MMPI is an effective tool in therapeutic intervention. Other factors which have been related to therapeutic success among college students have been therapist variables such as empathy, genuineness, and positive regard (Schauble & Pierce, 1974), and the level of directiveness and exploration exhibited by the therapist (Gomes-Schwartz & Schwartz, 1978). Important client variables include willingness to become involved in the therapeutic process (Gomes-Schwartz, 1978; Strupp, 1980), willingness to explore the problem (Schauble & Pierce, 1974), and the initial level of distress experienced by the client (Gomes-Schwartz & Schwartz, 1978).

Anderson & Kunce, 1984; Andrews, 1973; Baird, 1979; Cooke & Kiesler, 1967; Dietzel & Abeles, 1975; Dougherty, 1976; Elliotty et al., 1987; Finn & Tonsager, 1992; Gallagher, 1952; Gerstein & Hotelling, 1987; Glenwick & Arata, 1977; Gomes-Schwartz, 1978; Gomes-Schwartz & Schwartz, 1978; Greenfield & Fey, 1956; Hardt & Kamiya, 1978; Hawkes, 1950; Jansen & Robb, 1970; Joanning, 1976; Johnsgard & Muench, 1965; Keithly et al., 1980; Kleinmuntz, 1960; Plotkin & Rice, 1981; Propst, 1980; Schauble & Pierce, 1974; Scheibe, 1965; Schonfield & Donner, 1972; Sell & Torres-Henry, 1979; Shipley & Fazio, 1973; Strupp, 1980; Strupp & Bloxom, 1975; Strupp & Hadley, 1979; Subotnik, 1972a,b.

Specific Topics

Therapist Variables

MMPI data have provided useful information on a variety of therapist variables that influence treatment outcome. For example, Ottomanelli (1978) examined the relationship between paraprofessional and professional counselor assignment and patient improvement, as measured by the MMPI. While patients assigned to a professional counselor showed significant decreases on the D and Sc scales, patients assigned to paraprofessional counselors did not exhibit significant decreases on any MMPI scales. Other therapist variables that have been studied include: amount of therapist contact, therapist expectancies, and perceptions of patient likeability.

Schmidt and Miller (1983) investigated the effect of the amount of therapist contact on patient outcome. In an 8-week program of behavioral management, cognitive restructuring, and assertiveness training, depressed outpatients were treated either individually by a single therapist, in small groups, in a large group, or with bibliotherapy. All treated groups improved substantially over the course of treatment, while waiting-list controls remained unchanged. There were no significant differences among treated groups, nor did the groups change significantly during the follow-up period. The effectiveness of this program was supported, but was not related to the amount of therapist contact.

Data analyses by Martin et al. (1976) indicated that therapist expectancies of clinical improvement were more predictive of patient adjustment than were patient expectancies. In further investigations of the effect of therapist expectancies on treatment outcomes, Martin et al. (1977a, b) found that general and patient-specific expectancies were associated with patient improvement as measured by the MMPI. Patient-specific expectancies were more closely correlated with outcome, though the combination of both expectancy measures was significantly predictive of treatment success. The data support a predictive, not causative, interpretation of the association between therapist expectancies and treatment outcome.

In a study of perceptions of patient likeability, Merbaum and Butcher (1982) elicited therapist nominations of "easy" and "difficult" patients and obtained MMPIs for each. Several factors differentiated easy from difficult patients, including significantly less pathology on the MMPI, a more favorable prognosis in psychotherapy, greater physical attractiveness if female, and less personality disorder. Therapists' affective response is discussed as a "nonspecific" treatment factor that may affect treatment outcome. Martin and Sterne (1976) found additional support for the contention that patients who are liked tend to improve more than less-liked patients. This was found to be true when the therapists' ratings of improvement were used as a criterion, but not when objective measures, such as the MMPI, were used. It was suggested that objective outcome measures be used in conjunction with therapists' ratings in an effort to guard against extraneous influences in the judgment of outcome.

Barret-Lennard, 1962; Barrington, 1961; Bondy, 1970; Carson & Heine, 1962; Carson & Llewellyn, 1966; Frayn, 1968; Garfield & Bergin, 1971a; Gomes-Schwartz & Schwartz, 1978; Heikkinen & Wegner, 1973; Martin & Sterne, 1976; Martin et al., 1976, 1977a, b; Matarazoo & Wiens, 1966; Matarazoo et al., 1963; McNair et al., 1962; McNeil & Cohler, 1957; Melnick, 1972; Merbaum & Butcher, 1982; Ottomanelli, 1978; L. Pancheri et al., 1988; Parsons et al., 1959; Pierce & Schauble, 1970; Rice, 1965; Roback & Strassberg, 1975; Schmidt & Miller, 1983; Sines, Silver, & Lucero, 1961; Sundberg, 1952; Van der Veen & Stoler, 1965; Wogan, 1965.

Therapist/Client Compatibility

MMPI data have proved to be a useful source of information on therapist–client compatibility. For example, a study by Baird (1979) found that subjects with more neurotic profiles chose therapist-directed therapies, while those with more characterological profiles preferred patient-directed approaches. Peake (1979) investigated the importance of therapist–client agreement for therapy outcome. Preparations to reduce clients' ambiguity about the relationship aspects of therapy were not found to improve agreement on the quality of the relationship conjointly experienced. Furthermore, an inconsistent relationship was found between agreement for therapy outcome and actual therapy outcome, as measured by the MMPI. Dougherty (1976) investigated patient–therapist matching for the prediction of optimal therapeutic outcomes. Three homogeneous typological categories of patients and therapists were identified, as well as two groups of therapists homogeneous with respect to therapeutic orientation. Dougherty derived five regression equations for predicting outcomes for each patient and therapist group. Results indicated significant differences in outcomes for the deterioration-matched group with both its control and the optimally matched group, thus demonstrating the usefulness of carefully planned matching techniques.

Schauble and Pierce (1974) studied the relationship between therapist and client in-therapy behavior and successful therapy outcomes. Successful outcome was related to the therapist variables of empathy, positive regard, genuineness, and concreteness and the client variables of internalization–externalization and exploration. While the importance of therapist behaviors was consistent throughout, client variables were significantly related to success only in the later stages of therapy. Shapiro et al. (1976) confirmed the relationship between therapist and patient evaluations of each other as likable and physically attractive, and as either a good patient or a competent therapist and ratings of improvement by both parties.

Arbuckle, 1956; Baird, 1979; Berman et al., 1984; Borghi, 1968; Carr, 1970; Dietzel & Abeles, 1975; Dougherty, 1976; Gassner, 1970; Goldstein, 1962; Guerney, 1956; Lichtenstein, 1966; Martin et al., 1976; Maser, 1969; Melnick, 1972; Pancheri et al., 1988b; Peake, 1979; Persons & Marks, 1970; Rogers, 1967; Schauble & Pierce, 1974; Snyder & Snyder, 1961; Van der Veen,1965; Wogan, 1965, 1970.

The Prediction of Therapeutic Success

The prediction of therapy success and outcomes has been a widely explored topic. Therefore, the studies that are included in the following section are those which are not included more appropriately elsewhere.

An obvious measure of therapy success is the prediction of symptom reduction. Martin and Sterne (1975) studied the relationship between patient-held and therapist-held expectations and recovery from serious psychiatric disorders. Therapists', but not patients', expectations were significantly associated with symptom reduction. Patrick (1984) found that awareness of having problems and a willingness to disclose personal information is a primary factor in predicting the outcome of psychiatric hospitalization. Dicks and McHenry (1985) found that personality variables related to defensiveness and personal insight predicted success by discriminating high, moderate, and low success in a behavioral ladder program for male inmates in a state penitentiary.

Another component of therapy success is participation versus attrition. DuBrin and Zastowny (1988) examined literature on early attrition from psychotherapy, comparing descriptions of 242 continuers and 64 dropouts using the MMPI and time competence, inner-directed, and feeling scales. Compliance with therapeutic regimens also has been investigated within specific patient populations. For example, Kalichman et al. (1990) studied the use of the MMPI in predicting treatment participation of incarcerated rapists. Results indicated a significant relationship between MMPI profile group membership and treatment participation. Various scales predicted both attendance and clinicians' ratings of subjects' participation in their treatment groups. Pekarik et al. (1986) investigated personality and demographic characteristics of dropouts and completers in an alcohol treatment program. Dropouts scored higher on the Pd scale; for completers, Pd scores were correlated with age and Denial scores were correlated with intelligence. Pekarik et al. suggested that completers were consciously attempting to give socially appropriate answers, while dropouts were engaged in denial.

Prediction of therapy outcome frequently has been investigated within specific patient populations. Young et al. (1980) examined schizophrenic and nonschizophrenic inpatients randomly assigned to short- versus long-term hospitalization. Scores from intake MMPIs were predictive of outcome for long-term nonschizophrenics only; for schizophrenic groups, unreliability of responses on the MMPI reduced the potential for prediction. Flynn and Salomone (1977) studied MMPI and closure data for successful and unsuccessful clients in a rehabilitation program. Results indicated modest MMPI predictive ability and no improvement in the predictive powers of "optimal" predictors composites over the full, 13-scale MMPI. Ghiselli (1983) also explored whether therapeutic outcome for an alcohol treatment program could be predicted. The MMPI was administered before therapy began, and several predictors were identified. Ghiselli recommended a correlational-regression approach in the determination of what to expect from therapy and the use of a parametric-clinical approach to explain therapeutic success or failure.

Adams, 1962; Akerlind et al., 1992; Albert, 1970; Ananth et al., 1979; Aronoff & Evans, 1982; Ayer et al., 1966; Baiocco, 1991; Ban et al., 1969; Barrington, 1961; Berman et al., 1984; Blanchard, 1983; Blanchard et al., 1992; Blumenthal, 1982; Bradley et al., 1980; Brandwin & Kewman, 1982; Brennan et al., 1987; Briggs, 1958; Briggs & Yater, 1966; Burkovsky et al., 1988; Collet, 1987; Craig, 1984a, b; Devlin, 1953; Dicks & McHenry, 1985; Dobbs, 1970; Dolce et al., 1986; DuBrin & Zastowny, 1988; Endicott & Endicott, 1964; Evans & Blanchard, 1988; Faltz, 1969; Filstead et al., 1983; Fiske et al., 1964; Flynn & Salomone, 1977; Ford et al., 1983; Forsyth & Fairweather, 1961; Gallagher, 1954; Garfield & Bergin, 1971b; Garfield et al., 1971a, b; Ghiselli, 1983; Glasscock, 1955; Gomes-Schwartz, 1978; Gouws, 1961; Grace, 1964; Habrat & Walecka, 1991; Haertzen, 1952; Haertzen et al., 1968; Harris & Christiansen, 1946; Haase & Ivey, 1970; Heilbrun, 1971; Hoskins, 1966; Huber & Danahy, 1975; Jacob et al., 1983; Jenkins, 1952; Johnson et al., 1971; Johnson et al., 1970; Johnston & McNeal, 1965; Kalichman et al., 1990; Keegan & Lachar, 1979; Keithly et al., 1980; Khavin, 1985; King & Snow, 1989; Kleinke & Spangler, 1988; Klett & Vestre, 1967; Klinge et al., 1982; Klonoff et al., 1987; Knapp et al., 1991; Krasnoff, 1976, 1977; Kuperman et al., 1979a, b; Lacroix et al., 1986; Lanyon, 1966; Levinson & McLachlan, 1973; Lowe, 1967; Lowe & Thomas, 1976; Marks et al., 1963; Martin & Sterne, 1975; Mascia, 1969; McCreary et al., 1979; McWilliams & Brown, 1977; Miller & Gottlieb, 1974; Moore et al., 1986; Muzekari, 1965; Oostdam & Duivenvoorden, 1983; Ottomanelli, 1977; Patrick, 1984; Pearson & Swenson, 1951; Pekarik et al., 1986; Perconte & Griger, 1991; Peterson, 1954; Pierce, 1968; Pumroy & Kogan, 1958; Rapaport, 1958; Reich et al., 1985; Robinson

& Little, 1982; Rosen et al., 1971; Sander, 1975; Sandness, 1967; Scapinello & Blanchard, 1987; Schofield & Briggs, 1958; Schofield et al., 1954; Shapiro et al., 1976; Sheppard et al., 1988; Sinnett, 1961; Skoog et al., 1984; Sladen & Mozdzierz, 1985; Sloane, 1976; Snowden, 1984; Stelmachers, 1963; Stoddard et al., 1988; Straus & Hess, 1993; Sulzer & Schiele, 1962; Sutker et al., 1976; Svanum & Dallas, 1981; Svanum & McAdoo, 1989; Sweet, 1981; Tibilova & Tsytsareva, 1988; Tsushima et al., 1991; Turner et al., 1986; Uomoto et al., 1988; Villanueva et al., 1988; Wadden, 1983; Walker et al., 1987; Walters et al., 1982; Williams, 1987; Williams et al., 1986; R. B. Williams, 1986; Windle, 1952; Wirt, 1955; Young et al., 1980; Zubin & Windle, 1954.

The Prediction of Premature Termination

Several attempts have been made to determine whether the MMPI may be used to predict those clients who will prematurely discontinue therapy. Although some have argued that there are no differences in MMPI scores between dropouts and persisters (Craig, 1984a, b; Evans & Blanchard, 1988; Nacev, 1980), several consistent observations have been made. First, differences in Pd scores have been consistently observed between the two groups (Clemens & Kahn, 1990; Huber & Danahy, 1975; Pekarik et al., 1986), often in conjunction with differences in Ma scores (Keegan & Lachar, 1979; Robinson & Little, 1982; Tsushima et al., 1991), suggesting that dropouts are often more impulsive, rebellious, and demonstrate poor judgment regarding the consequences of their actions. Second, differences in scores for the D scale suggest that dropouts may be pessimistic regarding the future and may lack confidence in their abilities to succeed (Blumenthal, 1982; Clemens & Kahn, 1990; Fals Stewart & Schafer, 1993). Finally, differences in Si scores suggest that the dropouts may have difficulty developing supportive social relationships and expressing their feelings openly in a therapeutic environment (Blumenthal, 1982; Fals Stewart & Schafer, 1993; Sacks & Levy, 1979). Based on these findings, it is likely that the MMPI may be used to identify clients who are at greater risk for treatment attrition.

Blumenthal, 1982; Borghi, 1965, 1968; Chaffin, 1992; Clemens & Kahn, 1990; Craig, 1984a, b; Daniels et al., 1963; DeLeon, 1984; DeLeon & Schwartz, 1984; DuBrin & Zastowny, 1988; Evans & Blanchard, 1988; Fals-Stewart & Schafer, 1993; Firestone & Witt, 1982; Gallagher, 1952; Horton & Kriauciunas, 1970; Huber & Danahy, 1975; Keegan & Lachar, 1979; King & Snow, 1989; Krakowski & Smart, 1974; Krasnoff, 1976, 1977; McAdoo & Roeske, 1973; McWilliams & Brown, 1977; Munley et al., 1994; Nacev, 1980; Pekarik et al., 1986; Robinson & Little, 1982; Sacks & Levy, 1979; Sheppard et al., 1988; Sladen & Mozdzierz, 1985; Tsushima et al., 1991.

Bibliography

Abse, D. W., Dahlstrom, W. G., & Tolley, A. G. (1960). Evaluation of tranquilizing drugs in the management of acute mental disturbance. *American Journal of Psychiatry* 116, 973–980.

Adams, H. B. (1962). Three measures of ego strength and prognosis for psychotherapy. *Journal of Clinical Psychology* 18, 490–494.

Adams, H. B. (1964). Therapeutic potentialities of sensory deprivation procedures. *International Mental Health Research Newsletter* 6, 7–9.

Adams, H. B., Cooper, G. D., & Carrera, R. N. (1972). Individual differences in behavioral reactions of psychiatric patients to brief partial sensory deprivation. *Perceptual and Motor Skills* 34, 199–217.

Adams, H. B., Robertson, M. H., & Cooper, G. D. (1966). Sensory deprivation and personality change. *Journal of Nervous and Mental Disease* 143, 256–265.

Aitken, R. C., Daly, R. J., Lister, J. A., & O'Connor, P. J. (1971). Treatment of flying phobia in aircrew. *American Journal of Psychotherapy* 25, 530–542.

Akerlind, I., Hornquist, J. O., & Bjurulf, P. (1992). Psychological factors in the long-term prognosis of chronic low back pain patients. *Journal of Clinical Psychology* 48, 596–605.

Albert, G. (1970). Sentence completions as a measure of progress in therapy. *Journal of Contemporary Psychotherapy* 3, 31–34.

Alexander, J. F. (1968). Perspectives of psychotherapy process: Dependency, interpersonal relationships, and sex differences. *Dissertation Abstracts* 49, 5197B.

Al-Issa, I., & Kraft, T. (1967). Personality factors in behaviour therapy. *Canadian Psychologist* 8, 218–222.

Alpher, V. S. (1992). Changes in identity and self-organization in psychotherapy of multiple personality disorder. *Psychotherapy* 29, 570–579.

Amini, F., Zilberg, N. J., Burke, E. L., & Salasnek, S. (1982). A controlled study of inpatient vs. outpatient treatment of delinquent drug abusing adolescents: One year results. *Comprehensive Psychiatry* 23, 436–444.

Ananth, J., Engelsmann, F., Kiriakos, R., & Kolivakis, T. (1979). Prediction of lithium response. *Acta Psychiatrica Scandinavica* 60, 279–286.

Ananth, J., Engelsmann, F., & Kiriakos, R. (1980). Evaluation of lithium response: Psychometric findings. *Canadian Journal of Psychiatry* 25, 151–154.

Andersen, A. L. (1949). Personality changes following prefrontal lobotomy in a case of severe psychoneurosis. *Journal of Consulting Psychology* 13, 105–107.

Anderson, A. V. (1959). Predicting response to group psychotherapy. *Dissertation Abstracts* 20, 1073.

Anderson, W. P. & Kunce, J. T. (1984). Diagnostic implications of markedly elevated MMPI Sc scale scores for nonhospitalized clients. *Journal of Clinical Psychology* 40, 925–930.

Andrews, J. M. (1973). A study of the effects of a filmed, vicarious, desensitization procedure in the treatment of manifest anxiety and test anxiety in community college students. *Dissertation Abstracts International* 33, 5399A.

Anger-Diaz, B. (1987). Efectos terapeuticos de un curso en computacion sobre la conducta de pacientes esquizofrenicos. (Therapeutic effects of a computer course on the behavior of schizophrenic patients.) *Salud Mental* 10, 72–80.

Angers, W. P., & Paulson, P. C. (1964). Cooperation between counseling and health services. *Journal of School Health* 34, 49–53.

Anker, J. M. (1961). Chronicity of neuropsychiatric hospitalization: A predictive scale. *Journal of Consulting Psychology* 25, 425–432.

Anzel, A. S. (1970). A-B typing and patient socioeconomic and personality characteristics in a quasi-therapeutic situation. *Journal of Consulting and Clinical Psychology* 35, 102–115.

Apostal, R. A. (1971). Personality descriptions of mental health center patients for use as pre-therapy information. *Mental Hygiene* 55, 119–120.

Arbuckle, D. S. (1956). Client perception of counselor personality. *Journal of Counseling Psychology* 3, 93–96.

Archer, R. P. (1994). Minnesota Multiphasic Personality Inventory-Adolescent. In M. E. Maruish (Ed.), *The use of psychological testing for treatment planning and outcome assessment* (pp. 423–452). Hillsdale, NJ: Lawrence Erlbaum Associates.

Archer, R. P., Gordon, R. A., Zillmer, E. A., & McClure, S. (1985). Characteristics and correlates of MMPI change within an adult psychiatric inpatient setting. *Journal of Clinical Psychology* 41, 739–746.

Archibald, H. C., & Tuddenham, R. D. (1965). Persistent stress reaction after combat—a 20-year follow-up. *Archives of General Psychiatry* 12, 475–481.

Aronoff, G. M., & Evans, W. O. (1982). The prediction of treatment outcome at a multidisciplinary pain center. *Pain* 14, 67–73.

Artunkal, S., & Togrol, B. (1964). Psychological studies in hyperthyroidism. In M. P. Cameron & M. O'Connor (Eds.), *Brain–thyroid relationships with special reference to thyroid disorders.* Boston: Little, Brown.

Ashby, J. D., Ford, D. H., Guerney, B. G., & Guerney, L. F. (1957). Effects on clients of a reflective and a leading type of psychotherapy. *Psychological Monographs* 71 (24, Whole No. 453).

Ayer, M. J., Thoreson, R. W., & Butler, A. J. (1966). Predicting rehabilitation success with the MMPI and demographic data. *Personnel and Guidance Journal* 44, 631–637.

Azrin, N. H., & Besalel, V. A. (1981). An operant reinforcement method of treating depression. *Journal of Behavior Therapy and Experimental Psychiatry* 12, 145–151.

Baiocco, G. (1991). Indici predittivi psicometrici e psicofisiologici in biofeedback training. (Psychophysiological and psychometric predictive signs in biofeedback training.) *Rivista di Psichiatria* 26, 339–343.

Baird, P. (1979). Relationships between certain MMPI factors and psychotherapeutic preferences. *Psychological Reports* 44, 1317–1318.

Baker, R. R. (1968). The effects of psychotropic drugs on psychological testing. *Psychological Bulletin* 69, 377–387.

Balance, W. D., Sandberg, S. S., & Bringmann, W. G. (1971). Acceptance of trait-descriptive vs. "medical model" oriented feedback statements. *Psychological Reports* 29, 539–544.

Balson, P. M. (1971). The use of behavior therapy techniques in crisis-intervention: A case report. *Journal of Behavior Therapy and Experimental Psychiatry* 2, 297–300.

Ban, T. A., Lehmann, H. E., & Green, A. A. (1969). Conditioning in the prediction of therapeutic outcome in depressions. *Conditional Reflex* 4, 115–123.

Bannister, D., & Beech, H. R. (1961). An evaluation of the Feldman prognosis scale for shock therapy. *Journal of Mental Science* 107, 503–508.

Barrett, C. L. (1969). Systematic desensitization versus implosive therapy. *Journal of Abnormal Psychology* 74, 587–592.

Barrett-Lennard, G. T. (1962). Dimensions of therapist response as causal factors in therapeutic change. *Psychological Monographs* 76 (43, Whole No. 562).

Barrington, B. (1961). Prediction from counselor behavior of client perception and of case outcome. *Journal of Counseling Psychology* 8, 37–42.

Barron, F. (1953a). Some test correlates of response to psychotherapy. *Journal of Consulting Psychology* 17, 235–241.

Barron, F. (1953b). An ego-strength scale which predicts response to psychotherapy. *Journal of Consulting Psychology* 17, 327–333.

Barron, F., & Leary, T. F. (1955). Changes in psychoneurotic patients with and without psychotherapy. *Journal of Consulting Psychology* 19, 239–245.

Barth, K., Nielsen, G., Haver, B., & Havik, O. E. (1988). Comprehensive assessment of change in patients treated with short-term dynamic psychotherapy: An overview: A 2-year follow-up study of 34 cases. *Psychotherapy and Psychosomatics* 50, 141–150.

Baughman, E. E., Shands, H. C., & Hawkins, D. R. (1959). Intensive psychotherapy and personality change: Psychological test evaluation of a single case. *Psychiatry* 22, 296–301.

Bean, K. L., & Karasievich, G. O. (1975). Psychological test results at three stages of inpatient alcoholism treatment. *Journal of Studies on Alcohol* 36, 838–852.

Beardsley, J. V., & Puletti, F. (1971). Personality (MMPI) and cognitive (WAIS) changes after levodopa treatment: Occurrence in patients with Parkinson's disease. *Archives of Neurology* 25, 145–150.

Beasley, J. D., Grimson, R. C., Bicker, A. A., & Closson, W. J. (1991). Follow-up of a cohort of alcoholic patients through 12 months of comprehensive biobehavioral treatment. *Journal of Substance Abuse Treatment* 8, 133–142.

Beausoleil, R., & Rioux, S. (1983). Traitement multi-dimensionnel pour patients souffrant de maux de dos chroniques: une etude comparative. (Multi-dimensional treatment for patients suffering from chronic low-back pain: A comparative study.) *Revue de Modification du Comportement* 13, 107–116.

Bednar, R. L., & Weinberg, S. L. (1970). Clinical judgments of client pathology and subsequent client improvement. *Journal of Clinical Psychology* 26, 443–446.

Bell, R. L. (1961). Factors influencing attitudes toward hospital discharge in neuropsychiatric patients. *Dissertation Abstracts* 22, 2067.

Bellak, L., & Rosenberg, S. (1966). Effects of antidepressant drugs on psychodynamics. *Psychosomatics* 7, 106–114.

Bellur, S. & Hermann, B. P. (1984). Emotional and cognitive effects of anticonvulsant medications. *Clinical Neuropsychology* 6, 21–23.

Berdie, R. F. (1954). Changes in self-ratings as a method of evaluating counseling. *Journal of Counseling Psychology* 1, 49–54.

Berdie, R. F. (1968). Perhaps mode of response does not explain intra-individual variability. *Psychological Reports* 23, 40–42.

Bergin, A. E. (1966). Some implications of psychotherapy research for therapeutic practice. *Journal of Abnormal Psychology* 71, 235–246.

Bergin, A. E., & Garfield, S. L. (Eds.). (1971). *Handbook of psychotherapy and behavior change: An empirical analysis.* New York: John Wiley & Sons.

Bergin, A. E., & Jasper, L. G. (1969). Correlates of empathy in psychotherapy: A replication. *Journal of Abnormal Psychology* 74, 477–481.

Bergin, A. E., & Strupp, H. H. (1972). *Changing frontiers in the science of psychotherapy.* Chicago: Aldine-Atherton.

Berman, J. J., Meyer, J., & Coats, G. (1984). Effects of program characteristics on treatment outcome: An interrupted time-series analysis. *Journal of Studies on Alcohol* 45, 405–410.

Bernard, J. L. & Bernard, M. L. (1984). The abusive male seeking treatment: Jekyll and Hyde. *Family Relations Journal of Applied Family and Child Studies* 33, 543–547.

Bernard, J. L., Kinzie, W. B., Tollman, G. A., & Webb, R. A. (1965). Some effects of a brief course in the psychology of adjustment on a psychiatric admissions ward. *Journal of Clinical Psychology* 21, 322–326.

Berzins, J. I., Ross, W. F., & Cohen, D. I. (1970). Relation of the A-B distinction and trust–distrust sets to addict patients' self-disclosures in brief interviews. *Journal of Consulting and Clinical Psychology* 34, 289–296.

Berzins, J. I., Bednar, R. L., & Severy, L. J. (1975). The problems of intersource consensus in measuring therapeutic outcomes: New data and multivariate perspectives. *Journal of Abnormal Psychology* 84, 10–19.

Biasco, F., Fritch, C. O., & Redfering, D. L. (1983). Personality differences between successfully and unsuccessfully treated drug abusers. *Social Behavior and Personality* 11, 105–111.

Biggers, W. H. (1966). Obesity: Affective changes in the fasting state. *Archives of General Psychiatry* 14, 218–221.

Bierenbaum, H., Nichols, M. P., & Schwartz, A. J. (1976). Effects of varying session length and frequency in brief emotive psychotherapy. *Journal of Consulting and Clinical Psychology* 44, 790–798.

Biondi, M., Costantini, A., Gualdi, M., & Pennacchi, D. (1985). Terapia farmacologica della cataratta: personalita e effetto placebo. (Pharmacological treatment of cataracts: Personality and the placebo effect.) *Medicina Psicosomatica* 30, 331–342.

Birk, L., Huddleston, W., Miller, E., & Cohler, B. (1971). Avoidance conditioning for homosexuality. *Archives of General Psychiatry* 25, 314–323.

Birk, L., Miller, E., & Cohler, B. (1970). Group psychotherapy for homosexual men by male-female cotherapists. *Acta Psychiatrica Scandinavica* 218(Suppl.), 1–38.

Black, C. J., & Petty, N. E. (1977). Psychotherapy in the treatment of vocal cord nodes. *Perceptual and Motor Skills* 45, 1302.

Blanchard, E. B. (1982). Sequential comparisons of relaxation training and biofeedback in the treatment of three kinds of chronic headache or, the machines may be necessary some of the time. *Behaviour Research and Therapy* 20, 469–481.

Blanchard, E. B. (1983). Nonpharmacologic treatment of chronic headache: Prediction of outcome. *Neurology* 33, 1596–1603.

Blanchard, E. B. (1985). Behavioral treatment of 250 chronic headache patients: A clinical replication series. *Behavior Therapy* 16, 308–327.

Blanchard, E. B., Scharff, L., Payne, A., & Schwarz, S. P. (1992). Prediction of outcome from cognitive-behavioral treatment of irritable bowel syndrome. *Behaviour Research and Therapy* 30, 647–650.

Blank, L. (1965). *Psychological evaluation in psychotherapy: Ten case histories.* Chicago: Aldine.

Blum, K., Trachtenberg, M. C., & Ramsay, J. C. (1988). Improvement of inpatient treatment of the alcoholic as a function of neurotransmitter restoration: A pilot study. *International Journal of the Addictions* 23, 991–998.

Blumenthal, J. A. (1982). Physiological and psychological variables predict compliance to prescribed exercise therapy in patients recovering from myocardial infarction. *Psychosomatic Medicine* 44, 519–527.

Bobrov, A. E., Shurygin, A. N., & Krasil'nikov, S. V. (1993). Study of the effectiveness of combined use of monoaminoxidase inhibitors and psychotherapy in the treatment of chronic alcoholism. *Journal of Russian and East European Psychiatry* 26, 3–11.

Bolding, O. T., & Willcutt, H. C. (1969). Physiological and psychological evaluation of the estrogen deprived patient. *Journal of the Medical Association of Alabama* 39, 459–463.

Bolding, O. T., & Willcutt, H. C. (1970). Weight loss and psychological observations of gynecological patients. *Alabama Journal of Medical Science* 7, 87–91.

Bondy, S. B. (1970). Completed psychotherapies: An investigation of the communications of values, therapeutic outcome, and selected therapist variables. *Dissertation Abstracts International* 30, 5227A.

Borghi, J. H. (1965). An investigation of treatment attrition in psychotherapy. *Dissertation Abstracts* 26, 1770.

Borghi, J. H. (1968). Premature termination of psychotherapy and patient-therapist expectations. *American Journal of Psychotherapy* 22, 460–473.

Boudewyns, P. A. (1974). Is "milieu therapy" in a short-term inpatient psychiatric setting worth the money? *International Mental Health Research Newsletter* 16, 7–8.

Boudewyns, P. A., & Wilson, A. E. (1972). Implosive therapy and desensitization therapy using free association in the treatment of inpatients. *Journal of Abnormal Psychology* 79, 259–268.

Bozzetti, L. P. (1972). Group psychotherapy with addicted smokers. *Psychotherapy and Psychosomatics* 20, 172–175.

Bradley, I., Poser, E. G., & Johnson, J. A. (1980). Outcome expectation ratings as predictors of success in weight reduction. *Journal of Clinical Psychology* 36, 500–502.

Brandwin, M. A., & Kewman, D. G. (1982). MMPI indicators of treatment response to spinal epidural stimulation in patients with chronic pain and patients with movement disorders. *Psychological Reports* 51, 1059–1064.

Brennan, A. F., Barrett, C. L., & Garretson, H. D. (1987). The prediction of chronic pain outcome by psychological variables. *International Journal of Psychiatry in Medicine* 16, 373–387.

Brick, H., Doub, W. H., & Perdue, W. C. (1962). Effects of amitriptyline on depressive and anxiety states in penitentiary inmates. *Diseases of the Nervous System* 23, 572–578.

Brick, H., Doub, W. H., & Perdue, W. C. (1965). A comparison of the effects of amitripyline and protriptyline on anxiety and depressive states in female prisoners. *International Journal of Neuropsychiatry* 1, 325–326.

Brick, H., Doub, W. H., & Perdue, W. C. (1966). Effects of tybamate on depressive and anxiety states in penitentiary inmates—a preliminary report. *International Journal of Neuropsychiatry* 2, 637–644.

Briggs, P. F. (1958). Prediction of rehospitalization using the MMPI. *Journal of Clinical Psychology* 14, 83–84.

Briggs, P. F., & Yater, A. C. (1966). Counseling and psychometric signs as determinants in the vocational success of discharged psychiatric patients. *Journal of Clinical Psychology* 22, 100–104.

Brill, N. Q., Koegler, R. R., Epstein, L. J., & Forgy, E. W. (1964). Controlled study of psychiatric outpatient therapy. *Archives of General Psychiatry* 10, 581–595.

Burdick, B. M. & Holmes, C. B. (1980). Use of the lithium scale with an outpatient psychiatric sample. *Psychological Reports* 47, 69–70.

Burish, T. G. (1981). Improved cognitive functioning in central diabetes insipidus following therapy with a vasopressin analogue. *Clinical Neuropsychology* 3, 13–15.

Burke, E. J., Hickling, E. J., Alfonso, M. P., & Blanchard, E. B. (1985). The adjunctive use of biofeedback and relaxation in the treatment of severe rheumatoid arthritis: A preliminary investigation. *Clinical Biofeedback and Health An International Journal* 8, 28–36.

Burkovsky, G. V., Vuks, A. Y., Iovlev, B. V., & Korabelnikov, K. V. (1988). (Informative value of clinical, personality and psychosocial characteristics of schizophrenic patients in relation to predicting the results of restorative therapy.) *Zhurnal Nevropatologii i Psikhiatrii imeni S. S. Korsakova* 88, 97–102.

Butcher, J. N. (1987). Computerized clinical and personality assessment using the MMPI. In J. N. Butcher (Ed.), *Computerized psychological assessment: A practitioner's guide* (pp. 161–197). New York: Basic Books.

Butcher, J. N. (1990). *The MMPI-2 in psychological treatment.* New York: Oxford.

Butcher, J. N., & Williams, C. L. (1992). *Essentials of MMPI-2 and MMPI-A interpretation.* Minneapolis, MN: University of Minnesota Press.

Butter, H. J. & Dutil, C. (1985). The assessment of a psychosocial treatment with chronic schizophrenic patients using neuropsychopharmacological indices. *Progress in Neuro Psychopharmacology and Biological Psychiatry* 9, 593–597.

Cabeen, C. W., & Coleman, J. C. (1961). Group therapy with sex offenders: Description and evaluation of group therapy program in an institutional setting. *Journal of Clinical Psychology* 17, 123–129.

Cabras, P. L., La Malfa, G. P., Giovannini, F., & Giardinelli, L. (1985). Applicazione del training autogeno alle psicosomatosi gastrointestinali. (Application of autogenic training to gastrointestinal psychosomatic diseases.) *Medicina Psicosomatica* 30, 315–329.

Caditz, S. B. (1961). Effects of a forestry camp experience of the personality of delinquent boys. *Journal of Clinical Psychology* 17, 78–81.

Caine, T. M. (1965). Changes in symptom, attitude, and trait measures among chronic neurotics in a therapeutic community. In G. A. Foulds (Ed.), *Personality and personal illness.* London: Tavistock.

Campbell, D. R., & Kimball, R. R. (1985). "Using MMPI lithium response scales": Drs. Campbell and Kimball reply. *American Journal of Psychiatry* 142, 1389.

Campbell, D. R., & Sinha, B. K. (1983). Psychotherapy and chronic hemodialysis. *International Journal for the Advancement of Counselling* 6, 47–60.

Canter, F. M. (1971). Authoritarian attitudes, degree of pathology and preference of structured versus unstructured psychotherapy in hospitalized mental patients. *Psychological Reports* 28, 231–234.

Capwell, D. F. (1945). Personality patterns of adolescent girls: II, Delinquents and non-delinquents. *Journal of Applied Psychology* 29, 289–297.

Carp, A. (1950). MMPI performance and insulin shock therapy. *Journal of Abnormal and Social Psychology* 45, 721–726.

Carr, J. E. (1970). Differentiation similarity of patient and therapist and the outcome of psychotherapy. *Journal of Abnormal Psychology* 76, 361–369.

Carr, J. E., & Whittenbaugh, J. A. (1965). Perception of "improvement" and interjudge reliability in therapy-outcome studies. *Proceedings of the 73rd Annual Convention of the APA*, 197–198.

Carr, J. E., & Whittenbaugh, J. A. (1969). Sources of disagreement in the perception of psychotherapy outcomes. *Journal of Clinical Psychology* 25, 16–21.

Carson, R. C., & Heine, R. W. (1962). Similarity and success in therapeutic dyads. *Journal of Consulting Psychology* 26, 38–43.

Carson, R. C., & Llewellyn, C. E. (1966). Similarity in therapeutic dyads: A reevaluation. *Journal of Consulting Psychology* 30, 458.

Cartwright, D. S. (1956). Note on "Changes in psychoneurotic patients with and without psychotherapy." *Journal of Consulting Psychology* 20, 403–404.

Cartwright, D. S., Kirtner, W. L., & Fiske, D. W. (1963). Method factors in changes associated with psychotherapy. *Journal of Abnormal and Social Psychology* 66, 164–175.

Cavanagh, R., Clifford, J. S., & Gregory, W. L. (1989). The use of bromocriptine for the treatment of attention deficit disorder in two chemically dependent patients. *Journal of Psychoactive Drugs* 21, 217–220.

Cernovsky, Z. (1984). Es scale level and correlates of MMPI elevation: Alcohol abuse vs. MMPI scores in treated alcoholics. *Journal of Clinical Psychology* 40, 1502–1509.

Chabot, D. R. (1969). An investigation of the effects of an increased emotional state on the reliability of the MMPI in an adolescent population. *Dissertation Abstracts* 29, 2629B.

Chaffin, M. (1992). Factors associated with treatment completion and progress among intrafamilial sexual abusers. *Child Abuse and Neglect* 16, 251–264.

Christensen, C. M., & MacDonald, J. (1960). Directed cognition and personality change. *Alberta Journal of Educational Research* 6, 211–217.

Cionini, L., & Giovannoni, A. (1984). L'EMG Biofeedback Training nel trattamento dell'impotenza psicogena: un caso clinico. (EMG biofeedback training in the treatment of psychogenic impotence: A clinical case.) *Medicina Psicosomatica* 29, 29–42.

Clark, C. M. (1961). Changes in response patterns of counseling institute trainees. *Dissertation Abstracts* 21, 811.

Clark, M. E. (1995). *MMPI-2 TRT Content and Content Component scales: Clinical correlates and outcome prediction for men with chronic pain*. Unpublished doctoral dissertation, University of South Florida.

Clemens, C., & Kahn, M. W. (1990). Selecting substance abusers for long-term treatment. *International Journal of the Addictions* 25, 33–42.

Cleveland, S. E. (1989). Personality factors in the mediation of drug response. In S. Fisher & R. P. Greenberg, (Eds.), *The limits of biological treatments for psychological distress: Comparisons with psychotherapy and placebo* (pp. 235–262). Hillsdale, NJ: Lawrence Erlbaum Associates.

Cline, D. W., & Rouzer, D. L. (1971). The nonphysician as primary therapist in hospital psychiatry. *American Journal of Psychiatry* 128, 407–411.

Coche, E. & Flick, A. (1975). Problem-solving training groups for hospitalized psychiatric patients. *Journal of Psychology* 91, 19–29.

Cochrane, C. M., Prange, A. J., & Abse, D. W. (1963). Reserpine-produced changes in the direction of aggressive drives. *Proceedings of the 3rd World Congress of Psychiatry* 3, 370–373.

Cogswell, J. F. (1960). The effects of prochlorperazine (Compazine) on delusional behavior. *Dissertation Abstracts* 20, 3374.

Cohen, C. P., Johnson, D. L., & Hanson, P. G. (1971). Interpersonal changes among psychiatric patients in human relations training. *Journal of Personality Assessment* 35, 472–479.

Cole, C. E., Patterson, R. M., Craig, J. B., Thomas, W. E., Ristine, L. P., Stahly, M., & Pasamanick, B. (1959). A controlled study of the efficacy of iproniazid in treatment of depression. *Archives of General Psychiatry* 1, 513–518.

Collet, L. (1987). "MMPI and headache: A special focus on differential diagnosis, prediction of treatment outcome and patient: Treatment matching": Commentary. *Pain* 29, 267–268.

Collet, L., Cottraux, J., & Ladouceur, R. (1987). Cognitive therapy of depression and counterdemand effects: A pilot study. *Psychological Reports* 60, 555–560.

Colligan, R. C., Ferdinande, R. J., Lucas, A. R., & Duncan, J. W. (1983). A one-year followup study of adolescent patients hospitalized with anorexia nervosa. *Journal of Developmental and Behavioral Pediatrics* 4, 278–279.

Conwell, D. V., Kurth, C. J., & Murphy, P. G. (1955). Use of psychologic tests in determining prognosis and treatment in geriatric mental illness. *Journal of the American Geriatrics Society* 3, 232–238.

Cooke, M. K., & Kiesler, D. J. (1967). Prediction of college students who later require personal counseling. *Journal of Counseling Psychology* 14, 346–349.

Cooper, G. D., & York, M. W. (1969). Rehabilitation potential of domiciliary members under 45 years of age. *Newsletter for Research in Psychology* 11, 5–7.

Costello, R. M., Hulsey, T. L., Schoenfeld, L. S., & Ramamurthy, S. (1987). P-A-I-N: A four-cluster MMPI typology for chronic pain. *Pain* 30, 199–209.

Costello, R. M., Schoenfeld, L. S., Ramamurthy, S., & Hobbs-Hardee, B. (1989). Sociodemographic and clinical correlates of P-A-I-N. *Journal of Psychosomatic Research* 33, 315–321.

Coursey, R. D., Frankel, B. L., Gaarder, K. R., & Mott, D. E. (1980). A comparison of relaxation techniques with electrosleep therapy for chronic, sleep-onset insomnia: A sleep-EEG study. *Biofeedback and Self Regulation* 5, 57–73.

Craig, R. J. (1984a). Personality dimensions related to premature termination from an inpatient drug abuse treatment program. *Journal of Clinical Psychology* 40, 351–355.

Craig, R. J. (1984b). Can personality tests predict treatment dropouts? *International Journal of the Addictions* 19, 665–674.

Crebelli, M., Delle Chiaie, R., & Valletta, M. (1983). L'EMG biofeedback training nella terapia dell'ansia cronica. Uno studio su 119 pazienti. (EMG biofeedback in chronic anxiety therapy: A study of 119 cases.) *Rivista di Psichiatria* 18, 201–221.

Croake, J. W., & Hinckle, D. E. (1983). Adlerian family counseling education. *Individual Psychology Journal of Adlerian Theory, Research and Practice* 39, 247–258.

Crumpton, E., Cantor, J. M., & Batiste, C. (1960). A factor analytic study of Barron's ego strength scale. *Journal of Clinical Psychology* 16, 383–391.

Curlee, J. (1971). Sex differences in patient attitudes toward alcoholism treatment. *Quarterly Journal of Studies on Alcohol* 32, 643–650.

Custers, A. (1973). (Experiencing in the therapeutic process: Study of the relation between experiencing change and personality change in client-centered psychotherapy.) *Psychologica Belgica* 13, 125–138.

Cutler, N. R., & Heiser, J. F. (1978). Retrospective diagnosis of hypomania following successful treatment of episodic violence with lithium: A case report. *American Journal of Psychiatry* 135, 753–754.

Dahlstrom, W. G. (1972). *Personality systematics and the problem of types.* New York: Learning Press.

Dahlstrom, W. G. (1975). Recommendations for patient measures in evaluating psychotherapy: Test batteries and inventories. In M. B. Parloff & I. E. Waskow (Eds.), *Psychotherapy change measures: Report of the Clinical Research Branch, NIMH Outcome Measures Project.* Washington, D.C.: U.S. Government Printing Office.

Dahlstrom, W. G., & Craven, D. D. (1952). The MMPI and stuttering phenomena in young adults. *American Psychologist* 7, 341.

Dahlstrom, W. G., Welsh, G. S., & Dahlstrom, L. E. (1975). *An MMPI handbook: Volume II, research applications.* Minneapolis: University of Minnesota Press.

Dana, R. H. (1957). MMPI performance and electroshock treatment. *Journal of Clinical Psychology* 13, 350–355.

Danet, B. N. (1968a). Self-confrontation by videotape in group psychotherapy. *Dissertation Abstracts* 28, 3058B.

Danet, B. N. (1968b). Self-confrontation in psychotherapy reviewed. Videotape playback as a clinical and research tool. *American Journal of Psychotherapy* 22, 245–257.

Daniels, R. S., Margolis, P. M., & Carson, R. C. (1963). Hospital discharges against medical advice. *Archives of General Psychiatry* 8, 120–130.

Davis, G. L. & Hoffman, R. G. (1991). MMPI and CPI scores of child molesters before and after incarceration-for-treatment. *Journal of Offender Rehabilitation* 17, 77–85.

Davis, K. L. (1968). The sensitivity of selected instruments to personality changes produced by group counseling. *Dissertation Abstracts* 28, 3968A.

Decourcy, P. (1971). The hazard of short-term psychotherapy without assessment: A case history. *Journal of Personality Assessment* 35, 285–288.

Deforest, F. D., & Johnson, L. S. (1981). Modification of stimulation seeking behavior in psychopaths using hypnotic sensory imagery conditioning. *American Journal of Clinical Hypnosis* 23, 184–194.

DeLeon, G. (1984). Program-based evaluation research in therapeutic communities. *National Institute on Drug Abuse Research Monograph Series* 51, 69–87.

DeLeon, G., & Jainchill, N. (1982). Male and female drug abusers: Social and psychological status 2 years after treatment in a therapeutic community. *American Journal of Drug and Alcohol Abuse* 8, 465–497.

DeLeon, G., & Schwartz, S. (1984). Therapeutic communities: What are the retention rates? *American Journal of Drug and Alcohol Abuse* 10, 267–284.

Delle Chiaie, R., Guerani, G., & Biondi, M. (1981). EMG BFB con segnale di rinforzo musicale nella terapia dell'ansia cronica. (EMG-BFB with musical reinforcement in the treatment of anxiety neurosis.) *Rivista di Psichiatria* 16, 455–472.

Delzotti, L., Pancheri, P., & Morbidelli, S. (1983). Risultati clinici del follow-up fino a tre anni in pazienti trattati con EMG o thermal biofeedback. (Follow-up: Clinical outcomes three years after in patients treated with EMG or thermal biofeedback.) *Rivista di Psichiatria* 18, 222–242.

De Piano, F. A., De Piano, L. C., Carter, W., & Wanlass, R. L. (1984). Physical fitness training: Adjunctive treatment for the depressed, low self esteem and muscular tense patient. *Psychotherapy in Private Practice* 2, 75–83.

Denson, R., & Sydiaha, D. (1970). A controlled study of LSD treatment in alcoholism and neurosis. *British Journal of Psychiatry,* 116, 443–445.

Der, D. F., & Lewington, P. (1990). Rational self-directed hypnotherapy: A treatment for panic attacks. *American Journal of Clinical Hypnosis* 32, 160–167.

DeShazo, D., & Kissiah, C. W. (1971). The effectiveness of relaxation therapy in tension reduction. *Newsletter for Research in Psychology* 13, 10–11.

Destounis, N., Pinto, A., Johnson, C., & Cooper, M. (1965). Clinical trial of isocarboxazid. *Current Therapeutic Research* 7, 257–261.

Devlin, J. P. (1953). A study of verbalized self-attitudes and reactions to social frustration as methods of predicting success in brief psychotherapy.*Pennsylvania State College Abstracts* 15, 544.

Diamond, S., & Montrose, D. (1984). The value of biofeedback in the treatment of chronic headache: A four-year retrospective study. *Headache* 24, 5–18.

Dicks, R. H., & McHenry, J. D. (1985). Predictors of outcomes in a performance ladder program. *Journal of Offender Counseling, Services and Rehabilitation* 9, 57–70.

Dietzel, C. S., & Abeles, N. (1975). Client-therapist complementarity and therapeutic outcome. *Journal of Counseling Psychology* 22, 264–272.

Dimascio, A., Meyer, R. E., & Stifler, L. (1968). Effects of imipramine of individuals varying in level of depression. *American Journal of Psychiatry* 124(Suppl.), 55–58.

Dimascio, A., Gardos, G., Harmatz, J., & Shader, R. (1969). Tybamate—an examination of its actions in "high" and "low" anxious normals. *Diseases of the Nervous System* 30, 758–763.

Distler, L. S., May, P. R., & Tuma, A. H. (1964). Anxiety and ego strength as predictors of response to treatment in schizophrenic patients. *Journal of Consulting Psychology* 28, 170–177.

Ditman, K. S., Moss, T., Forgy, E., Zunin, L., Funk, W., & Lynch, R. (1970). Characteristics of alcoholics volunteering for lysergide treatment. *Quarterly Journal of Studies on Alcohol* 31, 414–422.

Dobbs, N. J. (1970). Predicting length of psychiatric hospitalization using demographic and psychological test data. *Dissertation Abstracts International* 31, 2276B.

Dodd, J. (1970). A retrospective analysis of variables related to duration of treatment in a university psychiatric clinic. *Journal of Nervous and Mental Disease* 151, 75–84.

Dolce, J. J., Crocker, M. F., & Doleys, D. M. (1986). Prediction of outcome among chronic pain patients. *Behaviour Research and Therapy* 24, 313–319.

Donnelly, E. F., Goodwin, F. K., Waldman, I. N., & Murphy, D. L. (1978). Prediction of antidepressant responses to lithium. *American Journal of Psychiatry* 135, 552–556.

Donnelly, E. F., Murphy, D. L., Waldman, I. N., & Goodwin, F. K. (1979). Prediction of antidepressant responses to imipramine. *Neuropsychobiology,* 5, 94–101.

Donovan, D. M., & O'Leary, M. R. (1979). Depression, hypomania, and expectation of future success among alcoholics. *Cognitive Therapy and Research* 3, 141–154.

Dorr, D. (1981). Conjoint psychological testing in marriage therapy: New wine in old skins. *Professional Psychology* 12, 549–555.

Dougherty, F. E. (1976). Patient-therapist matching for prediction of optimal and minimal therapeutic outcome. *Journal of Consulting and Clinical Psychology* 44, 889–897.

Drake, L. E. (1954). MMPI profiles and interview behavior. *Journal of Counseling Psychology,* 1, 92–95.

Drake, L. E. (1956). Interpretation of MMPI profiles in counseling male clients. *Journal of Counseling Psychology* 3, 83–88.

Dubois, A. M. (1983). Etude comparative en double aveugle de deux traitements psychanalytiques. (A double-blind study of two types of psychiatric treatments.) *Genitif* 5, 91–101.

DuBrin, J. R., & Zastowny, T. R. (1988). Predicting early attrition from psychotherapy: An analysis of a large private-practice cohort. Special Issue: Psychotherapy and the new health care systems. *Psychotherapy* 25, 393–408.

Dunlap, N. G. (1961). Alcoholism in women: Some antecedents and correlates of remission in middle-class members of Alcoholics Anonymous. *Dissertation Abstracts* 22, 1904.

Dymond, R. F. (1955). Adjustment changes in the absence of psychotherapy. *Journal of Consulting Psychology* 19, 103–107.

Edelman, M. (1969). Anxiety level and the repression-sensitization dimension in desensitization therapies. *Dissertation Abstracts International* 30, 2417B.

Edelman, R. I. (1970). Effects of progressive relaxation on autonomic processes. *Journal of Clinical Psychology* 26, 421–425.

Edelman, R. I. (1971). Desensitization and physiological arousal. *Journal of Personality and Social Psychology* 17, 259–266.

Edwards, D., Bucky, S. F., & Schuckit, M. (1977). Personality and attitudinal change for alcoholics treated at the Navy's Alcohol Rehabilitation Center. *Journal of Community Psychology* 5, 180–185.

Edwards, D. W., & Roundtree, G. A. (1981). Assessment of short-term treatment groups with adjudicated first offender shoplifters. *Journal of Offender Counseling, Services and Rehabilitation* 6, 89–102.

Edwards, J., DiClemente, C., & Samuels, M. L. (1985). Psychological characteristics: A pretreatment survival marker of patients with testicular cancer. *Journal of Psychosocial Oncology* 3, 79–94.

Edwin, D., Andersen, A. E., & Rosell, F. (1988). Outcome prediction of MMPI in subtypes of anorexia nervosa. *Psychosomatics* 29, 273–282.

Ehrle, R. A., & Auvenshine, C. D. (1964). Anxiety level, need for counseling, and client improvement in an operational setting. *Journal of Counseling Psychology* 11, 286–287.

Elkins, G. R. (1984). Hypnosis in the treatment of myofibrositis and anxiety: A case report. *American Journal of Clinical Hypnosis* 27, 26–30.

Ellertsen, B. (1988). Migrene og tensjonshodepine. Psykofysiologi, personlighet og behandling. (Migraine and tension headache: Psychophysiology, personality, and therapy.) *Tidsskrift for Norsk Psykologforening* 25, 664–668.

Elliott, T. R., Anderson, W. P., & Adams, N. A. (1987). MMPI indicators of long-term therapy in a college counseling center. *Psychological Reports* 60, 79–84.

Ells, E. M. (1967). MMPI stability: Hospital discharge vs. outpatient intake. *Newsletter for Research in Psychology* 9, 10–11.

Endicott, N. A., & Endicott, J. (1963). "Improvement" in untreated psychiatric patients. *Archives of General Psychiatry* 9, 575–585.

Endicott, N. A., & Endicott, J. (1964). Prediction of improvement in treated and untreated patients using the Rorschach prognostic rating scale. *Journal of Consulting Psychology* 28, 342–348.

Ends, E. J., & Page, C. W. (1957). A study of three types of group psychotherapy with hospitalized male inebriates. *Quarterly Journal of Studies on Alcohol* 18, 263–277.

Ends, E. J., & Page, C. W. (1959). Group psychotherapy and concomitant psychological change. *Psychological Monographs* 73 (10, Whole No. 480).

Epstein, S. J., & Deyoub, P. L. (1981). Hypnotherapy for fear of choking: Treatment implications of a case report. *International Journal of Clinical and Experimental Hypnosis* 29, 117–127.

Evans, D. D., & Blanchard, E. B. (1988). Prediction of early termination from the self-regulatory treatment of chronic headache. *Biofeedback and Self Regulation* 13, 245–256.

Exner, J. E., & Murillo, L. G. (1977). A long term follow-up of schizophrenics treated with regressive ECT. *Diseases of the Nervous System* 38, 162–168.

Eyberg, S. M., & Robinson, E. A. (1982). Parent-child interaction training: Effects on family functioning. *Journal of Clinical Child Psychology* 11, 130–137.

Fairweather, G. W., Simon, R., Gebhard, M. E., Weingarten, W., Holland, J. L., Sanders, R., Stone, C. D., & Reahl, J. E. (1960). Relative effectiveness of psychotherapeutic programs: A multicriteria comparison of four programs for three different patient groups. *Psychological Monographs* 74 (5, Whole No. 492).

Fals Stewart, W., & Schafer, J. (1993). MMPI correlates of psychotherapy compliance among obsessive–compulsives. *Psychopathology* 26, 1–5.

Faltz, C. A. (1969). Prediction of hospital readmission and work adjustment among released psychiatric patients. *Dissertation Abstracts* 29, 3084B.

Faravelli, C., & Albanesi, G. (1987). Agoraphobia with panic attacks: 1-year prospective follow-up. *Comprehensive Psychiatry* 28, 481–487.

Faravelli, C., & Sacchetti, E. (1984). Subjective side effects during treatment with clomipramine: Relationship to symptoms, plasma levels and personality. *IRCS Medical Science Psychology and Psychiatry* 12, 1111–1112.

Fardan, L. D., & Tyson, Y. (1985). Drew program for obesity treatment. 89th Annual Convention and Scientific Assembly of the National Medical Association (1984, Montreal, Canada). *Journal of the National Medical Association* 77, 737–741.

Fava, M., Rosenbaum, J. F., Pava, J. A., & McCarthy, M. K. (1993). Anger attacks in unipolar depression: I. Clinical correlates and response to fluoxetine treatment. *American Journal of Psychiatry* 150, 1158–1163.

Fazio, A. F. (1972). Implosive therapy with semiclinical phobias. *Journal of Abnormal Psychology* 80, 183–188.

Feldman, M. J. (1951). A prognosis scale for shock therapy. *Psychological Monographs* 65 (10, Whole No. 327).

Feldman, M. J. (1952). The use of the MMPI profile for prognosis and evaluation of shock therapy. *Journal of Consulting Psychology* 16, 376–382.

Feldman, M. J. (1958). An evaluation scale for shock therapy. *Journal of Clinical Psychology* 14, 41–45.

Ferreira, J. G. deA. (1953). The MMPI in the study of lobotomized persons. *Medicinia Contemporanea* 71, 531–536.

Filstead, W. J., Drachman, D. A., Rossi, J. J., & Getsinger, S. H. (1983). The relationship of MMPI subtype membership to demographic variables and treatment outcome among substance misusers. *Journal of Studies on Alcohol* 44, 917–922.

Finn, S. E., & Tonsager, M. E. (1992). Therapeutic effects of providing MMPI-2 test feedback to college students awaiting therapy. *Psychological Assessment* 4, 278–287.

Firestone, P., & Witt, J. E. (1982). Characteristics of families completing and prematurely discontinuing a behavioral parent-training program. *Journal of Pediatric Psychology* 7, 209–222.

Fischer, R., Ristine, L. P., & Wisecup, P. (1969). Increase in gustatory acuity and hyperarousal in schizophrenia. *Biological Psychiatry* 1, 209–218.

Fiske, D. W., & Goodman, G. (1965). The posttherapy period. *Journal of Abnormal Psychology* 70, 169–179.

Fiske, D. W., Cartwright, D. S., & Kirtner, W. L. (1964). Are psychotherapeutic changes predictable? *Journal of Abnormal and Social Psychology* 69, 418–426.

Flanagan, D. A., & Wagner, H. L. (1991). Expressed emotion and panic-fear in the prediction of diet treatment compliance. *British Journal of Clinical Psychology* 30, 231–240.

Fleeson, W., Glueck, B., Heistad, G., King, J. E., Lykken, D., Meehl, P., & Mena, A. (1958). The ataraxic effect of two phenothiazine drugs on an outpatient population. *Medical Bulletin of the University of Minnesota* 29, 274–286.

Flemenbaum, A., & Schiele, B. C. (1971). The antidepressant properties of A-25794: A pilot study. *Current Therapeutic Research* 13, 53–56.

Fleming, M. (1981). A study of pre- and postsurgical transsexuals: MMPI characteristics. *Archives of Sexual Behavior* 10, 161–170.

Flores, P. J. (1982). Modifications of Yalom's interactional group therapy model as a mode of treatment for alcoholism. *Group* 6, 3–16.

Florez, B, H. (1979). Group psychotherapy in cancer patients. *Revista Latinoamericana de Psicologia* 11, 47–63.

Floyd, W. A. (1974). The use of the MMPI in marital counseling and research. *Journal of Family Counseling* 2, 16–21.

Flynn, J. D. (1971). An analysis of feasibility and nonfeasibility of vocational rehabilitation applicants as measured by the projective occupational attitudes test. *Dissertation Abstracts International* 32, 1210B.

Flynn, R. J., & Salomone, P. R. (1977). Performance of the MMPI in predicting rehabilitation outcome: A discriminant analysis, double cross-validation assessment. *Rehabilitation Literature* 38, 12–15.

Follingstad, D. R. (1980). A reconceptualization of issues in the treatment of abused women: A case study. *Psychotherapy Theory, Research and Practice* 17, 294–303.

Ford, D. H. (1959). Research approaches to psychotherapy. *Journal of Counseling Psychology* 6, 55–60.

Ford, M. R., Stroebel, C. F., Strong, P., & Szarek, B. L. (1982). Quieting response training: Treatment of psychophysiological disorders in psychiatric inpatients. *Biofeedback and Self Regulation* 7, 331–339.

Ford, M. R., Stroebel, C. F., Strong, P., & Szarek, B. L. (1983). Quieting response training: Predictors of long-term outcome. *Biofeedback and Self Regulation* 8, 393–408.

Forman, B. (1960). The effect of differential treatment on attitudes, personality traits, and behavior of adult parolees. *Dissertation Abstracts* 21, 1652.

Forrest, G. L., Bortner, T. W., & Bakker, C. B. (1967). The role of personality variables in response to chlorpromazine, dextoamphetamine and placebo. *Journal of Psychiatric Research* 5, 281–288.

Forsyth, R. P. (1965). MMPI and demographic correlates of post-hospital adjustment in neuropsychiatric patients. *Psychological Reports* 16, 355–366.

Forsyth, R. P., & Fairweather, G. W. (1961). Psychotherapeutic and other hospital treatment criteria: The dilemma. *Journal of Abnormal and Social Psychology* 62, 598–604.

Foulds, G. A. (1959). The relative stability of personality measures compared with diagnostic measures. *Journal of Mental Science* 105, 783–787.

Fowler, R. D., Teel, S. K., & Coyle, F. A. (1967). The measurement of alcoholic response to treatment by Barron's ego-strength scale. *Journal of Psychology* 67, 65–68.

Fox, B., & Di Scipio, W. J. (1968). An exploratory study in the treatment of homosexuality by combining principles from psychoanalytical theory and conditioning: Theoretical and methodological considerations. *British Journal of Medical Psychology* 41, 273–282.

Fracchia, J., Sheppard, C., & Merlis, S. (1974a). Treatment patterns in psychiatry: Clinical and personality features of elderly hospitalized patients during milieu, single-drug and multiple-drug programs. *Journal of the American Geriatrics Society* 22, 212–216.

Fracchia, J., Sheppard, C., & Merlis, S. (1974b). Psychological characteristics of long-term mental patients: Some implications for treatment. *Comprehensive Psychiatry* 15, 495–501.

Frankel, A., & Murphy, J. (1974). Physical fitness and personality in alcoholism: Canonical analysis of measures before and after treatment. *Quarterly Journal of Studies on Alcohol* 35, 1272–1278.

Frankel, B. L. (1978). Treatment of hypertension with biofeedback and relaxation techniques. *Psychosomatic Medicine* 40, 276–293.

Frayn, D. H. (1968). A relationship between rated ability and personality traits in psychotherapists. *American Journal of Psychiatry* 124, 1232–1237.

Frederiksen, N., & Gilbert, A. C. F. (1960). Replication of a study of differential predictability. *Educational and Psychological Measurement* 20, 759–767.

Freeman, C. W., Calsyn, D. A., Paige, A. B., & Halar, E. M. (1980). Biofeedback with low back pain patients. *American Journal of Clinical Biofeedback* 3, 118–122.

Freedman, N., Rosen, B., Engelhardt, D. M., & Margolis, R. (1967). Prediction of psychiatric hospitalization: I. The measurement of hospitalization proneness. *Journal of Abnormal Psychology* 72, 468–477.

Friedman, C., De Mowbray, M. S., & Hamilton, A. (1961). Imipramine (Tofranil) in depressive states: A controlled trial with in-patients. *Journal of Mental Science* 107, 948–953.

Fry, P. S. (1984). Cognitive training and cognitive-behavioral variables in the treatment of depression in the elderly. *Clinical Gerontologist* 3, 25–45.

Fryer, D. G., & Timberlake, W. H. (1963). A trial of imipramine (Tofranil) in depressed patients with chronic physical disease. *Journal of Chronic Diseases* 16, 173–178.

Fryrear, J. L., & Stephens, B. C. (1988). Group psychotherapy using masks and video to facilitate intrapersonal communication. *Arts in Psychotherapy* 15, 227–234.

Fuchs, C. Z., & Rehm, L. P. (1977). A self-control behavior therapy program for depression. *Journal of Consulting and Clinical Psychology* 45, 206–215.

Fullerton, D. T., Lohrenz, F. N., Fahs, H., & Wenzel, F. (1968). Adrenal cortical activity in depression. *Comprehensive Psychiatry* 9, 233–239.

Gallagher, J. J. (1952). An investigation into factors differentiating college students who discontinue non-directive counseling from college students who continue counseling. *Pennsylvania State College Abstracts* 14, 445.

Gallagher, J. J. (1953a). MMPI changes concomitant with client-centered therapy. *Journal of Consulting Psychology* 17, 334–338.

Gallagher, J. J. (1953b). Manifest anxiety changes concomitant with client-centered therapy. *Journal of Consulting Psychology* 17, 443–446.

Gallagher, J. J. (1953c). The problem of escaping clients in nondirective counseling. In W. U. Snyder (Ed.), *Group report of a program of research in psychotherapy*. State College, PA: Pennsylvania State University Press.

Gallagher, J. J. (1954). Test indicators for therapy prognosis. *Journal of Consulting Psychology* 18, 409–413.

Garfield, S. L., & Bergin, A. E. (1971a). Personal therapy, outcome and some therapist variables. *Psychotherapy* 8, 251–253.

Garfield, S. L., & Bergin, A. E. (1971b). Therapeutic conditions and outcome. *Journal of Abnormal Psychology* 77, 108–114.

Garfield, S. L., Prager, R. A., & Bergin, A. E. (1971a). Evaluation of outcome in psychotherapy. *Journal of Consulting and Clinical Psychology* 37, 307–313.

Garfield, S. L., Prager, R. A., & Bergin, A. E. (1971b). Evaluating outcome in psychotherapy: A hardy perennial. *Journal of Consulting and Clinical Psychology* 37, 320–322.

Garvey, M. J., Johnson, R. A., Valentine, R. H., & Schuster, V. (1983). Use of an MMPI scale to predict antidepressant response to lithium. *Psychiatry Research* 10, 17–20.

Gassner, S. M. (1970). Relationship between patient-therapist compatibility and treatment effectiveness. *Journal of Consulting and Clinical Psychology* 34, 408–414.

Geer, J. H. (1964). Phobia treated by reciprocal inhibition. *Journal of Abnormal and Social Psychology* 69, 642–645.

Gelfand, D. M., Gelfand, S., & Rardin, M. W. (1965). Some personality factors associated with placebo responsivity. *Psychological Reports* 17, 555–562.

Gendlin, E. T. (1962). Client-centered development and work with schizophrenics. *Journal of Counseling Psychology* 9, 205–211.

Gendlin, E. T., & Rychlak, J. F. (1970). Psychotherapeutic processes. *Annual Review of Psychology* 21, 155–190.

Gendlin, E. T., Beebe, J., Cassens, J., & Oberlander, M. (1968). Focusing ability in psychotherapy, personality, and creativity. In J. Shlien (Ed.), *Research in psychotherapy: Vol. 3*. Washington, D.C.: American Psychological Association.

Gerstein, L. H., & Hotelling, K. (1987). Length of group treatment and changes in women with bulimia. *Journal of Mental Health Counseling* 9, 162–173.

Getter, H., & Sundland, D. M. (1962). The Barron ego strength scale and psychotherapeutic outcome. *Journal of Consulting Psychology* 26, 195.

Ghiselli, W. B. (1983). Clinical and statistical issues related to predicting therapeutic outcome. *Journal of Clinical Psychology* 39, 651–657.

Gibbs, J. J., Wilkens, B., & Lauterbach, C. G. (1957). A controlled clinical psychiatric study of chlorpromazine. *Journal of Clinical and Experimental Psychopathology* 18, 269–283.

Gibson, R. L. (1956). A factor analysis of measures of change following client-centered therapy. *Pennsylvania State University Abstracts* 18, 415.

Gibson, R. L., Snyder, W. U., & Ray, W. S. (1955). A factor analysis of measures of change following client-centered therapy. *Journal of Counseling Psychology* 2, 83–90.

Giebink, J. W., & Stover, D. O. (1969). Adjustment, mental health opinions, and proficiency of child care personnel. *Journal of Consulting and Clinical Psychology* 33, 532–535.

Giedt, F. H. (1961). Predicting suitability for group psychotherapy. *American Journal of Psychotherapy* 15, 582–591.

Glasscock, E. M. (1955). An investigation of the value of the MMPI as a prognostic instrument. *Dissertation Abstracts* 15, 874.

Glenwick, D. S., & Arata, C. L. (1977). Assertiveness training in a college companion program: Effects on student volunteers and rehabilitation center clients. *Rehabilitation Psychology* 24, 225–231.

Gligor, A., & Tryon, W. (1973). An evaluation of the integration of male and female patients in a psychiatric hospital. *Newsletter for Research in Mental Health and Behavioral Sciences* 15, 18–19.

Goldstein, A. P. (1960). Patients' expectancies and non-specific therapy as a basis for (un)spontaneous remission. *Journal of Clinical Psychology* 16, 399–403.

Goldstein, A. P. (1962). *Therapist-patient expectancies in psychotherapy*. New York: Pergamon.

Goldstein, B. J., & Brauzer, B. (1971). Comparison of Molindone and placebo in anxious depressed patients. *Current Therapeutic Research* 13, 344–349.

Goldstein, B. J., & Weer, D. M. (1970). Comparative evaluation of benzoctamine and diazepam in treatment of anxiety. *Journal of Clinical Pharmacology* 10, 194–198.

Goldstein, I. B., Shapiro, D., Thananopavarn, C., & Sambhi, M. P. (1982). Comparison of drug and behavioral treatments of essential hypertension. *Health Psychology* 1, 7–26.

Goldstein, L., Graedon, J., Willard, D., Goldstein, F., & Smith, R. R. (1970). A comparative study of the effects of methaqualone and glutethimide on sleep in male chronic
insomniacs. *Journal of Clinical Pharmacology* 10, 258–268.

Gomes-Schwartz, B. (1978). Effective ingredients in psychotherapy: Prediction of outcome
from process variables. *Journal of Consulting and Clinical Psychology* 46, 1023–1035.

Gomes-Schwartz, B., & Schwartz, J. M. (1978). Psychotherapy process variables distinguishing the inherently helpful person from the professional psychotherapist. *Journal of
Consulting and Clinical Psychology* 46, 196–197.

Gonda, T. A. (1964). Prediction of short-term outcome of electroconvulsive therapy. *Journal of Nervous and Mental Disease* 138, 587–594.

Gondra, J. M. (1975). The relationship of the self/ideal congruence index to change during therapy and to personality adjustment. *Revista de Psicologia General y Aplicada*
30, 585–607.

Good, P. K. E. (1957). A psychological study of the effects of regressive electroshock therapy.
Dissertation Abstracts 17, 2064.

Goorney, A. B. (1970). Treatment of aviation phobias by behavior therapy. *British Journal
of Psychiatry* 117, 535–544.

Gordon, M. H. (1958). Analysis of project one. Mimeographed materials, Research Conference, Veterans Administration Hospital, Downey, IL.

Gordon, T., Grummon, D. L., Rogers, C. R., & Seeman, J. (1954). Developing a program
of research in psychotherapy. In C. R. Rogers & J. Seeman (Eds.), *Psychotherapy and
personality*. Chicago: University of Chicago Press.

Gouws, D. J. (1961). Prediction of relapse for psychiatric patients. *Journal of Consulting
Psychology* 25, 142–145.

Grace, D. P. (1964). Predicting progress of schizophrenics in a work-oriented rehabilitation program. *Journal of Consulting Psychology* 28, 560.

Graham, J. R. (1987). *The MMPI: A practical guide (2nd edition)*. New York: Oxford.

Graham, J. R. (1990). *MMPI-2: Assessing personality and psychopathology*. New: Oxford.

Graham, J. R., Lilly, R. S., Konick, D. S., Paolino, A. F., & Friedman, I. (1973). MMPI
changes associated with short-term psychiatric hospitalization. *Journal of Clinical
Psychology* 29, 69–73.

Grazzi, L., Frediani, F., Zappacosta, B., & Boiardi, A. (1988). Psychological assessment in
tension headache before and after biofeedback treatment. *Headache* 28, 337–338.

Greene, R. L., & Clopton, J. R. (1994). Minnesota Multiphasic Personality Inventory-2.
In M. E. Maruish (Ed.), *The use of psychological testing for treatment planning and
outcome assessment* (pp. 137–159). Hillsdale, NJ: Lawrence Erlbaum Associates.

Greenfield, N. S. (1958). Personality patterns of patients before and after application for
psychotherapy. *Journal of Consulting Psychology* 22, 280.

Greenfield, N. S., & Fey, W. F. (1956). Factors influencing utilization of psychotherapeutic
services in male college students. *Journal of Clinical Psychology* 12, 276–279.

Grof, S., Soskin, R. A., Richards, W. A., & Kurland, A. A. (1973). DPT as an adjunct in
psychotherapy of alcoholics. *International Pharmacopsychiatry* 8, 104–115.

Grosz, H. J., & Wagoner, R. (1971). MMPI and EPPS profiles of high and low verbal
interactors in therapy groups. *Psychological Reports* 28, 951–955.

Guck, T. P., Meilman, P. W., & Skultety, F. M. (1987). Pain Assessment Index: Evaluation following multidisciplinary pain treatment. *Journal of Pain and Symptom Management* 2, 23–27.

Guck, T. P., Meilman, P. W., Skultety, F. M., & Poloni, L. D. (1988). Pain-patient Minnesota Multiphasic Personality Inventory (MMPI) subgroups: Evaluation of long-term
treatment outcome. *Journal of Behavioral Medicine* 11, 159–169.

Guenther, R. M. (1983). The role of nutritional therapy in alcoholism treatment. *International Journal of Biosocial Research* 4, 5–18.

Guerney, L. F. (1956). Differential effects of certain therapist characteristics on client reactions to psychotherapy. *Dissertation Abstracts* 16, 1493.

Guthrie, D., Moeller, T., & Guthrie, R. (1983). Biofeedback and its application to the stabilization and control of diabetes mellitus. *American Journal of Clinical Biofeedback* 6, 82–87.

Haase, R. F., & Ivey, A. E. (1970). Influence of client pretesting on counseling outcome. *Journal of Consulting and Clinical Psychology* 34, 128.

Habrat, E., & Walecka, W. (1991). Cechy osobowosci jako czynnik predykcyjny przy stosowaniu lekow prezeciwdepresyjnych w depresjach endogennych. (Personality patterns as a prognostic factor for pharmacotherapy of endogenous depression.) *Psychiatria Polska* 25, 105–110.

Haertzen, C. A. (1952). The value of the MMPI as a predictor of discharge of mentally sick patients at the Rochester State Hospital. *Blocks and Blots* 2, 4–5.

Haertzen, C. A., & Hill, H. E. (1959). Effects of morphine and pentobarbital on differential MMPI profiles. *Journal of Clinical Psychology* 15, 434–437.

Haertzen, C. A., Hill, H. E., & Monroe, J. J. (1968). MMPI scales for differentiating and predicting relapse in alcoholics, opiate addicts, and criminals. *International Journal of the Addictions* 3, 91–106.

Hales, W. M., & Simon, W. (1948). MMPI patterns before and after insulin shock therapy. *American Journal of Psychiatry* 105, 254–258.

Hall, W. E., Libby, A., & Steele, H. T. (1972). Evaluation of a milieu therapy psychiatric ward: MMPI findings. *Newsletter for Research in Psychology* 14, 26–30.

Hankoff, L. D., Gundlach, R. H., Paley, H. M., & Rudorfer, L. (1964). Diphenhydramine as an anti-depressant: A negative finding. *Diseases of the Nervous System* 25, 547–552.

Hanlon, T. E., Michaux, M. H., Ota, K. Y., Shaffer, J. W., & Kurland, A. A. (1965). The comparative effectiveness of eight phenothiazines. *Psychopharmacologia* 7, 89–106.

Hanlon, T. E., Ota, K. Y., Agallianos, D. D., Berman, S. A., Bethon, G. D., Kobler, F., & Kurland, A. A. (1969). Combined drug treatment of newly hospitalized, acutely ill psychiatric patients. *Diseases of the Nervous System* 30, 104–116.

Hardt, J. V., & Kamiya, J. (1978). Anxiety change through electroencephalographic alpha feedback seen only in high anxiety subjects. *Science* 201, 79–81.

Harris, R. E. (1945). Measured personality characteristics of convulsive therapy patients: A study of diagnostic and prognostic criteria. *Psychological Bulletin* 42, 535.

Harris, R. E., & Christiansen, C. (1946). Prediction of response to brief psychotherapy. *Journal of Psychology* 21, 269–284.

Harris, R. E., Bowman, K. M., & Simon, A. (1948). Studies in electonarcosis therapy: III. Psychological test findings. *Journal of Nervous and Mental Disease* 107, 371–376.

Hathaway, S. R. (1948). Some considerations relative to non-directive counseling as therapy. *Journal of Clinical Psychology* 4, 226–231.

Hathaway, S. R., & Harmon, L. R. (1946). Clinical counseling in emotional and social rehabilitation. *Journal of Clinical Psychology* 2, 151–157.

Havik, O. E. (1982). Psykologiske testkarakteristika hos tre kategorier korttidspasienter. (Psychological test findings in three categories of patients accepted for psychotherapy of short duration.) *Tidsskrift for Norsk Psykologforening* 19, 535–541.

Hawkes, G. R. (1950). Use of the MMPI in screening college students for counseling purposes. *Journal of Educational Psychology* 41, 116–121.

Hecht, S., & Kroeber, T. C. (1955). A study in prediction of attitudes of patients towards brief psychotherapy. *American Psychologist* 10, 370.

Hedayat, M. M., & Kelly, D. B. (1991). Relationship of MMPI Dependency and Dominance scale scores to staff's ratings, diagnoses, and demographic data for day-treatment clients. *Psychological Reports* 68, 259–266.

Hedstom, L. J. (1966). Prediction of duration of psychotherapy by the MMPI and ratings of initial interview behavior and socioeconomic status. *Dissertation Abstracts* 26, 6848.

Heikkinen, C. A., & Wegner, K. W. (1973). MMPI studies of counselors: A review. *Journal of Counseling Psychology* 20, 275–279.

Heilbrun, A. B. (1971). Prediction of rehabilitation outcome in chronic court-case alcoholics. *Quarterly Journal of Studies on Alcohol* 32, 328–333.

Heller, A., Zahourek, R., & Whittington, H. G. (1971). Effectiveness of antidepressant drugs: A triple-blind study comparing imipramine, desipramine, and placebo. *American Journal of Psychiatry* 127, 1092–1095.

Helweg, G. C. (1971). The relationships between selected personality characteristics and perceptions of directive and nondirective psychotherapeutic approaches. *Dissertation Abstracts International* 32, 2396B.

Hennessy, R. M.(1971). Treatment outcome of process and reactive schizophrenics. *Dissertation Abstracts International* 31, 4338B.

Henriques, E., Arsenian, J., Cutter, H., & Samaraweera, A. B. (1972). Personality characteristics and drug of choice. *International Journal of the Addictions* 7, 73–76.

Henry, B. W., Overall, J. E., & Woodward, J. A. (1976). Actuarial justification for choice of drug treatment for psychiatric patients. *Diseases of the Nervous System* 37, 555–557.

Hess, H. (1992). Affektives Erleben im Gruppenprozess und Therapieerfolg. / Affective response in group therapy process and outcome. *Psychotherapie Psychosomatik Medizinische Psychologie* 42, 120–126.

Hickling, E. J., Sison, G. F., & Vanderploeg, R. D. (1986). Treatment of posttraumatic stress disorder with relaxation and biofeedback training. *Biofeedback and Self Regulation* 11, 125–134.

Hirsch, I., & Walder, L. (1969). Training mothers in groups as reinforcement therapists for their own children. *Proceedings of the 77th Annual Convention of the APA* 4, 561–562.

Hisli, N. (1987). Effect of patients' evaluation of group behavior on therapy outcome. Special Issue: Integration of research and practice in the field of group psychotherapy. *International Journal of Group Psychotherapy* 37, 119–124.

Hjemboe, S., Almagor, M., & Butcher, J. N. (1992). Empirical assessment of marital distress: The Marital Distress Scale for the MMPI-2. In C. D. Spielberger & J. N. Butcher (Eds.), *Advances in personality assessment*, Vol. 9 (pp. 141–152). Hillsdale, NJ: Lawrence Erlbaum Associates.

Hogan, R. (1969). Development of an empathy scale. *Journal of Consulting and Clinical Psychology* 33, 307–316.

Holcomb, W. R. (1986). Stress inoculation therapy with anxiety and stress disorders of acute psychiatric inpatients. *Journal of Clinical Psychology* 42, 864–872.

Hollister, L. E., & Overall, J. E. (1965). Reflections on the specificity of action of antidepressants. *Psychosomatics* 6, 361–365.

Hollister, L. E., Overall, J. E., & Johnson, M. (1963). Evaluation of desipramine in depressive states. *Journal of New Drugs* 3, 161–166.

Hollister, L. E., Overall, J. E., Johnson, M., Pennington, V., Katz, G., & Shelton, J. (1964). *Journal of Nervous and Mental Disease* 139, 370–375.

Holmes, G. R., & Heckel, R. V. (1970). Psychotherapy with the first Negro male on one southern university campus: A case study. *Journal of Consulting and Clinical Psychology* 34, 297–301.

Holt, S. M. (1955). Prognostic factors in psychoneurosis mixed type. *Dissertation Abstracts,* 15, 1118.

Horowitz, S. L. (1970). Strategies within hypnosis for reducing phobic behavior. *Journal of Abnormal Psychology* 75, 104–112.

Horton, A. M., & Johnson, C. H. (1980). Rational-emotive therapy and depression: A clinical case study. *Perceptual and Motor Skills* 51, 853–854.

Horton, M., & Kriauciunas, R. (1970). MMPI differences between terminators and continuers in youth counseling. *Journal of Counseling Psychology* 17, 98–101.

Hoskins, J. E. (1966). A study of certain characteristics which have predictive value for vocational adjustment in a rehabilitation workshop. *Dissertation Abstracts* 26, 4797.

House, K. M., & Martin, R. L. (1975). MMPI delineation of a subgroup of depressed patients refractory to lithium carbonate therapy. *American Journal of Psychiatry* 132, 644–646.

Howard, L., Reardon, J. P., & Tosi, D. J. (1982). Modifying migraine headache through rational stage directed hypnotherapy: A cognitive-experiential perspective. *International Journal of Clinical and Experimental Hypnosis* 30, 257–269.

Huber, N. A. & Danahy, S. (1975). Use of the MMPI in predicting completion and evaluating changes in a long-term alcoholism treatment program. *Journal of Studies on Alcohol* 36, 1230–1237.

Hudgens, A. J. (1979). Family-oriented treatment of chronic pain. *Journal of Marital and Family Therapy* 5, 67–78.

Hundziak, M., & Pasamanick, B. (1964). Occupational and industrial therapy in the treatment of psychiatric patients: A controlled study of efficacy in an intensive treatment institution. *Genetic Psychology Monographs* 69, 3–48.

Hunt, D. D., & Hampson, J. L. (1980). Follow-up of 17 biologic male transsexuals after sex-reassignment surgery. *American Journal of Psychiatry* 137, 432–438.

Hunt, J. McV., Ewing, T. N., LaForge, R., & Gilbert, W. M. (1959). An integrated approach to research on therapeutic counseling with samples of results. *Journal of Counseling Psychology* 6, 46–54.

Hurt, S. W., Reznikoff, M., & Clarkin, J. F. (1991). *Psychological assessment, psychiatric diagnosis, & treatment planning.* New York: Brunner/Mazel.

Hutzell, R. R. (1984). Logoanalysis for alcoholics. *International Forum for Logotherapy* 7, 40–45.

Hutzler, J. C., Keen, J., Molinari, V., & Carey, L. (1981). Super-obesity: A psychiatric profile of patients electing gastric stapling for the treatment of morbid obesity. *Journal of Clinical Psychiatry* 42, 458–462.

Jacob, R. G., Turner, S. M., Szekely, B. C., & Eidelman, B. H. (1983). Predicting outcome of relaxation therapy in headaches: The role of "depression". *Behavior Therapy* 14, 457–465.

Jacobs, A., Edelman, M., & Wolpin, M. (1971). Effects of differential anxiety level and the repression-sensitization dimension in desensitization therapy. *Proceedings of the 79th Annual Convention of the APA* 6, 427–428.

Jacobs, M. A., Heim, E., & Chassan, J. B. (1966). Intensive design in the study of differential therapeutic effects. *Comprehensive Psychiatry* 7, 278–289.

Jacobson, J. L., & Wirt, R. D. (1969). MMPI profiles associated with outcomes of group psychotherapy with prisoners. In J. N. Butcher (Ed.), *MMPI: Research developments and clinical applications.* New York: McGraw-Hill.

Janecek, J., Schiele, B. C., & Vestre, N. D. (1963). Pargyline and tranylcypromine in the treatment of hospitalized depressed patients. *Journal of New Drugs* 3, 309–316.

Janecek, J., Vestre, N. D., Schiele, B. C., & Zimmermann, R. (1966). Oxazepam in the treatment of anxiety states: A controlled study. *Journal of Psychiatric Research* 4, 199–206.

Jansen, D. G., & Nickles, L. A. (1973). Variables that differentiate between single- and multiple-admission psychiatric patients at a state hospital over a 5-year period. *Journal of Clinical Psychology* 29, 83–85.

Jansen, D. G., & Robb, G. P. (1970). Differences between counseled and noncounseled students on the MMPI. *Journal of Clinical Psychology* 26, 391–393.

Jenkins, W. L. (1952). The MMPI applied to the problem of prognosis in schizophrenia. *Dissertation Abstracts* 12, 381.

Jeske, J. O. (1973). Identification and therapeutic effectiveness in group therapy. *Journal of Counseling Psychology* 20, 528–530.

Joanning, H. (1976). Behavioral rehearsal in group treatment of socially nonassertive individuals. *Journal of College Student Personnel* 17, 313–318.

Johnsgard, K. W., & Muench, G. A. (1965). Group therapy with normal college students. *Psychotherapy: Theory, Research and Practice* 2, 114–116.

Johnson, D. T., & Spielberger, C. D. (1968). The effects of relaxation training and the passage of time on measures of state- and trait-anxiety. *Journal of Clinical Psychology* 24, 20–23.

Johnson, G., Martin, P. L., & Vogler, R. E. (1970). Prediction of rehospitalization of family-care patients using the MMPI. *Psychological Reports* 26, 273–274.

Johnson, G., Fox, J., Schaefer, H. H., & Ishikawa, W. (1971). Predicting rehospitalization from community placement. *Psychological Reports* 29, 475–478.

Johnson, R. W., & Sandness, D. G. (1966). Are rehabilitation follow-up studies biased? *Rehabilitation Counseling Bulletin* 9, 95–101.

Johnston, G. A. (1993). Megavitamins and psychotherapy: Effective, economical and time-saving treatment: A three year study. *Journal of Orthomolecular Medicine* 8, 104–120.

Johnston, R. P., & McNeal, B. F. (1964). Combined MMPI and demographic data in predicting length of neuropsychiatric hospital stay. *Journal of Consulting Psychology* 28, 64–70.

Johnston, R. P., & McNeal, B. F. (1965). Residual psychopathology in released psychiatric patients and its relation to readmission. *Journal of Abnormal Psychology* 70, 337–342.

Johnston, R. P., & McNeal, B. F. (1967). Statistical vs. clinical prediction: Length of neuropsychiatric hospital stay. *Journal of Abnormal Psychology* 72, 335–340.

Jones, R. J. (1956). A controlled investigation of the effects of reserpine (Serpasil) on adjustment and tension in hospitalized male psychotics. *Dissertation Abstracts* 16, 1495.

Judson, A. J., & MacCasland, B. W. (1960). The effects of chlorpromazine on psychological test scores. *Journal of Consulting Psychology* 24, 192.

Jurjevich, R. M. (1966a). Short interval test-retest stability of MMPI, CPI, Cornell Index, and Symptom Check List. *Journal of General Psychology* 74, 201–206.

Jurjevich, R. M. (1966b). The regression toward the mean in MMPI, CPI and Symptom Check List. *Educational and Psychological Measurement* 26, 661–664.

Jurko, M. F., Andy, O. J., & Giurintano, L. P. (1974). Changes in the MMPI as a function of thalamotomy. *Journal of Clinical Psychology* 30, 569–570.

Kahn, M. W. (1953). The role of perceptual consistency and generality change in Rorschach and psychotherapy behavior. In W. U. Snyder (Ed.), *Group report of a program of research in psychotherapy*. State College, PA: Pennsylvania State University Press.

Kahn, R. B., Schramm, N. T., & Daoud, F. (1979). Another alternative: A 90-day contractual detoxification treatment program. *Drug Forum* 7, 51–58.

Kalichman, S. C., Shealy, L., & Craig, M. E. (1990). The use of the MMPI in predicting treatment participation among incarcerated adult rapists. *Journal of Psychology and Human Sexuality* 3, 105–119.

Kaplan, F. (1966). Effects of anxiety and defense in a therapy-like situation. *Journal of Abnormal Psychology* 71, 449–458.

Kaplan, M. F. (1967). Interview interaction of repressors and sensitizers. *Journal of Consulting Psychology* 31, 513–516.

Kaplan, R. (1972). Phenytoin, metronidazole and multivitamins in the treatment of alcoholism. *Quarterly Journal of Studies on Alcohol* 33, 97–104.

Kaufmann, P. (1950). Changes in the MMPI as a function of psychiatric therapy. *Journal of Consulting Psychology* 14, 458–464.

Keegan, J. F., & Lachar, D. (1979). The MMPI as a predictor of early termination from polydrug abuse treatment. *Journal of Personality Assessment* 43, 379–384.

Keegan, J. F., Dewey, D., & Lucas, C. P. (1987). MMPI correlates of medical compliance in a weight control program. *International Journal of Eating Disorders* 6, 439–442.

Keilson, M. V., Dworkin, F. H., & Gelso, C. J. (1979). The effectiveness of time-limited psychotherapy in a university counseling center. *Journal of Clinical Psychology* 35, 631–636.

Keithly, L. J., Samples, S. J., & Strupp, H. H. (1980). Patient motivation as a predictor of process and outcome in psychotherapy. *Psychotherapy and Psychosomatics* 33, 87–97.

Kellner, R. (1967). The evidence in favour of psychotherapy. *British Journal of Medical Psychology* 40, 341–358.

Kelly, D. H., Walter, C. J., Mitchell-Heggs, N., & Sargant, W. (1972). Modified leucotomy assessed clinically, physiologically and psychologically at six weeds and eighteen months. *British Journal of Psychiatry* 120, 19–29.

Kelly, E. E. (1966). Member personality and group counseling interaction. *Journal of Psychology* 63, 89–97.

Kelly, E. L., Miller, J. G., Marquis, D. G., Gerard, R. W., & Uhr, L. (1958). Personality differences and continued meprobamate and prochlorperazine administration. *Archives of Neurology and Psychiatry* 80, 241–246.

Kennedy, B. P., & Minami, M. (1993). The Beech Hill Hospital/Outward Bound Adolescent Chemical Dependency Treatment Program. *Journal of Substance Abuse Treatment* 10, 395–406.

Khanna, J. L., Pratt, S., Burdizk, E. G., & Chaddha, R. L. (1963). A study of certain effects of tranylcypromine, a new antidepressant. *Journal of New Drugs* 3, 227–232.

Khavin, A. B. (1985). (Individual-psychological factors in prediction of help to stutterers.) *Voprosy Psikhologii* 2, 133–135.

Kidd, A. H. (1968). The ego strength scale and the Goldberg scale in evaluating clinic outpatients. *Journal of Clinical Psychology* 24(Suppl.), 438–439.

Kiesler, D. J. (1971). Patient experiencing and successful outcome in individual psychotherapy of schizophrenics and psychoneurotics. *Journal of Consulting and Clinical Psychology* 37, 370–385.

Kiesler, D. J., Klein, M. H., Mathieu, P. L., & Schoeninger, D. (1967). Constructive personality change for therapy and control patients. In C. R. Rogers (Ed.), *The therapeutic relationship and its impact: A study of psychotherapy with schizophrenics*. Madison, WI: University of Wisconsin Press.

King, S. A., & Snow, B. R. (1989). Factors for predicting premature termination from a multidisciplinary inpatient chronic pain program. *Pain* 39, 281–287.

Kinsman, R. A., Dirks, J. F., & Dahlem, N. W. (1980). Noncompliance to prescribed-as-needed (PRN) medication use in asthma: Usage patterns and patient characteristics. *Journal of Psychosomatic Research* 24, 97–107.

Kleinke, C. L., & Spangler, A. S. (1988). Predicting treatment outcome of chronic back pain patients in a multidisciplinary pain clinic: Methodological issues and treatment implications. *Pain* 33, 41–48.

Kleinmuntz, B. (1960). Identification of maladjusted college students. *Journal of Counseling Psychology* 7, 209–211.

Kleinmuntz, B. (1961a). The college maladjustment scale (MT): Norms and predictive validity. *Educational and Psychological Measurement* 21, 1029–1033.

Kleinmuntz, B. (1961b). Screening: Identification or prediction? *Journal of Counseling Psychology* 8, 279–280.

Klett, W. G. (1965). An investigation into the effect of historically based inferences in group psychotherapy on the behavior of withdrawn psychiatric patients. *Newsletter for Research in Psychology* 7, 44–46.

Klett, W. G. (1966). The effect of historically based inferences on the behavior of withdrawn psychiatric patients. *Journal of Clinical Psychology* 22, 427–429.

Klett, W. G., & Vestre, N. D. (1967). Demographic and prognostic characteristics of psychiatric patients classified by gross MMPI measures. *Proceedings of the 75th Annual Convention of the APA* 2, 205–206.

Kline, M. V. (1952). Visual imagery and a case of experimental hypnotherapy. *Journal of General Psychology* 46, 159–167.

Kline, N. S., & Schacter, F. (1965). Nortriptyline in private practice. *Canadian Psychiatric Association Journal* 10, 59–66.

Klinge, V., Culbert, J., & Piggott, L. R. (1982). Efficacy of psychiatric inpatient hospitalization for adolescents as measured by pre- and post-MMPI profiles. *Journal of Youth and Adolescence* 11, 493–502.

Klonoff, H., Fleetham, J., Tayor, R., & Clark, C. (1987). Treatment outcome of obstructive sleep apnea: Physiological and neuropsychological concomitants. *Journal of Nervous and Mental Disease* 175, 208–212.

Knapp, J. E., Templer, D. I., Cannon, W. G., & Dobson, S. (1991). Variables associated with success in an adolescent drug treatment program. *Adolescence* 26, 305–317.

Koch, H. C. (1983). Changes in personal construing in three psychotherapy groups and a control group. *British Journal of Medical Psychology* 56, 245–254.

Koch, J., & Greger, J. (1985). Erfahrungen bei der Kombination eines Kommunikationstrainings mit dynamischer Gruppenpsychotherapie. (Experience gained with communication training combined with group-centred dynamic psychotherapy.) *Psychiatrie, Neurologie und medizinische Psychologie* 37, 339–346.

Kodman, F., & Sedlacek, G. (1962). MMPI changes following a course in mental hygiene. *Mental Hygiene* 46, 95–97.

Koss, M. P. (1980). A multivariate analysis of long-term stay in private practice psychotherapy. *Journal of Clinical Psychology* 36, 991–993.

Kraft, T. (1969). Behaviour therapy or personality therapy. *Psychotherapy and Psychosomatics* 17, 217–225.

Kraft, T. (1970). Successful treatment of "Drinamyl" addicts and associated personality changes. *Canadian Psychiatric Association Journal* 15, 223–227.

Kraft, T., & Wijesinghe, B. (1970). Systematic desensitization of social anxiety in the treatment of alcoholism: A psychometric evaluation of change. *British Journal of Psychiatry* 117, 443–444.

Krakowski, M., & Smart, R. G. (1974). Social and psychological characteristics of heroin addicts dropping out of methadone treatment. *Canadian Psychiatric Association Journal* 19, 41–47.

Krasnoff, A. (1976). Differences between alcoholics who complete or withdraw from treatment. *Journal of Studies on Alcohol* 37, 1666–1671.

Krasnoff, A. (1977). Failure of MMPI scales to predict treatment completion. *Journal of Studies on Alcohol* 38, 1440–1442.

Kraus, A. R. (1959). Experimental study of the effect of group psychotherapy with chronic psychotic patients. *International Journal of Group Psychotherapy* 9, 293–302.

Krupitskii, E. M., Burakov, A. M., Karandashova, G. F., & Lebedev, V. B. (1993). A method of treating affective disorders in alcoholics. *Journal of Russian and East European Psychiatry* 26, 26–37.

Kunce, J. T., & Worley, B. (1966). Relationship of circular pencil mazes with cognitive and emotional distress. *Journal of Clinical Psychology* 22, 303–305.

Kuperman, S. K., Golden, C. J., & Blume, H. G. (1979a). Predicting pain treatment results by personality variables in organic and functional patients. *Journal of Clinical Psychology* 35, 832–837.

Kuperman, S. K., Osmon, D., Golden, C. J., & Blume, H. G. (1979b). Prediction of neurosurgical results by psychological evaluation. *Perceptual and Motor Skills* 48, 311–315.

Kurland, A. A. (1967). The therapeutic potential of LSD in medicine. In R. C. DeBold & R. C. Leaf (Eds.), *LSD, man and society*. Middletown, CT: Wesleyan University Press.

Kurland, A. A., Destounis, N., Shaffer, J. W., & Pinto, A. (1967a). A critical study of isocarboxazid (Marplan) in the treatment of depressed patients. *Journal of Nervous and Mental Disease* 145, 292–305.

Kurland, A. A., Unger, S., Shaffer, J. W., & Savage, C. (1967b). Psychedelic therapy utilizing LSD in the treatment of the alcoholic patient: A preliminary report. *American Journal of Psychiatry* 123, 1202–1209.

Kurland, A. A., Pinto, A., Dim, B. H., & Babikow, P. W. (1968). Thiazesim (SQ-10,496) in the treatment of depressed patients. *Current Therapeutic Research* 10, 201–206.

Lacroix, J. M., Clarke, M. A., Bock, J. C., & Doxey, N. C. (1986). Predictors of biofeedback and relaxation success in multiple-pain patients: Negative findings. *International Journal of Rehabilitation Research* 9, 376–378.

Lafave, H.G., March, B.W., & Kargas, A.K. (1965). Desipramine and imipramine in an out-patient setting: A comparative study. *American Journal of Psychiatry* 122, 698–701.

Land, H. M. (1986). Child abuse: Differential diagnosis, differential treatment. *Child Welfare* 65, 33–44.

Lane, J. B. (1985). Using MMPI lithium response scales. *American Journal of Psychiatry* 142, 1388–1389.

Lanyon, R. I. (1966). The MMPI and prognosis in stuttering therapy. *Journal of Speech and Hearing Disorders* 31, 186–191.

Lanyon, R. I., Primo, R.V., Terrell, F., & Wenar, A. (1972). An aversion-desensitization treatment for alcoholism. *Journal of Consulting and Clinical Psychology* 38, 394–398.

Lapuc, P. S., & Harmatz, M. G. (1970). Verbal conditioning and therapeutic change. *Journal of Consulting and Clinical Psychology* 35, 70–78.

Lavellee, Y. J., Lamontagne, Y., Annable, L., & Fontaine, F. (1982). Characteristics of chronically anxious patients who respond to EMG feedback training. *Journal of Clinical Psychiatry* 43, 229–230.

Lawlis, G. F. (1970). Vocational counseling: A therapeutic encounter. *Rehabilitation Research and Practice Review* 1, 25–39.

Lawson, H. H., Kahn, M. W., & Heiman, E. M. (1982). Psychopathology, treatment outcome and attitude toward mental illness in Mexican American and European patients. *International Journal of Social Psychiatry* 28, 20–26.

Leak, G. K. (1980). Effects of highly structured versus nondirective group counseling approaches on personality and behavioral measures of adjustment in incarcerated felons. *Journal of Counseling Psychology* 27, 520–523.

Leary, T., & Coffey, H. S. (1955). The prediction of interpersonal behavior in group psychotherapy. *Psychodrama and Group Psychotherapy Monographs* 28, 1–35.

Leary, T. R., Presnell, M. M., Weil, G., Schwitzgebel, R., & Kinne, S. (1965). A new behavior change program using psilocybin. *Psychotherapy: Theory, Research, and Practice* 2, 61–72.

Lebo, D., Toal, R.A., & Brick, H. (1958). Manifest anxiety in prisoners before and after CO_2. *Journal of Consulting Psychology* 22, 51–55.

Lerner, A. (1953). An experiment in group counseling with male alcoholic inmates. *Federal Probation* 17, 32–9.

Levee, J. R. (1963). A pilot investigation into the effects of an interpersonal therapy approach upon mental patients in a general hospital short-term psychiatric setting. *Dissertation Abstracts* 24, 1245.

Levinson, T., & McLachlan, J. F. (1973). Factors relating to outcome in the treatment of alcohol addiction at the Donwood Institute. *Toxicomanies* 6, 203–221.

Levis, D. J., & Carrera, R. (1967). Effects of ten hours of implosive therapy in the treatment of outpatient: A preliminary report. *Journal of Abnormal Psychology* 72, 504–508.

Levitt, E. A. (1975). Procedural issues in the systematic desensitization of air-travel phobia. *New Zealand Psychologist* 4, 2–9.

Lewinsohn, P. M. (1965). Dimensions of MMPI change. *Journal of Clinical Psychology* 21, 37–43.

Lewinsohn, P. M., & Nichols, R. C. (1964). The evaluation of changes in psychiatric patients during and after hospitalization. *Journal of Clinical Psychology* 20, 272–279.

Lewinsohn, P. M., & Nichols, R. C. (1967). Dimensions of change in mental hospital patients. *Journal of Clinical Psychology* 23, 498–503.

Lewinsohn, P. M., & Shaw, D. A. (1969). Feedback about interpersonal behavior as an agent of behavior change: A case study in the treatment of depression. *Psychotherapy and Psychosomatics* 17, 82–88.

Lewinsohn, P. M., Weinstein, M. S., & Alper, T. (1970). A behavioral approach to the group treatment of depressed persons: A methodological contribution. *Journal of Clinical Psychology* 26, 525–532.

Lichtenstein, E. (1966). Personality similarity and therapeutic success: A failure to replicate. *Journal of Consulting Psychology* 30, 282.

Lichtenstein, E., & Bryan, J. H. (1966). Short-term stability of MMPI profiles. *Journal Consulting Psychology* 30, 172–174.

Lick, J. R., & Heffler, D. (1977). Relaxation training and attention placebo in the treatment of severe insomnia. *Journal of Consulting and Clinical Psychology* 45, 153–161.

Liederman, P. C., Green, R., & Liederman, V. R. (1967). Outpatient group therapy with geriatric patients. *Geriatrics* 22, 148–153.

Linder, L. H. (1981). Group behavioral treatment of agoraphobia: A preliminary report. *Comprehensive Psychiatry* 22, 226–233.

Loevinger, J., & Ossorio, A. (1959). Evaluation of therapy by self-report: A paradox. *Journal of Abnormal and Social Psychology* 58, 392–394.

Lomont, J. F., Gilner, F. H., Spector, N. J., & Skinner, K. K. (1969). Group assertion training and group insight therapies. *Psychological Reports* 25, 463–470.

Lorandos, D. A. (1990). Change in adolescent boys at Teen Ranch: A five-year study. *Adolescence* 25, 509–516.

Lorr, M., McNair, D. M., Weinstein, G. J., Michaux, W. W., & Raskin, A. (1961). Meprobamate and chlorpromazine in psychotherapy: Some effects on anxiety and hostility of outpatients. *Archives of General Psychiatry* 4, 381–389.

Love, A. W., & Peck, C. L. (1987). The MMPI and psychological factors in chronic low back pain: A review. *Pain* 28, 1–12.

Love, J. W. (1958). A study of personality changes attending personal counseling. *Dissertation Abstracts* 18, 1107.

Lowe, C. M. (1967). Prediction of posthospital work adjustment by the use of psychological tests. *Journal of Counseling Psychology* 14, 248–252.

Lowe, W. C., & Thomas, S. D. (1976). Assessing alcoholism treatment effectiveness: A comparison of three evaluative measures. *Journal of Studies on Alcohol* 37, 883–889.

Luborsky, L. (1971). Perennial mystery of poor agreement among criteria for psychotherapy outcome. *Journal of Consulting and Clinical Psychology* 37, 316–319.

Luckey, W. T., & Schiele, B. C. (1967). A comparison of haloperidol and trifluoperazine: A double-blind, controlled study on chronic schizophrenic outpatients. *Diseases of the Nervous System* 28, 181–186.

Mabli, J., Nesbitt, K. L., Glick, S., & Tilbrook, J. (1985). FCI Fort Worth substance abuse evaluation: A pilot study. *Federal Probation* 49, 40–45.

Malan, D. H., Bacal, H. A., Heath, E. S., & Balfour, F. H. G. (1968). A study of psychodynamic changes in untreated neurotic patients: I. Improvements that are questionable on dynamic criteria. *British Journal of Psychiatry* 114, 525–551.

Mandell, A. J., Markham, C. H., Tallman, F. F., & Mandell, M. P. (1962). Motivation and ability to move. *American Journal of Psychiatry* 119, 544–549.

Manos, N., & Vasilopoulou, E. (1984). Evaluation of psychoanalytic psychotherapy outcome. *Acta Psychiatrica Scandinavica* 70, 28–35.

Marks, J., Stauffacher, J. C., & Lyle, C. (1963). Predicting outcome in schizophrenia. *Journal of Abnormal and Social Psychology* 66, 117–127.

Martin, C. V., & Alvord, J. R. (1966). Long-term effects of intensive short-term treatment of the character and personality disorders. *Corrective Psychiatry and Journal of Social Therapy* 12, 433–442.

Martin, D. V., & Caine, T. M. (1963). Personality change in the treatment of chronic neurosis in a therapeutic community. *British Journal of Psychiatry* 109, 267–272.

Martin, P. J., & Sterne, A. L. (1975). Prognostic expectations and treatment outcome. *Journal of Consulting and Clinical Psychology* 43, 572–576.

Martin, P. J. & Sterne, A. L. (1976). Subjective objectivity: Therapists' affection and successful psychotherapy. *Psychological Reports* 38, 1163–1169.

Martin, P. J., Sterne, A. L., Moore, J. E., & Friedmeyer, M. H. (1976). Patient's and therapists' expectancies and treatment outcome: An elusive relationship reexamined. *Research Communications in Psychology, Psychiatry and Behavior* 1, 301–314.

Martin, P. J., Moore, J. E., & Sterne, A. L. (1977a). Therapists as prophets: Their expectancies and treatment outcome. *Psychotherapy Theory, Research and Practice* 14, 188–195.

Martin, P. J., Moore, J. E., Sterne, A. L., & McNairy, R. M. (1977b). Therapists prophesy. *Journal of Clinical Psychology* 33, 502–510.

Mascia, G. V. (1969). A study of the prediction of alcoholics' responsiveness to treatment. *Dissertation Abstracts International* 30, 2912B.

Maser, A. L. (1969). The effect of client response and counselor personality on counselor response, and the effect of counselor response on client response. *Dissertation Abstracts* 29, 2096A.

Matarazzo, J. D., Weitman, M., & Saslow, G. (1963). Interview content and interviewer speech duration. *Journal of Clinical Psychology* 19, 463–472.

Matarazzo, J. D., & Wiens, A. N. (1966). Interviewer effects on interviewee speech and silence durations. *Proceedings of the 74th Annual Convention of the American Psychological Association* 1, 45–46.

Mathias, R. E., & Sindberg, R. M. (1986). Time limited group therapy in minimum security. *Journal of Offender Counseling, Services and Rehabilitation* 11, 7–17.

Matson, J. L. (1982). The treatment of behavioral characteristics of depression in the mentally retarded. *Behavior Therapy* 13, 209–218.

May, P. R. A. (Ed.). (1968). *Treatment in schizophrenia: A comparative study of five treatment methods*. New York: Science House.

May, P. R. A., & Distler, L. S. (1968). The use of psychological tests to measure treatment outcome in schizophrenic patients. In P. R. A. May (Ed.), *Treatment in schizophrenia: A comparative study of five treatment methods*. New York: Science House.

May, P. R. A., & Tuma, A. H. (1964). Choice of assessment of treatment outcome. *Journal of Psychiatric Research* 2, 199–209.

McAdoo, W. G., & Roeske, N. A. (1973). A comparison of defectors and continuers in a child guidance clinic. *Journal of Consulting and Clinical Psychology* 40, 328–334.

McArthur, D. L., Cohen, M. J., Gottlieb, H. J., & Naliboff, B. D. (1987). Treating chronic low back pain: I. Admissions to initial follow-up. *Pain* 29, 1–22.

McCabe, O. L., Savage, C., Kurland, A., & Unger, S. (1972). Psychedelic (LSD) therapy of neurotic disorders: Short term effects. *Journal of Psychedelic Drugs* 5, 18–28.

McCall, R. J. (1973). MMPI factors that differentiate remediably from irremediably obese women. *Journal of Community Psychology* 1, 34–36.

McCall, R. J. (1974). Group therapy with obese women of varying MMPI profiles. *Journal of Clinical Psychology* 30, 466–470.

McClellan, T. A., & Stieper, D. R. (1971). A structured approach to group marriage counseling. *Mental Hygiene* 55, 77–84.

McCreary, C., Turner, J., & Dawson, E. (1979). The MMPI as a predictor of response to conservative treatment for low back pain. *Journal of Clinical Psychology* 35, 278–284.

McDonald, I. M., Perkins, M., & Marjerrison, G. (1966). A controlled comparison of amitriptyline and electroconvulsive therapy in the treatment of depression. *American Journal of Psychiatry* 122, 1427–1431.

McFarlane, A. H., Bellissimo, A., & Upton, E. (1982). "Atypical" anorexia nervosa: Treatment and management on a behavioral medicine unit. *Psychiatric Journal of the University of Ottawa* 7, 158–162.

McHugh, R. B., & Sivanich, G. (1963). Assessing the temporal stability of profile groups in a comparative experimental survey. *Psychological Reports* 13, 145–146.

McKeever, W. F., May, P. R. A., & Tuma, A. H. (1965). Prognosis in schizophrenia: Prediction of length of hospitalization from psychological test variables. *Journal of Clinical Psychology* 21, 214–221.

McNair, D. M., Callahan, R. M., & Lorr, M. (1962). Therapist "type" and patient response to psychotherapy. *Journal of Consulting Psychology* 26, 425–429.

McNamara, J. R., & Andrasik, F. (1982). Recidivism follow-up for residents released from a forensic psychiatry behavior change treatment program. *Journal of Psychiatric Treatment and Evaluation* 4, 423–426.

McNeil, E. B., & Cohler, J. R. (1957). The effect of personal needs on counselors' perception and behavior. *Papers of the Michigan Academy of Science, Arts, and Letters* 42, 281–288.

McReynolds, W. T. (1969). The treatment of chronic and acute anxiety in a psychiatric population. *Newsletter for Research in Psychology* 11, 10–11.

McWilliams, J., & Brown, C. C. (1977). Treatment termination variables, MMPI scores and frequencies of relapse in alcoholics. *Journal of Studies on Alcohol* 38, 477–486.

Meehl, P. E. (1955). Psychotherapy. *Annual Review of Psychology* 6, 357–377.

Melnick, B. (1972). Patient–therapist identification in relation to both patient and therapist variables and therapy outcome. *Journal of Consulting and Clinical Psychology* 38, 97–104.

Melson, S. J. (1982). Short-term intensive group psychotherapy for patients with "functional" complaints. *Psychosomatics* 23, 689–695.

Meltzoff, J., & Kornreich, M. (1970). *Research in psychotherapy*. New York: Atherton Press.

Mena, A. (1965). Evaluation of regressive electroshock treatments in chronic paranoid schizophrenics. *Dissertation Abstracts* 25, 6763.

Mena, A., Heistad, G., & Schiele, B. C. (1964). A comparison of tranylcypromine alone with tranylcypromine plus trifluoperazine in the treatment of chronic outpatients: A double blind controlled study. *Journal of Neuropsychiatry* 5, 542–550.

Mendlesohn, R. M., Penman, A. S., & Schiele, B. C. (1959). Massive chlorpromazine therapy: The nature of behavioral changes. *Psychiatric Quarterly* 33, 55–76.

Merbaum, M., & Butcher, J. N. (1982). Therapists' liking of their psychotherapy patients: Some issues related to severity of disorder and treatability. *Psychotherapy Theory, Research and Practice* 19, 69–76.

Merzbacher, C. F. (1979). A diet and exercise regimen: Its effect upon mental acuity and personality, a pilot study. *Perceptual and Motor Skills* 48, 367–371.

Metzen, J. D. (1971). Efficacy of eating as the response antagonistic to anxiety in the group desensitization of "normal" snake phobic subjects. *Dissertation Abstracts International* 32, 3011B.

Meyer, R. G. (1993). *The clinician's handbook: Integrated diagnostics, assessment, and intervention in adult and adolescent psychopathology* (3rd edition). Boston, MA: Allyn & Bacon.

Michaux, M. H., Chelst, M. R., Foster, S. A., & Pruim, R. J. (1972). Day and full-time psychiatric treatment: A controlled comparison. *Current Therapeutic Research* 14, 279–292.

Mick, R. M. (1956). A study of resistance during psychotherapy. *Dissertation Abstracts* 16, 1174.

Miller, T. W. (1990). *Chronic pain*, Vols. 1 & 2. Madison, CT: International Universities Press.

Miller, W. H., & Gottlieb, F. (1974). Predicting behavioral treatment outcome in disturbed children: A preliminary report of the Responsivity Index of Parents (RIP). *Behavior Therapy* 5, 210–214.

Miller, W. R. (1978). Behavioral treatment of problem drinkers: A comparative outcome study of three controlled drinking therapies. *Journal of Consulting and Clinical Psychology* 46, 74–86.

Miller, W. R., & DiPilato, M. (1983). Treatment of nightmares via relaxation and desensitization: A controlled evaluation. *Journal of Consulting and Clinical Psychology* 51, 870–877.

Miner, M. H., Marques, J. K., Day, D. M., & Nelson, C. (1990). Impact of relapse prevention in treating sex offenders: Preliminary findings. *Annals of Sex Research* 3, 165–185.

Minsel, W. R. (1972). Further investigation on the effects and processes of client-centered counseling therapy. *Zeitschrift für Klinische Psychologie* 3, 232–250.

Mirabel-Sarron, C., Morell, C., & Samuel Lajeunesse, B. (1993). Apport de la therapie cognitive de Beck dans les depressions chroniques et resistantes aux antidepresseurs. (Beck's cognitive therapy for patients with pharmacotherapy-resistant chronic depression.) *Annales Medico Psychologiques* 151, 697–701.

Modlin, H. C. (1947). A study of the MMPI in clinical practice with notes on the Cornell Index. *American Journal of Psychiatry* 103, 758–769.

Mogar, R. E., & Savage, C. (1963). Personality change associated with psychedelic (LSD) therapy: A preliminary report. *Psychotherapy: Theory, Research, and Practice* 1, 154–162.

Molinari, E., Valtolina, G., Peri, G., & Pedrabissi, L. (1991). Cambiamenti psicologici in un trattamento combinato dell'obesita. (Psychological changes in a combined treatment for obesity.) *Ricerche di Psicologia* 15, 97–127.

Monroe, J. J., & Hill, H. E. (1958). The Hill-Monroe Inventory for prediciting acceptability for psychotherapy in the institutionalized narcotic addict. *Journal of Clinical Psychology* 14, 31–6.

Moos, R. H. (1968). Differential effects of ward settings on psychiatric patients. *Journal of Nervous and Mental Disease* 147, 386–393.

Monsen, J., Odegard P., & Melgard, T. (1989a). Alvorlige psykiske forstyrrelser og forandringer etter inngaende psykoterapi: Resultater fra Toyen-prosjektet. (Major psychological disorders and changes after intensive psychotherapy: Findings from the Toyen-project, Oslo.) *Tidsskrift for Norsk Psykologforening* 26, 616–626.

Monsen, J., Odegard, P., & Melgard, T. (1989b). Major psychological disorders and changes after intensive psychotherapy: Findings from the Toyen project, Oslo. *Psychoanalysis and Psychotherapy* 7, 171–180.

Moore, J. E., Armentrout, D. P., Parker, J. C., & Kivlahan, D. R. (1986). Empirically derived pain-patient MMPI subgroups: Prediction of treatment outcome. *Journal of Behavioral Medicine* 9, 51–63.

Moran, M. (1978). Systems releasing action therapy with alcoholics: An experimental evaluation. *Journal of Clinical Psychology* 34, 769–774.

Moreland, K. L., & Dahlstrom, W. G. (1983). Professional training with and use of the MMPI. *Professional Psychology Research and Practice* 14, 218–223.

Morrison, T. L., Edwards, D. W., & Weissman, H. N. (1994). The MMPI and MMPI-2 as predictors of psychiatric diagnosis in an outpatient sample. *Journal of Personality Assessment* 62, 17–30.

Mowrer, O. H. (Ed.). (1953). *Psychotherapy: Theory and research.* New York: Ronald.

Moxley, A. W., & Satz, P. (1970). Effects of statistical information on clinical judgment. *Proceedings of the 78th Annual Convention of the American Psychological Association* 5, 545–546.

Mugutdinov, T. M. (1987). A method for treating neuroses. *Soviet Neurology and Psychiatry* 20, 38–45.

Muller, B. (1964). Further evidence for the validity of the Mental Status Schedule (MSS). *American Psychologist* 19, 516.

Muller, N., Gunther, W., Horn, B., & Laakmann, G. (1988). Psychopathological changes in a patient with rhythmic midtemporal discharges after antiepileptic medication. *Biological Psychiatry* 23, 741–745.

Munjack, D. (1976). Behavioural treatment of orgasmic dysfunction: A controlled study. *British Journal of Psychiatry* 129, 497–502.

Munjack, D. J. (1985). Imipramine versus propranolol for the treatment of panic attacks: A pilot study. *Comprehensive Psychiatry* 26, 80–89.

Munley, P. H., Bains, D. S., Frazee, J., & Schwartz, L. T. (1994). Inpatient PTSD treatment: A study of pretreatment measures, treatment dropout, and therapist ratings of response to treatment. *Journal of Traumatic Stress* 7, 319–325.

Murillo, L. G., & Exner, J. E. (1973). The effect of regressive ECT with process schizophrenics. *American Journal of Psychiatry* 130, 269–273.

Muzekari, L. H. (1965). The MMPI in predicting treatment outcome in alcoholism. *Journal of Consulting Psychology* 20, 281.

Myatt, M. F. (1952). A study of the relationship between motivation and test performance of patients in a rehabilitation ward. *Dissertation Abstracts* 12, 339.

Nacev, V. (1980). Dependency and ego-strength as indicators of patients' attendance in psychotherapy. *Journal of Clinical Psychology* 36, 691–695.

Naliboff, B. D., McCreary, C. P., McArthur, D. L., & Cohen, M. J. (1988). MMPI changes following behavioral treatment of chronic low back pain. *Pain* 35, 271–277.

Nathan, R. G., Robinson, D., Cherek, D. R., & Sebastian, C. S. (1986). Alternative treatments for withdrawing the long-term benzodiazepine user: A pilot study. *International Journal of the Addictions* 21, 195–211.

Nawas, M. M. (1971). "Existential" anxiety treated by systematic desensitization: A case study. *Journal of Behavior Therapy and Experimental Psychiatry* 2, 291–295.

Nelson-Gray, R. O., Herbert, J. D., Herbert, D. L., & Sigmon, S. T. (1989). Effectiveness of matched, mismatched, and package treatments of depression. *Journal of Behavior Therapy and Experimental Psychiatry* 20, 281–294.

Newburger, H. M. (1963). Psychotherapy and anxiety: A sociometric study. *Group Psychotherapy* 16, 1–7.

Newburger, H. M., & Schauer, G. (1953). Sociometric evaluation of group psychotherapy. *Group Psychotherapy* 6, 7–20.

Newmark, C. S. (1971). MMPI: Comparison of the oral form presented by a live examiner and the booklet form. *Psychological Reports* 29, 797–798.

Newmark, C. S., Finkelstein, M., & Frerking, R. A. (1974). Comparison of the predictive validity of two measures of psychotherapy prognosis. *Journal of Personality Assessment* 38, 144–148.

Nezu, A. M. (1986). Efficacy of a social problem-solving therapy approach for unipolar depression. *Journal of Consulting and Clinical Psychology* 54, 196–202.

Nichols, M. P. (1974). Outcome of brief cathartic psychotherapy. *Journal of Consulting and Clinical Psychology* 42, 403–410.

Nielsen, G. (1982). Endringer hos pasienter i korttidsterapi: En prosjektpresentasjon. (Changes in patients receiving psychotherapy of short duration: Presentation of an evaluation study.) *Tidsskrift for Norsk Psykologforening* 19, 359–364.

Nielsen, G. (1984). Evaluering av pasienter i dynamisk korttidspsykoterapi: En prosjekt-illustrasjon. (Evaluation of patients in brief dynamic psychotherapy.) *Nordisk Psykologi* 36, 65–74.

Nielsen, G., Barth, K., Haver, B., & Havik, O. E. (1988). Forlopet etter korttids dynamisk psykoterapi: Er bedringen varig? En oppfolging av pasienter i Bergen-prosjektet. (Patterns of change after brief dynamic psychotherapy: Is improvement maintained?) *Tidsskrift for Norsk Psykologforening* 25, 147–154.

Nielsen, G., Havik, O. E., Barth, K., & Haver, B. (1989). Testkorrelater til bedring i korttids dynamisk psykoterapi. (Some test correlates of response to brief dynamic psychotherapy.) *Tidsskrift for Norsk Psykologforening* 26, 156–164.

Nigl, A. J., & Jackson, B. (1979). Electromyograph biofeedback as an adjunct to standard psychiatric treatment. *Journal of Clinical Psychiatry* 40, 433–436.

Nocita, A., & Stiles, W. B. (1986). Client introversion and counseling session impact. *Journal of Counseling Psychology* 33, 235–241.

Novac, A. (1986). Improvement in tardive dyskinesia and MMPI scores with propranolol. *Journal of Clinical Psychiatry* 47, 218–219.

Nussbaum, K., & Michaux, W. W. (1963). Response to humor in depression: A predictor and evaluator of patient change. *Psychiatric Quarterly* 37, 527–539.

Nussbaum, K., Wittig, B.A., & Hanlon, T.E. (1963). Intravenous nialamide in the treatment of depressed female patients. *Comprehensive Psychiatry* 4, 105–116.

Ochoa Mangado, E., Lopez Ibor Alino, J. J., Perez de los Cobos Peris, J. C., & Cebollada Gracia, A. (1992). Tratamiento de deshabituacion con naltrexona en la dependencia de opiaceos. (Withdrawal treatment with naltrexone in opiate dependence.) *Actas Luso Espanolas de Neurologia, Psiquiatria y Ciencias Afines* 20, 215–229.

Olson, G. W. (1962). Appplication of an objective method for measuring the action of antidepressant medications. *American Journal of Psychiatry* 118, 1044–1045.

O'Neil, P. M., Roitzsch, J. C., Giacinto, J. P., & Miller, W. C. (1983). Testing for differences between alcoholics who accept or refuse disulfiram. *Digest of Alcoholism Theory and Application* 2, 49–50.

Onorato, V. A., & Tsushima, W. T. (1983). EMG, MMPI, and treatment outcome in the biofeedback therapy of tension headache and posttraumatic pain. *American Journal of Clinical Biofeedback* 6, 71–81.

Oostdam, E. M., & Duivenvoorden, H. J. (1983). Predictability of the result of surgical intervention in patients with low back pain. *Journal of Psychosomatic Research* 27, 273–281.

Osborne, D. (1985). The MMPI in psychiatric practice. *Psychiatric Annals* 15, 542–545.

Ottomanelli, G. A. (1976). Follow-up of a token economy applied to civilly committed narcotic addicts. *International Journal of the Addictions* 11, 793–806.

Ottomanelli, G. A. (1977). MMPI and Pyp prediction compared to base rate prediction of six-month behavioral outcome for methadone patients. *British Journal of Addiction* 72, 177–186.

Ottomanelli, G. A. (1978). Patient improvement, measured by the MMPI and Pyp, related to paraprofessional and professional counselor assignment. *International Journal of the Addictions* 13, 503–507.

Ottomanelli, G., Wilson, P., & Whyte, R. (1978). MMPI evaluation of 5-year methadone treatment status. *Journal of Consulting and Clinical Psychology* 46, 579–582.

Overall, J. E., Hollister, L. E., Pokorny, A. D., Casey, J. F., & Katz, G. (1962). Drug therapy in depressions, controlled evaluation of imipramine, isocarboxazid, dextro-amphetamine-amobarbital and placebo. *Clinical Pharmacology and Therapeutics* 3, 16–22.

Overall, J. E., Hollister, L. E., & Meyer, F. (1964). Imipramine and thiorodazine in depressed and schizophrenic patients. Are there specific antidepressant drugs? *Journal of the American Medical Association* 189, 605–608.

Overall, J. E., Hollister, L. E., Shelton, J., Johnson, M., & Kimball, I. (1966). Tranylcypromine compared with dextro-amphetamine in hospitalized depressed patients. *Diseases of the Nervous System* 27, 653–659.

Overall, J. E., Brown, D., Williams, J. D., & Neill, L. T. (1973). Drug treatment of anxiety and depression in detoxified alcoholic patients. *Archives of General Psychiatry* 29, 218–221.

Pacella, B. L., Piotrowski, C., & Lewis, N. D. C. (1947). The effects of electric convulsive therapy on certain personality traits in psychiatric patients. *American Journal of Psychiatry* 104, 83–91.

Pancheri, L., Costantini, E., de Angelis, G., & Iannucci, C. (1988a). Valutazioni dell'esperienza di una psicoterapia cognitiva effettuata in ambito universitario: Impatto del setting e variabili correlate all'interruzione precoce della terapia. (Patients' and therapists' perceptions of a cognitive therapy in a university clinic: Influence of the setting and variables related to patient attrition.) *Rivista di Psichiatria* 23, 103–114.

Pancheri, P. (1982). Ansia di stato, ACTH, prolattina, GH e cortisolo in corso di terapia di rilassamento con EMG-biofeedback. (State anxiety, ACTH, cortisol growth hormone, prolactin during electromyographic (frontal) biofeedback relaxation training.) *Rivista di Psichiatria* 17, 422–461.

Pancheri, P., Bellaterra, M., Reda, G., & Polizzi, C. A. (1988a). Infarto acuto del miocardio (IMA): Valutazione dello stato d'ansia, della risposta degli ormoni dello stress e del decorso clinico in pazienti trattati e non trattati con bromazepam. (Acute myocardial infarction (AMI): State anxiety, stress hormone response and clinical course in patients treated and not treated with bromazepam.) *Rivista di Psichiatria* 23, 1–14.

Pancheri, P., Carilli, L., Gismondi, R., & Kotzalidis, G. D. (1988b). Miglioramento dei sintomi negativi della schizofrenia cronica residua con trattamento mediante CCK-8: Uno studio controllato in doppio cieco. (Negative symptom improvement in CCK-8 treated chronic residual schizophrenics: A double-blind controlled study.) *Rivista di Psichiatria* 23, 17–33.

Panton, J. H. (1979). MMPI profiles associated with outcomes of intensive psychotherapeutic counseling with youthful first offender prison inmates. *Research Communications in Psychology, Psychiatry and Behavior* 4, 383–395.

Parker, C. A. (1961). The predictive use of the MMPI in a college counseling center. *Journal of Counseling Psychology* 8, 154–158.

Parsons, O. A., Altrocchi, J., & Spring, F. E. (1959). Discrepancies in interpersonal perception, adjustment and therapeutic skill. *Perceptual Motor Skills* 18, 697–702.

Passini, F. T. (1977). Alpha wave biofeedback training therapy in alcoholics. *Journal of Clinical Psychology* 33, 292–299.

Patrick, J. (1984). Predicting outcome of psychiatric hospitalization: A comparison of attitudinal and psychopathological measures. *Journal of Clinical Psychology* 40, 546–549.

Pauker, J. D. (1965). MMPI profile stability in a psychiatric, inpatient population. *Journal of Clinical Psychology* 21, 281–282.

Pauker, J. D. (1966a). Stability of MMPI profiles of female psychiatric inpatients. *Journal of Clinical Psychology* 22, 209–212.

Pauker, J. D. (1966b). Stability of MMPI scales over five testings within a one-month period. *Educational and Psychological Measurement* 26, 1063–1067.

Peake, T. H. (1979). Therapist-patient agreement and outcome in group therapy. *Journal of Clinical Psychology* 35, 637–646.

Pearce, K. I. (1970). A comparison of care given by family practitioners and psychiatrists in a teaching hospital psychiatric unit. *American Journal of Psychiatry* 127, 835–840.

Pearson, J. S. (1950) Prediction of the response of schizophrenic patients to electroconvulsive therapy. *Journal of Clinical Psychology* 6, 285–287.

Pearson, J. S., & Swenson, W. M. (1951). A note on extended findings with the MMPI in predicting response to electroconvulsive therapy. *Journal of Clinical Psychology* 7, 288.

Pekarik, G., Jones, D. L., & Blodgett, C. (1986). Personality and demographic characteristics of dropouts and completers in a nonhospital residential alcohol treatment program. *International Journal of the Addictions* 21, 131–137.

Pena-Ramos, A., & Hornberger, R. (1979). MMPI and drug treatment in alcohol withdrawal. *Journal of Clinical Psychiatry* 40, 361–364.

Peniston, E. G., & Kulkosky, P. J. (1991). Alpha-theta brainwave neuro-feedback therapy for Vietnam veterans with combat-related post-traumatic stress disorder. *Medical Psychotherapy an International Journal* 4, 47–60.

Peniston, E. G., Hughes, R. B., & Kulkosky, P. J. (1986). EMG biofeedback-assisted relaxation training in the treatment of reactive depression in chronic pain patients. *Psychological Record* 36, 471–481.

Pennington, V. M. (1964). The phenotropic action of perphenazine-amitriptyline. *American Journal of Psychiatry* 120, 1115–1116.

Perconte, S. T., & Griger, M. L. (1991). Comparison of successful, unsuccessful, and relapsed Vietnam veterans treated for posttraumatic stress disorder. *Journal of Nervous and Mental Disease* 179, 558–562.

Perez, F., & Satz, P. (1971). The effects of feedback on clinical prediction. *Proceedings of the 79th Annual Convention of the American Psychological Association* 6, 465–466.

Perez-Solera, A. (1992). Tratamiento de trastornos hipocondriacos mediante un cambio de atribucion: Estudio del tratamiento y sequimiento a 1 ano, de un grupo de 4 pacientes. (Treatment in hypochondriacal disorders through a change in attributions: Treatment study in a group of four patients and follow-up for 1 year.) *Analisis y Modificacion de Conducta* 18, 279–290.

Persons, R. W. (1965). Psychotherapy with sociopathic offenders: An empirical evaluation. *Journal of Clinical Psychology* 21, 205–207.

Persons, R. W. (1966). Psychological and behavioral change in delinquents following psychotherapy. *Journal of Clinical Psychology* 22, 337–340.

Persons, R. W., & Marks, P. A. (1970). Self-disclosure with recidivists: A study of interviewer–interviewee matching. *Proceedings of the 77th Annual Convention of the American Psychological Association* 4, 531–532.

Peterson, D. R. (1954). Predicting hospitalization of psychiatric outpatients. *Journal of Abnormal and Social Psychology* 49, 260–265.

Petretic-Jackson, P., & Jackson, T. (1990). Assessment and crisis intervention with rape and incest victims: Strategies, techniques, and case illustrations. In A. R. Roberts (Ed.), *Crisis intervention handbook: Assessment, treatment and research* (pp. 124–152). Belmont, CA: Wadsworth.

Pickens, R. (1979). MMPI correlates of performance on a behavior therapy ward. *Behaviour Research and Therapy* 17, 17–24.

Pierce, R. M. (1968). Comment on the prediction of posthospital work adjustment with psychological tests. *Journal of Counseling Psychology* 15, 386–387.

Pierce, R. M., & Schauble, P.G. (1970). A note on the role of facilitative responsibility in the therapeutic relationship. *Journal of Clinical Psychology* 26, 250–252.

Pierloot, R. A., Wellens, W., & Houben, M. E. (1975). Elements of resistance to a combined medical and psychotherapeutic program in anorexia nervosa: An overview. *Psychotherapy and Psychosomatics* 26, 101–117.

Piotrowski, C., Sherry, D., & Keller, J. W. (1985). Psychodiagnostic test usage: A survey of the Society for Personality Assessment. *Journal of Personality Assessment* 49, 115–119.

Pino, C. J. (1971). Relation of a trainability index to T-group outcomes. *Journal of Applied Psychology* 55, 439–442.

Plotkin, W. B., & Rice, K. M. (1981). Biofeedback as a placebo: Anxiety reduction facilitated by training in either suppression or enhancement of alpha brainwaves. *Journal of Consulting and Clinical Psychology* 49, 590–596.

Pokorny, A. D., & Overall, J. E. (1961). Preliminary report on VA cooperative study No. 5: chemotherapy of depression. In *Transactions of the Sixth Research Conference on Cooperative Chemotherapy Studies in Psychiatry and Broad Research Approaches to Mental Illness*. Washington, D.C.: Veterans Administration Department of Medicine and Surgery.

Poulos, C. J. (1981). What effects do corrective nutritional practices have on alcoholics? *Journal of Orthomolecular Psychiatry* 10, 61–64.

Prager, R. A., & Garfield, S. L. (1972). Client initial disturbance and outcome in psychotherapy. *Journal of Consulting and Clinical Psychology* 38, 112–117.

Prange, A. J., Cochrane, C. M., Abse, D. W., & Boswell, J. I. (1963). A double blind clinical trial of chlorpromazine and reserpine in acute mental disturbance. *Journal of New Drugs* 3, 85–95.

Price, R. H., & Curlee-Salisbury, J. (1975). Patient–treatment interactions among alco-holics. *Journal of Studies on Alcohol* 36, 659–669.

Price, S. C. (1981). Group treatment of erectile dysfunction for men without partners: A controlled evaluation. *Archives of Sexual Behavior* 10, 253–268.

Propst, L. R. (1980). A comparison of the cognitive restructuring psychotherapy paradigm and several spiritual approaches to mental health. *Journal of Psychology and Theology* 8, 107–114.

Pumroy, D. K. (1961). Some counseling behavior correlates of the social desirability scale. *Journal of Counseling Psychology* 8, 49–53.

Pumroy, D. K., & Kogan, W. S. (1958). A validation of measures that predict the efficacy of shock therapy. *Journal of Clinical Psychology* 14, 46–47.

Pustell, T. E. (1958). A note on use of the MMPI in college counseling. *Journal of Counseling Psychology* 5, 69–70.

Raab, E., Rickels, K., & Moore, E. (1964). A double-blind evaluation of tybamate in anxious neurotic medical clinical patients. *American Journal of Psychiatry* 120, 1005–1007.

Rae, J. B. (1972). The influence of the wives on the treatment outcome of alcoholics: A follow-up study at two years. *British Journal of Psychiatry* 120, 601–613.

Ramos-Platon, M. J., & Sierra, J. E. (1992). Changes in psychopathological symptoms in sleep apnea patients after treatment with nasal continuous positive airway pressure. *International Journal of Neuroscience* 62, 173–195.

Rapaport, G. M. (1958). "Ideal self" instructions, MMPI profile changes, and the prediction of clinical improvement. *Journal of Consulting Psychology* 22, 459–463.

Rashkis, H. A., & Shaskan, D. A. (1946). The effects of group psychotherapy on personality inventory scores. *American Journal of Orthopsychiatry* 16, 345–349.

Reardon, J. P., Tosi, D. J., & Gwynne, P. H. (1977). The treatment of depression through Rational Stage Directed Hypnotherapy (RSDH): A case study. *Psychotherapy Theory, Research and Practice* 14, 95–103.

Rehm, L. P. (1979). A comparison of self-control and assertion skills treatments of depression. *Behavior Therapy* 10, 429–442.

Rehm, L. P. (1981). An evaluation of major components in a self-control therapy program for depression. *Behavior Modification* 5, 459–489.

Rehm, L. P., & Marston, A. R. (1968). Reduction in social anxiety through modifications of self-reinforcement: An instigation therapy technique. *Journal of Consulting and Clinical Psychology* 32, 565–574.

Reich, J., Steward, M. S., Tupin, J. P., & Rosenblatt, R. M. (1985). Prediction of response to treatment in chronic pain patients. *Journal of Clinical Psychiatry* 46, 425–427.

Reynolds, B. S. (1981). Dating skills training in the group treatment of erectile dysfunction for men without partners. *Journal of Sex and Marital Therapy* 7, 184–194.

Reznikoff, M., & Toomey, L. C. (1965). An evaluation of some possible prognostic indicators of response to phenothiazine treatment of acute schizophrenic psychoses. *International Journal of Neuropsychiatry* 1, 352–358.

Rice, L. M. (1965). Therapist's style of participation and case outcome. *Journal of Consulting Psychology* 29, 155–160.

Rickels, K., Clark, T., Ewing, J., & Klingensmith, W. (1959). Evalutation of tranquilizing drugs in medical outpatients (a controlled study of amobarbital, meprobamate, prochlorperazine, and placebo). *Journal of the American Medical Association* 171, 1649–1656.

Ries, H. A. (1966). The MMPI K scale as a predictor of prognosis. *Journal of Clinical Psychology* 22, 212–213.

Riklan, M., Halgin, R., Maskin, M., & Weissman, D. (1973). Psychological studies of longer range L-dopa therapy in parkinsonism. *Journal of Nervous and Mental Disease* 157, 452–464.

Ritchey, R. E. (1968). Evaluation of schizophrenics in a ward halfway house program. *Proceedings of the 76th Annual Convention of the American Psychological Association* 3, 499–500.

Rittenhouse, J. D. (1970). Endurance of effect: Family unit treatment compared to identified patient treatment. *Proceedings of the 78th Annual Convention of the American Psychological Association* 5, 535–536.

Roback, H. B. (1972). Experimental comparisons of outcomes in insight- and non-insight-oriented therapy groups. *Journal of Consulting and Clinical Psychology* 38, 411–417.

Roback, H. B., & Strassberg, D. S. (1975). Relationship between perceived therapist-offered conditions and therapeutic movement in group psychotherapy. *Small Group Behavior* 6, 345–352.

Roberts, J. M. (1959). Prognostic factors in the electroshock treatment of depressive states: II, The application of specific tests. *Journal of Mental Science* 105, 693–703.

Robertson, M. (1965). Therapeutic effectiveness of verbal communication under conditions of perceptual isolation. *Proceedings of the 73rd Annual Convention of the American Psychological Association,* 259–260.

Robin, A. A., & Wiseberg, S. (1958). A controlled trial of methylphenidate (Ritalin) in depressive states. *Journal of Neurology, Neurosurgery, and Psychiatry* 21, 55–57.

Robinson, K. D., & Little, G. L. (1982). One-day dropouts from correctional drug treatment. *Psychological Reports* 51, 409–410.

Robinson, M. E., Swimmer, G. I., & Rallof, D. (1989). The P-A-I-N MMPI classification system: A critical review. *Pain* 37, 211–214.

Rogers, C. R. (Ed.). (1967). *The therapeutic relationship and its impact: A study of psychotherapy with schizophrenics.* Madison: University of Wisconsin Press.

Rogers, J. H., McCarthy, S. M., & Wood, K. A. (1993). Community meeting participation as an indicator of treatment progress: The crisis stabilization unit. *Therapeutic Communities International Journal for Therapeutic and Supportive Organizations* 14, 165–178.

Rosen, A. (1953). Test–retest stability of MMPI scales for a psychiatric population. *Journal of Consulting Psychology* 17, 217–221.

Rosen, A. C., & Golden, J. S. (1975). The encounter-sensitivity training group as an adjunct to medical education. *International Review of Applied Psychology* 24, 61–70.

Rosen, B., Engelhardt, D. M., Freedman, N., Margolis, R., & Klein, D. F. (1971). The hospitalization proneness scale as a predictor of response to phenothiazine treatment: II, Delay of psychiatric hospitalization. *Journal of Nervous and Mental Disease* 152, 405–411.

Rosenheim, H. D., & Dunn, R. W. (1977). The effectiveness of rational behavior therapy in a military population. *Military Medicine* 142, 550–552.

Rosenthal, T. L. (1967). Stimulus modality and aerophobia: cautions for desensitization therapy. *American Journal of Clinical Hypnosis* 9, 269–274.

Ross, E. K., & Priest, R. G. (1970). The effect of hydroxyzine on phenothiazine therapy. *Diseases of the Nervous System* 31, 412–414.

Ross, W. F., McReynolds, W. T., & Berzins, J. I. (1974). Effectiveness of marathon group psychotherapy with hospitalized female narcotics addicts. *Psychological Reports* 34, 611–616.

Roulet, N., Alvarez, R. R., Duffy, J. P., Lenkoski, L. D., & Bidder, T. G. (1962). Imipramine in depression, a controlled study. *American Journal of Psychiatry* 119, 427–431.

Ruble, P. E. (1961). Psychic energizers in neurologically debilitated patients. *Journal of Neuropsychiatry* 2(Suppl.), 66–68.

Ruja, D. H. (1951). Personality changes following prefrontal lobotomy in 25 schizophrenic patients. *American Psychologist* 6, 499.

Rush, A. J., & Watkins, J. T. (1981). Group versus individual cognitive therapy: A pilot study. *Cognitive Therapy and Research* 5, 95–103.

Russell, M. W., & Bennett, R. N. (1972). Some suggestive data regarding group therapy and corrective therapy in treating voluntary alcoholics. *Newsletter for Research in Psychology* 14, 21–22.

Sacks, J. G., & Levy, N. M. (1979). Objective personality changes in residents of a therapeutic community. *American Journal of Psychiatry* 136, 796–799.

Sanchez, V. C., Lewinsohn, P. M., & Larson, D. W. (1980). Assertion training: Effectiveness in the treatment of depression. *Journal of Clinical Psychology* 36, 526–529.

Sander, K. (1973). The influence of pretherapy variables of clients on self-exploratory behavior in counseling therapy. *Zeitschrift fur Klinische Psychologie und Psychotherapie* 21, 40–45.

Sander, K. (1975). The influence of personality traits on treatment outcomes in client-centered psychotherapy. *Zeitschrift fur Klinische Psychologie. Forschung und Praxis* 4, 137–147.

Sandifer, M. G., Wilson, L. C., & Gambill, J. M. (1965). The influence of case selection and dosage in an antidepressant drug trial. *British Journal of Psychiatry* 111, 142–148.

Sandness, D. G. (1967). The MMPI as a predictor in vocational rehabilitation. *Dissertation Abstracts* 27, 3681B.

Sands, P. M. (1965). Application of the Interpersonal Problems Attitude Survey in a patients' training laboratory. *Dissertation Abstracts* 26, 2326.

Sanso, T. P. (1984). Personalidad y evolucion ponderal durante el tratamiento de sujetos con sobrepeso. (Personality and weight evolution during the treatment of overweight people.) *Analisis y Modificacion de Conducta* 10, 463–481.

Santucci, P. A. (1963). Treating depression as a decrease in functional capacity. *Maryland Medical Journal* 12, 546–552.

Sappington, A. A., & Michaux, M. H. (1975). Prognostic patterns in self-report, relative report, and professional evaluation measures for hospitalized and day-care patients. *Journal of Consulting and Clinical Psychology* 43, 904–910.

Sauer, J., & Schnetzer, M. (1978). Personality structure of asthmatic persons and its change due to different treatment methods in the development of a cure. *Zeitschrift fur Klinische Psychologie und Psychotherapie* 26, 171–180.

Savage, C., Fadiman, J., Mogar, R., & Allen, M. H. (1966). The effects of psychedelic (LSD) therapy on values, personality, and behavior. *International Journal of Neuropsychiatry* 2, 241–254.

Savage, C., Savage, E., Fadiman, J., & Harman, W. (1964). LSD: Therapeutic effects of the psychedelic experience. *Psychological Reports* 14, 111–120.

Scapinello, K. F., & Blanchard, R. (1987). Historical items in the MMPI: Note on evaluating treatment outcomes for a criminal population. *Psychological Reports* 61, 775–778.

Schauble, P. G., & Pierce, R. M. (1974). Client in-therapy behavior: A therapist guide to progress. *Psychotherapy Theory, Research and Practice* 11, 229–234.

Scheibe, K. E. (1965). College students spend eight weeks in a mental hospital: A case report. *Psychotherapy: Theory, Research, and Practice* 2, 117–120.

Schiele, B. C., Janecek, J., & Zimmerman, R. (1969). A double-blind comparison of trifluperidol and trifluoperazine in acute schizophrenic patients. *Comprehensive Psychiatry* 10, 355–360.

Schmidt, M. M., & Miller, W. R. (1983). Amount of therapist contact and outcome in a multidimensional depression treatment program. *Acta Psychiatrica Scandinavica* 67, 319–332.

Schoenberg, B., & Carr, A. C. (1963). An investigation of criteria for brief psychotherapy of neurodermatitis. *Psychosomatic Medicine* 25, 253–263.

Schofield, W. (1950). Changes in response to the MMPI following certain therapies. *Psychological Monographs* 64 (Serial No. 311).

Schofield, W. (1953). A further study of the effects of therapies on MMPI responses. *Journal of Abnormal and Social Psychology* 48, 67–77.

Schofield, W. (1964). *Psychotherapy: The purchase of friendship.* Englewood Cliffs, NJ: Prentice-Hall.

Schofield, W. (1966). The structured personality inventory in measurement of effects of psychotherapy. In L. A. Gottschalk & A. H. Auerbach (Eds.), *Methods of research in psychotherapy,* pp. 536–550. New York: Appleton-Century-Crofts.

Schofield, W., & Briggs, P. F. (1958). Criteria of therapeutic response in hospitalized psychiatric patients. *Journal of Clinical Psychology* 14, 227–232.

Schofield, W., Hathaway, S. R., Hastings, D. W., & Bell, D. M. (1954). Prognostic factors in schizophrenia. *Journal of Consulting Psychology* 18, 155–166.

Schonfield, J., & Donner, L. (1972). The effect of serving as a psychotherapist on students with different speciality preferences. *Journal of Medical Education* 47, 203–209.

Schork, E. J., Eckert, E. D., & Halmi, K. A. (1994). The relationship between psychopathology, eating disorder diagnosis, and clinical outcome at 10-year follow-up in anorexia nervosa. *Comprehensive Psychiatry* 35, 113–123.

Schroeder, D. J., & Piercy, D. C. (1979). A comparison of MMPI two-point codes in four alcoholism treatment facilities. *Journal of Clinical Psychology* 35, 656–663.

Schroeder, H., & Craine, L. (1971). Relationships among measures of fear and anxiety for snake phobics. *Journal of Consulting and Clinical Psychology* 36, 443.

Schweizer, E., Rickels, K., Case, G., & Greenblatt, D. J. (1990). Long-term therapeutic use of benzodiazepines: II. Effects of gradual taper. *Archives of General Psychiatry* 47, 908–915.

Scita, F., Fontana, S., Scorsonelli, M., & Nouarini, A. (1988). Trattamento di 11 casi di ipertensione arteriosa labile tramite EMG biofeedback. (Treatment of 11 cases of essential hypertension with EMG biofeedback.) *Medicina Psicosomatica* 33, 29–43.

Scott, A. B., Schlottmann, R. S., Brunetti, D. G., & Mihura, J. L. (1992). Treatment correlates of the MMPI subtle and obvious scores. *Psychological Reports* 71, 1357–1358.

Segal, B. (1971). Further investigation of personality correlates of the A-B scale. *Psychotherapy: Theory, Research, and Practice* 8, 37.

Sell, J. M., & Torres-Henry, R. (1979). Testing practices in university and college counseling centers in the United States. *Professional Psychology* 10, 774–779.

Seltzer, S., Dewart, D., Pollack, R. L., & Jackson, E. (1983). The effects of dietary tryptophan on chronic maxillofacial pain and experimental pain tolerance. *Journal of Psychiatric Research* 17, 181–186.

Shacter, H. (1947). Personality profiles of psychoneurotics before and after treatment. *American Psychologist* 2, 420.

Shaffer, J. W. (1963). Chlordiazepoxide (Librium) and acquiescent response set. *Psychological Reports* 13, 463–465.

Shaffer, J. W., Hanlon, T. E., Wolf, S., Foxwell, N. H., & Kurland, A. A. (1962). Nialamide in the treatment of alcoholism. *Journal of Nervous and Mental Disease* 135, 222–232.

Shaffer, J. W., Freinek, W. R., & McCusker, J. K. (1964a). A comparison of modaline sulfate (W-3207) and imipramine in the treatment of depression. *Journal of New Drugs* 4, 288–294.

Shaffer, J. W., Freinek, W. R., Wolf, S., Foxwell, N. H., & Kurland, A. A. (1964b). Replication of a study of nialamide in the treatment of convalescing alcoholics with emphasis on prediction of response. *Current Therapeutic Research* 6, 521–531.

Shands, H. C., Baughman, E. E., & Hawkins, D. R. (1959). A study of the "transactional" psychotherapy. *Psychiatry* 22, 289–295.

Shapiro, A. K., & Shapiro, E. (1968). Treatment of Gilles de la Tourette's syndrome with haloperidol. *British Journal of Psychiatry* 114, 345–350.

Shapiro, A. K., Struening, E., Shapiro, E., & Barten, H. (1976). Prognostic correlates of psychotherapy in psychiatric outpatients. *American Journal of Psychiatry* 133, 802–808.

Shapiro, D.A. (1969). Empathy, warmth, and genuineness in psychotherapy. *British Journal of Social and Clinical Psychology* 8, 350–361.

Shaw, J. A., Donley, P., Morgan, D. W., & Robinson, J. A. (1975). Treatment of depression in alcoholics. *American Journal of Psychiatry* 132, 641–644.

Shea, M. J. (1972). A follow-up study into adulthood of adolescent psychiatric patients in relation to internalizing and externalizing symptoms, MMPI configurations, social competence, and life history variables. *Dissertation s International* 33, 2822B.

Sheppard, D., Smith, G. T., & Rosenbaum, G. (1988). Use of MMPI subtypes in predicting completion of a residential alcoholism treatment program. *Journal of Consulting and Clinical Psychology* 56, 590–596.

Sher, T. G., Baucom, D. H., & Larus, J. M. (1990). Communication patterns and response to treatment among depressed and nondepressed maritally distressed couples. *Journal of Family Psychology* 4, 63–79.

Sherer, M., Haygood, J. M., & Alfano, A. M. (1984). Stability of psychological test results in newly admitted alcoholics. *Journal of Clinical Psychology* 40, 855–857.

Sherman, A. R. (1972). Real-life exposure as a primary therapeutic factor in the desensitization treatment of fear. *Journal of Abnormal Psychology* 79, 19–28.

Shipley, C. R., & Fazio, A. F. (1973). Pilot study of treatment for psychological depression. *Journal of Abnormal Psychology* 82, 372–376.

Shostrom, E. L., & Knapp, R. R. (1966). The relationship of a measure of self-actualization (POI) to a measure of pathology (MMPI) and to therapeutic growth. *American Journal of Psychotherapy* 20, 193–202.

Shrauger, J. S., & Katkin, E. S. (1970). The use of nonspecific underlying motivational factors in the systematic desensitization of specific marital and interpersonal fears: A case study. *Journal of Abnormal Psychology* 75, 221–226.

Siegman, A. W., & Pope, B. (1965). Personality variables associated with productivity and verbal influence in the initial interview. *Proceedings of the 73rd Annual Convention of the American Psychological Association*, 273–274.

Sifneos, P. E. (1969). Learning to solve emotional problems—a controlled study of short-term anxiety-provoking psychotherapy. *International Psychiatry Clinics* 6, 87–99.

Sikes, M.P., Faibish, G., & Valles, J. (1965). Evaluation of an intensive alcoholic treatment program. *Proceedings of the 73rd Annual Convention of the American Psychological Association*, 275–276.

Silver, S. N. (1976). Outpatient treatment for sexual offenders. *Social Work* 21, 134–140.

Simon, W., & Gilberstadt, H. (1954). MMPI patterns before and after carbon dioxide inhalation therapy. *Journal of Nervous and Mental Disease* 119, 523–529.

Simon, W., Wirt, R. D., Wirt, A. L., Holloran, A. V., Hinckley, R. G., Lund, J. B., & Hopkins, G. W. (1958). A controlled study of the short-term differential treatment of schizophrenia. *American Journal of Psychiatry* 114, 1077–1085.

Simono, R. B. (1968). Anxiety and involvement in counseling. *Journal of Counseling Psychology* 15, 497–499.

Simonsen, E. (1985). Evaluering af et gruppeterapiforlob bedomt ud fra MMPI og interview. (Evaluation of group therapy with the MMPI and an interview.) *Nordisk Psykiatrisk Tidsskrift* 39, 455–462.

Simopoulos, A. M., Pinto, A., Babikow, P. W., & Kurland, A. A. (1968). Evaluation of antidepressant properties of A-10, 749. *Current Therapeutic Research* 10, 570–575.

Simopoulos, A. M., Pinto, A., Babikow, P. W., Kurland, A. A., & Savage, C. (1970). Psychotomimetic properties and therapeutic potentials of dexoxadrol on convalescing alcoholics. *Diseases of the Nervous System* 31, 203–207.

Sines, L. K., & Silver, R. J. (1960). MMPI correlates of ward placement among state hospital patients. *Journal of Clinical Psychology* 16, 404–406.

Sines, L. K., Silver, R. J., & Lucero, R. J. (1961). The effect of therapeutic intervention by untrained "therapists." *Journal of Clinical Psychology* 17, 394–396.

Sinnett, E. R. (1961). The prediction of irregular discharge among alcoholic patients. *Journal of Social Psychology* 55, 231–235.

Sinnett, E. R., Stimpert, W. E., & Straight, E. (1965). A five-year follow-up study of psychiatric patients. *American Journal of Orthopsychiatry* 35, 573–580.

Sivanisch, G. (1961). Test-retest changes during the course of hospitalization among some frequentual occurring MMPI profiles. *Dissertation Abstracts* 21, 2787.

Skolnick, N. J., & Zuckerman, M. (1979). Personality change in drug abusers: A comparison of therapeutic community and prison groups. *Journal of Consulting and Clinical Psychology* 47, 768–770.

Skoog, D. K., Andersen, A. E., & Laufer, W. S. (1984). Personality and treatment effectiveness in anorexia nervosa. *Journal of Clinical Psychology* 40, 955–961.

Sladen, B. J., & Mozdzierz, G. J. (1985). An MMPI scale to predict premature termination from inpatient alcohol treatment. *Journal of Clinical Psychology* 41, 855–862.

Slawson, P. F. (1965). Psychodrama as a treatment for hospitalized patients: A controlled study. *American Journal of Psychiatry* 122, 530–533.

Sloane, R. B. (1976). Patient characteristics and outcome in psychotherapy and behavior therapy. *Journal of Consulting and Clinical Psychology* 44, 330–339.

Smith, J. R. (1963). Personality and interpersonal factors associated with the duration of marriage counseling. *Dissertation Abstracts* 24, 886.

Smith, J. R. (1967). Suggested scales for prediction of client movement and the duration of marriage counseling. *Sociology and Social Research* 52, 63–71.

Smith, J. W., Johnson, L. C., & Burdick, J. A. (1971). Sleep, psychological and clinical changes during alcohol withdrawal in NAD-treated alcoholics. *Quarterly Journal of Studies on Alcohol* 32, 982–994.

Smith, R. C., & Porier, G. W. (1971). Factors influencing administrative disposition of psychiatric patients. *Journal of Clinical Psychology* 27, 54–59.

Smith, W. L., & Duerksen, D. L. (1979). Personality and the relief of chronic pain: Predicting surgical outcome. *Clinical Neuropsychology* 1, 35–38.

Snowden, L., & Cotler, S. (1974). The effectiveness of paraprofessional ex-addict counselors in a methadone treatment program. *Psychotherapy Theory, Research and Practice* 11, 331–338.

Snowden, L. R. (1984). Treatment participation and outcome in a program for problem drinker-drivers. *Evaluation and Program Planning* 7, 65–71.

Snyder, D. K. (1990). Assessing chronic pain with the Minnesota Multiphasic Personality Inventory (MMPI). In T. W. Miller (Ed.), *Chronic pain* (pp. 215–257). Madison, CT: International Universities Press.

Snyder, W. U., & Snyder, B. J. (1961). *The psychotherapy relationship*. New York: Macmillan.

Solomon, R. (1983). Use of the MMPI with multiple personality patients. *Psychological Reports* 53, 1004–1006.

Solyom, L., Kenny, F., & Ledwidge, B. (1969). Evaluation of a new treatment paradigm for phobias. *Canadian Psychiatric Association Journal* 14, 3–9.

Solyom, L., Heseltine, G. R., McClure, D. J., Ledwidge, B., & Kenny, F. (1971). A comparative study of aversion relief and systematic desensitization in the treatment of phobias. *British Journal of Psychiatry* 119, 299–303.

Soskin, R. A. (1970). Personality and attitude change after two alcoholism treatment programs: Comparative contributions of lysergide and human relations training. *Quarterly Journal of Studies on Alcohol* 31, 920–931.

Soskin, R. A. (1973). The use of LSD in time-limited psychotherapy. *Journal of Nervous and Mental Disease* 157, 410–419.

Sowles, R. C., & Gill, J. H. (1970). Institutional and community adjustment of delinquents following counseling. *Journal of Consulting and Clinical Psychology* 34, 398–402.

Speer, D. C. (1970). Effects of marathon group therapy: short-term MMPI changes. *Comparative Group Studies* 1, 397–404.

Spielberger, C. D., Weitz, H., & Denny, J. P. (1962). Group counseling and the academic performance of anxious college freshmen. *Journal of Counseling Psychology* 9, 195–204.

Spreche, D. (1963). A quantitative comparison of ECT with hexafluorodiethyl ether. *Journal of Neuropsychiatry* 5, 132–137.

Spreen, O., & Strauss, E. (1991). *A compendium of neuropsychological tests: Administration, norms, and commentary.* New York: Oxford.

Stampfl, T. G., & Levis, D. J. (1973). *Implosive therapy: Theory and technique.* New York: General Learning Press.

Stanley, W. J., & Fleming, H. (1962). A clinical comparison of phenelzine and ECT in the treatment of depressive illness. *Journal of Mental Science* 108, 708–710.

Staudenmayer, H., Kinsman, R. A., & Jones, N. F. (1978). Attitudes toward respiratory illness and hospitalization in asthma: Relationships with personality, symptomatology, and treatment response. *Journal of Nervous and Mental Disease* 166, 624–634.

Stava, L. (1984). The use of hypnotic uncovering techniques in the treatment of pedophilia. *International Journal of Clinical and Experimental Hypnosis* 32, 350–355.

Stein, M. K., Downing, R. W., & Rickels, K. (1978). Self-estimates in anxious and depressed outpatients treated with pharmacotherapy. *Psychological Reports* 43, 487–492.

Steinbook, R. M., & Chapman, A. B. (1970). Lithium responders: An evaluation of psychological test characteristics. *Comprehensive Psychiatry* 11, 524–530.

Stelmachers, Z. T. (1963). Stereotyped and individualized information and their relative contribution to predictive accuracy. *Dissertation Abstracts* 24, 395.

Stephens, J. H., & Shaffer, J. W. (1970). A controlled study of the effects of diphenylhydantoin on anxiety, irritability, and anger in neurotic outpatients. *Psychopharmacologia* 17, 169–181.

Stewart, H., & Cole, S. (1968). Emerging concepts for briefer psychotherapy—a review. *Psychological Reports* 22, 619–629.

Stieper, D. R., & Wiener, D. N. (1959). The problem of interminability in outpatient psychotherapy. *Journal of Consulting Psychology* 23, 237–242.

Stieper, D. R., & Wiener, D. N. (1965). *Dimensions of psychotherapy: An experimental and clinical approach.* Chicago: Aldine.

Stimpert, W. E., Sinnett, E. R., & Wilkins, D. M. (1966). A description of psychiatric patients five years after treatment. *Social Work* 11, 78–86.

Stip, E., Duguay, R., Edmond, A., & Leouffre, P. (1991). Etude de l'effet placebo dans une population quebecoise de sujet souffrant d'impuissance erectile et psychogene. (Treatment of male psychogenic impotency with placebo in Quebec.) *Psychologie Medicale* 23, 183–187.

Stockey, M. R. (1961). A comparison of the effectiveness of group-counseling, individual-counseling, and employment among adolescent boys with adjustment problems. *Dissertation Abstracts* 22, 491.

Stoddard, V. M., Tsushima, W. T., & Heiby, E. (1988). MMPI predictors of outpatient medical utilization rates following psychotherapy. Special Issue: Psychotherapy and the new health care systems. *Psychotherapy* 25, 370–376.

Stone, J. L., McDaniel, K. D., Hughes, J. R., & Hermann, B. P. (1986). Episodic dyscontrol disorder and paroxysmal EEG abnormalities: Successful treatment with carbamazepine. *Biological Psychiatry* 21, 208–212.

Stone, L. A. (1965). Measured personality correlates of a judged prognosis scale. *Proceedings of the 73rd Annual Convention of the American Psychological Association*, 277–278.

Stone, W. N., & Tieger, M. E. (1971). Screening for T-groups: The myth of healthy candidates. *American Journal of Psychiatry* 127, 1485–1490.

Stoudenmire, J. (1972). Effects of muscle relaxation training on state and trait anxiety in introverts and extraverts. *Journal of Personality and Social Psychology* 24, 273–275.

Straus, B., & Hess, H. (1993). Interpersonale Probleme, interpersonale Orientierung und Behandlungserfolg nach stationarer Gruppenpsychotherapie. (Interpersonal problems, interpersonal orientation and treatment success following inpatient group psychotherapy.) *Psychotherapie Psychosomatik Medizinische Psychologie* 43, 82–92.

Strauss, R. S. (1968). The MMPI and types of hospital discharge. *Dissertation Abstracts* 28, 5196.

Strupp, H. H. (1980). Success and failure in time-limited psychotherapy: Further evidence (Comparison 4). *Archives of General Psychiatry* 37, 947–954.

Strupp, H. H., & Bloxom, A. L. (1975). An approach to defining a patient population in psychotherapy research. *Journal of Counseling Psychology* 22, 231–237.

Strupp, H. H., & Hadley, S. W. (1979). Specific vs nonspecific factors in psychotherapy: A controlled study of outcome. *Archives of General Psychiatry* 36, 1125–1136.

Subotnik, L. (1972a). "Spontaneous remission" of deviant MMPI profiles among college students. *Journal of Consulting and Clinical Psychology* 38, 191–201.

Subotnik, L. (1972b). Spontaneous remission: Fact or artifact? *Psychological Bulletin* 77, 32–48.

Sullivan, P. L., Miller, C., & Smelser, W. (1958). Factors in length of stay and progress in psychotherapy. *Journal of Consulting Psychology* 22, 1–9.

Sulzer, E. S. (1959). The psychological effects of promazine on chronic psychiatric patients. *Dissertation Abstracts* 20, 1075.

Sulzer, E. S., & Schiele, B. C. (1962). The prediction of response to tranylcypromine plus trifluoperazine by the MMPI. *American Journal of Psychiatry* 119, 69–70.

Sundberg, N. D. (1952). The relationship of psychotherapeutic skill and experience to knowledge of other people. *Dissertation Abstracts* 12, 390.

Sutker, P. B., Cohen, G. H., & Allain, A. N. (1976). Prediction of successful response to multimodality treatment among heroin addicts. *International Journal of the Addictions* 11, 861–879.

Svanum, S., & Dallas, C. L. (1981). Alcoholic MMPI types and their relationship to patient characteristics, polydrug abuse, and abstinence following treatment. *Journal of Personality Assessment* 45, 278–287.

Svanum, S., & McAdoo, W. G. (1989). Predicting rapid relapse following treatment for chemical dependence: A matched-subjects design. *Journal of Consulting and Clinical Psychology* 57, 222–226.

Sweet, J. J. (1981). The MMPI in evaluation of response to treatment of chronic pain. *American Journal of Clinical Biofeedback* 4, 121–130.

Sweet, J. J. (1985). The Millon Behavioral Health Inventory: Concurrent and predictive validity in a pain treatment center. *Journal of Behavioral Medicine* 8, 215–226.

Szalanski, J. (1975). Psychodrama used to correct self-attitudes in minors. *Psychologia Wychowawcza* 18, 249–257.

Tanner, B. A. (1971). A case report on the use of relaxation and systematic desensitization to control multiple compulsive behaviors. *Journal of Behavior Therapy and Experimental Psychiatry* 2, 267–272.

Tanner, B. A. (1973). The modification of male homosexual behavior by avoidance learning. *Dissertation Abstracts International* 33, 3923B.

Tanner, B. A. (1974). A comparison of automated aversive conditioning and a waiting list control in the modification of homosexual behavior in males. *Behavior Therapy* 5, 29–32.

Taulbee, E. S. (1958). Relationship between certain personality variables and continuation in psychotherapy. *Journal of Consulting Psychology* 22, 83–89.

Taulbee, E. S. (1961). The relationship between Rorschach flexor and extensor M responses and the MMPI and psychotherapy. *Journal of Projective Techniques* 25, 447–479.

Tavola, T., Gala, C., Conte, G., & Invernizzi, G. (1992). Traditional Chinese acupuncture in tension-type headache: A controlled study. *Pain* 48, 325–329.

Taylor, A. J. (1966). An evaluation of group psychotherapy—a research report. *New Zealand Medical Journal* 65, 120–122.

Teitelbaum, S. H., & Suinn, R. M. (1964). Group therapy program with orthopedic patients. *Group Psychotherapy* 17, 49–55.

Terwilliger, J. S., & Fiedler, F. E. (1958). An investigation of determinants inducing individuals to seek personal counseling. *Journal of Consulting Psychology* 22, 288.

Thorpe, J. G. (1962). The current status of prognostic test indicators of electroconvulsive therapy. *Psychosomatic Medicine* 24, 554–568.

Thurstin, A. H., Alfano, A. M., & Sherer, M. (1986). Pretreatment MMPI profiles of A.A. members and nonmembers. *Journal of Studies on Alcohol* 47, 468–471.

Tibilova, A. U., & Tsytsareva, I. V. (1988). Prognostic significance of personality features in psychotherapy of depressive elderly patients. *Trudy Leningradskogo Nauchno Issledovatel'skogo Psikhonevrologicheskogo Instituta im V M Bekhtereva* 121, 131–137.

Toms, E. C. (1961). A comparative study of selected tranquilizers in the treatment of psychiatric patients. *Journal of Nervous and Mental Disease* 132, 425–431.

Toomey, T. C., Ghia, J. N., Mao, W., & Gregg, J. M. (1977). Acupuncture and chronic pain mechanisms: The moderating effects of affect, personality, and stress on response to treatment. *Pain* 3, 137–145.

Tosi, D. J., Howard, L., & Gwynne, P. H. (1982). The treatment of anxiety neurosis through rational stage directed hypnotherapy: A cognitive experiential perspective. *Psychotherapy Theory, Research and Practice* 19, 95–101.

Tosi, D. J., Eshbaugh, D. M., & Murphy, M. A. (1993). *A clinician's guide to the personality profiles of alcohol and drug abusers: Typological descriptions using the MMPI.* Springfield, IL: Charles C Thomas.

Tredici, L. M., Vestre, N. D., & Schiele, B. C. (1966). The antidepressant properties in IN-1060: a preliminary report. *Journal of New Drugs* 6, 278–283.

Truax, C. B. (1971). Normalization of verbal productivity and improvement in depressive status in schizophrenics. *Journal of Clinical Psychology* 27, 537–539.

Truax, C. B., & Carkhuff, R. R. (1965). Personality change in hospitalized mental patients during group psychotherapy as a function of the use of alternate sessions and vicarious therapy pretraining. *Journal of Clinical Psychology* 21, 225–228.

Truax, C. B., Carkhuff, R. R., & Kodman, F. (1965). Relationships between therapist-offered conditions and patient change in group psychotherapy. *Journal of Clinical Psychology* 21, 327–329.

Truax, C. B., Schuldt, W. J., & Wargo, D. G. (1968). Self-ideal concept congruence and improvement in group psychotherapy. *Journal of Consulting and Clinical Psychology* 32, 47–53.

Truax, C. B., & Wargo, D. G. (1969). Effects of vicarious therapy pretraining and alternate sessions on outcome in group psychotherapy with outpatients. *Journal of Consulting and Clinical Psychology* 33, 440–447.

Trulson, M. E. (1986). Martial arts training: A novel "cure" for juvenile delinquency. *Human Relations* 39, 1131–1140.

Tsoi, M. M., Ho, P. C., & Poon, R. S. (1984). Pre-operation indicators and post-hysterectomy outcome. *British Journal of Clinical Psychology* 23, 151–152.

Tsushima, W. T., & Stoddard, V. M. (1990). Ethnic group similarities in the biofeedback treatment of pain. *Medical Psychotherapy An International Journal* 3, 69–75.

Tsushima, W. T., Pang, D. B., & Stoddard, V. M. (1987). Sex similarities and differences in the biofeedback treatment of chronic pain. *Clinical Biofeedback and Health An International Journal* 10, 45–50.

Tsushima, W. T., Stoddard, V. M., Tsushima, V. G., & Daly, J. (1991). Characteristics of treatment drop-outs among two samples of chronic headache patients. *Journal of Clinical Psychology* 47, 199–205.

Tucker, L.R. (1963). Implications of factor analysis of three way matrices for measurements of change. In C. W. Harris (Ed.). *Problems in measuring change*. Madison, WI: University of Wisconsin Press.

Turner, J. A., Herron, L., & Weiner, P. (1986). Utility of the MMPI Pain Assessment Index in predicting outcome after lumbar surgery. *Journal of Clinical Psychology* 42, 764–769.

Tyre, T. E., D'Auria, P., Yanchar, R., & Tyre, C. (1987). The use of biofeedback in adjunctive care of the cancer patient. *Clinical Biofeedback and Health An International Journal* 10, 135–141.

Uhlenhuth, E. H., & Duncan, D. B. (1968). Subjective change with medical student therapists: I, Course of relief in psychoneurotic outpatients. *Archives of General Psychiatry* 18, 428–438.

Uhlenhuth, E. H., & Duncan, D. B. (1968). Subjective change with medical student therapists: II, Some determinants of change in psychoneurotic outpatients. *Archives of General Psychiatry* 18, 532–540.

Uhlenhuth, E. H., & Park, L. C. (1963). The influence of medication (imipramine) and doctor in relieving depressed psychoneurotic outpatients. *Journal of Psychiatric Research* 2, 101–122.

Uhlenhuth, E. H., Lipman, R. S., & Covi, L. (1969). Combined pharmacotherapy and psychotherapy. *Journal of Nervous and Mental Disease* 148, 52–64.

Ullman, L. P., Krasner, L., & Gelfand, D. M. (1963). Changed content within a reinforced response class. *Psychological Reports* 12, 819–829.

Uomoto, J. M., Turner, J. A., & Herron, L. D. (1988). Use of the MMPI and MCMI in predicting outcome of lumbar laminectomy. *Journal of Clinical Psychology* 44, 191–197.

Unger, S., Kurland, A. A., Shaffer, J. W., Savage, C., Wolf, S., Leihy, R., McCabe, O. L.,

& Shock, H. (1968). LSD-type drugs and psychedelic therapy. In J. M. Shlien (Ed.), *Research in psychotherapy: Proceedings of the third conference* (pp. 521–535). Washington, D.C.: American Psychological Association.

Valliant, P. M., & Antonowicz, D. H. (1992). Rapists, incest offenders, and child molesters in treatment: Cognitive and social skills training. *International Journal of Offender Therapy and Comparative Criminology* 36, 221–230.

Van der Veen, F. (1965). Dimensions of the client and therapist behavior in relation to outcome. *Proceedings of the 73rd Annual Convention of the American Psychological Association*, 279–280.

Van der Veen, F. (1967). Basic elements in the process of psychotherapy: A research study. *Journal of Consulting Psychology* 31, 295–303.

Van der Veen, F., & Stoler, N. (1965). Therapist judgments, interview behavior and case outcome. *Psychotherapy: Theory, Research, and Practice* 2, 158–163.

Vein, A. M., & Airapetov, R. G. (1986). Nocturnal polygraphic studies of the treatment of depressed patients by sleep deprivation. *Soviet Neurology and Psychiatry* 19, 60–70.

Veldhuizen, J. F. (1972). The effect of institutional placement on delinquent adolescent girls: An MMPI and CPI sequence testing approach. *Dissertation Abstracts International* 32, 4232B.

Vernallis, F. F., Shipper, J. C., Butler, D. C., & Tomlimson, T. M. (1970). Saturation group psychotherapy in a weekend clinic: An outcome study. *Psychotherapy: Theory, Research, and Practice* 7, 144–152.

Vestre, N. D., Dehnel, L. L., & Schiele, B. C. (1969). A sequential comparison of amitriptyline, perphenazine, and the amitriptyline-perphenazine combination in recently admitted anergic schizophrenics. *Psychosomatics* 10, 296–303.

Viaille, H. D., (1964). Prediction of treatment outcome of chronic alcoholics in a state hospital. *Dissertation Abstracts* 24, 5534.

Vidor, M. (1951). Personality changes following pre-frontal leucotomy as reflected by the MMPI and the results of psychometric testing. *Journal of Mental Science* 97, 159–173.

Villanueva, M. R., Roman, D. D., & Tuley, M. R. (1988). Determining forensic rehabilitation potential with the MMPI: Practical implications for residential treatment populations. *American Journal of Forensic Psychology* 6, 27–35.

Volsky, T., Magoon, T. M., Norman, W. T., & Hoyt, D. P. (1965). *The outcomes of counseling and psychotherapy: Theory and research*. Minneapolis: University of Minnesota Press.

Wadden, T. A. (1983). Predicting treatment response to relaxation therapy for essential hypertension. *Journal of Nervous and Mental Disease* 171, 683–689.

Wadden, T. A. (1984). Relaxation therapy for essential hypertension: Specific or nonspecific effects? *Journal of Psychosomatic Research* 28, 53–61.

Wadden, T. A., & Lucas, R. A. (1980). MMPI as a predictor of weight loss. *Psychological Reports* 46, 984–986.

Wagner, E. E., & Dobbins, R. D. (1967). MMPI profiles of parishioners seeking pastoral counseling. *Journal of Consulting Psychology* 31, 83–84.

Walfish, S., Massey, R., & Krone, A. (1990a). MMPI profiles of cocaine-addicted individuals in residential treatment: Implications for practical treatment planning. *Journal of Substance Abuse Treatment* 7, 151–154.

Walfish, S., Massey, R., & Krone, A. (1990b). Conducting psychological evaluations with AA-oriented alcoholism treatment programs: Implications for practical treatment planning. In J. N. Butcher & C. D. Spielberger (Eds.), *Advances in personality assessment*, Vol. 8 (pp. 161–185), Hillsdale, NJ: Lawrence Erlbaum Associates.

Walker, D. E., Blankenship, V., Ditty, J. A., & Lynch, K. P. (1987). Prediction of recovery for closed-head-injured adults: An evaluation of the MMPI, the Adaptive Behavior Scale, and a "Quality of Life" Rating Scale. *Journal of Clinical Psychology* 43, 699–707.

Walls, R. T., Miller, J. J., & Cox, J. (1970). Delay of reinforcement and training choice behavior for rehabilitation clients. *Rehabilitation Counseling Bulletin* 14, 69–77.

Walters, G. D., Solomon, G. S., & Walden, V. R. (1982). Use of the MMPI in predicting psychotherapeutic persistence in groups in male and female outpatients. *Journal of Clinical Psychology* 38, 80–83.

Watkins, J. T. (1967). The effects of manifest anxiety on verbal conditioning in a quasi-therapy setting. *Dissertation Abstracts* 28, 2635B.

Watson, C. G. (1968). Prediction of length of hospital stay from MMPI scales. *Journal of Clinical Psychology* 24, 444–447.

Watson, G., & Comrey, A. L. (1954). Nutritional replacement for mental illness. *Journal of Psychology* 38, 251–264.

Watt, G. D. (1949). An evaluation of non-directive counseling in the treatment of delinquents. *Journal of Educational Research* 42, 343–352.

Weckowicz, T. E., Yonge, K. A., Cropley, A. J., & Muir, W. (1971). Objective therapy predictors in depression: A multivariate approach. *Journal of Clinical Psychology* 27, 3–29.

Weintraub, W., & Aronson, H. (1963). Clinical judgment in psychopharmacological research. *Journal of Neuropsychiatry* 5, 65–70.

Weiss, M. F. (1973). The treatment of insomnia through the use of electrosleep: An EEG study. *Journal of Nervous and Mental Disease* 157, 108–120.

Weiss, R. W., & Russakoff, S. (1977). Relationship of MMPI scores of drug-abusers to personal variables and type of treatment program. *Journal of Psychology* 96, 25–29.

Weiss, S. W. (1957). The efficacy of isonicotinic acid hydrozoid with schizophrenic criminals. *Dissertation Abstracts* 17, 900.

Weiss, W. U., & Waldrop, R. S. (1972). Some characteristics of individuals who remain in an institution for the aged. *Developmental Psychology* 6, 182.

Welkowitz, J. (1960). Behavior patterns in group psychotherapy sessions in two Veterans Administration hospitals. *Dissertation Abstracts* 20, 4202.

Welsh, G. S., & Roseman, M. (1955). A graphic method for showing therapeutic change by use of MMPI factor scales. *American Psychologists* 10, 568.

Wesson, D. R., Smith, D. E., Lerner, S. E., & Kettner, V. R. (1974). Treatment of polydrug users in San Francisco. *American Journal of Drug and Alcohol Abuse* 1, 159–179.

West, L. J. (1953). Measurement of changing psychopathology with the MMPI. *American Journal of Psychiatry* 109, 922–928.

Westendorp, F., & Brink, K. L. (1982). Characteristics of adolescents treated at six different treatment settings. *Adolescence* 17, 19–35.

Whitaker, D. L., & Wodarski, J. S. (1988). Treatment of sexual offenders in a community mental health center: An evaluation. Special Issue: Treatment of sex offenders in social work and mental health settings. *Journal of Social Work and Human Sexuality* 7, 49–68.

Whybrow, P. C., Prange, A. J., & Treadway, C. R. (1969). Mental changes accompanying thyroid gland dysfunction. A reappraisal using objective psychological measurement. *Archives of General Psychiatry* 20, 48–63.

Wieder, G. S. (1952). A comparative study of the relative effectiveness of two methods of teaching a thirty-hour course in psychology in modifying attitudes associated with racial, religious, and ethnic prejudices. *Dissertation Abstracts* 12, 163.

Wiener, D. N. (1946). Advisement factors in successful and unsuccessful rehabilitation trainess. *Advisement Bulletin No. 6.* Regional Veterans Administration Office, Minneapolis, MN.

Wiener, D. N., Feinberg, P., Nagobads, I. J., Westendorf, F., & Warren, P. W. (1963). Effects of withdrawal of tranquilizers — effects in chronic psychiatric outpatient users. *Archives of General Psychiatry* 9, 513–519.

Wiener, D. N., & Phillips, E. L. (1948). A study of progress in psychotherapy. *Journal of Clinical Psychology* 4, 201–206.

Wilkinson, A. E., Prado, W. M., Williams, W. O., & Schnadt, F. W. (1971). Psychological test characteristics and length of stay in alcoholism treatment. *Quarterly Journal of Studies on Alcohol* 32, 60–65.

Williams, C. L. (1982). Can the MMPI be useful to behavior therapists? *Behavior Therapist* 5, 83–84.

Williams, C. L. (1986). MMPI profiles from adolescents: Interpretive strategies and treatment considerations. *Journal of Child and Adolescent Psychotherapy* 3, 179–193.

Williams, D. E. (1987). MMPI and headache: A special focus on differential diagnosis, prediction of treatment outcome and patient: Treatment matching: Commentary. *Pain* 29, 269.

Williams, D. E., Thompson, J. K., Haber, J. D., & Raczynski, J. M. (1986). MMPI and headache: A special focus on differential diagnosis, prediction of treatment outcome, and patient-treatment matching. *Pain* 24, 143–158.

Williams, R. B. (1986). Psychosocial and physical predictors of anginal pain relief with medical management. *Psychosomatic Medicine* 48, 200–210.

Williams, S. G., & Baron, J. (1982). Effects of short-term intensive hospital psychotherapy on youthful drug abusers: I. Preliminary MMPI data. *Psychological Reports* 50, 79–82.

Wilson, I. C., Vernon, J. T., & Sandifer, M. G. (1963). A controlled study of treatments of depression. *Journal of Neuropsychiatry* 4, 331–337.

Wilson, I. C., Gambill, J. M., & Sandifer, M. G. (1964). A double blind study comparing imipramine (Tofranil) with desmethylimipramine (Pertofrane). *Psychosomatics* 5, 88.

Wilson, I. C., Rabon, A. M., & Merrick, H. A. (1966). Imipramine pamoate in the treatment of depression. *Psychosomatics* 7, 251–253.

Wilson, I. C., Rabon, A. M., & Merrick, H. A. (1967). Imipramine therapy in depressive syndromes: Prediction of therapeutic outcome. *Psychosomatics* 8, 203–207.

Wilson, S., & Kennard, D. (1978). The extraverting effect of treatment in a therapeutic community for drug abusers. *British Journal of Psychiatry* 132, 296–299.

Windle, C. (1952). Psychological tests in psychopathological prognosis. *Psychological Bulletin* 49, 451–482.

Winter, W. D., & Frederickson, W. K. (1956). The short-term effects of chlorpromazine on psychiatric patients. *Journal of Consulting Psychology* 20, 431–434.

Wirt, A. L. (1955). Predicition of commitment of hospitalized psychiatric patients. *Dissertation Abstracts* 15, 2581.

Wirt, R. D. (1956). Actuarial prediction. *Journal of Consulting Psychology* 20, 123–124.

Wirt, R. D., & Simon, W. (1959). *Differential treatment and prognosis in schizophrenia.* Springfield, IL: Charles C Thomas.

Wittenborn, J. R., & Plante, M. (1963). Patterns of response to placebo, iproniazid and electroconvulsive therapy among young depressed females. *Journal of Nervous and Mental Disease* 137, 155–161.

Wittenborn, J. R., Plante, M., Burgess, F., & Livermore, N. (1961). The efficacy of electroconvulsive therapy, iproniazid and placebo in the treatment of young depressed women. *Journal of Nervous and Mental Disease* 133, 316–332.

Wittenborn, J. R., Kiremitici, & Weber, E. S. (1973). The choice of alternative anti-depressants. *Journal of Nervous and Mental Disease* 156, 97–108.

Witton, K., & Ellsworth, R. B. (1962). Social and psychological (MMPI) changes 5–10 years after lobotomy. *Diseases of the Nervous System* 23, 440–444.

Wogan, M. (1965). A study of the relationship between personality similarity in psychotherapeutic dyads and the quality of the therapeutic experience. *Dissertation Abstracts* 26, 1787.

Wogan, M. (1970). Effect of therapist-patient personality variables on therapeutic outcome. *Journal of Consulting and Clinical Psychology* 35, 356–361.

Wojciechowski, F. L. (1984). Behavioral treatment of tension headache: A contribution to controlled outcome research methodology. *Gedrag Tijdschrift voor Psychologie* 12, 16–30.

Wolff, W. M. (1967). Psychotherapeutic persistence. *Journal of Consulting Psychology* 31, 429.

Wood, D. R., Reimherr, F. W., Wender, P. H., & Johnson, G. E. (1976). Diagnosis and treatment of minimal brain dysfunction in adults: A preliminary report. *Archives of General Psychiatry* 33, 1453–1460.

Yamamoto, J., & Goin, M. K. (1966). Social class factors relevant for psychiatric treatment. *Journal of Nervous and Mental Disease* 142, 332–339.

Yensen, R. (1976). MDA-assisted psychotherapy with neurotic outpatients: A pilot study. *Journal of Nervous and Mental Disease* 163, 233–245.

Young, R. C., Gould, E., Glick, I. D., & Hargreaves, W. A. (1980). Personality inventory correlates of outcome in a follow-up study of psychiatric hospitalization. *Psychological Reports* 46, 903–906.

Zeisset, R. M. (1968). Desensitization and relaxation in the modification of psychiatric patients' interview behavior. *Journal of Abnormal Psychology* 73, 18–24.

Ziegler, R., Kohutek, K., & Owen, P. (1978). A multimodal treatment approach for incarcerated alcoholics. *Journal of Clinical Psychology* 34, 1005–1009.

Zubin, J., & Windle, C. (1954). Psychological prognosis of outcome in the mental disorders. *Journal of Abnormal and Social Psychology* 49, 272–281.

Zuckerman, M., Sola, S., Masterson, J., & Angelone, J. V. (1975). MMPI patterns in drug abusers before and after treatment in therapeutic communities. *Journal of Consulting and Clinical Psychology* 43, 286–296.

Index